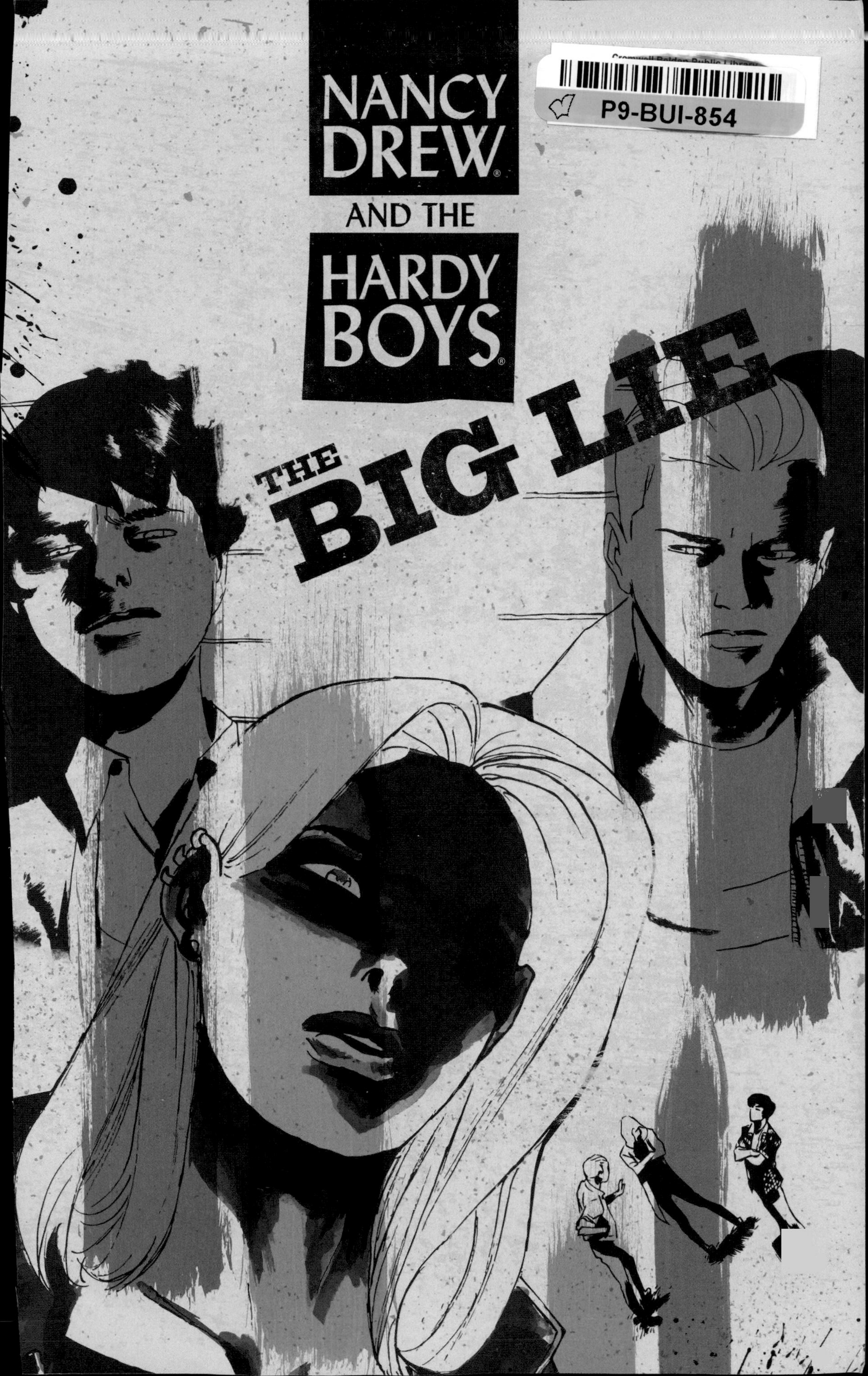
NANCY DREW®
AND THE
HARDY BOYS®
THE BIG LIE

WRITER
Anthony Del Col

ARTIST
Werther Dell'Edera

COLORIST
Stefano Simeone

LETTERER
Simon Bowland

COLLECTION
COVER ARTIST
Fay Dalton

EDITOR
Matt Idelson

ASSISTANT EDITOR
Matt Humphreys

COLLECTION DESIGN
Cathleen Heard

DYNAMITE®

f 📷 t 🐦 ▶ YouTube

Online at www.DYNAMITE.com
On Facebook /Dynamitecomics
On Instagram /Dynamitecomics
On Tumblr dynamitecomics.tumblr.com
On Twitter @dynamitecomics
On YouTube /Dynamitecomics

Paperback:
ISBN-13: 978-1-5241-0417-7

First Printing
10 9 8 7 6 5 4 3 2 1

Nick Barrucci, CEO / Publisher
Juan Collado, President / COO

Joe Rybandt, Executive Editor
Matt Idelson, Senior Editor
Anthony Marques, Associate Editor
Matt Humphreys, Assistant Editor
Kevin Ketner, Assistant Editor

Jason Ullmeyer, Art Director
Geoff Harkins, Senior Graphic Designer
Cathleen Heard, Graphic Designer
Alexis Persson, Graphic Designer

Chris Caniano, Digital Associate
Rachel Kilbury, Digital Assistant

Brandon Dante Primavera, V.P. of IT and Operations
Rich Young, Director of Business Development

Alan Payne, V.P. of Sales and Marketing
Janie Mackenzie, Marketing Coordinator
Pat O'Connell, Sales Manager

PEFC Certified
Printed on paper from
sustainably managed
forests and controlled
sources
PEFC/01-31-106   www.pefc.org

INTRO

Welcome to Bayport

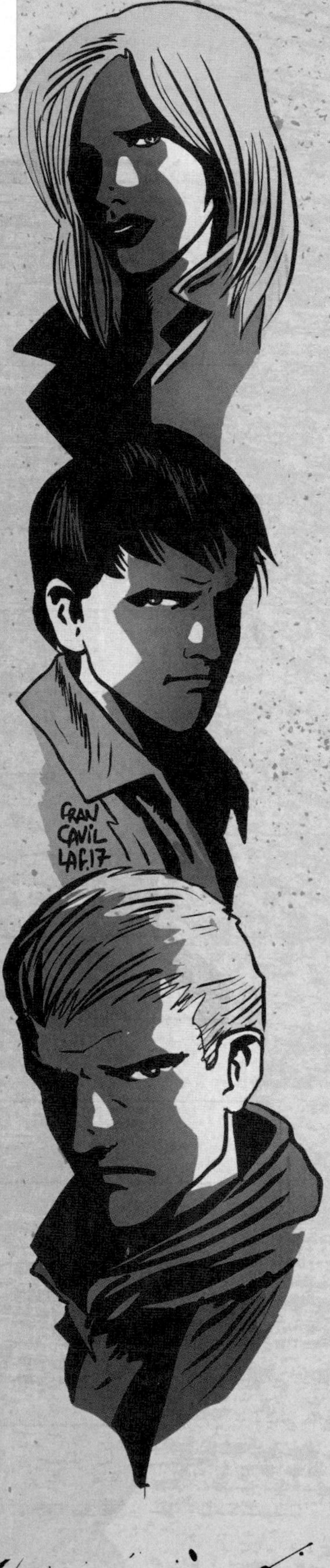
FRAN
CAVIL
LA F.17

When I did the variant cover for LIFE WITH ARCHIE #23 - that inspired the acclaimed zombie-horror series AFTERLIFE WITH ARCHIE — little did I know that I was going to start a little revolution and inspire several writers to take characters that had been living in that same slice of wholesome Americana for more than 70 years and spin them into new, unexpected territories.

For Roberto Aguirre-Sacasa, it was subverting the relationships of the classic Archie gang, who were forced to face the horrors of a devilish zombie invasion.

For Anthony Del Col, it was having Nancy Drew and the two Hardy boys face a real life crime story, turning the old, all-age mystery cases into a noir thriller.

THE BIG LIE is everything I love in a noir story. From the smoky lights of an interrogation room or an illegal gambling hideout to the mysterious relationships between the players (nobody can be trusted!) to the voice over/narration, everything oozes old pulp magazine but with a modern spin, a big part thanks also to the artwork of the talented Werther Dell'Edera.

The story kicks off with a murder, and things only get worse from there. Several threads are put into motion trying to figure out who killed who and who did what. Everything works so perfectly together while we, the readers, put the puzzle piece together along with Nancy and the Boys.

These are the Hardy Boys like you have never seen them before. This is the Nancy Drew like you have never seen her before. And this is to say that the book is not your grandparents' NANCY AND THE HARDY BOYS books. No wonder this was the sleeper hit book of the year and I can only hope this is the first of many more NEW mysteries for Nancy and the Hardy boys to come.

So put on that jazz vinyl you got stashed on the shelf, pour yourself something, and get ready to visit the dark side of Bayport. You're gonna like it here.

Francesco Francavilla

SPECIAL THANKS

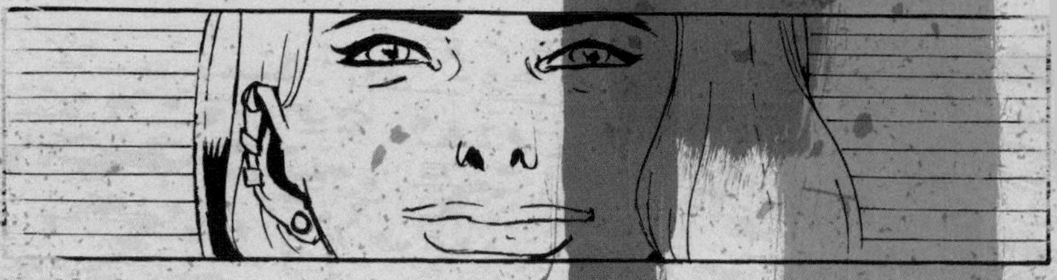

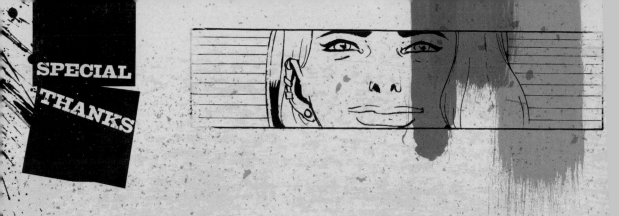

Nancy Drew & The Hardy Boys: The Big Lie

What is a good mystery without a few suspects? And what is a good book (hopefully you'll agree...) without a few people that had a hand in assisting?

Keith WTS Morris for his constant editorial guidance and insight; Laura Becker for believing in this project before anyone else did; Arlene Scanlan, Stephanie Voros and Samantha Metzger for not only approving this project but giving some great story ideas; Jenn Fischer of the Nancy Drew Sleuths for her insight into Nancy and gang; everyone at Dynamite (Juan, Nick, Joe, Alan, Janie, Keith, Jason, Cathleen, Pat, Denise, Kevin, Anthony M) for their roles large and small; assistant editor Matt "Chet Morton" Humphreys for his enthusiasm for Uber and family hugs; senior editor Matt Idelson for his editorial guidance, sarcastic wit, and — quite plainly — being a great editor from start to finish; all of my supporting characters in my families; and finally, my own personal femme fatale and Nancy Drew, Lisa Newal.

And, of course, thanks to Edward Stratemeyer (and his Syndicate writers) for initially creating these amazing characters that has survived for 90+ years now!

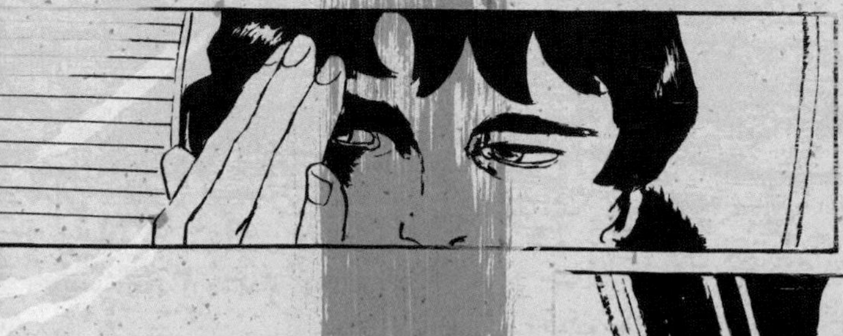

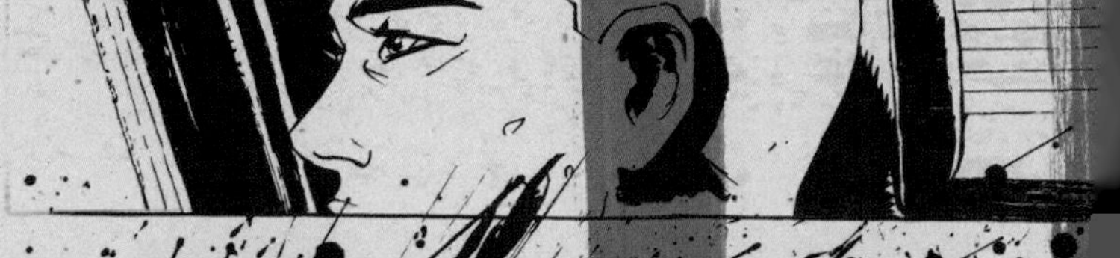

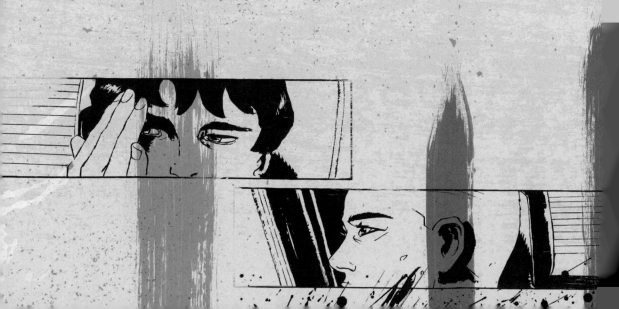

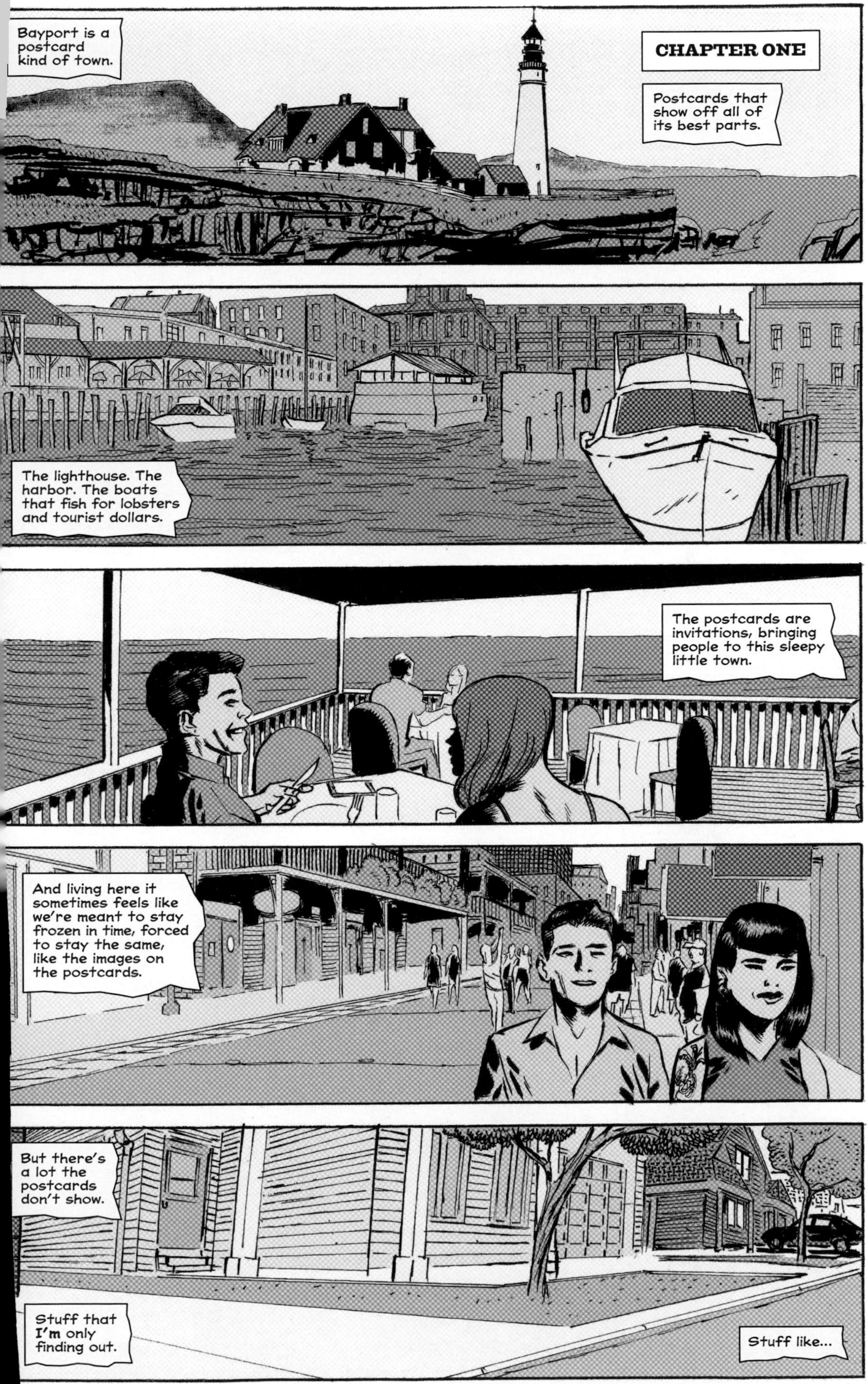
Bayport is a postcard kind of town.
CHAPTER ONE
Postcards that show off all of its best parts.
The lighthouse. The harbor. The boats that fish for lobsters and tourist dollars.
The postcards are invitations, bringing people to this sleepy little town.
And living here it sometimes feels like we're meant to stay frozen in time, forced to stay the same, like the images on the postcards.
But there's a lot the postcards don't show.
Stuff that I'm only finding out.
Stuff like...

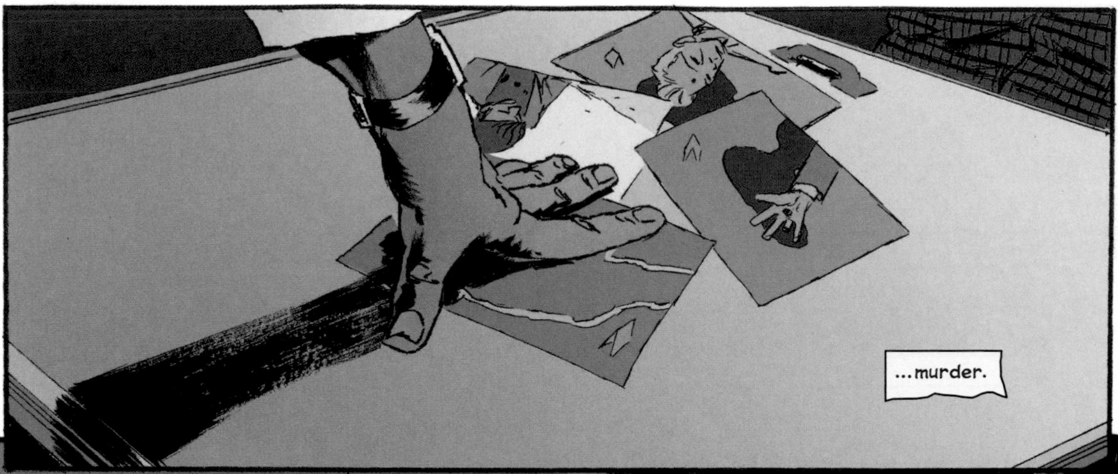
...murder.

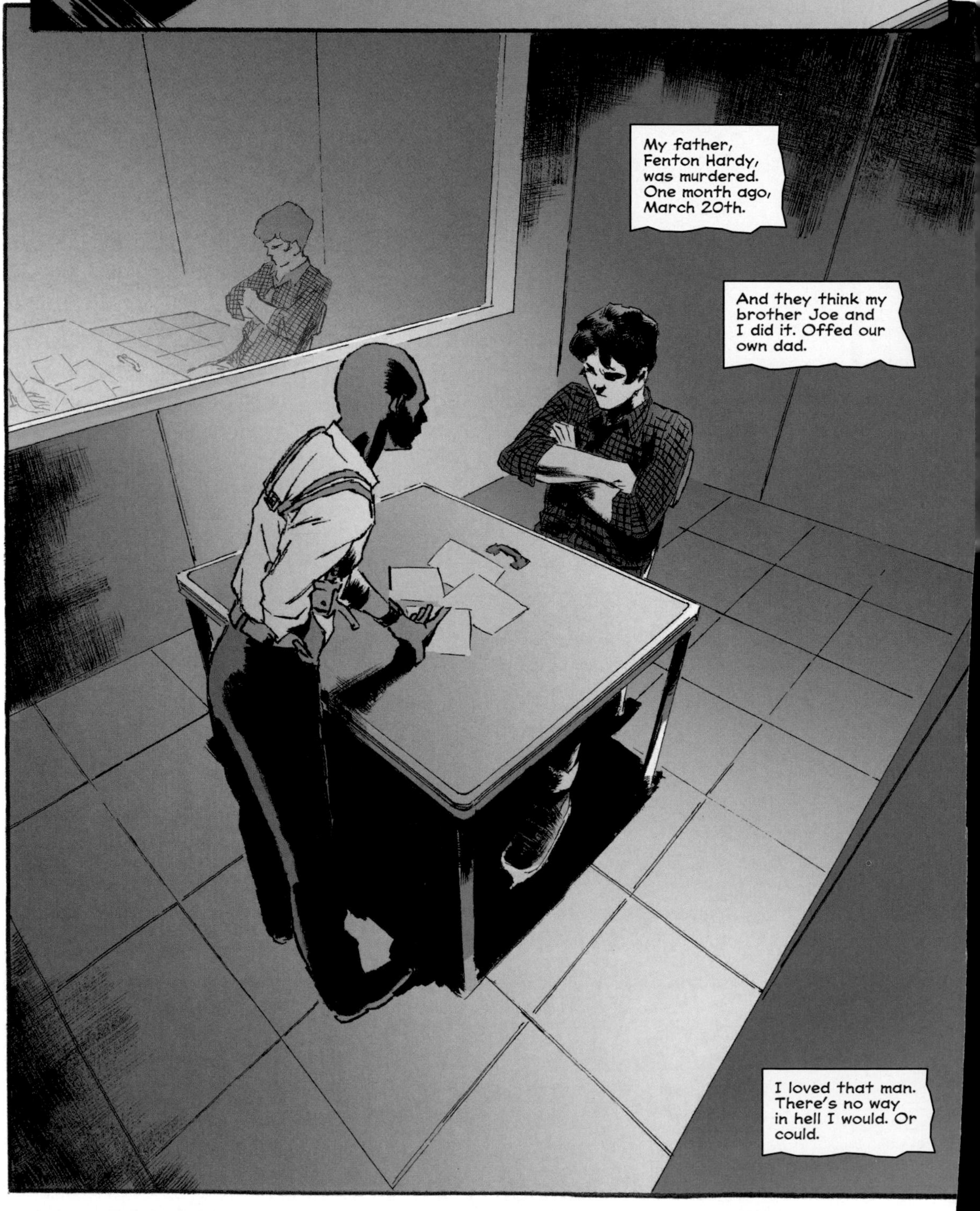
My father, Fenton Hardy, was murdered. One month ago, March 20th.
And they think my brother Joe and I did it. Offed our own dad.
I loved that man. There's no way in hell I would. Or could.

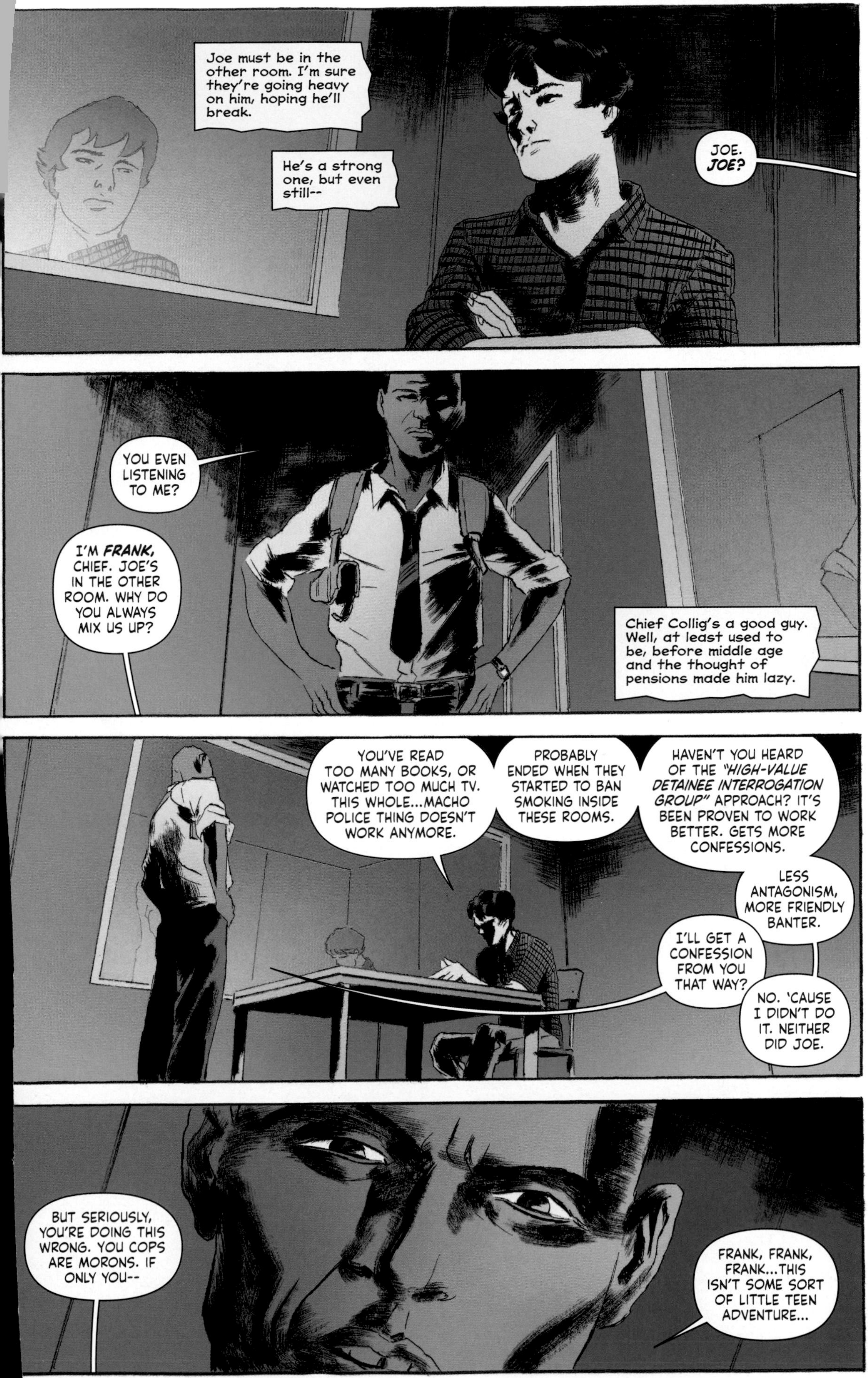
Joe must be in the other room. I'm sure they're going heavy on him, hoping he'll break.
He's a strong one, but even still--
JOE. JOE?
YOU EVEN LISTENING TO ME?
I'M FRANK, CHIEF. JOE'S IN THE OTHER ROOM. WHY DO YOU ALWAYS MIX US UP?
Chief Collig's a good guy. Well, at least used to be, before middle age and the thought of pensions made him lazy.
YOU'VE READ TOO MANY BOOKS, OR WATCHED TOO MUCH TV. THIS WHOLE...MACHO POLICE THING DOESN'T WORK ANYMORE.
PROBABLY ENDED WHEN THEY STARTED TO BAN SMOKING INSIDE THESE ROOMS.
HAVEN'T YOU HEARD OF THE "HIGH-VALUE DETAINEE INTERROGATION GROUP" APPROACH? IT'S BEEN PROVEN TO WORK BETTER. GETS MORE CONFESSIONS.
LESS ANTAGONISM, MORE FRIENDLY BANTER.
I'LL GET A CONFESSION FROM YOU THAT WAY?
NO. 'CAUSE I DIDN'T DO IT. NEITHER DID JOE.
BUT SERIOUSLY, YOU'RE DOING THIS WRONG. YOU COPS ARE MORONS. IF ONLY YOU--
FRANK, FRANK, FRANK...THIS ISN'T SOME SORT OF LITTLE TEEN ADVENTURE...

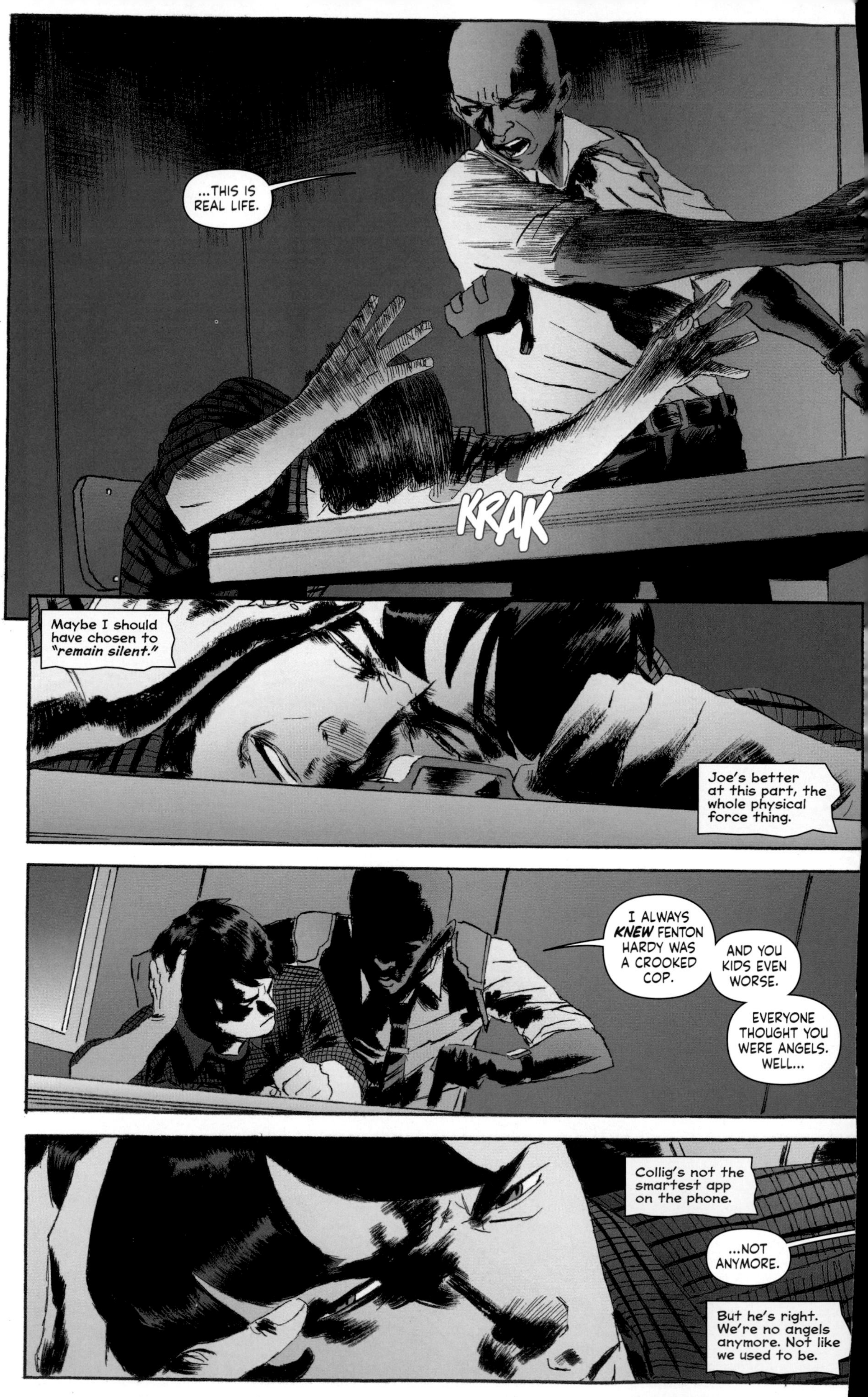
...THIS IS REAL LIFE.
KRAK
Maybe I should have chosen to "remain silent."
Joe's better at this part, the whole physical force thing.
I ALWAYS KNEW FENTON HARDY WAS A CROOKED COP.
AND YOU KIDS EVEN WORSE.
EVERYONE THOUGHT YOU WERE ANGELS. WELL...
Collig's not the smartest app on the phone.
...NOT ANYMORE.
But he's right. We're no angels anymore. Not like we used to be.

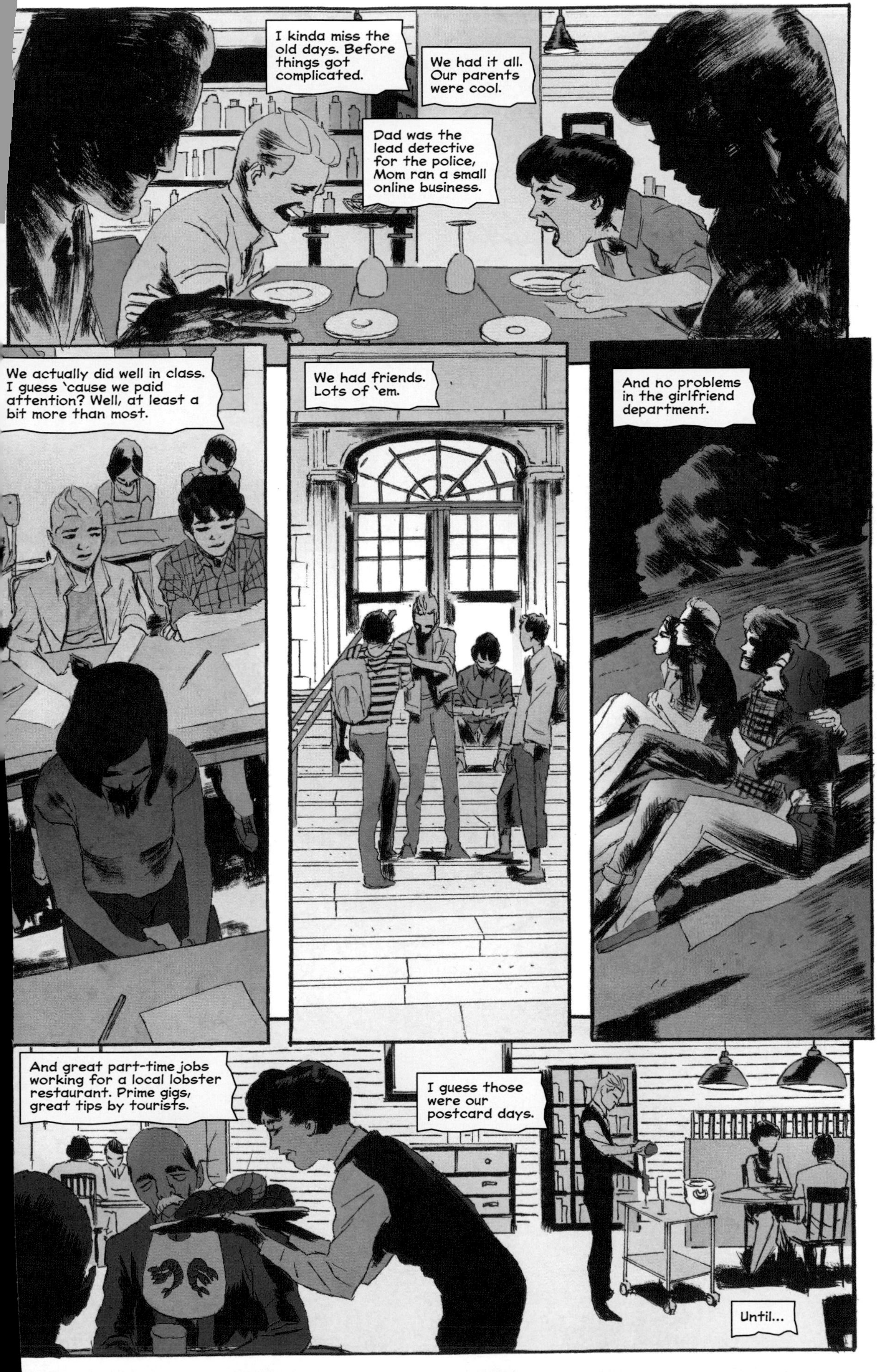
I kinda miss the old days. Before things got complicated.
We had it all. Our parents were cool.
Dad was the lead detective for the police, Mom ran a small online business.
We actually did well in class. I guess 'cause we paid attention? Well, at least a bit more than most.
We had friends. Lots of 'em.
And no problems in the girlfriend department.
And great part-time jobs working for a local lobster restaurant. Prime gigs, great tips by tourists.
I guess those were our postcard days.
Until...

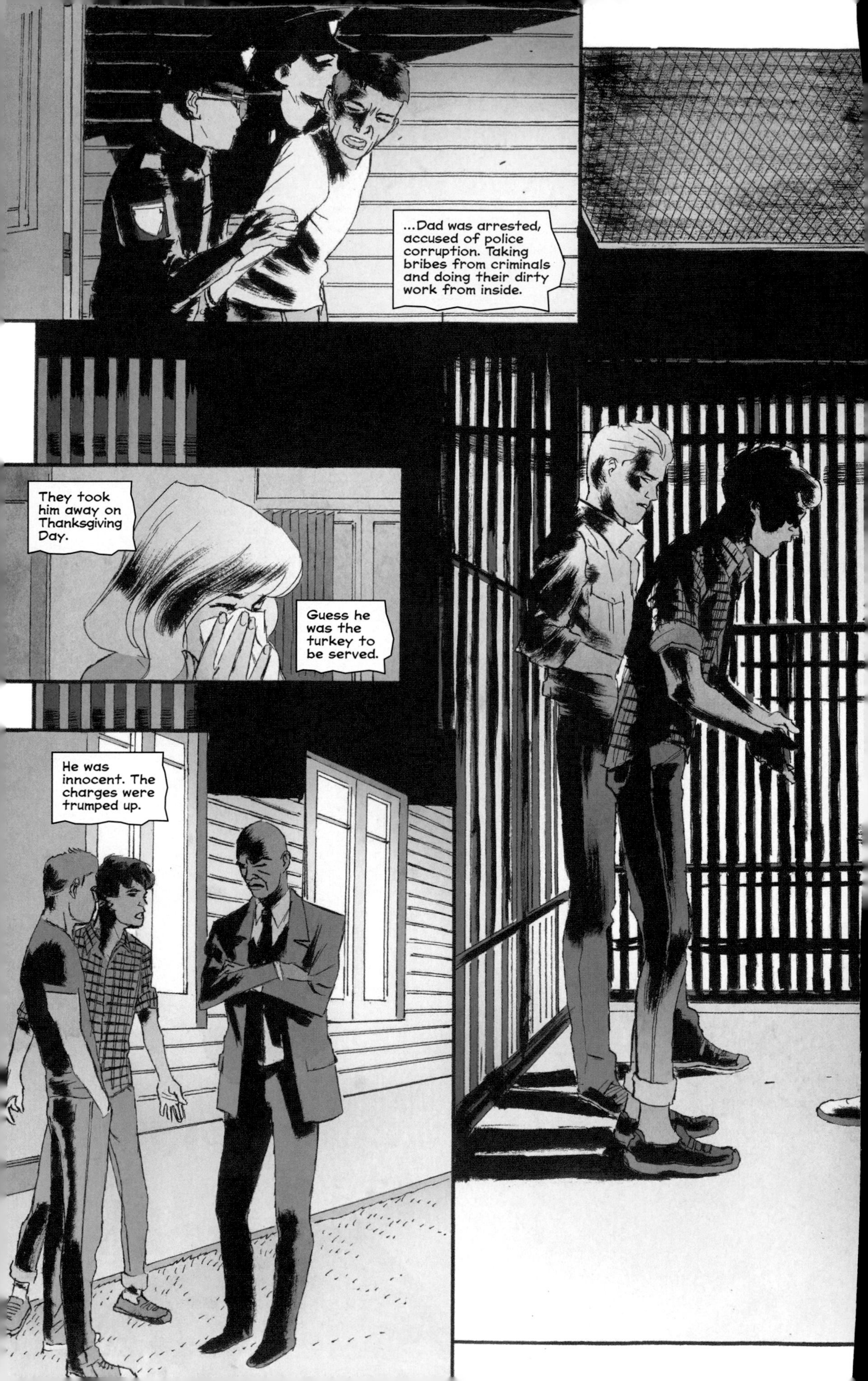
...Dad was arrested, accused of police corruption. Taking bribes from criminals and doing their dirty work from inside.
They took him away on Thanksgiving Day.
Guess he was the turkey to be served.
He was innocent. The charges were trumped up.

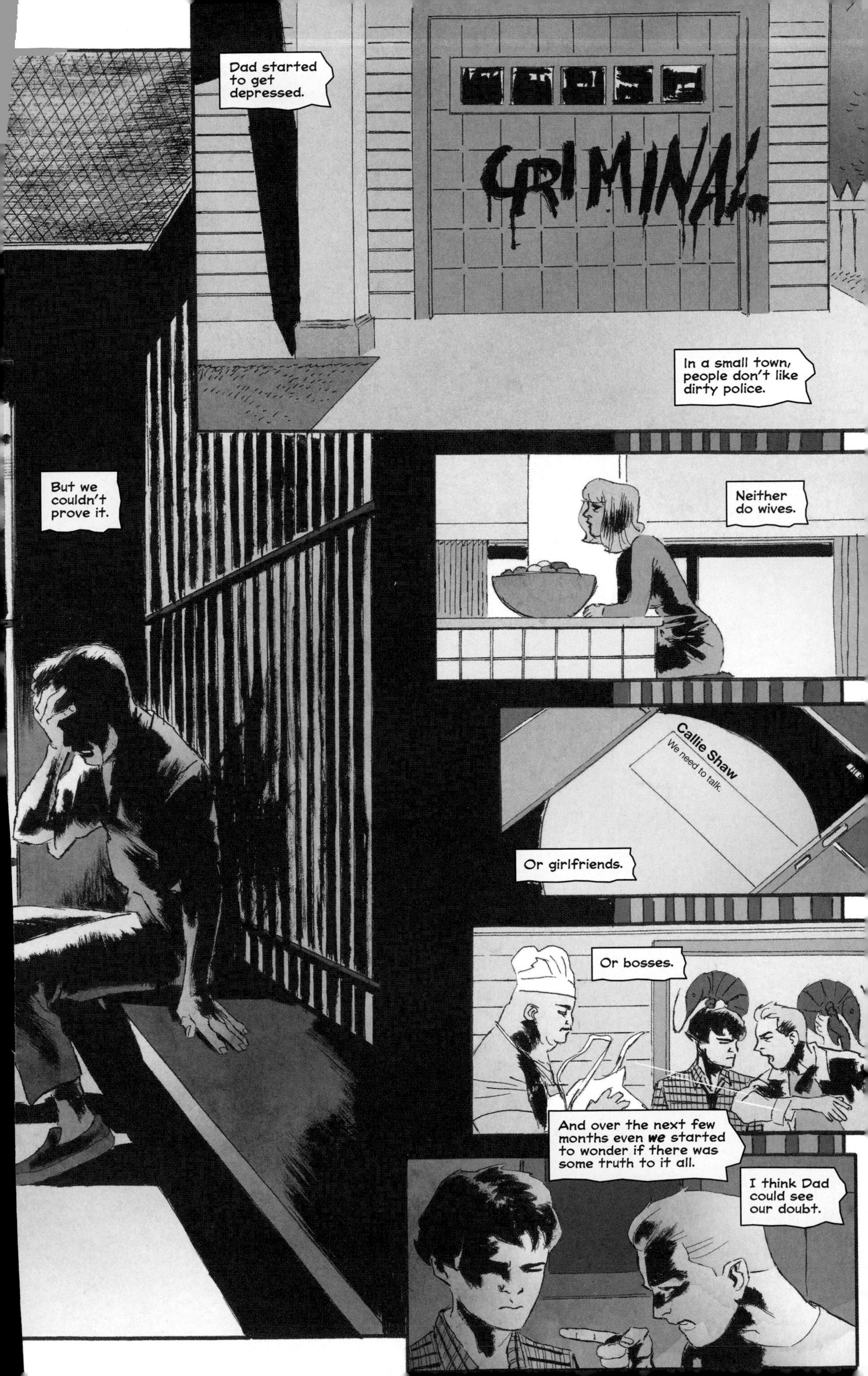

Dad started to get depressed.
CRIMINAL
In a small town, people don't like dirty police.
But we couldn't prove it.
Neither do wives.
Callie Shaw
We need to talk.
Or girlfriends.
Or bosses.
And over the next few months even *we* started to wonder if there was some truth to it all.
I think Dad could see our doubt.

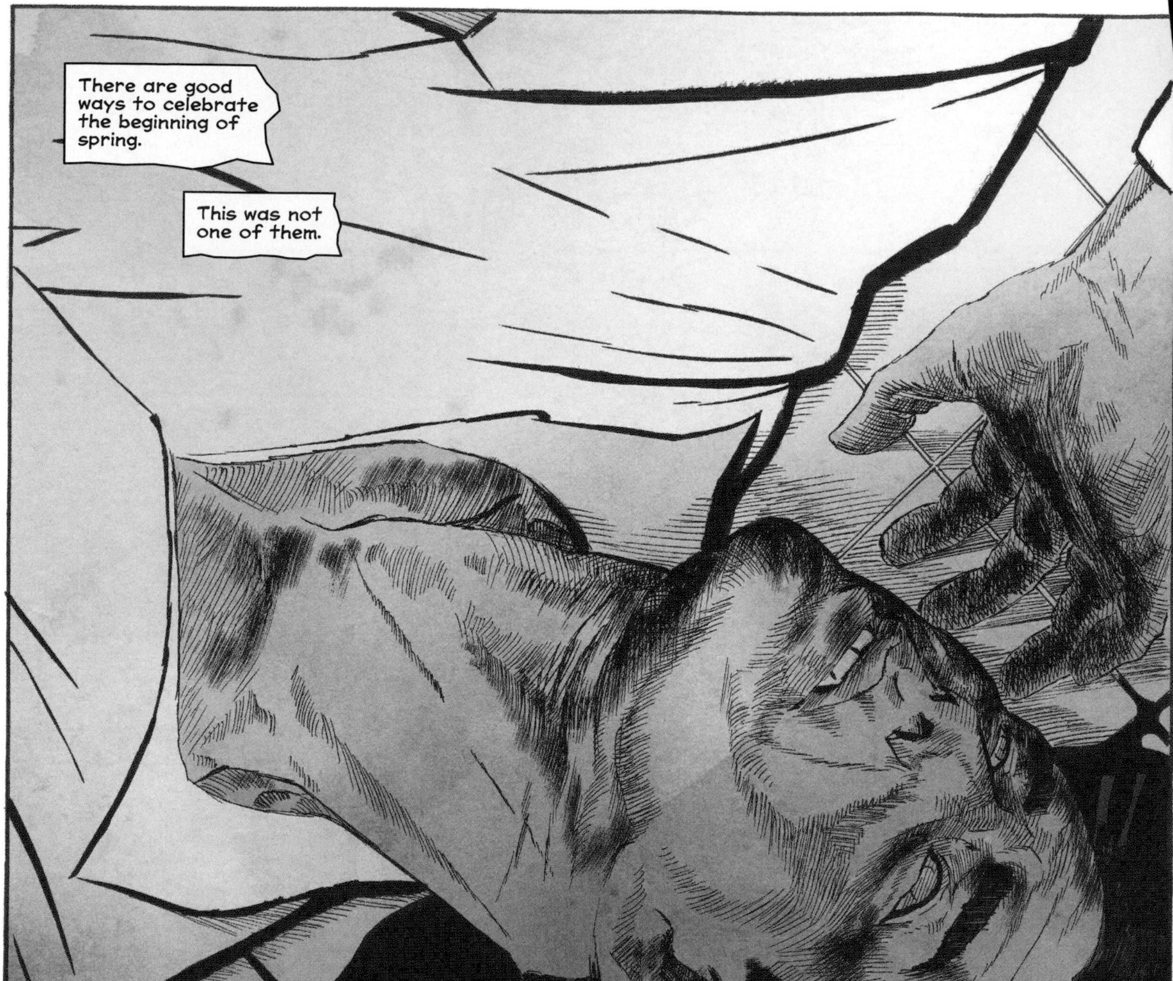
There are good ways to celebrate the beginning of spring.
This was not one of them.
Mom found him. Dead. Used his own gun to shoot himself in the head. Suicide note left in his typical Garamond font.
It said he wanted to stop serving as an embarrassment to the family.

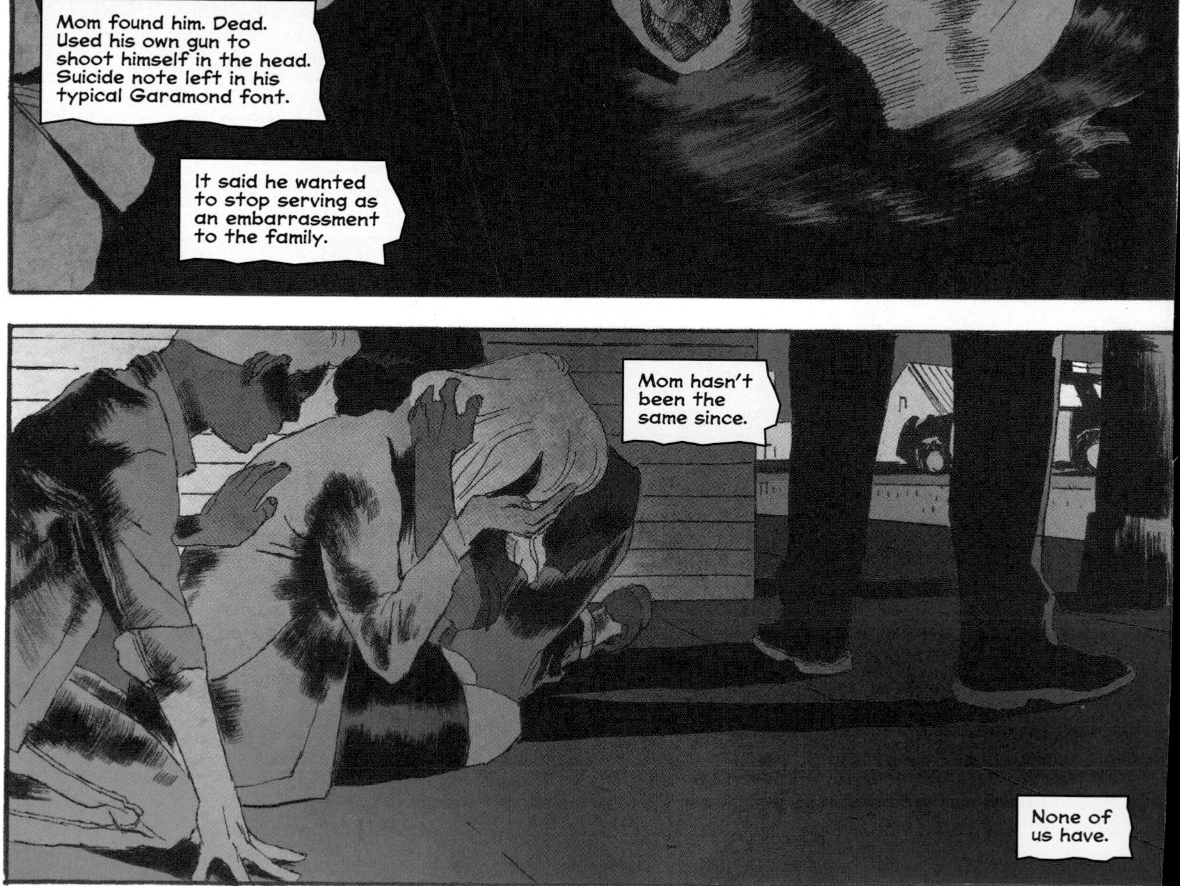
Mom hasn't been the same since.
None of us have.

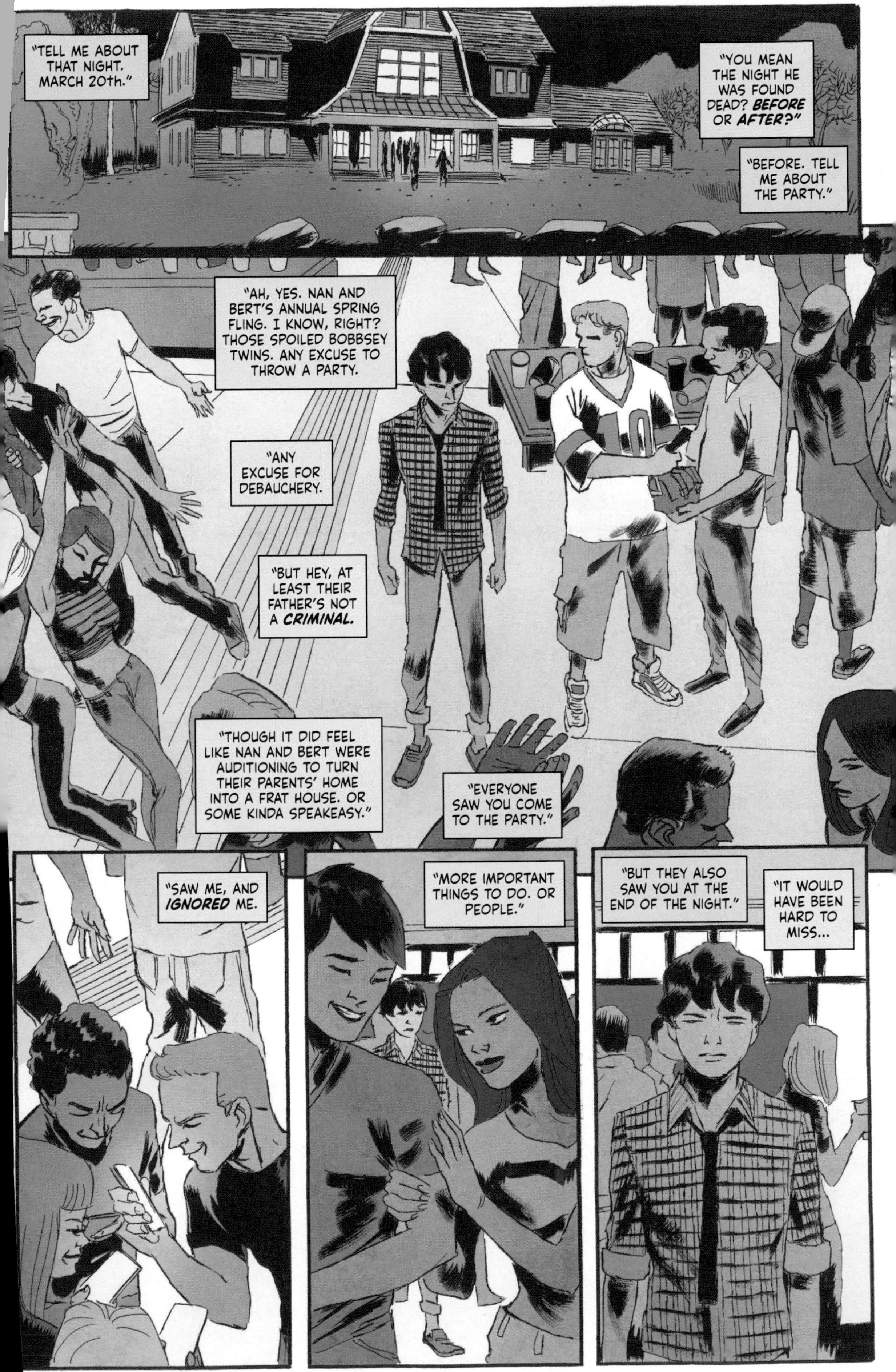
"TELL ME ABOUT THAT NIGHT. MARCH 20th."
"YOU MEAN THE NIGHT HE WAS FOUND DEAD? ***BEFORE*** OR ***AFTER?"***
"BEFORE. TELL ME ABOUT THE PARTY."
"AH, YES. NAN AND BERT'S ANNUAL SPRING FLING. I KNOW, RIGHT? THOSE SPOILED BOBBSEY TWINS. ANY EXCUSE TO THROW A PARTY.
"ANY EXCUSE FOR DEBAUCHERY.
"BUT HEY, AT LEAST THEIR FATHER'S NOT A ***CRIMINAL.***
"THOUGH IT DID FEEL LIKE NAN AND BERT WERE AUDITIONING TO TURN THEIR PARENTS' HOME INTO A FRAT HOUSE. OR SOME KINDA SPEAKEASY."
"EVERYONE SAW YOU COME TO THE PARTY."
"SAW ME, AND ***IGNORED*** ME.
"MORE IMPORTANT THINGS TO DO. OR PEOPLE."
"BUT THEY ALSO SAW YOU AT THE END OF THE NIGHT."
"IT WOULD HAVE BEEN HARD TO MISS...

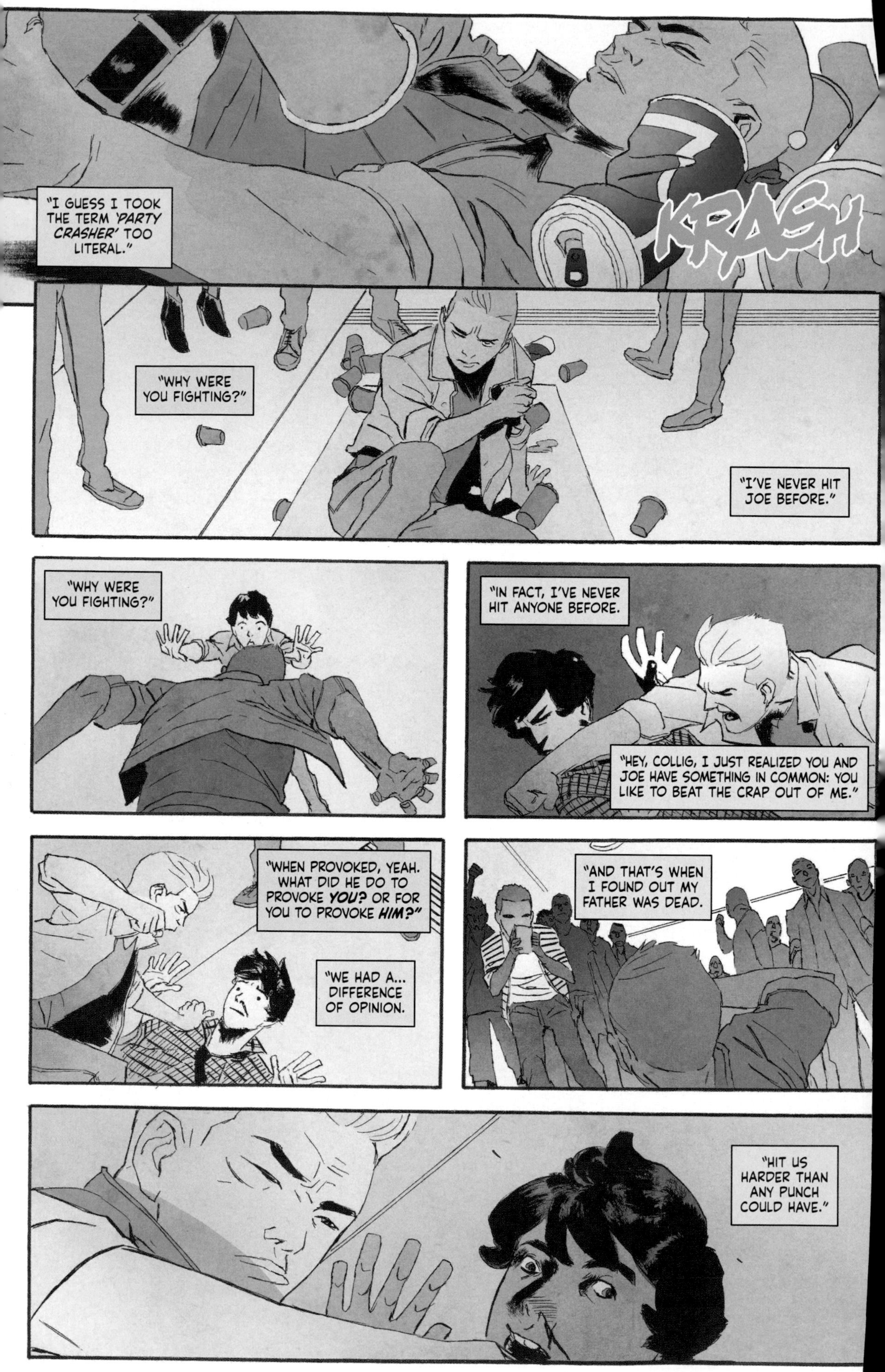
"I GUESS I TOOK THE TERM *'PARTY CRASHER'* TOO LITERAL."
KRASH
"WHY WERE YOU FIGHTING?"
"I'VE NEVER HIT JOE BEFORE."
"WHY WERE YOU FIGHTING?"
"IN FACT, I'VE NEVER HIT ANYONE BEFORE.
"HEY, COLLIG, I JUST REALIZED YOU AND JOE HAVE SOMETHING IN COMMON: YOU LIKE TO BEAT THE CRAP OUT OF ME."
"WHEN PROVOKED, YEAH. WHAT DID HE DO TO PROVOKE ***YOU?*** OR FOR YOU TO PROVOKE ***HIM?"***
"WE HAD A... DIFFERENCE OF OPINION.
"AND THAT'S WHEN I FOUND OUT MY FATHER WAS DEAD.
"HIT US HARDER THAN ANY PUNCH COULD HAVE."

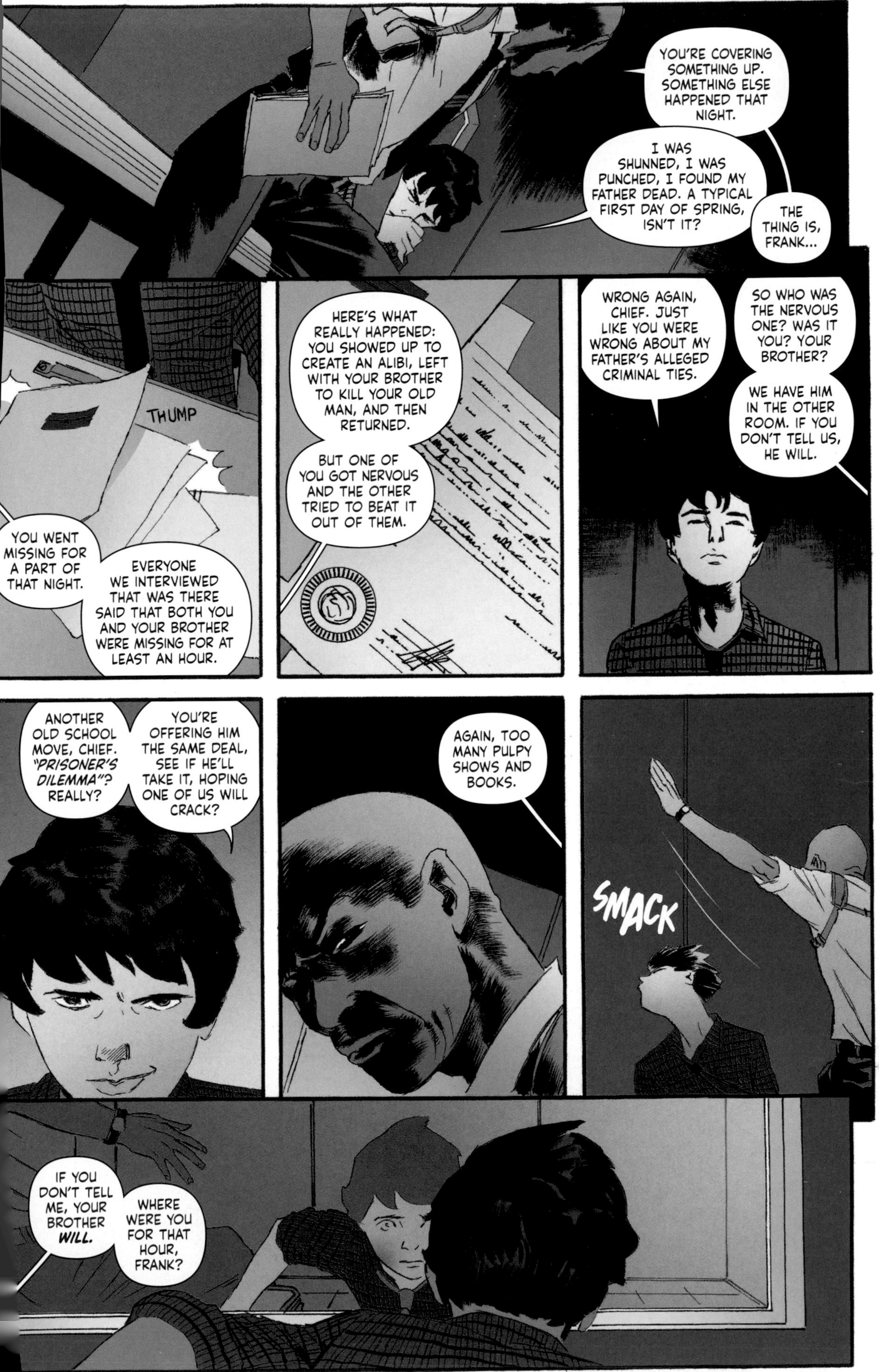
YOU'RE COVERING SOMETHING UP. SOMETHING ELSE HAPPENED THAT NIGHT.
I WAS SHUNNED, I WAS PUNCHED, I FOUND MY FATHER DEAD. A TYPICAL FIRST DAY OF SPRING, ISN'T IT?
THE THING IS, FRANK...
THUMP
YOU WENT MISSING FOR A PART OF THAT NIGHT.
EVERYONE WE INTERVIEWED THAT WAS THERE SAID THAT BOTH YOU AND YOUR BROTHER WERE MISSING FOR AT LEAST AN HOUR.
HERE'S WHAT REALLY HAPPENED: YOU SHOWED UP TO CREATE AN ALIBI, LEFT WITH YOUR BROTHER TO KILL YOUR OLD MAN, AND THEN RETURNED.
BUT ONE OF YOU GOT NERVOUS AND THE OTHER TRIED TO BEAT IT OUT OF THEM.
WRONG AGAIN, CHIEF. JUST LIKE YOU WERE WRONG ABOUT MY FATHER'S ALLEGED CRIMINAL TIES.
SO WHO WAS THE NERVOUS ONE? WAS IT YOU? YOUR BROTHER?
WE HAVE HIM IN THE OTHER ROOM. IF YOU DON'T TELL US, HE WILL.
ANOTHER OLD SCHOOL MOVE, CHIEF. *"PRISONER'S DILEMMA"*? REALLY?
YOU'RE OFFERING HIM THE SAME DEAL, SEE IF HE'LL TAKE IT, HOPING ONE OF US WILL CRACK?
AGAIN, TOO MANY PULPY SHOWS AND BOOKS.
SMACK
IF YOU DON'T TELL ME, YOUR BROTHER ***WILL.***
WHERE WERE YOU FOR THAT HOUR, FRANK?

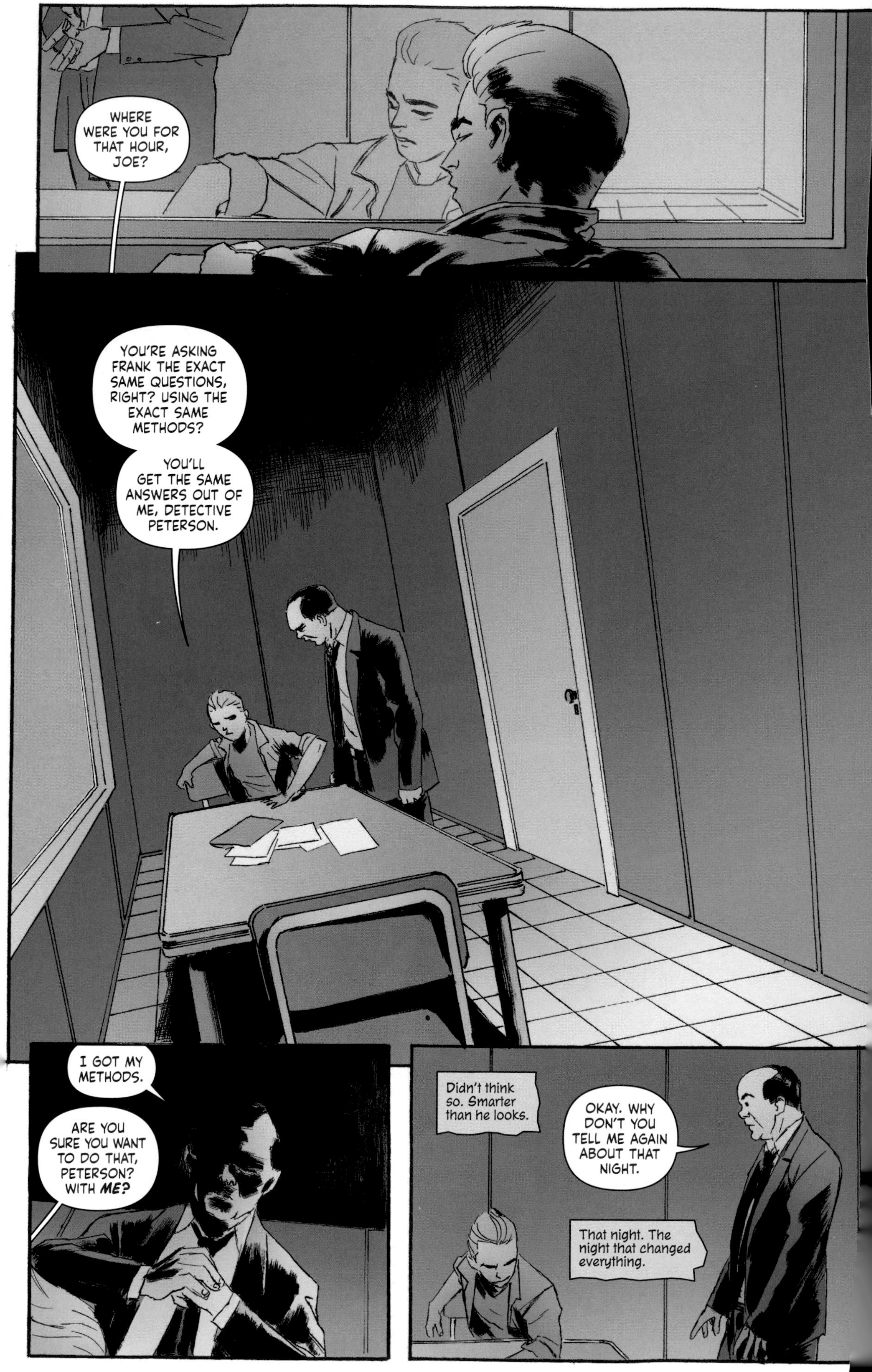
WHERE WERE YOU FOR THAT HOUR, JOE?
YOU'RE ASKING FRANK THE EXACT SAME QUESTIONS, RIGHT? USING THE EXACT SAME METHODS?
YOU'LL GET THE SAME ANSWERS OUT OF ME, DETECTIVE PETERSON.
I GOT MY METHODS.
ARE YOU SURE YOU WANT TO DO THAT, PETERSON? WITH *ME?*
Didn't think so. Smarter than he looks.
OKAY. WHY DON'T YOU TELL ME AGAIN ABOUT THAT NIGHT.
That night. The night that changed everything.

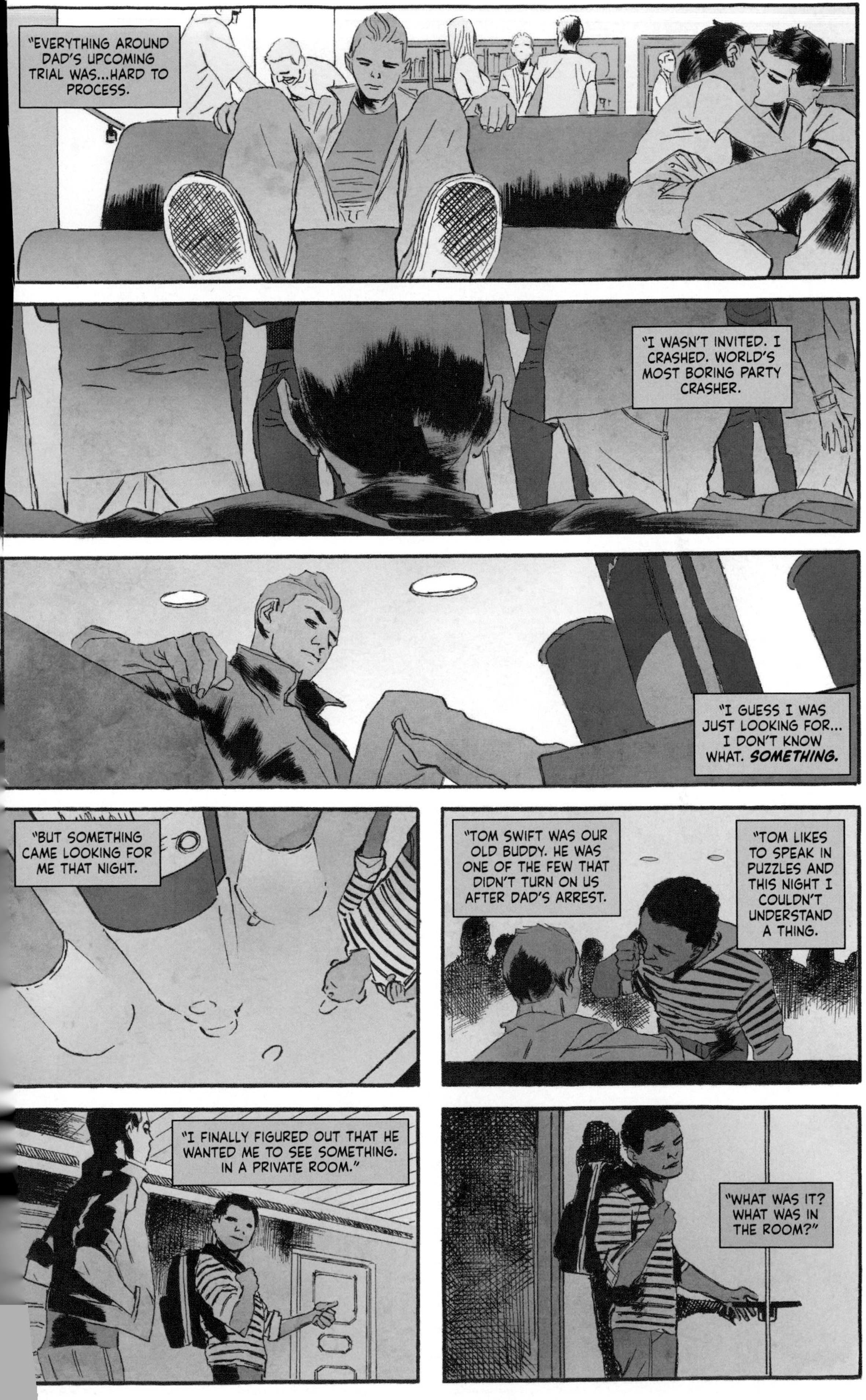
"EVERYTHING AROUND DAD'S UPCOMING TRIAL WAS...HARD TO PROCESS.
"I WASN'T INVITED. I CRASHED. WORLD'S MOST BORING PARTY CRASHER.
"I GUESS I WAS JUST LOOKING FOR... I DON'T KNOW WHAT. ***SOMETHING.***
"BUT SOMETHING CAME LOOKING FOR ME THAT NIGHT.
"TOM SWIFT WAS OUR OLD BUDDY. HE WAS ONE OF THE FEW THAT DIDN'T TURN ON US AFTER DAD'S ARREST.
"TOM LIKES TO SPEAK IN PUZZLES AND THIS NIGHT I COULDN'T UNDERSTAND A THING.
"I FINALLY FIGURED OUT THAT HE WANTED ME TO SEE SOMETHING. IN A PRIVATE ROOM."
"WHAT WAS IT? WHAT WAS IN THE ROOM?"

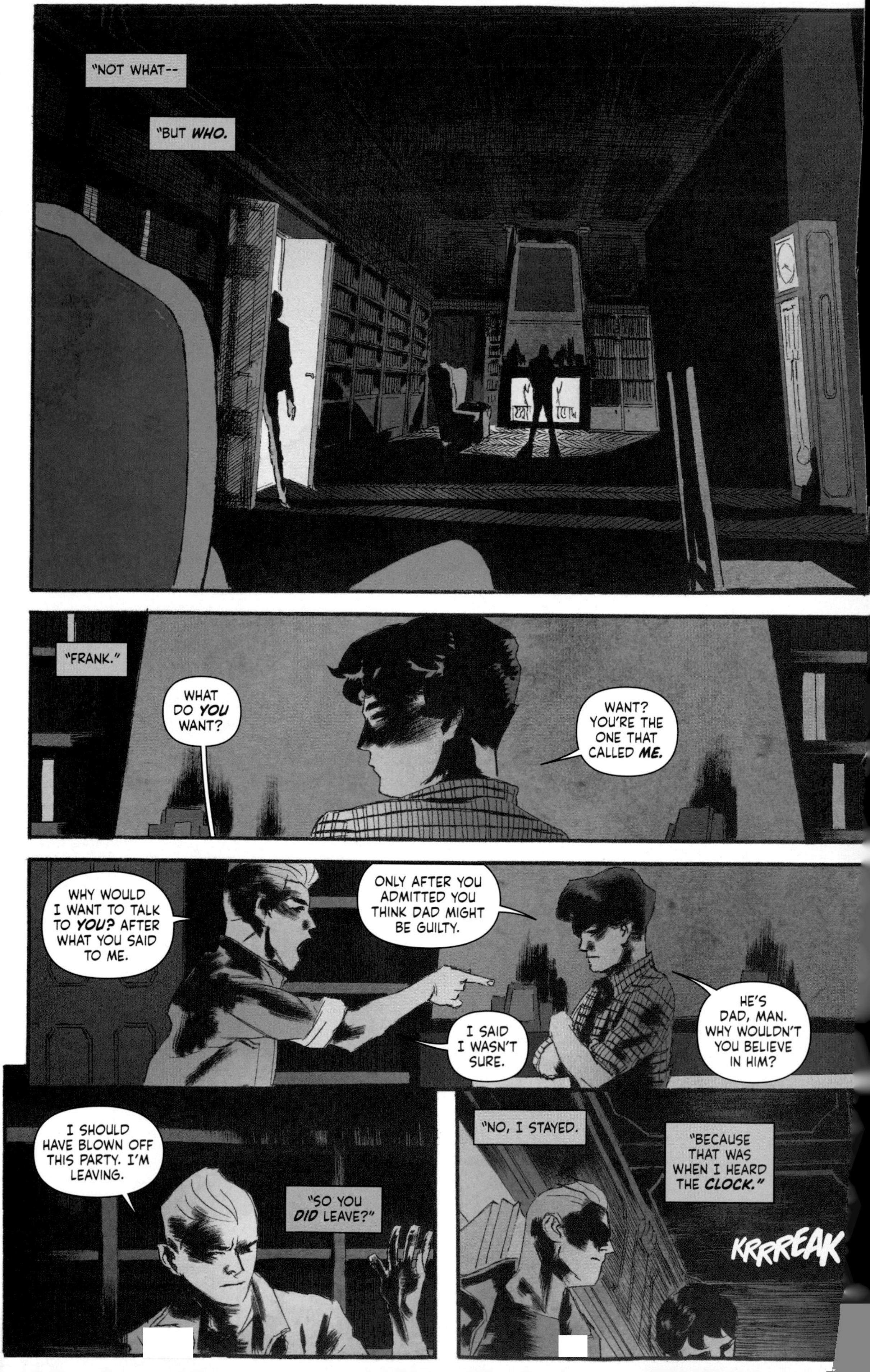
"NOT WHAT--
"BUT WHO.
"FRANK."
WHAT DO YOU WANT?
WANT? YOU'RE THE ONE THAT CALLED ME.
WHY WOULD I WANT TO TALK TO YOU? AFTER WHAT YOU SAID TO ME.
ONLY AFTER YOU ADMITTED YOU THINK DAD MIGHT BE GUILTY.
I SAID I WASN'T SURE.
HE'S DAD, MAN. WHY WOULDN'T YOU BELIEVE IN HIM?
I SHOULD HAVE BLOWN OFF THIS PARTY. I'M LEAVING.
"SO YOU DID LEAVE?"
"NO, I STAYED.
"BECAUSE THAT WAS WHEN I HEARD THE CLOCK."
KRRRREAK

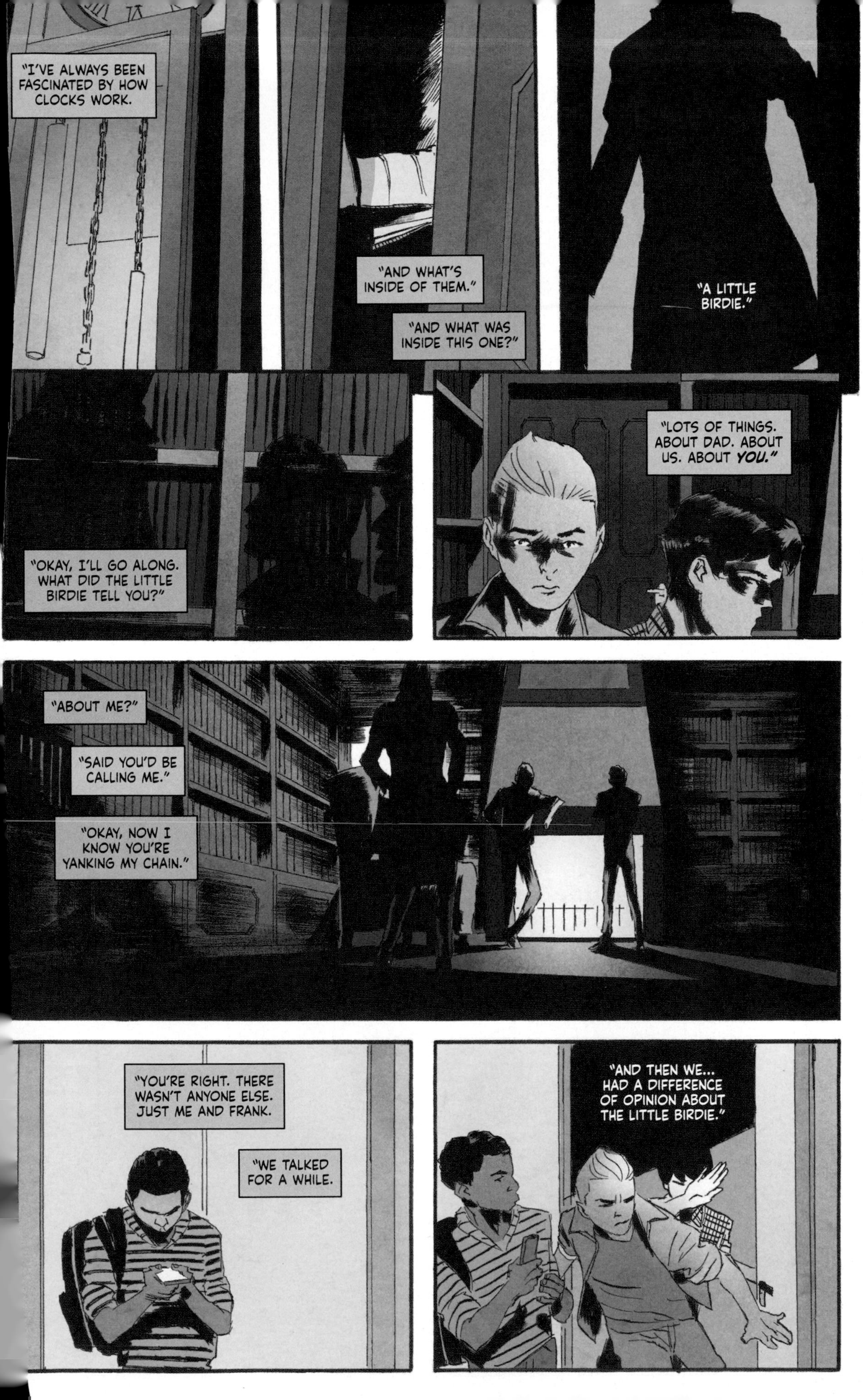
"I'VE ALWAYS BEEN FASCINATED BY HOW CLOCKS WORK.
"AND WHAT'S INSIDE OF THEM."
"AND WHAT WAS INSIDE THIS ONE?"
"A LITTLE BIRDIE."
"OKAY, I'LL GO ALONG. WHAT DID THE LITTLE BIRDIE TELL YOU?"
"LOTS OF THINGS. ABOUT DAD. ABOUT US. ABOUT YOU."
"ABOUT ME?"
"SAID YOU'D BE CALLING ME."
"OKAY, NOW I KNOW YOU'RE YANKING MY CHAIN."
"YOU'RE RIGHT. THERE WASN'T ANYONE ELSE. JUST ME AND FRANK.
"WE TALKED FOR A WHILE.
"AND THEN WE... HAD A DIFFERENCE OF OPINION ABOUT THE LITTLE BIRDIE."

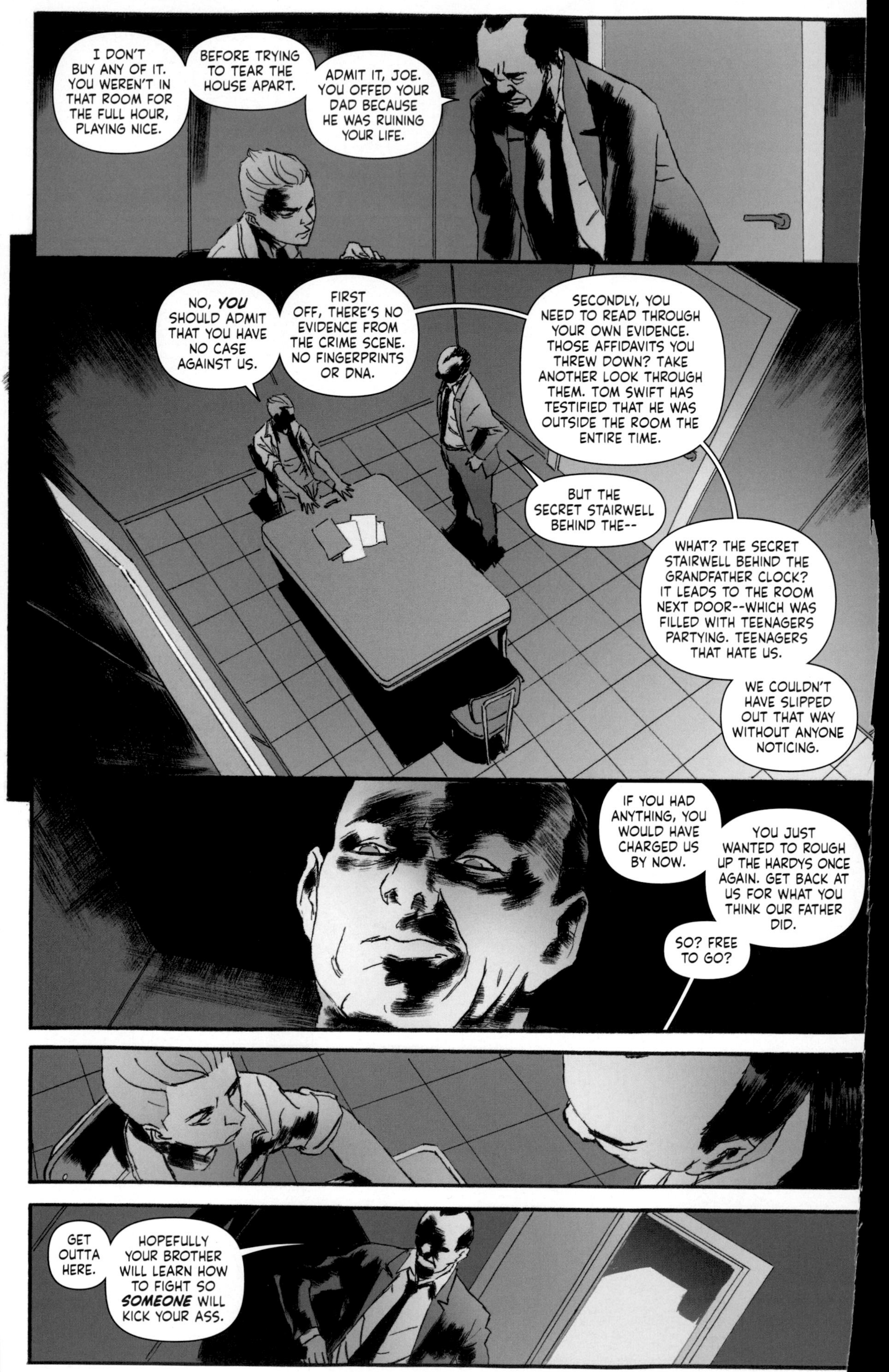
I DON'T BUY ANY OF IT. YOU WEREN'T IN THAT ROOM FOR THE FULL HOUR, PLAYING NICE.
BEFORE TRYING TO TEAR THE HOUSE APART.
ADMIT IT, JOE. YOU OFFED YOUR DAD BECAUSE HE WAS RUINING YOUR LIFE.
NO, *YOU* SHOULD ADMIT THAT YOU HAVE NO CASE AGAINST US.
FIRST OFF, THERE'S NO EVIDENCE FROM THE CRIME SCENE. NO FINGERPRINTS OR DNA.
SECONDLY, YOU NEED TO READ THROUGH YOUR OWN EVIDENCE. THOSE AFFIDAVITS YOU THREW DOWN? TAKE ANOTHER LOOK THROUGH THEM. TOM SWIFT HAS TESTIFIED THAT HE WAS OUTSIDE THE ROOM THE ENTIRE TIME.
BUT THE SECRET STAIRWELL BEHIND THE--
WHAT? THE SECRET STAIRWELL BEHIND THE GRANDFATHER CLOCK? IT LEADS TO THE ROOM NEXT DOOR--WHICH WAS FILLED WITH TEENAGERS PARTYING. TEENAGERS THAT HATE US.
WE COULDN'T HAVE SLIPPED OUT THAT WAY WITHOUT ANYONE NOTICING.
IF YOU HAD ANYTHING, YOU WOULD HAVE CHARGED US BY NOW.
YOU JUST WANTED TO ROUGH UP THE HARDYS ONCE AGAIN. GET BACK AT US FOR WHAT YOU THINK OUR FATHER DID.
SO? FREE TO GO?
GET OUTTA HERE.
HOPEFULLY YOUR BROTHER WILL LEARN HOW TO FIGHT SO ***SOMEONE*** WILL KICK YOUR ASS.

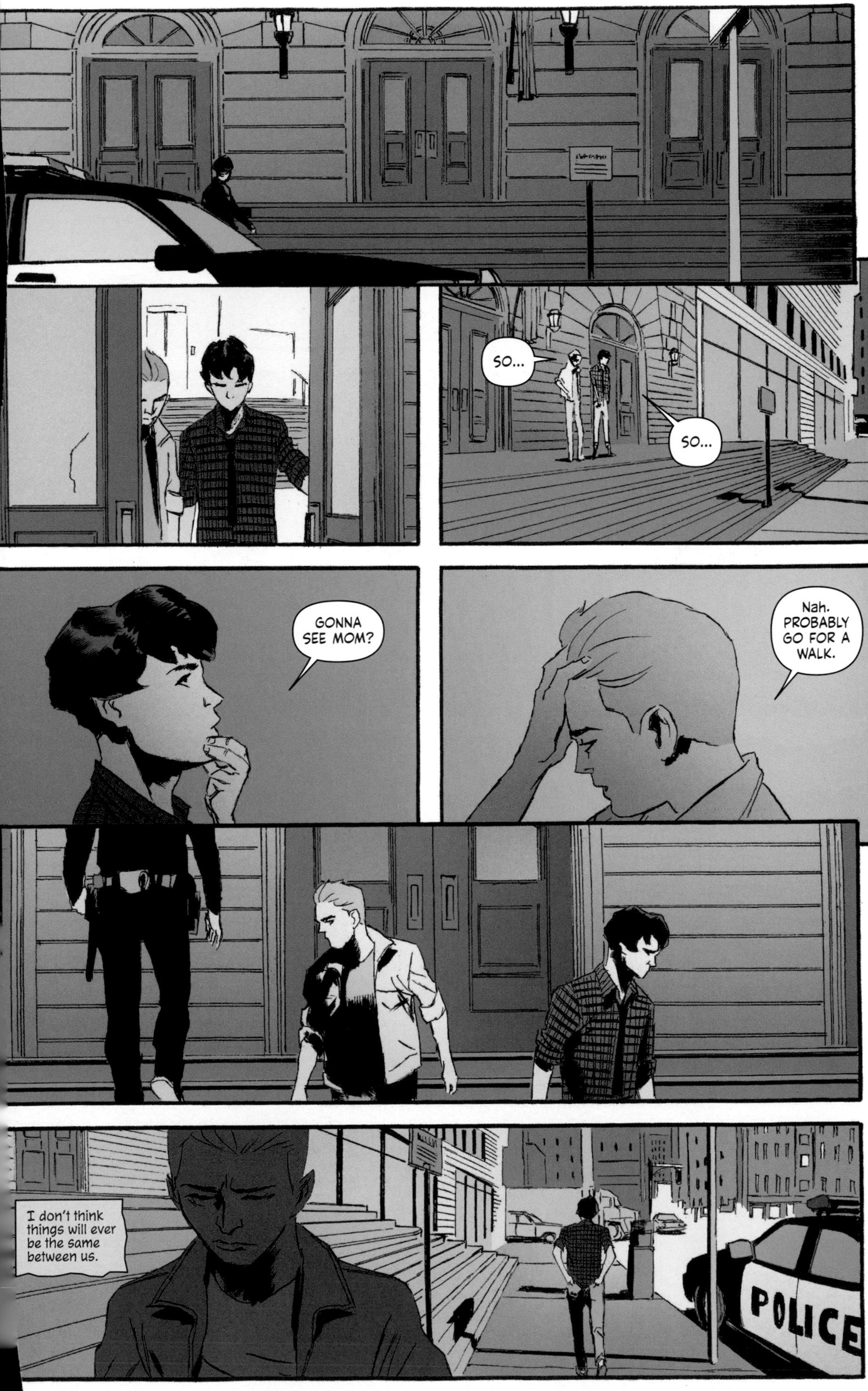
SO...
SO...
GONNA SEE MOM?
Nah. PROBABLY GO FOR A WALK.
I don't think things will ever be the same between us.
POLICE

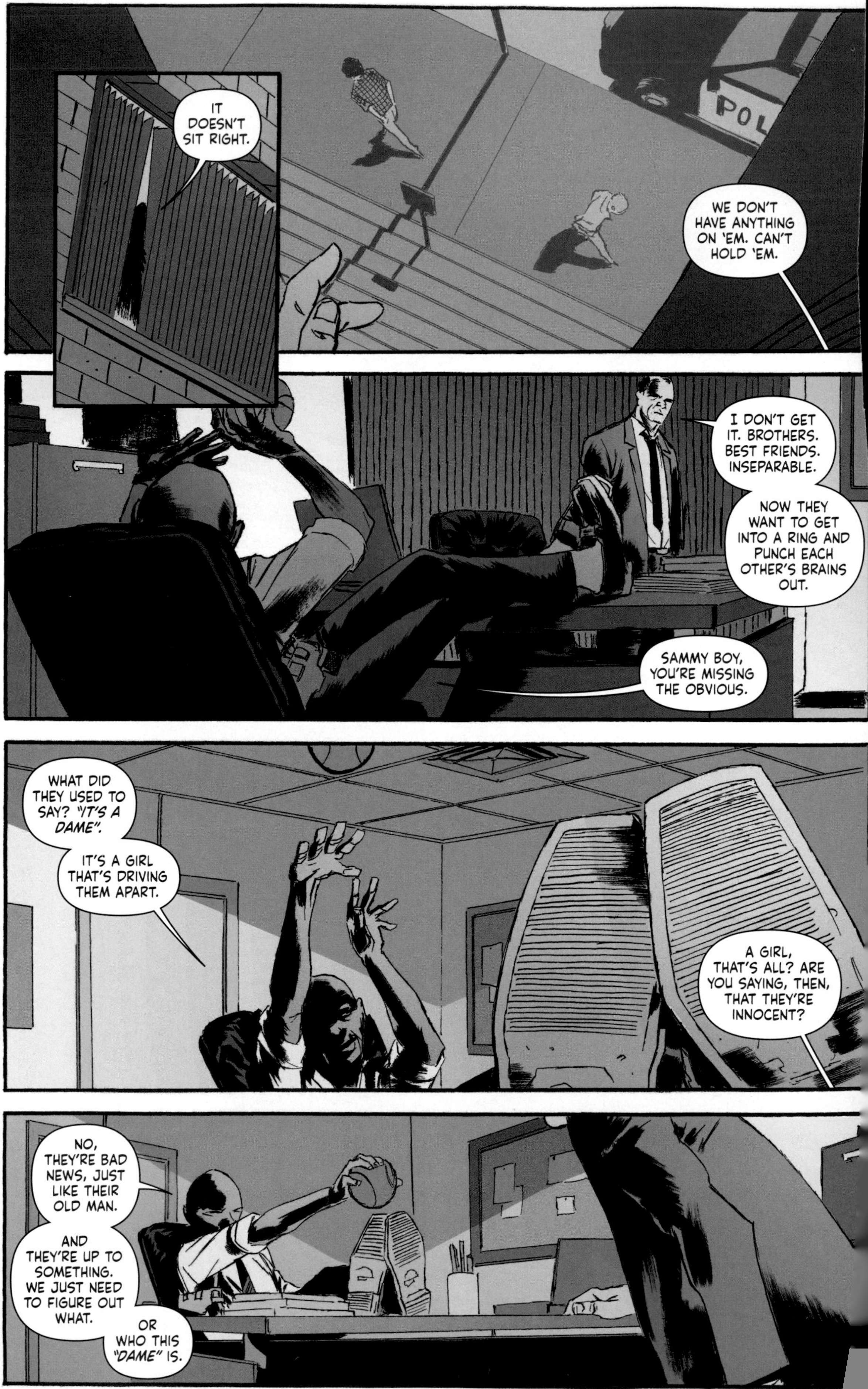
IT DOESN'T SIT RIGHT.
WE DON'T HAVE ANYTHING ON 'EM. CAN'T HOLD 'EM.
I DON'T GET IT. BROTHERS. BEST FRIENDS. INSEPARABLE.
NOW THEY WANT TO GET INTO A RING AND PUNCH EACH OTHER'S BRAINS OUT.
SAMMY BOY, YOU'RE MISSING THE OBVIOUS.
WHAT DID THEY USED TO SAY? *"IT'S A DAME"*.
IT'S A GIRL THAT'S DRIVING THEM APART.
A GIRL, THAT'S ALL? ARE YOU SAYING, THEN, THAT THEY'RE INNOCENT?
NO, THEY'RE BAD NEWS, JUST LIKE THEIR OLD MAN.
AND THEY'RE UP TO SOMETHING. WE JUST NEED TO FIGURE OUT WHAT.
OR WHO THIS *"DAME"* IS.

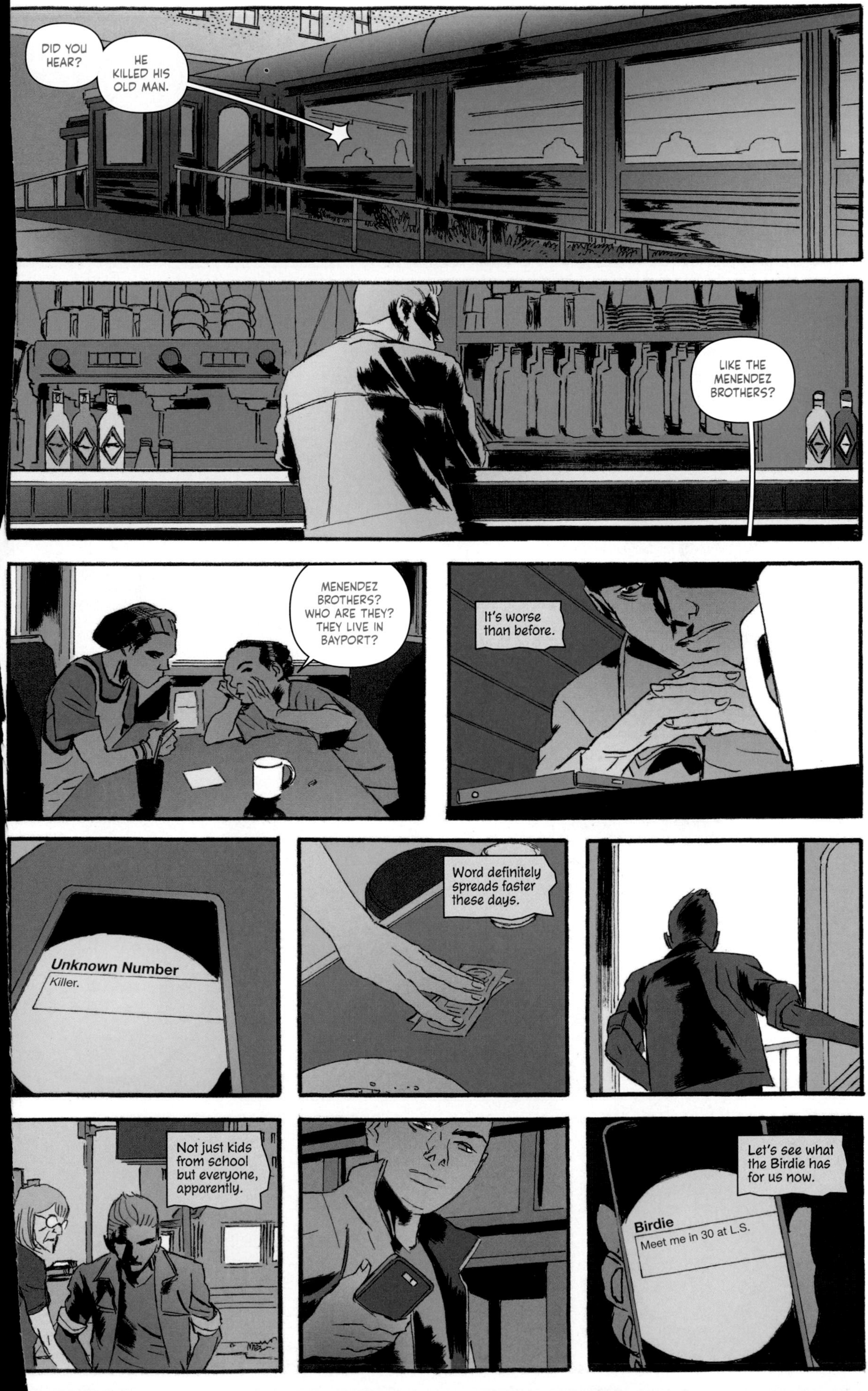

DID YOU HEAR?
HE KILLED HIS OLD MAN.
LIKE THE MENENDEZ BROTHERS?
MENENDEZ BROTHERS? WHO ARE THEY? THEY LIVE IN BAYPORT?
It's worse than before.
Unknown Number
Killer.
Word definitely spreads faster these days.
Not just kids from school but everyone, apparently.
Let's see what the Birdie has for us now.
Birdie
Meet me in 30 at L.S.

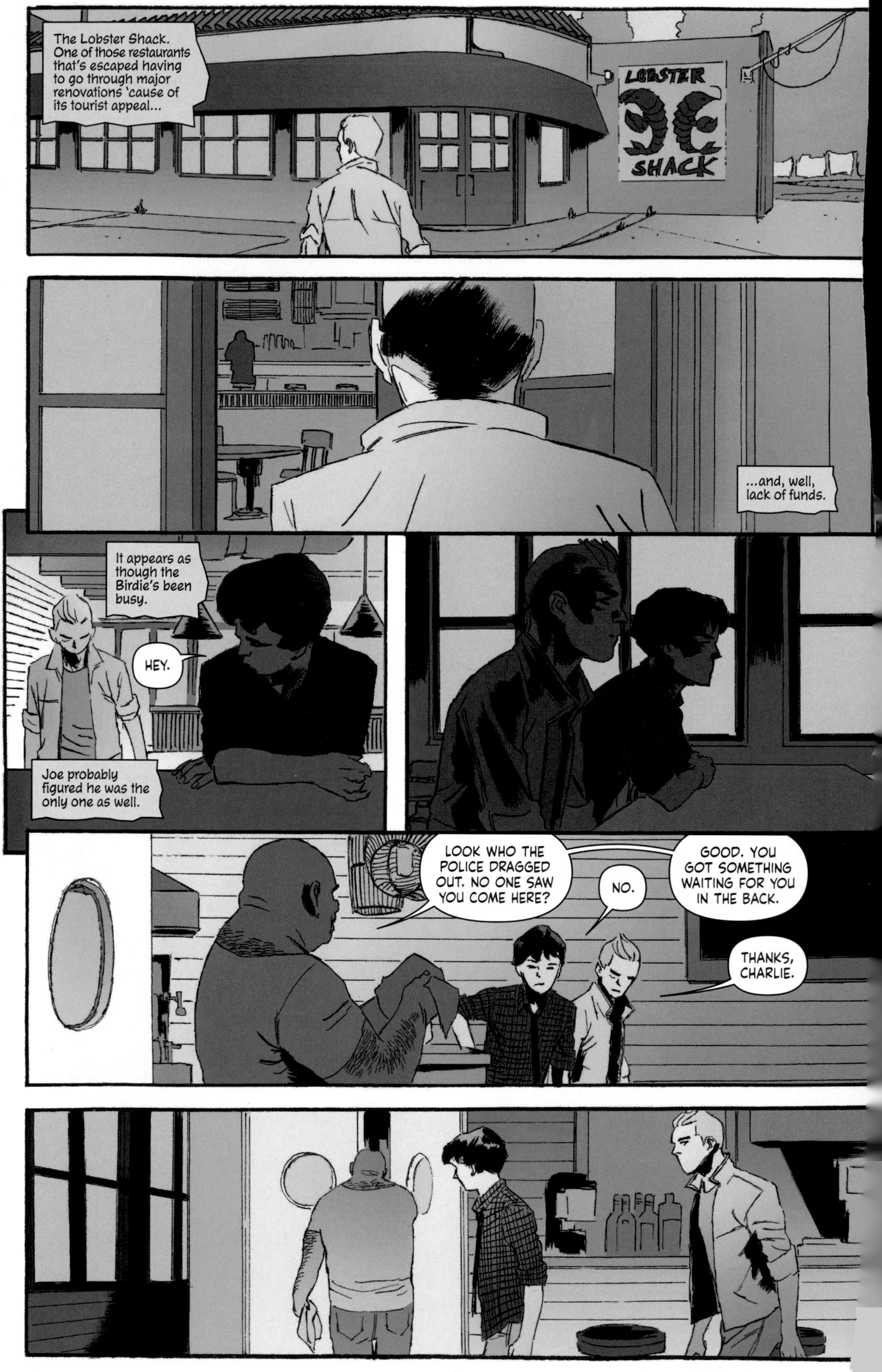
The Lobster Shack. One of those restaurants that's escaped having to go through major renovations 'cause of its tourist appeal...
LOBSTER SHACK
...and, well, lack of funds.
It appears as though the Birdie's been busy.
HEY.
Joe probably figured he was the only one as well.
LOOK WHO THE POLICE DRAGGED OUT. NO ONE SAW YOU COME HERE?
NO.
GOOD. YOU GOT SOMETHING WAITING FOR YOU IN THE BACK.
THANKS, CHARLIE.

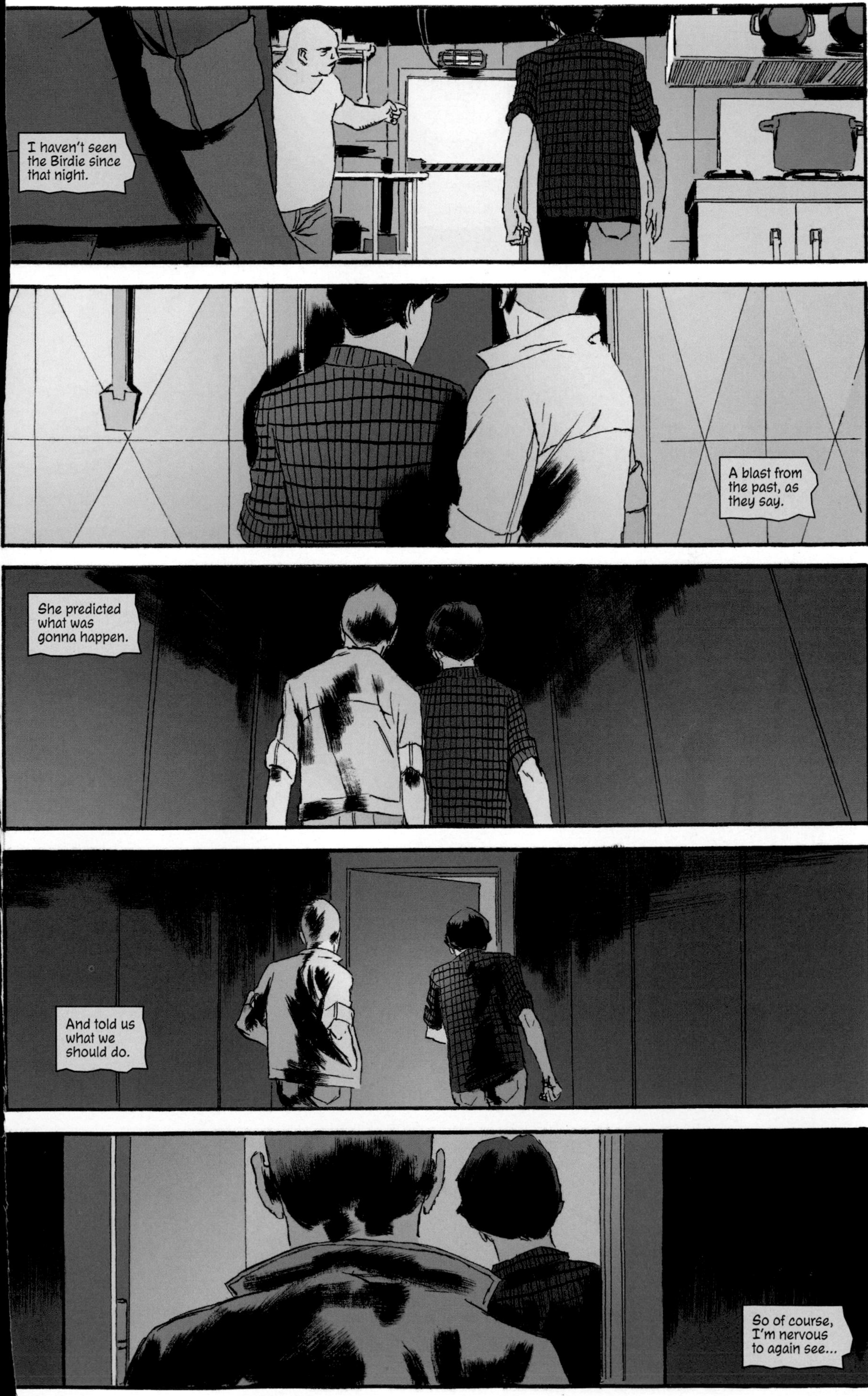
I haven't seen the Birdie since that night.
A blast from the past, as they say.
She predicted what was gonna happen.
And told us what we should do.
So of course, I'm nervous to again see...

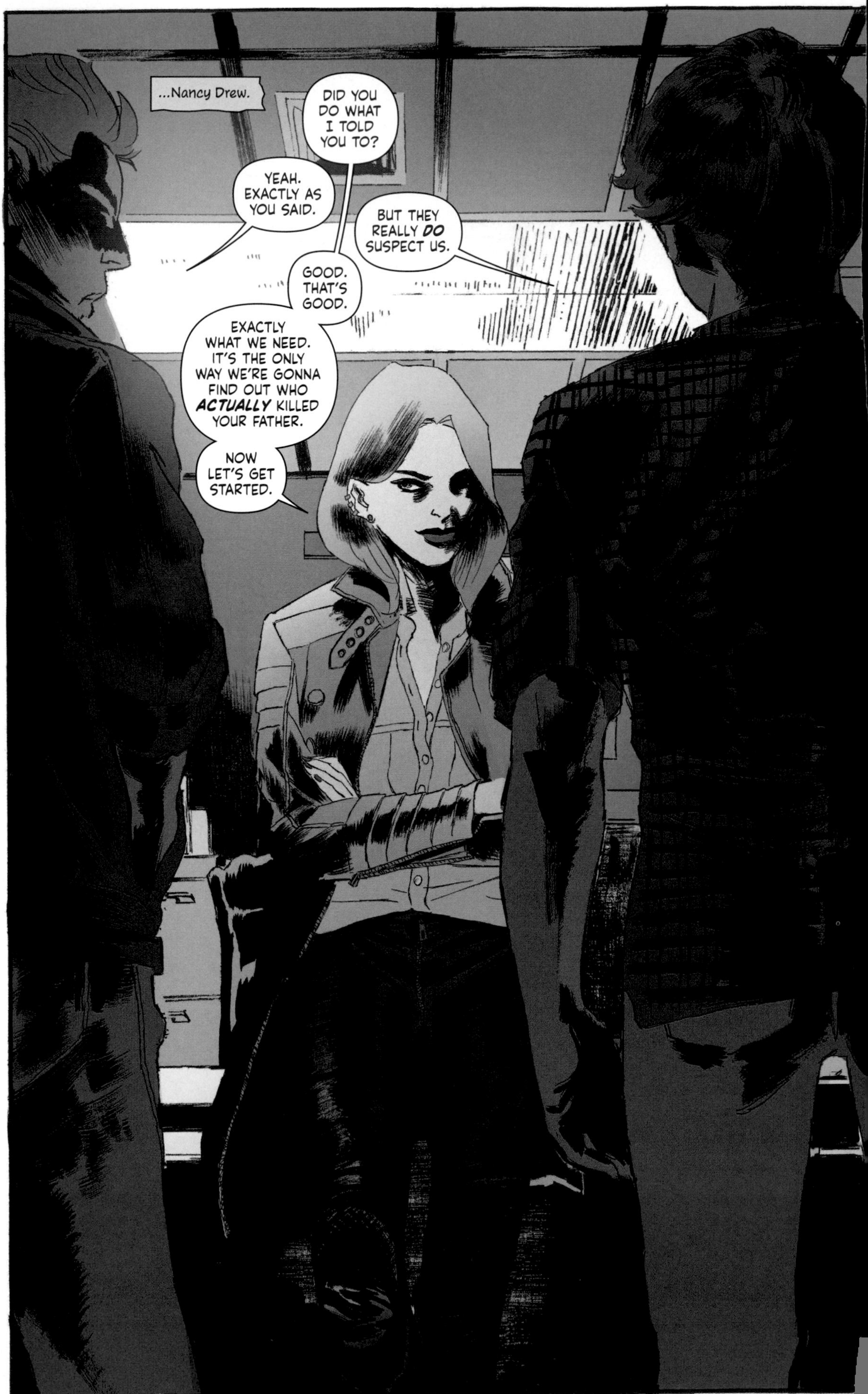
...Nancy Drew.
DID YOU DO WHAT I TOLD YOU TO?
YEAH. EXACTLY AS YOU SAID.
BUT THEY REALLY **DO** SUSPECT US.
GOOD. THAT'S GOOD.
EXACTLY WHAT WE NEED. IT'S THE ONLY WAY WE'RE GONNA FIND OUT WHO **ACTUALLY** KILLED YOUR FATHER.
NOW LET'S GET STARTED.

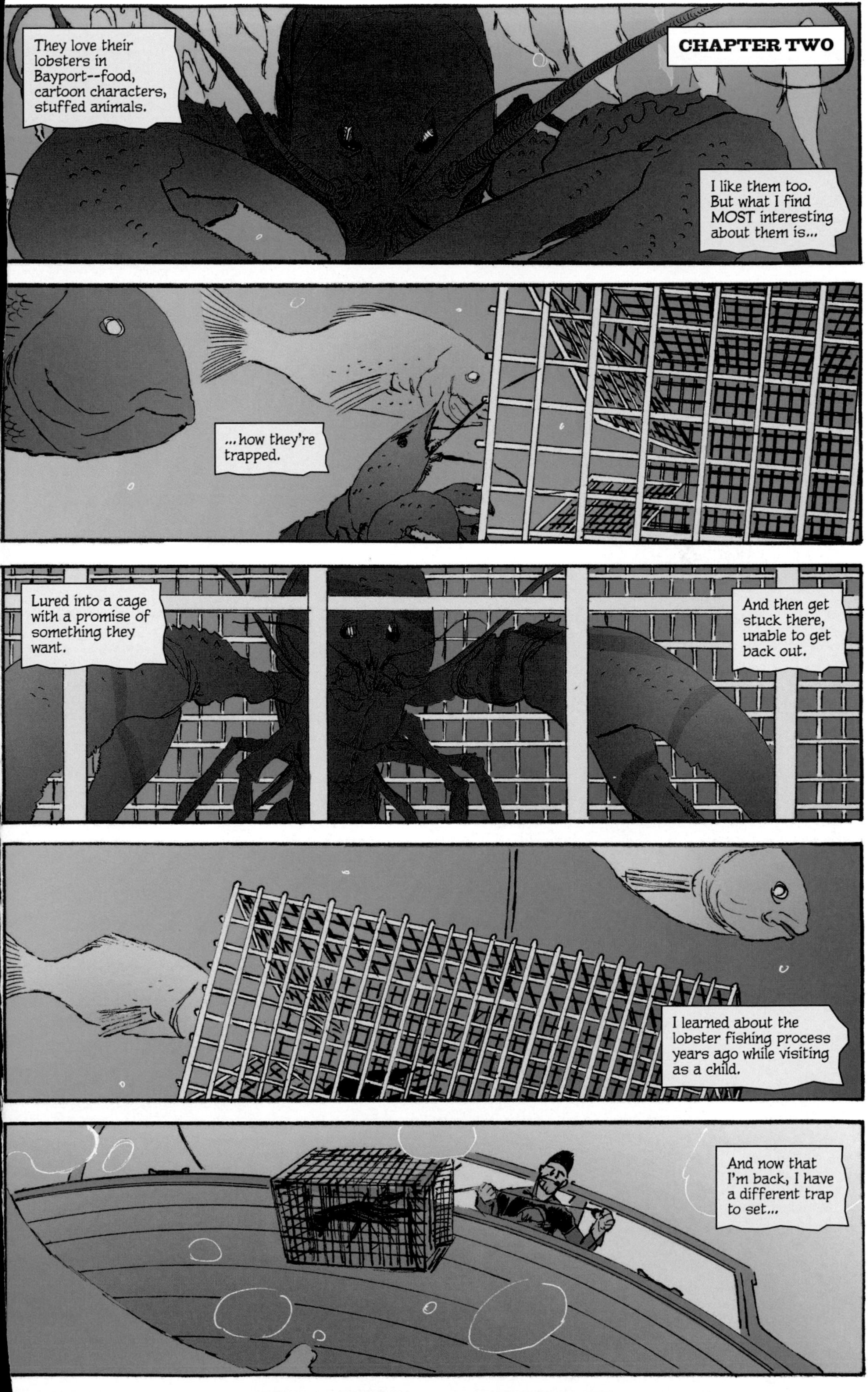
CHAPTER TWO
They love their lobsters in Bayport--food, cartoon characters, stuffed animals.
I like them too. But what I find MOST interesting about them is...
...how they're trapped.
Lured into a cage with a promise of something they want.
And then get stuck there, unable to get back out.
I learned about the lobster fishing process years ago while visiting as a child.
And now that I'm back, I have a different trap to set...

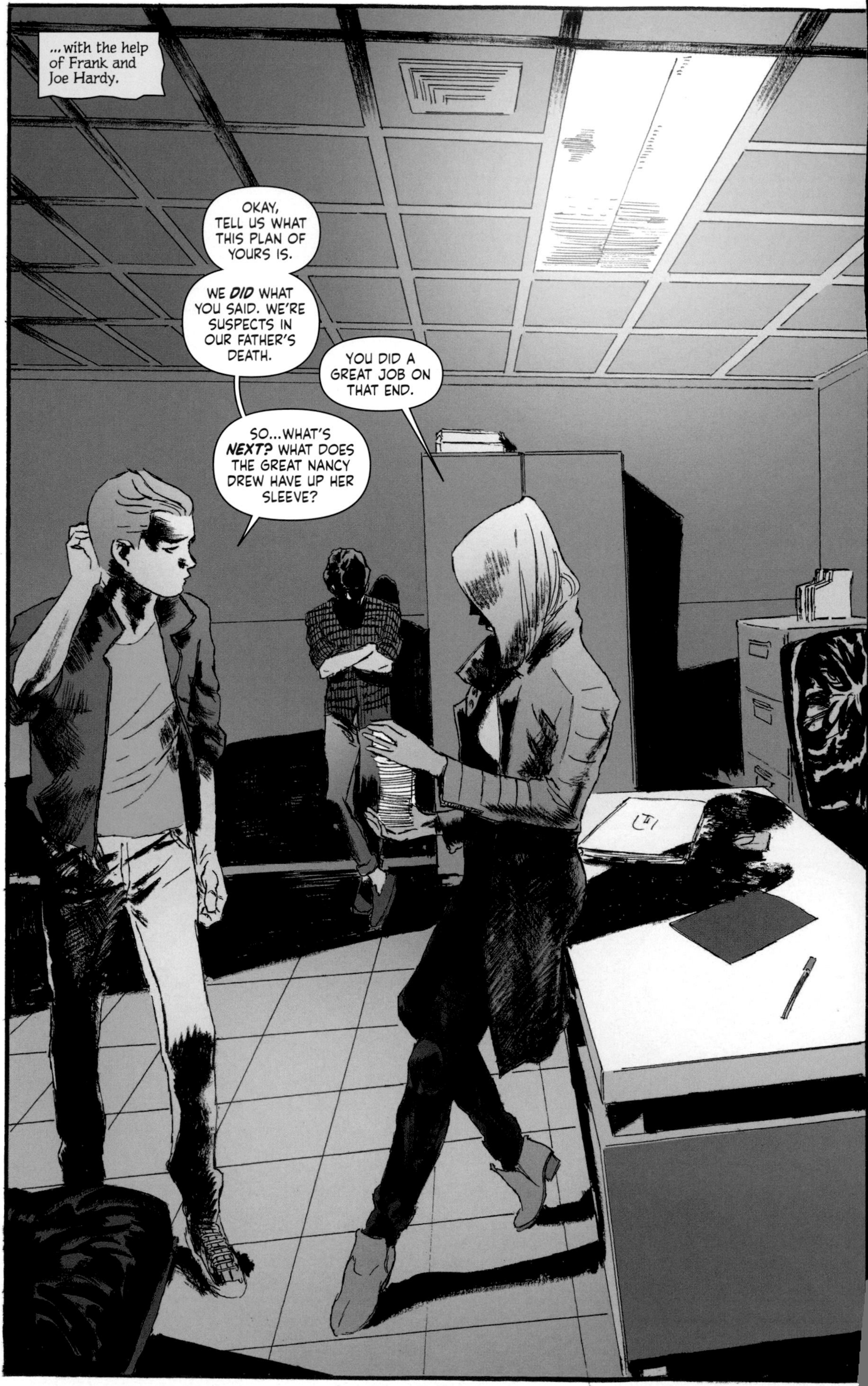
...with the help of Frank and Joe Hardy.
OKAY, TELL US WHAT THIS PLAN OF YOURS IS.
WE *DID* WHAT YOU SAID. WE'RE SUSPECTS IN OUR FATHER'S DEATH.
YOU DID A GREAT JOB ON THAT END.
SO...WHAT'S *NEXT?* WHAT DOES THE GREAT NANCY DREW HAVE UP HER SLEEVE?

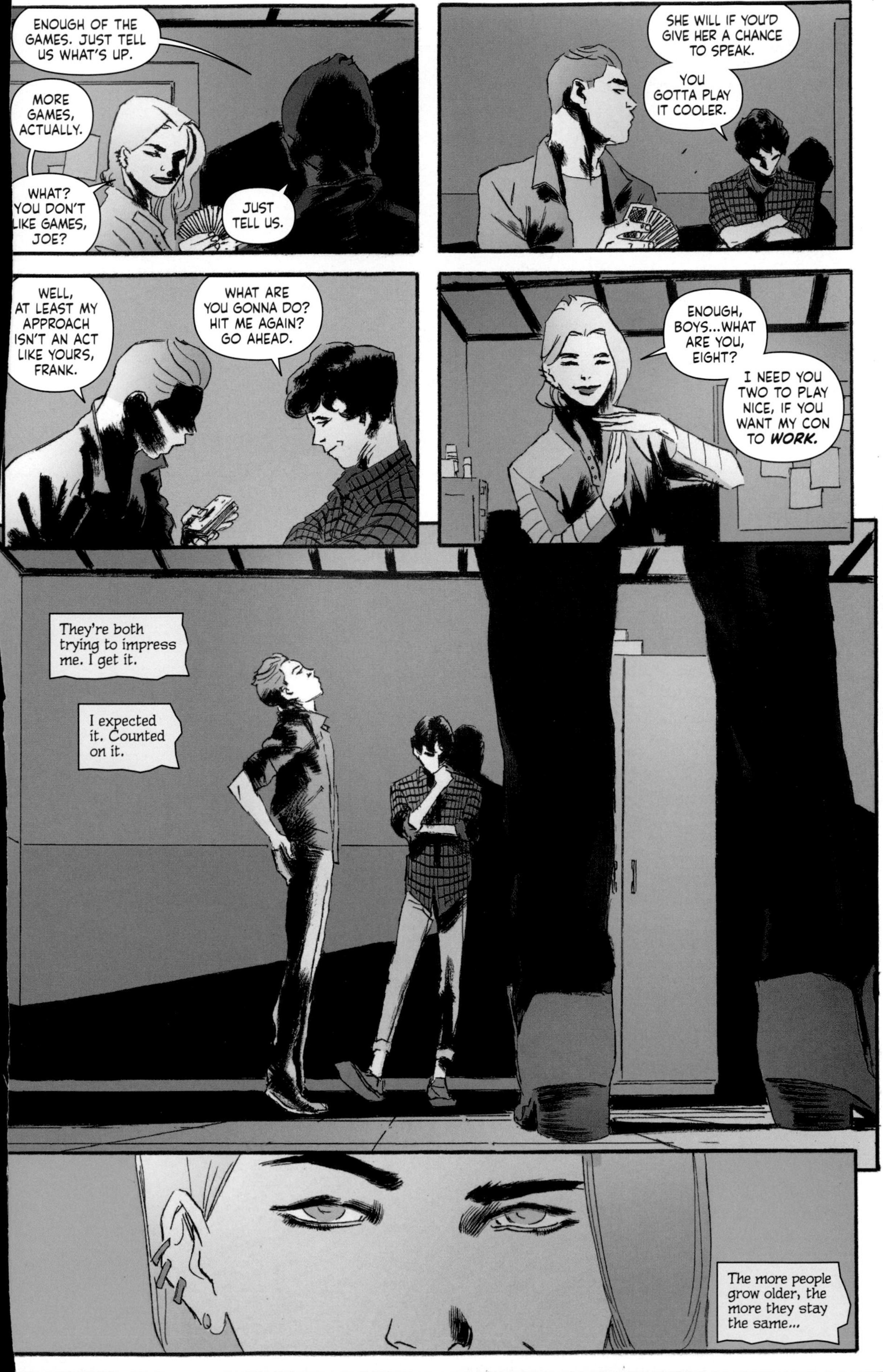
ENOUGH OF THE GAMES. JUST TELL US WHAT'S UP.
MORE GAMES, ACTUALLY.
WHAT? YOU DON'T LIKE GAMES, JOE?
JUST TELL US.
SHE WILL IF YOU'D GIVE HER A CHANCE TO SPEAK.
YOU GOTTA PLAY IT COOLER.
WELL, AT LEAST MY APPROACH ISN'T AN ACT LIKE YOURS, FRANK.
WHAT ARE YOU GONNA DO? HIT ME AGAIN? GO AHEAD.
ENOUGH, BOYS...WHAT ARE YOU, EIGHT?
I NEED YOU TWO TO PLAY NICE, IF YOU WANT MY CON TO WORK.
They're both trying to impress me. I get it.
I expected it. Counted on it.
The more people grow older, the more they stay the same...

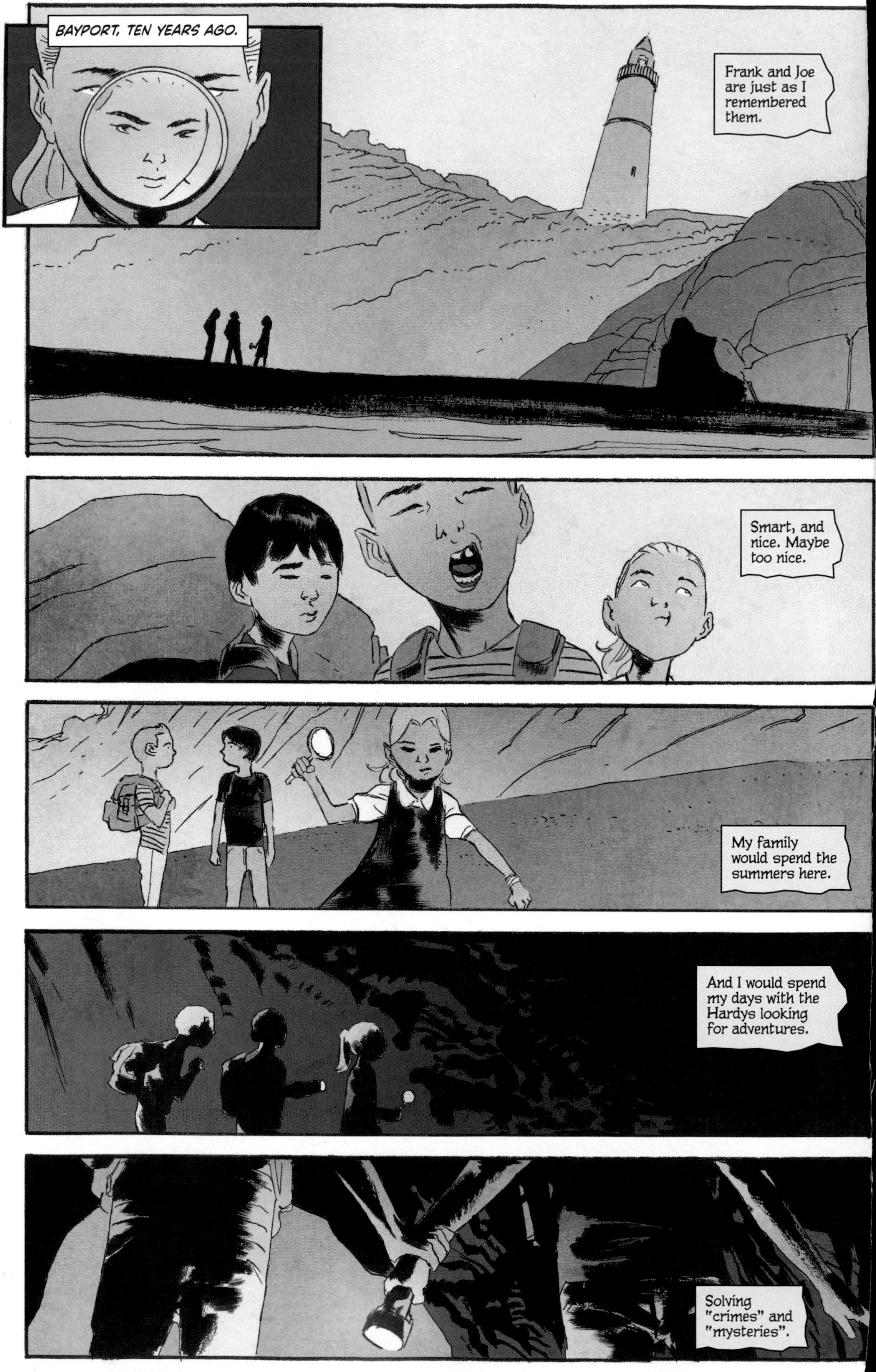
BAYPORT, TEN YEARS AGO.
Frank and Joe are just as I remembered them.
Smart, and nice. Maybe too nice.
My family would spend the summers here.
And I would spend my days with the Hardys looking for adventures.
Solving "crimes" and "mysteries".

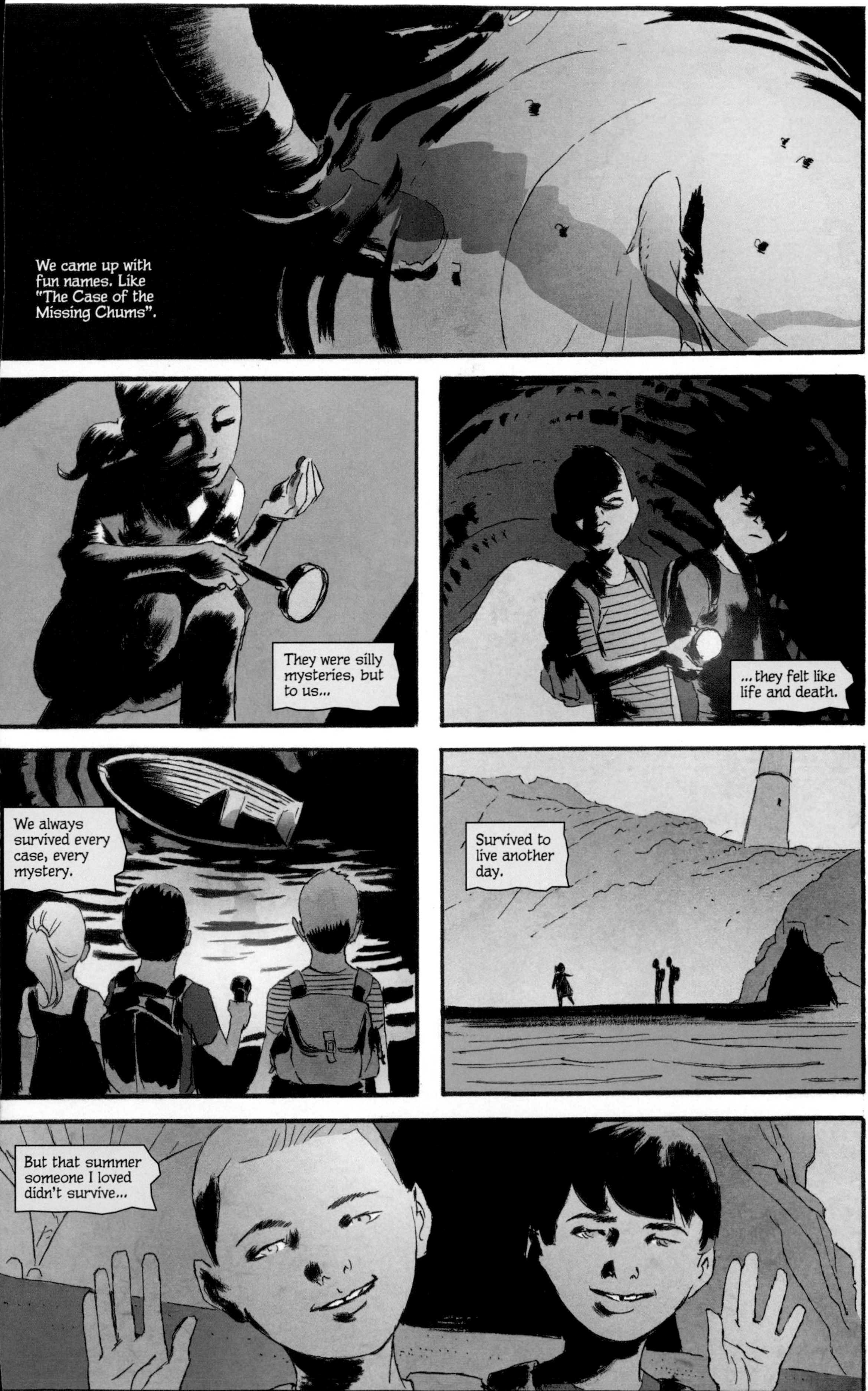
We came up with fun names. Like "The Case of the Missing Chums".
They were silly mysteries, but to us...
...they felt like life and death.
We always survived every case, every mystery.
Survived to live another day.
But that summer someone I loved didn't survive...

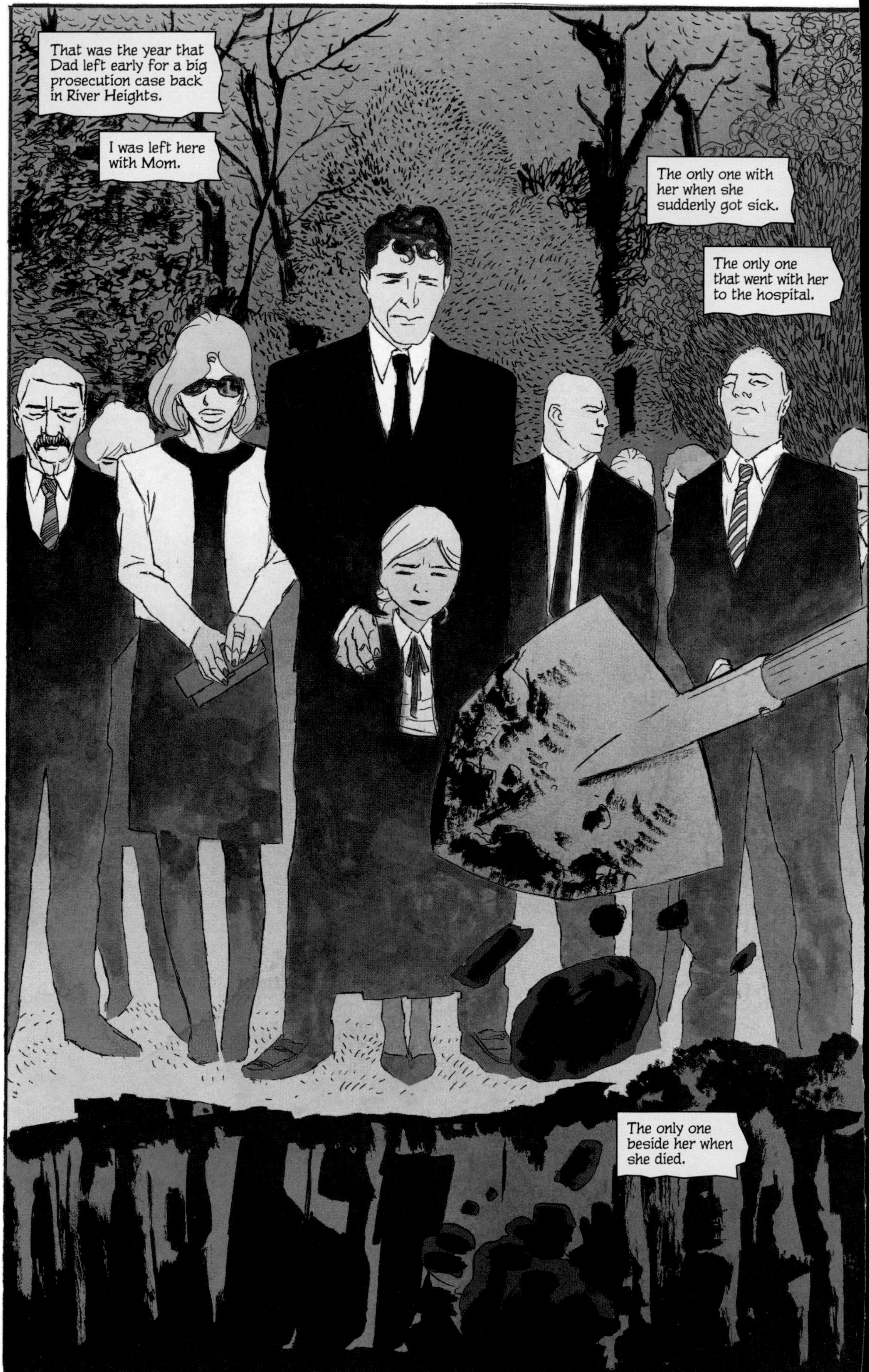
That was the year that Dad left early for a big prosecution case back in River Heights.
I was left here with Mom.
The only one with her when she suddenly got sick.
The only one that went with her to the hospital.
The only one beside her when she died.

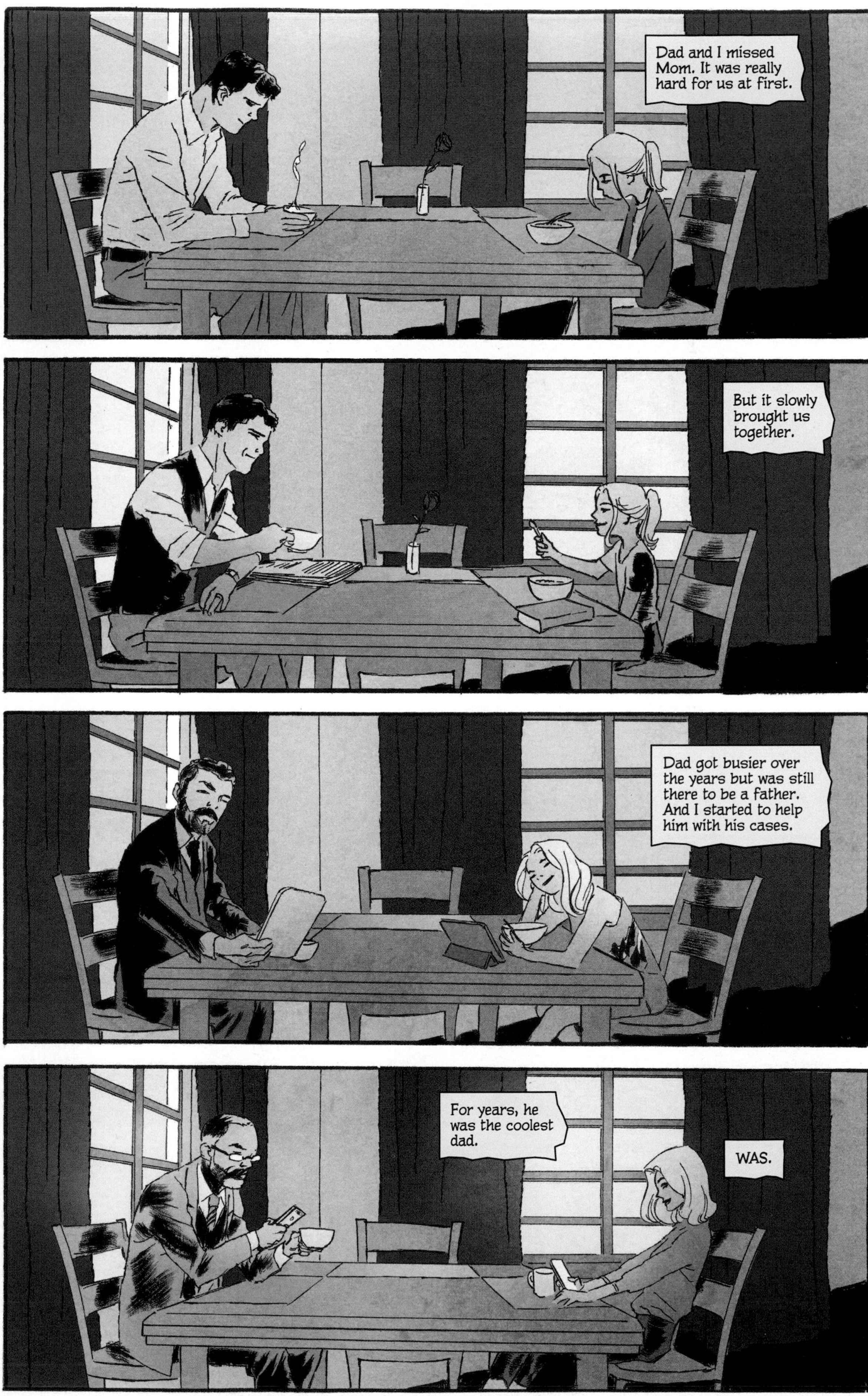
Dad and I missed Mom. It was really hard for us at first.
But it slowly brought us together.
Dad got busier over the years but was still there to be a father. And I started to help him with his cases.
For years, he was the coolest dad.
WAS.

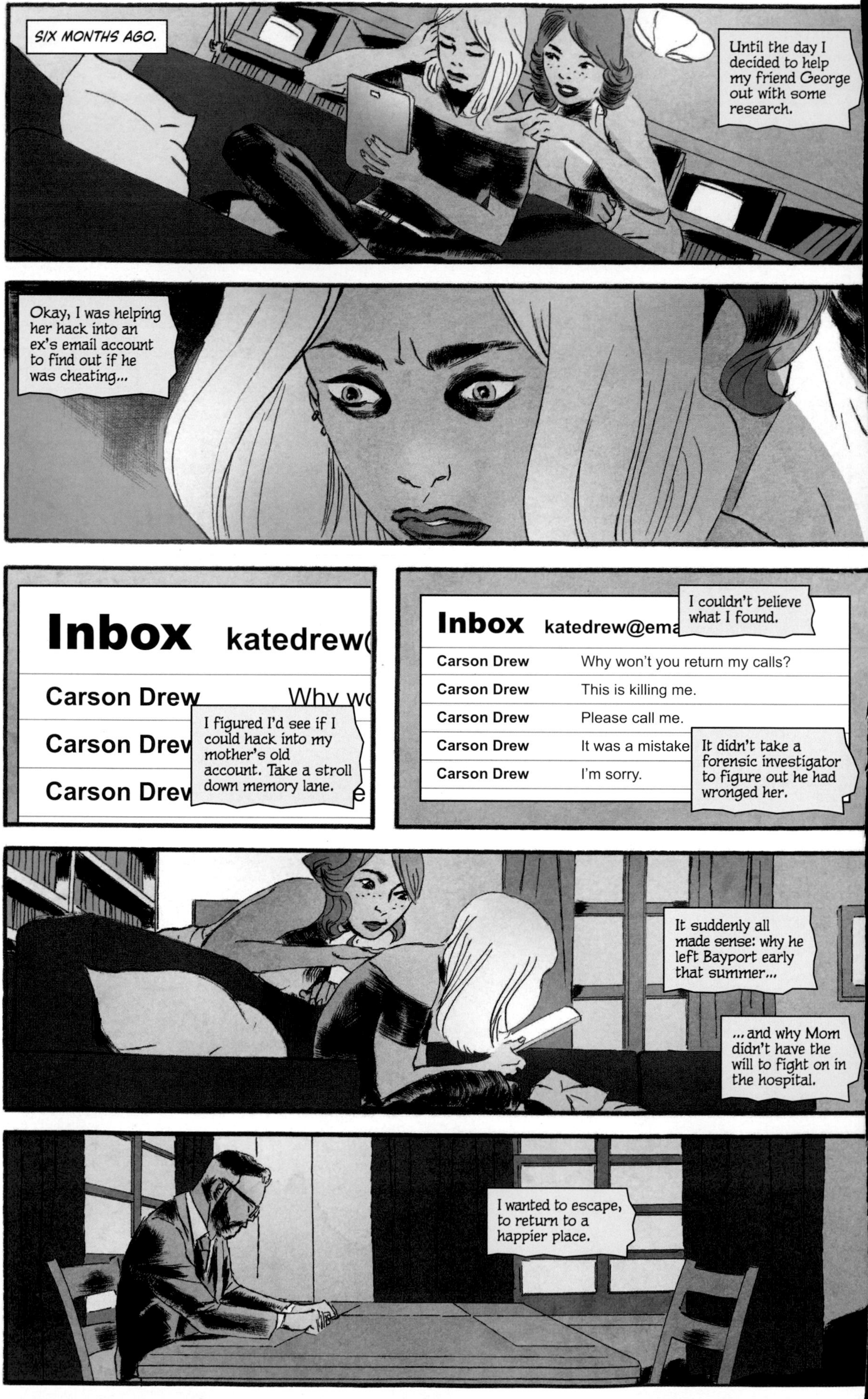
SIX MONTHS AGO.
Until the day I decided to help my friend George out with some research.
Okay, I was helping her hack into an ex's email account to find out if he was cheating...
Inbox katedrew(
Carson Drew
Why wo
Carson Drew
Carson Drew
I figured I'd see if I could hack into my mother's old account. Take a stroll down memory lane.
Inbox katedrew@ema
I couldn't believe what I found.
Carson Drew Why won't you return my calls?
Carson Drew This is killing me.
Carson Drew Please call me.
Carson Drew It was a mistake
Carson Drew I'm sorry.
It didn't take a forensic investigator to figure out he had wronged her.
It suddenly all made sense: why he left Bayport early that summer...
...and why Mom didn't have the will to fight on in the hospital.
I wanted to escape, to return to a happier place.

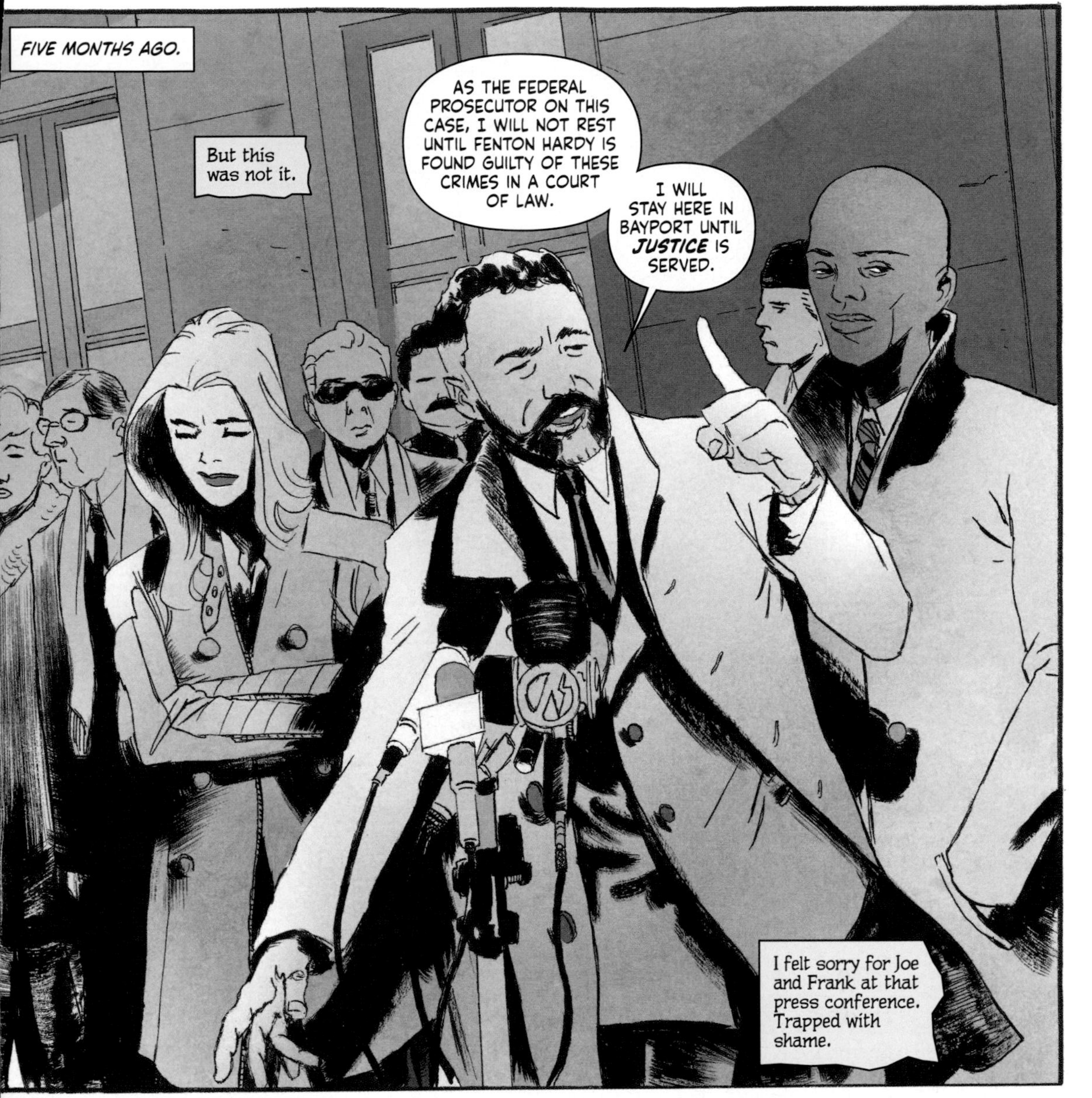
FIVE MONTHS AGO.
But this was not it.
AS THE FEDERAL PROSECUTOR ON THIS CASE, I WILL NOT REST UNTIL FENTON HARDY IS FOUND GUILTY OF THESE CRIMES IN A COURT OF LAW.
I WILL STAY HERE IN BAYPORT UNTIL JUSTICE IS SERVED.
I felt sorry for Joe and Frank at that press conference. Trapped with shame.

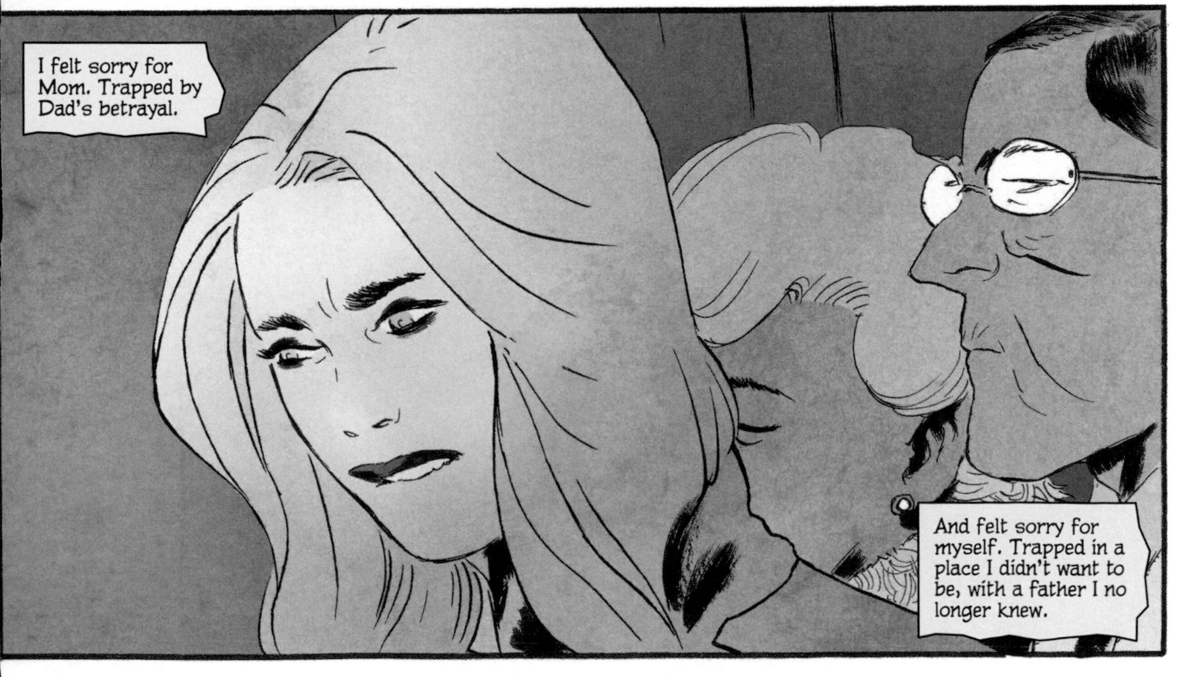
I felt sorry for Mom. Trapped by Dad's betrayal.
And felt sorry for myself. Trapped in a place I didn't want to be, with a father I no longer knew.

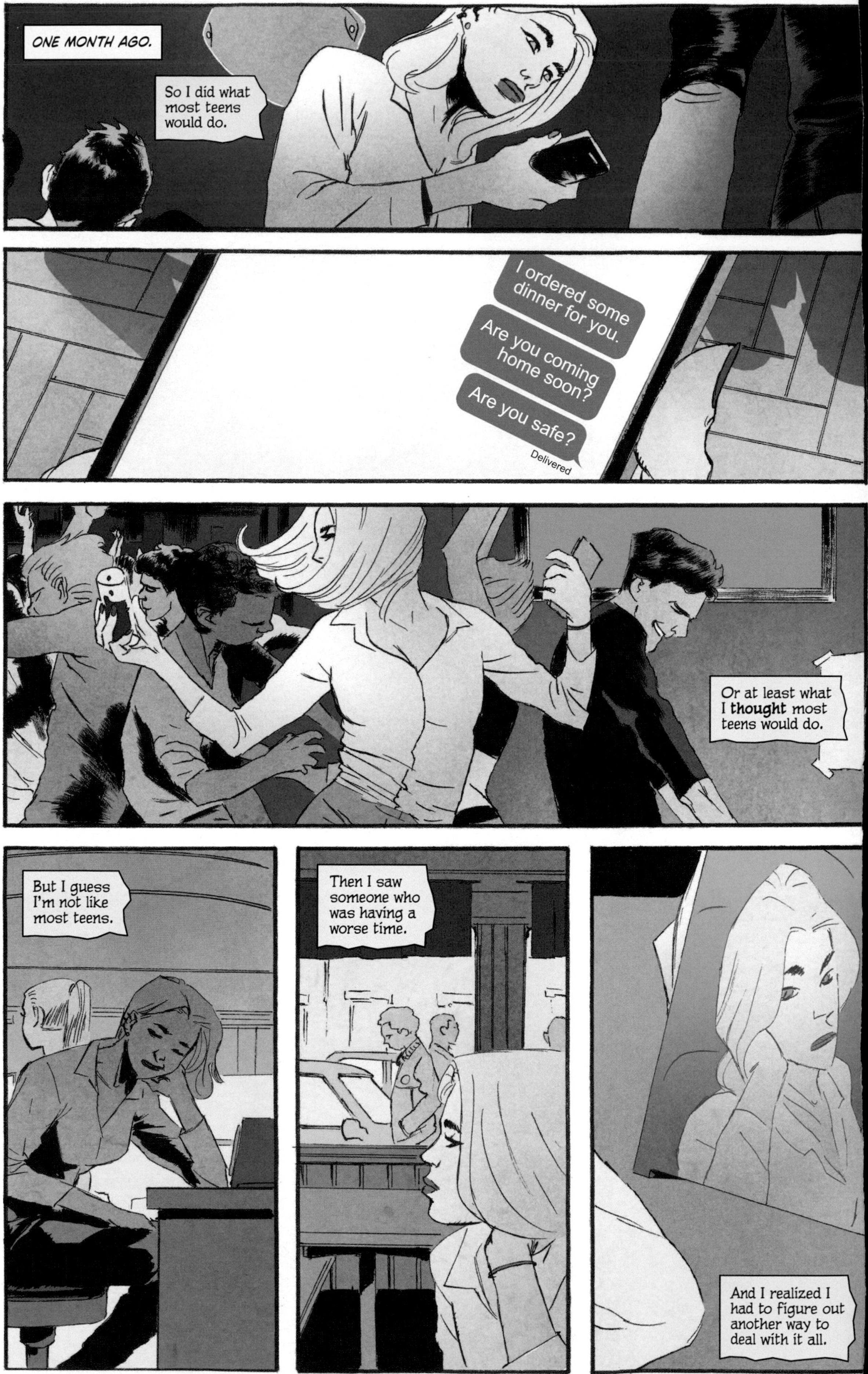
ONE MONTH AGO.
So I did what most teens would do.
I ordered some dinner for you.
Are you coming home soon?
Are you safe?
Delivered
Or at least what I **thought** most teens would do.
But I guess I'm not like most teens.
Then I saw someone who was having a worse time.
And I realized I had to figure out another way to deal with it all.

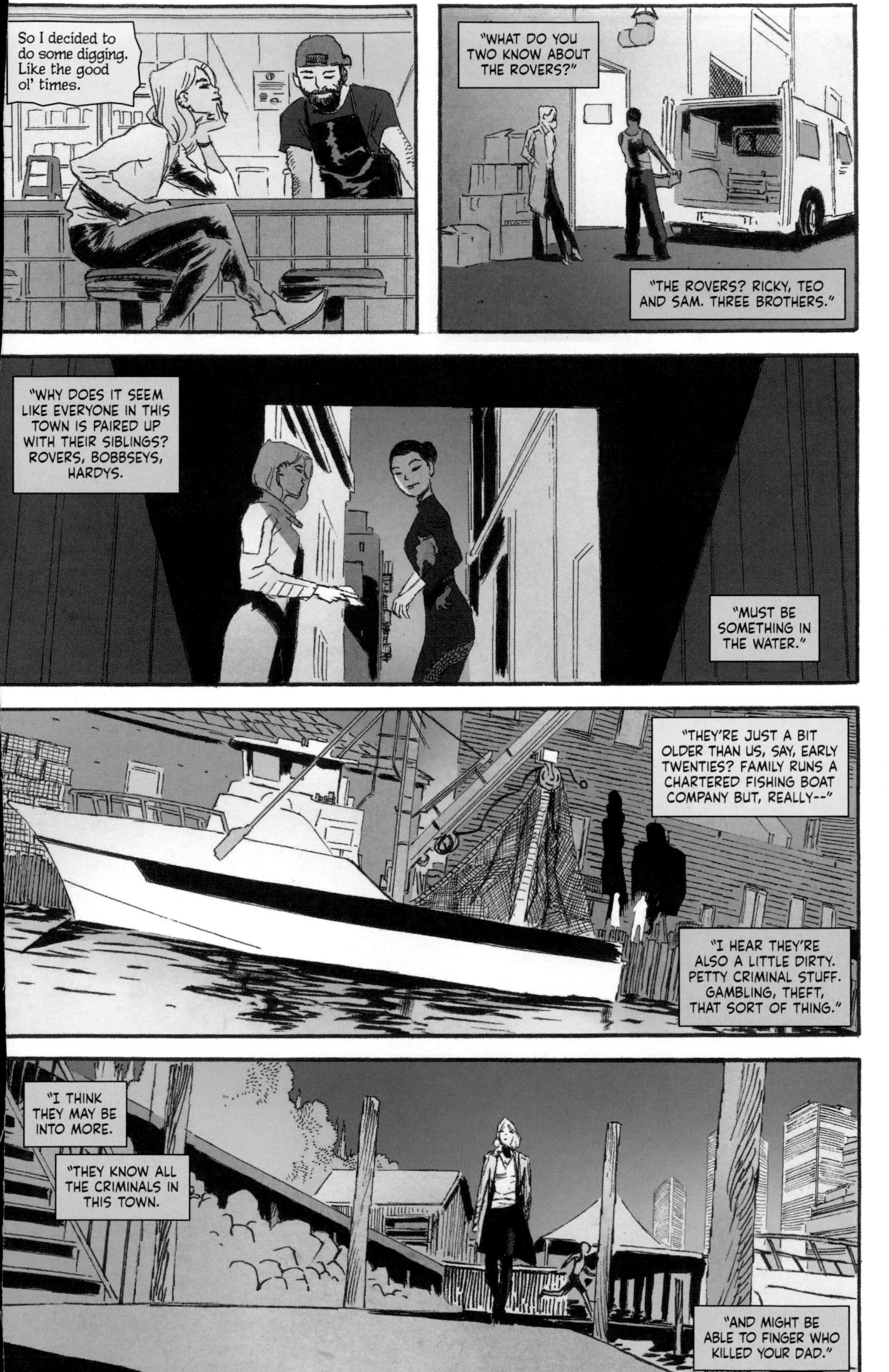
So I decided to do some digging. Like the good ol' times.
"WHAT DO YOU TWO KNOW ABOUT THE ROVERS?"
"THE ROVERS? RICKY, TEO AND SAM. THREE BROTHERS."
"WHY DOES IT SEEM LIKE EVERYONE IN THIS TOWN IS PAIRED UP WITH THEIR SIBLINGS? ROVERS, BOBBSEYS, HARDYS.
"MUST BE SOMETHING IN THE WATER."
"THEY'RE JUST A BIT OLDER THAN US, SAY, EARLY TWENTIES? FAMILY RUNS A CHARTERED FISHING BOAT COMPANY BUT, REALLY--"
"I HEAR THEY'RE ALSO A LITTLE DIRTY. PETTY CRIMINAL STUFF. GAMBLING, THEFT, THAT SORT OF THING."
"I THINK THEY MAY BE INTO MORE.
"THEY KNOW ALL THE CRIMINALS IN THIS TOWN.
"AND MIGHT BE ABLE TO FINGER WHO KILLED YOUR DAD."

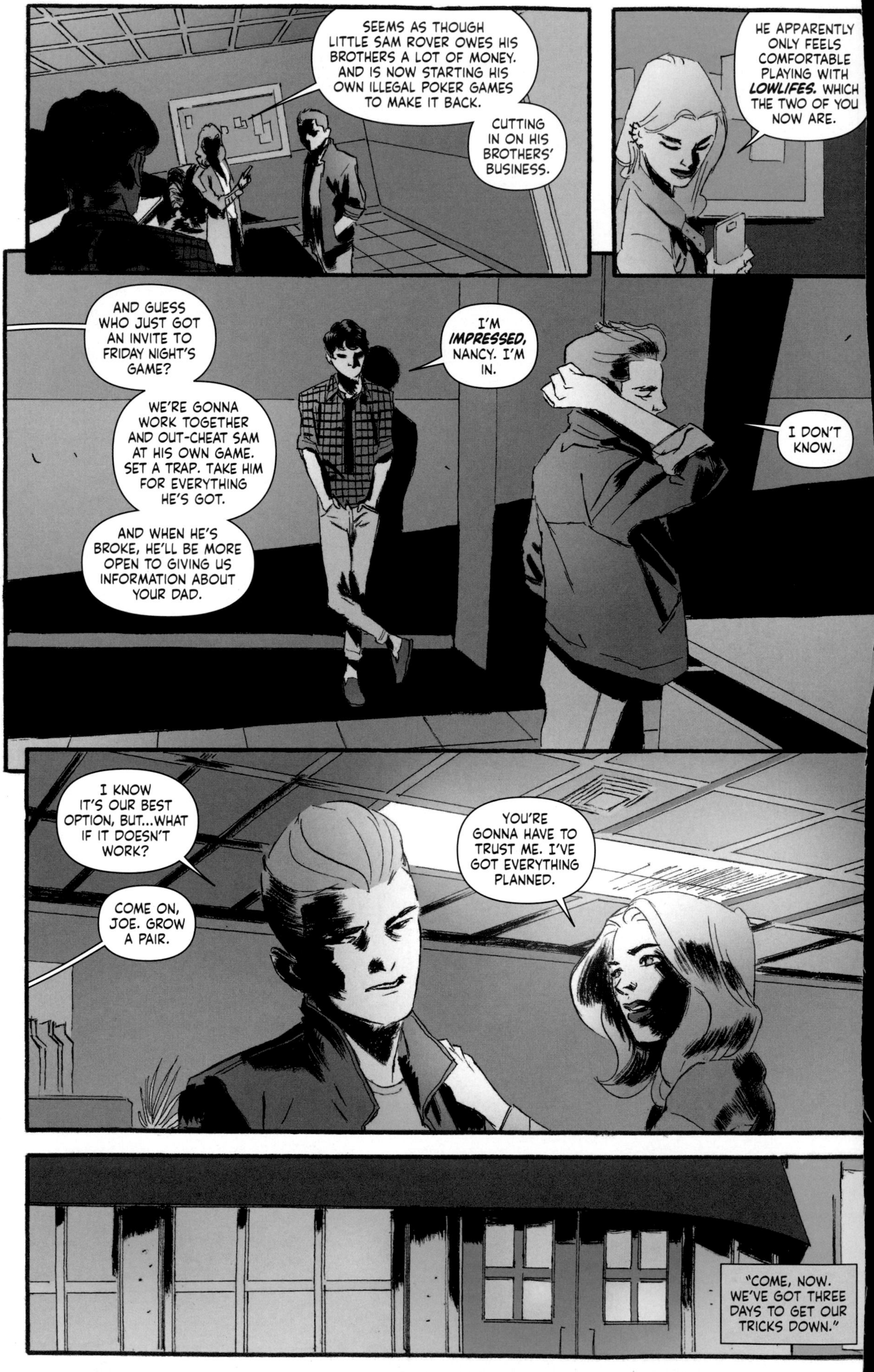
SEEMS AS THOUGH LITTLE SAM ROVER OWES HIS BROTHERS A LOT OF MONEY. AND IS NOW STARTING HIS OWN ILLEGAL POKER GAMES TO MAKE IT BACK.
CUTTING IN ON HIS BROTHERS' BUSINESS.
HE APPARENTLY ONLY FEELS COMFORTABLE PLAYING WITH ***LOWLIFES.*** WHICH THE TWO OF YOU NOW ARE.
AND GUESS WHO JUST GOT AN INVITE TO FRIDAY NIGHT'S GAME?
WE'RE GONNA WORK TOGETHER AND OUT-CHEAT SAM AT HIS OWN GAME. SET A TRAP. TAKE HIM FOR EVERYTHING HE'S GOT.
AND WHEN HE'S BROKE, HE'LL BE MORE OPEN TO GIVING US INFORMATION ABOUT YOUR DAD.
I'M ***IMPRESSED,*** NANCY. I'M IN.
I DON'T KNOW.
I KNOW IT'S OUR BEST OPTION, BUT...WHAT IF IT DOESN'T WORK?
COME ON, JOE. GROW A PAIR.
YOU'RE GONNA HAVE TO TRUST ME. I'VE GOT EVERYTHING PLANNED.
"COME, NOW. WE'VE GOT THREE DAYS TO GET OUR TRICKS DOWN."

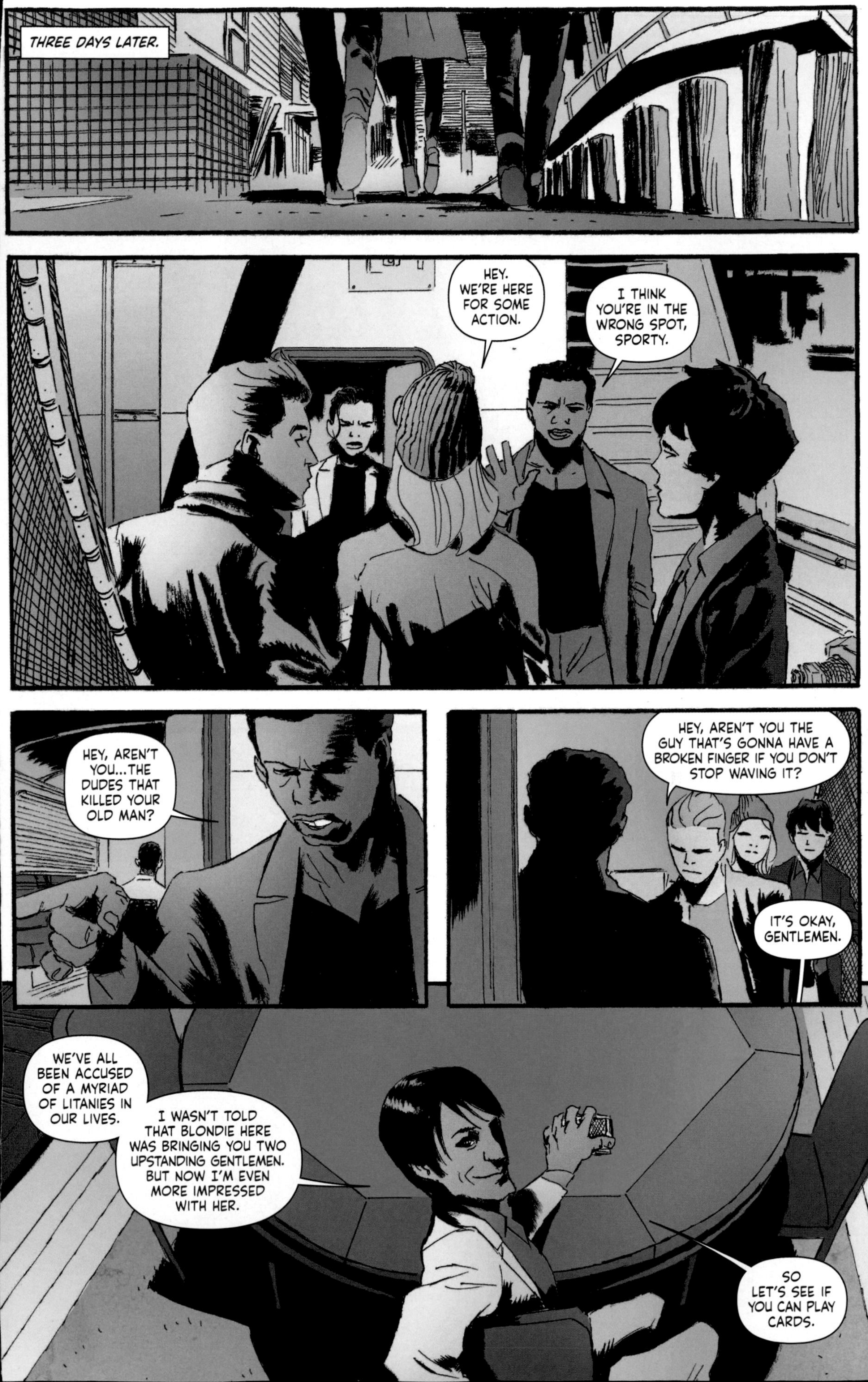

THREE DAYS LATER.
HEY. WE'RE HERE FOR SOME ACTION.
I THINK YOU'RE IN THE WRONG SPOT, SPORTY.
HEY, AREN'T YOU...THE DUDES THAT KILLED YOUR OLD MAN?
HEY, AREN'T YOU THE GUY THAT'S GONNA HAVE A BROKEN FINGER IF YOU DON'T STOP WAVING IT?
IT'S OKAY, GENTLEMEN.
WE'VE ALL BEEN ACCUSED OF A MYRIAD OF LITANIES IN OUR LIVES.
I WASN'T TOLD THAT BLONDIE HERE WAS BRINGING YOU TWO UPSTANDING GENTLEMEN. BUT NOW I'M EVEN MORE IMPRESSED WITH HER.
SO LET'S SEE IF YOU CAN PLAY CARDS.

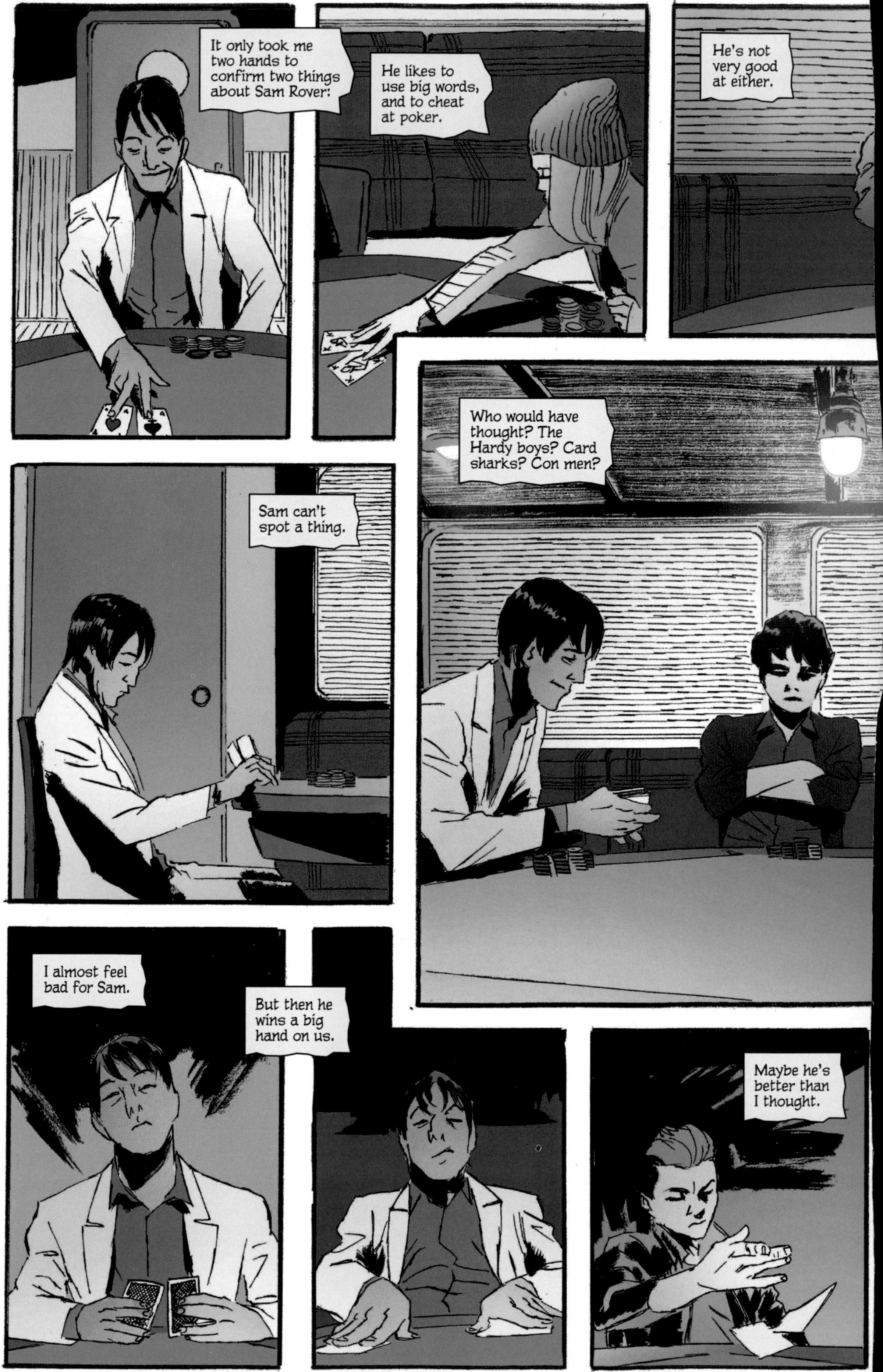
It only took me two hands to confirm two things about Sam Rover:
He likes to use big words, and to cheat at poker.
He's not very good at either.
Who would have thought? The Hardy boys? Card sharks? Con men?
Sam can't spot a thing.
I almost feel bad for Sam.
But then he wins a big hand on us.
Maybe he's better than I thought.

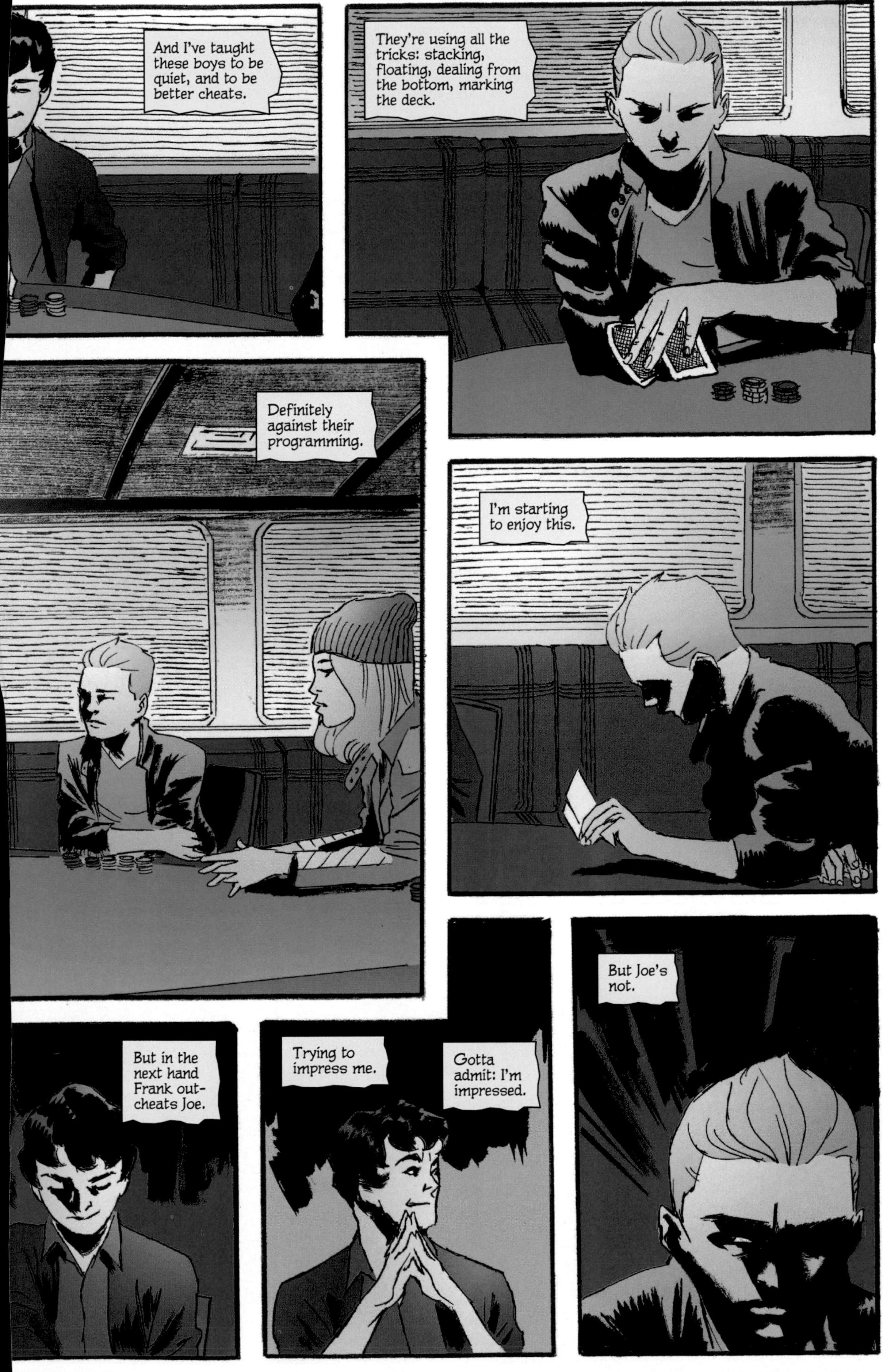
And I've taught these boys to be quiet, and to be better cheats.
They're using all the tricks: stacking, floating, dealing from the bottom, marking the deck.
Definitely against their programming.
I'm starting to enjoy this.
But in the next hand Frank out-cheats Joe.
Trying to impress me.
Gotta admit: I'm impressed.
But Joe's not.

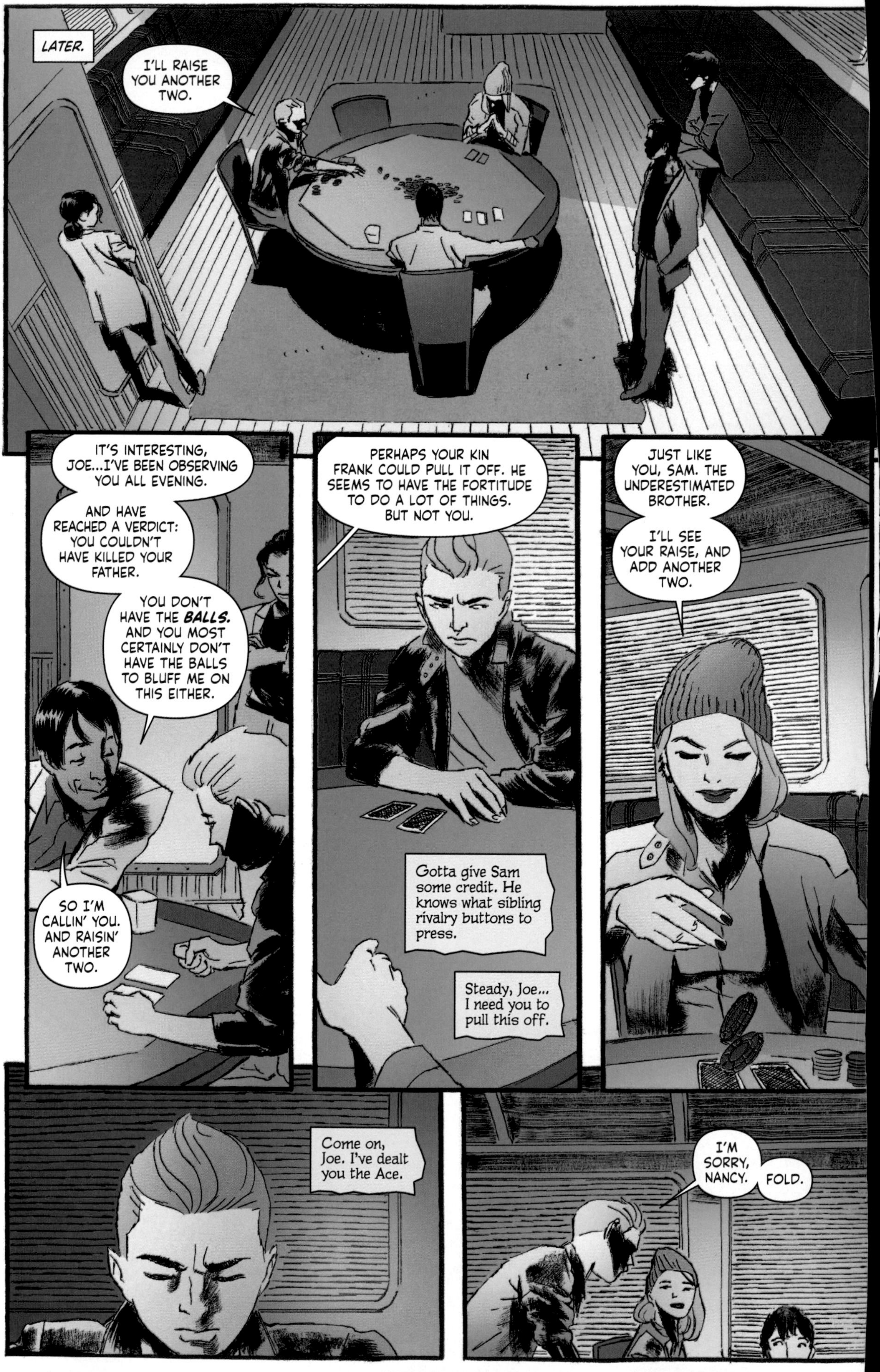
LATER.
I'LL RAISE YOU ANOTHER TWO.
IT'S INTERESTING, JOE...I'VE BEEN OBSERVING YOU ALL EVENING.
AND HAVE REACHED A VERDICT: YOU COULDN'T HAVE KILLED YOUR FATHER.
YOU DON'T HAVE THE ***BALLS.*** AND YOU MOST CERTAINLY DON'T HAVE THE BALLS TO BLUFF ME ON THIS EITHER.
SO I'M CALLIN' YOU. AND RAISIN' ANOTHER TWO.
PERHAPS YOUR KIN FRANK COULD PULL IT OFF. HE SEEMS TO HAVE THE FORTITUDE TO DO A LOT OF THINGS. BUT NOT YOU.
Gotta give Sam some credit. He knows what sibling rivalry buttons to press.
Steady, Joe... I need you to pull this off.
JUST LIKE YOU, SAM. THE UNDERESTIMATED BROTHER.
I'LL SEE YOUR RAISE, AND ADD ANOTHER TWO.
Come on, Joe. I've dealt you the Ace.
I'M SORRY, NANCY.
FOLD.

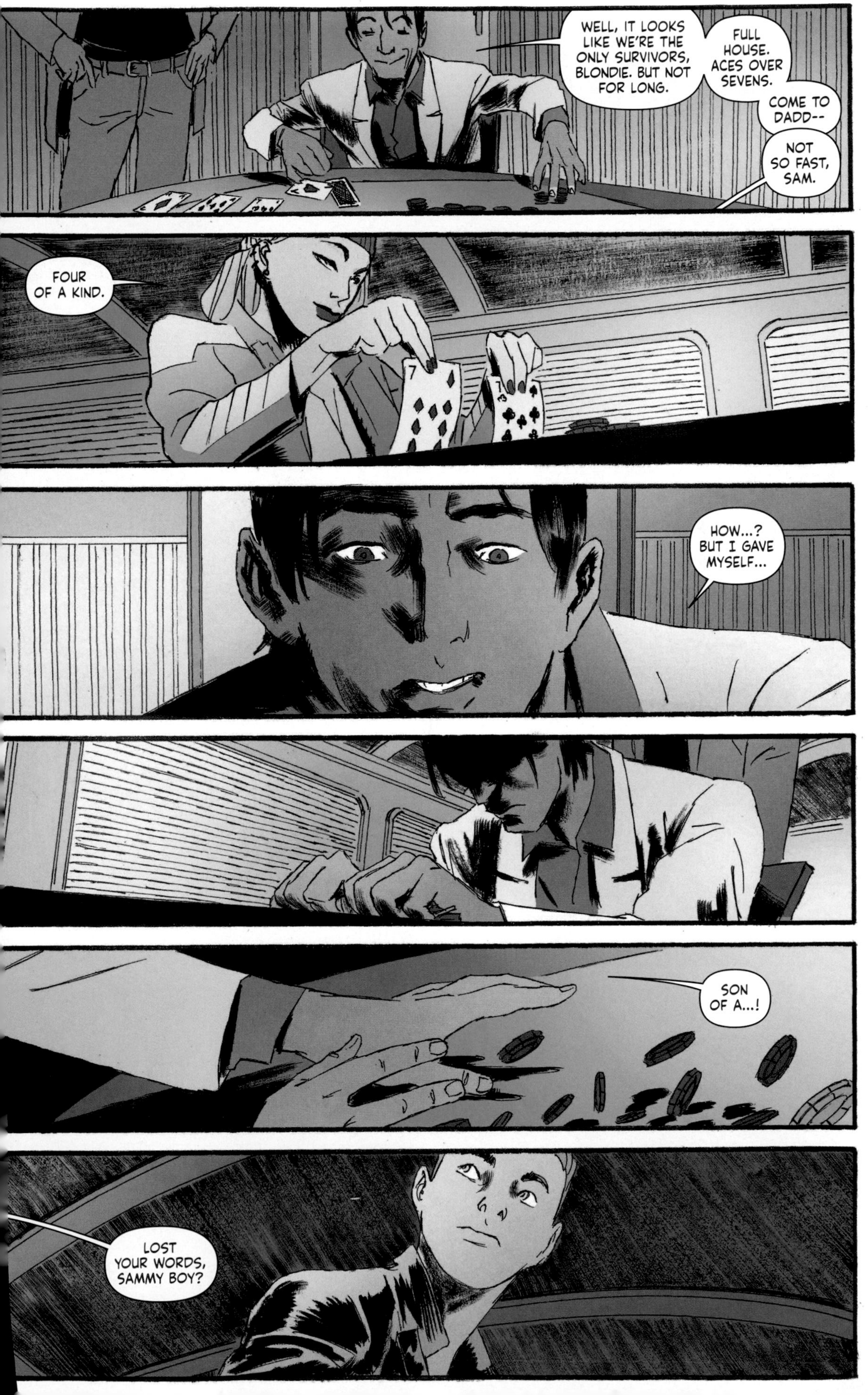
WELL, IT LOOKS LIKE WE'RE THE ONLY SURVIVORS, BLONDIE. BUT NOT FOR LONG.
FULL HOUSE. ACES OVER SEVENS.
COME TO DADD--
NOT SO FAST, SAM.
FOUR OF A KIND.
HOW...? BUT I GAVE MYSELF...
SON OF A...!
LOST YOUR WORDS, SAMMY BOY?

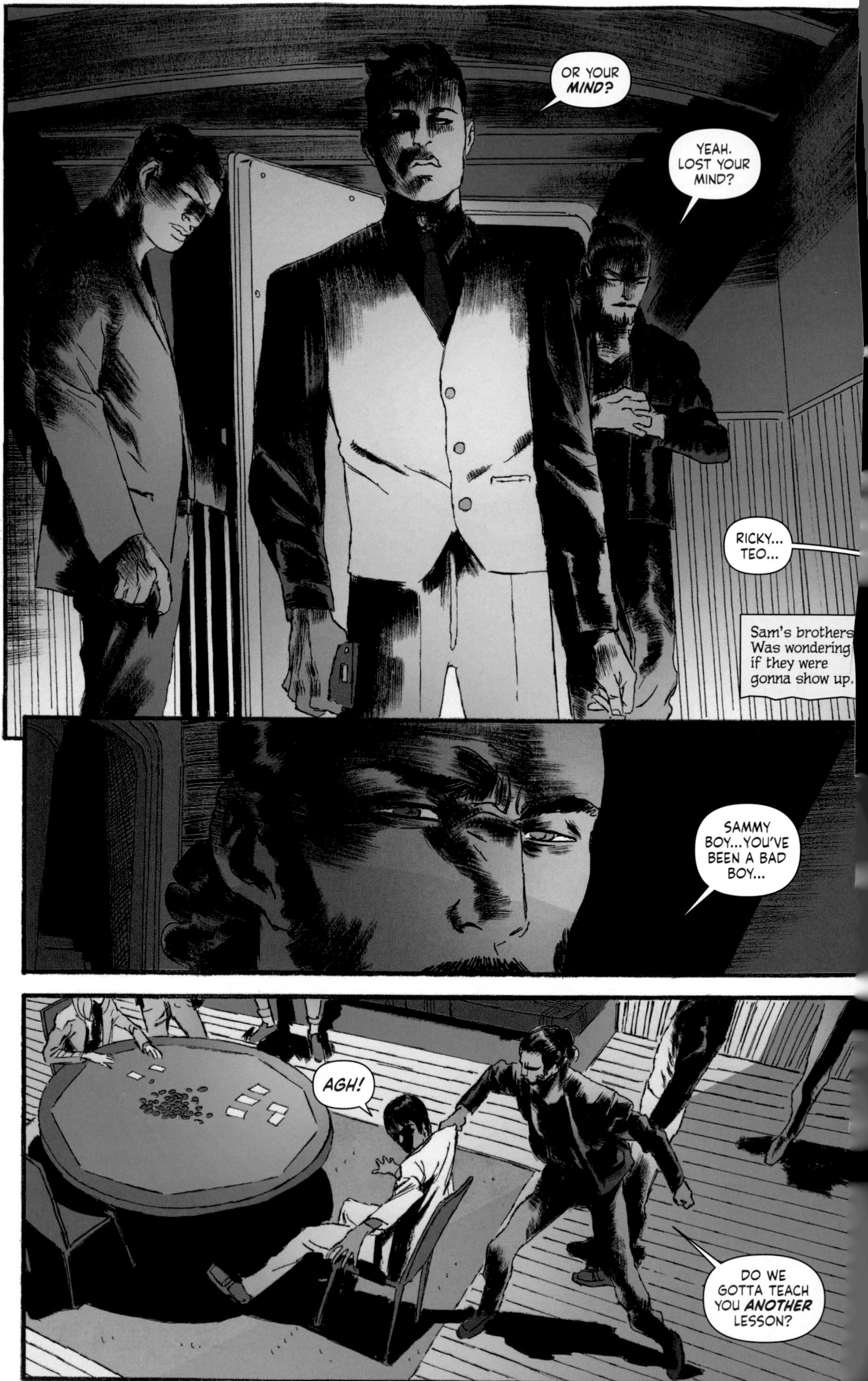
OR YOUR *MIND?*
YEAH. LOST YOUR MIND?
RICKY... TEO...
Sam's brothers. Was wondering if they were gonna show up.
SAMMY BOY...YOU'VE BEEN A BAD BOY...
AGH!
DO WE GOTTA TEACH YOU *ANOTHER* LESSON?

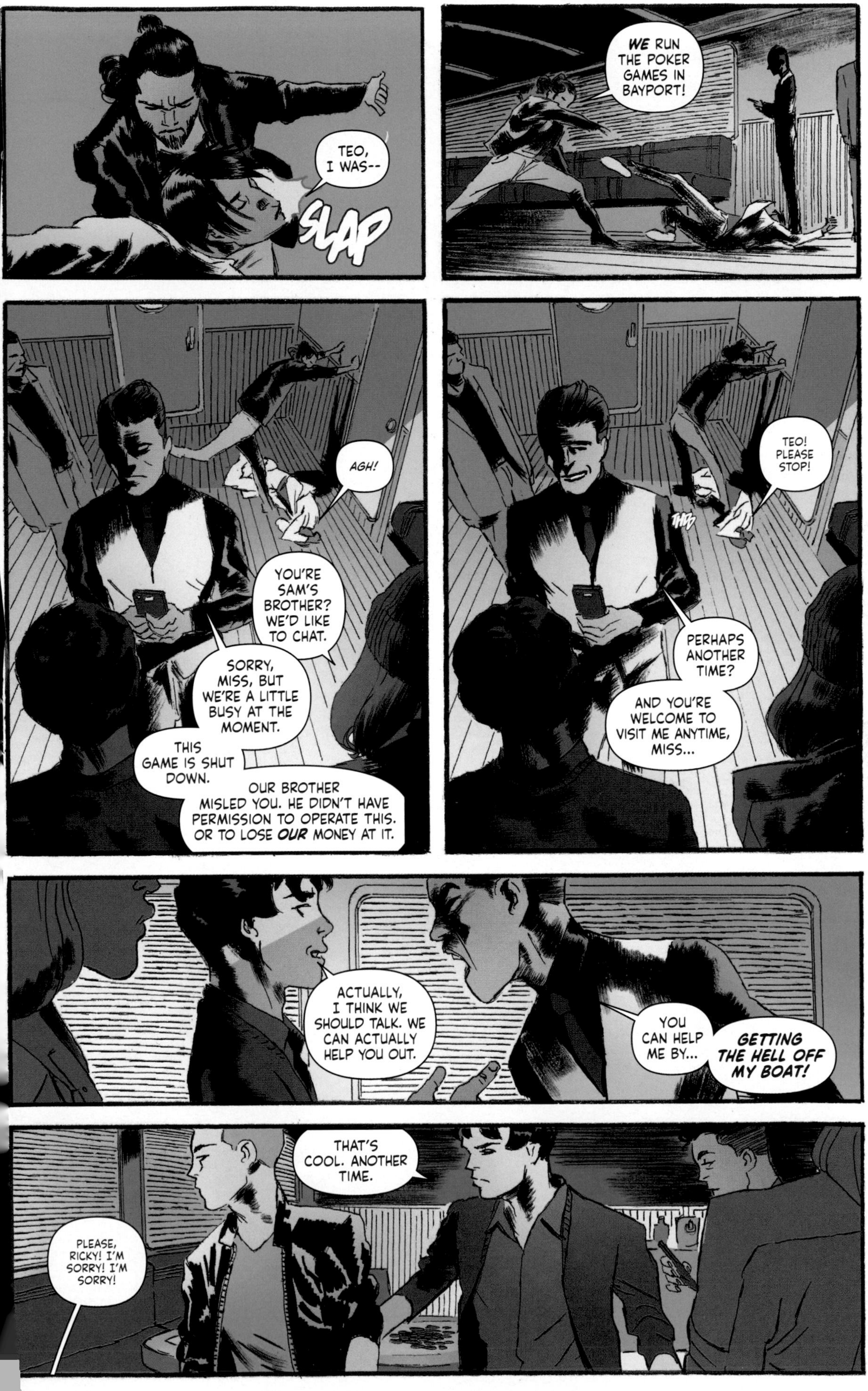
TEO, I WAS--
SLAP
WE RUN THE POKER GAMES IN BAYPORT!
AGH!
YOU'RE SAM'S BROTHER? WE'D LIKE TO CHAT.
SORRY, MISS, BUT WE'RE A LITTLE BUSY AT THE MOMENT.
THIS GAME IS SHUT DOWN.
OUR BROTHER MISLED YOU. HE DIDN'T HAVE PERMISSION TO OPERATE THIS. OR TO LOSE OUR MONEY AT IT.
TEO! PLEASE STOP!
PERHAPS ANOTHER TIME?
AND YOU'RE WELCOME TO VISIT ME ANYTIME, MISS...
ACTUALLY, I THINK WE SHOULD TALK. WE CAN ACTUALLY HELP YOU OUT.
YOU CAN HELP ME BY...
GETTING THE HELL OFF MY BOAT!
THAT'S COOL. ANOTHER TIME.
PLEASE, RICKY! I'M SORRY! I'M SORRY!

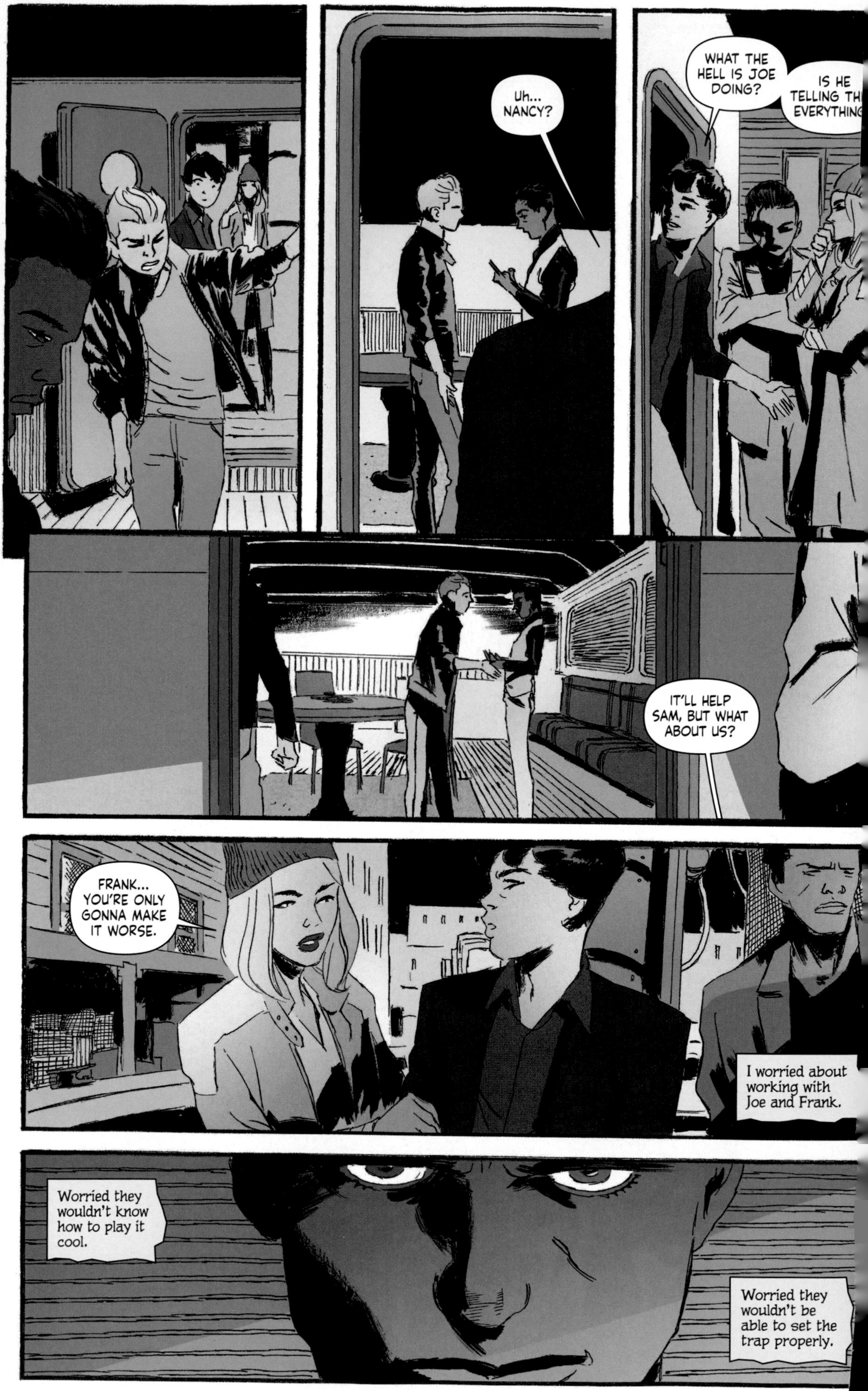
Uh... NANCY?
WHAT THE HELL IS JOE DOING?
IS HE TELLING TH EVERYTHING
IT'LL HELP SAM, BUT WHAT ABOUT US?
FRANK... YOU'RE ONLY GONNA MAKE IT WORSE.
I worried about working with Joe and Frank.
Worried they wouldn't know how to play it cool.
Worried they wouldn't be able to set the trap properly.

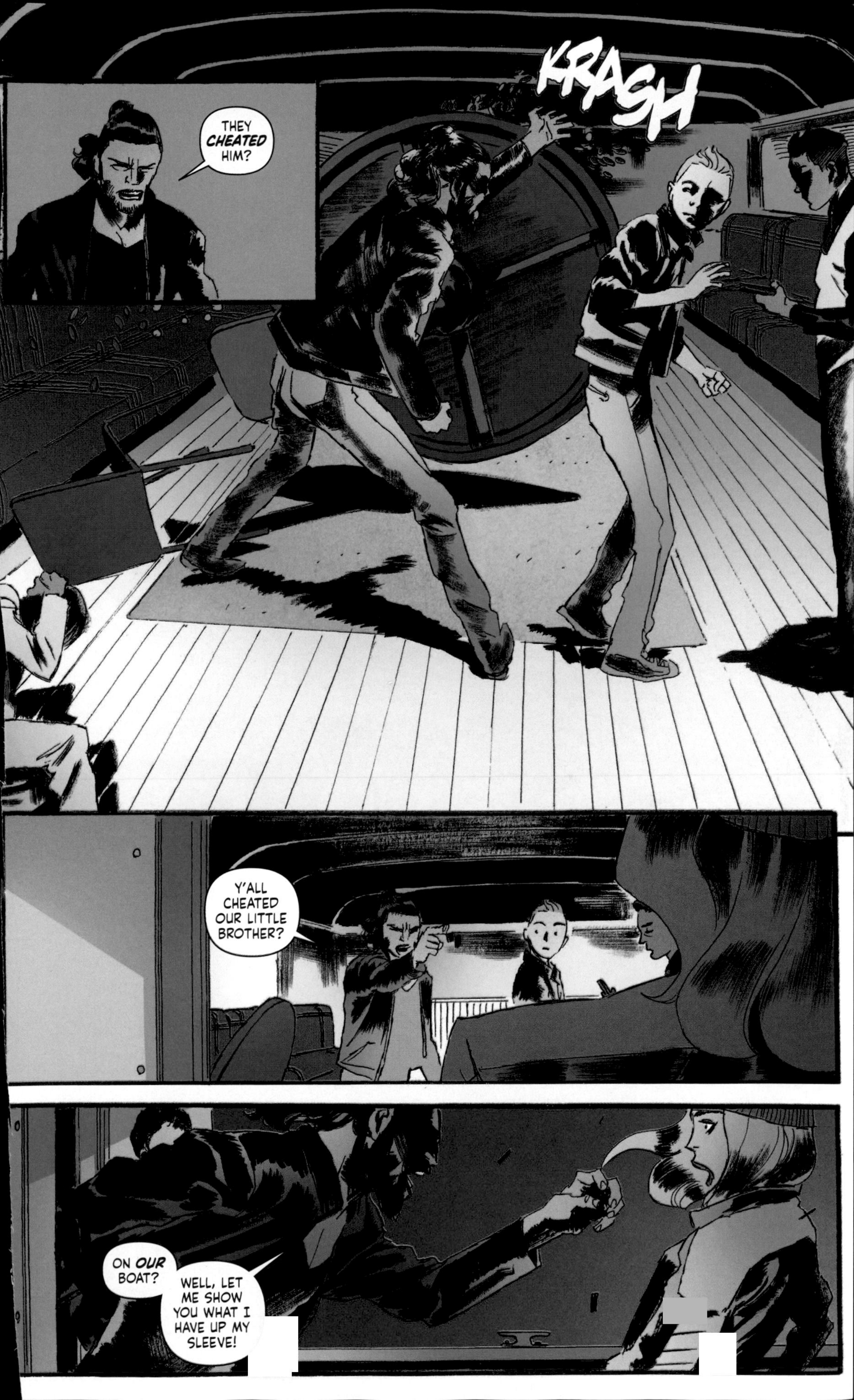
THEY *CHEATED* HIM?
KRASH
Y'ALL CHEATED OUR LITTLE BROTHER?
ON *OUR* BOAT?
WELL, LET ME SHOW YOU WHAT I HAVE UP MY SLEEVE!

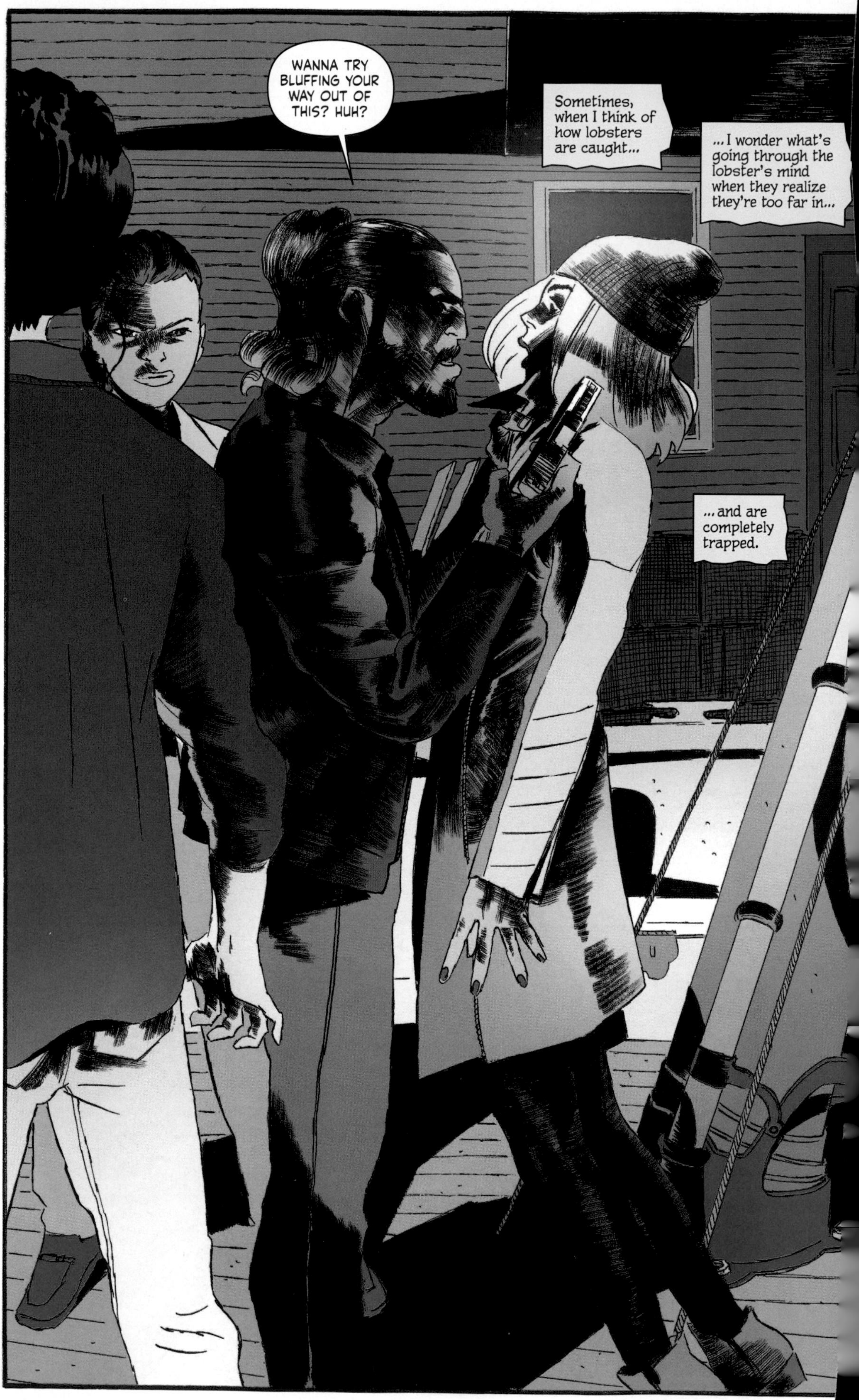
WANNA TRY BLUFFING YOUR WAY OUT OF THIS? HUH?
Sometimes, when I think of how lobsters are caught...
...I wonder what's going through the lobster's mind when they realize they're too far in...
...and are completely trapped.

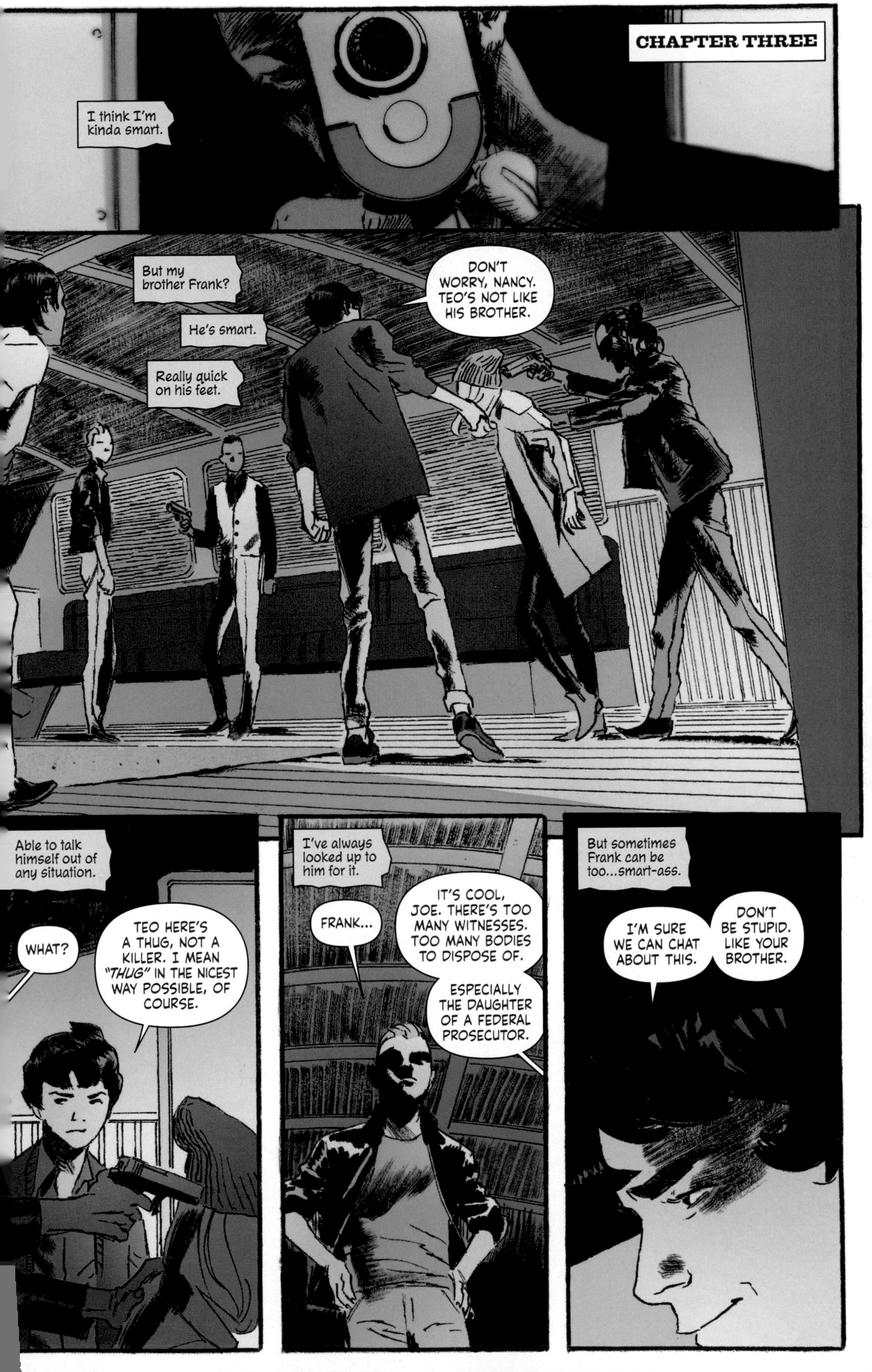
CHAPTER THREE
I think I'm kinda smart.
But my brother Frank?
He's smart.
Really quick on his feet.
DON'T WORRY, NANCY. TEO'S NOT LIKE HIS BROTHER.
Able to talk himself out of any situation.
WHAT?
TEO HERE'S A THUG, NOT A KILLER. I MEAN "THUG" IN THE NICEST WAY POSSIBLE, OF COURSE.
I've always looked up to him for it.
FRANK...
IT'S COOL, JOE. THERE'S TOO MANY WITNESSES. TOO MANY BODIES TO DISPOSE OF.
ESPECIALLY THE DAUGHTER OF A FEDERAL PROSECUTOR.
But sometimes Frank can be too...smart-ass.
I'M SURE WE CAN CHAT ABOUT THIS.
DON'T BE STUPID. LIKE YOUR BROTHER.

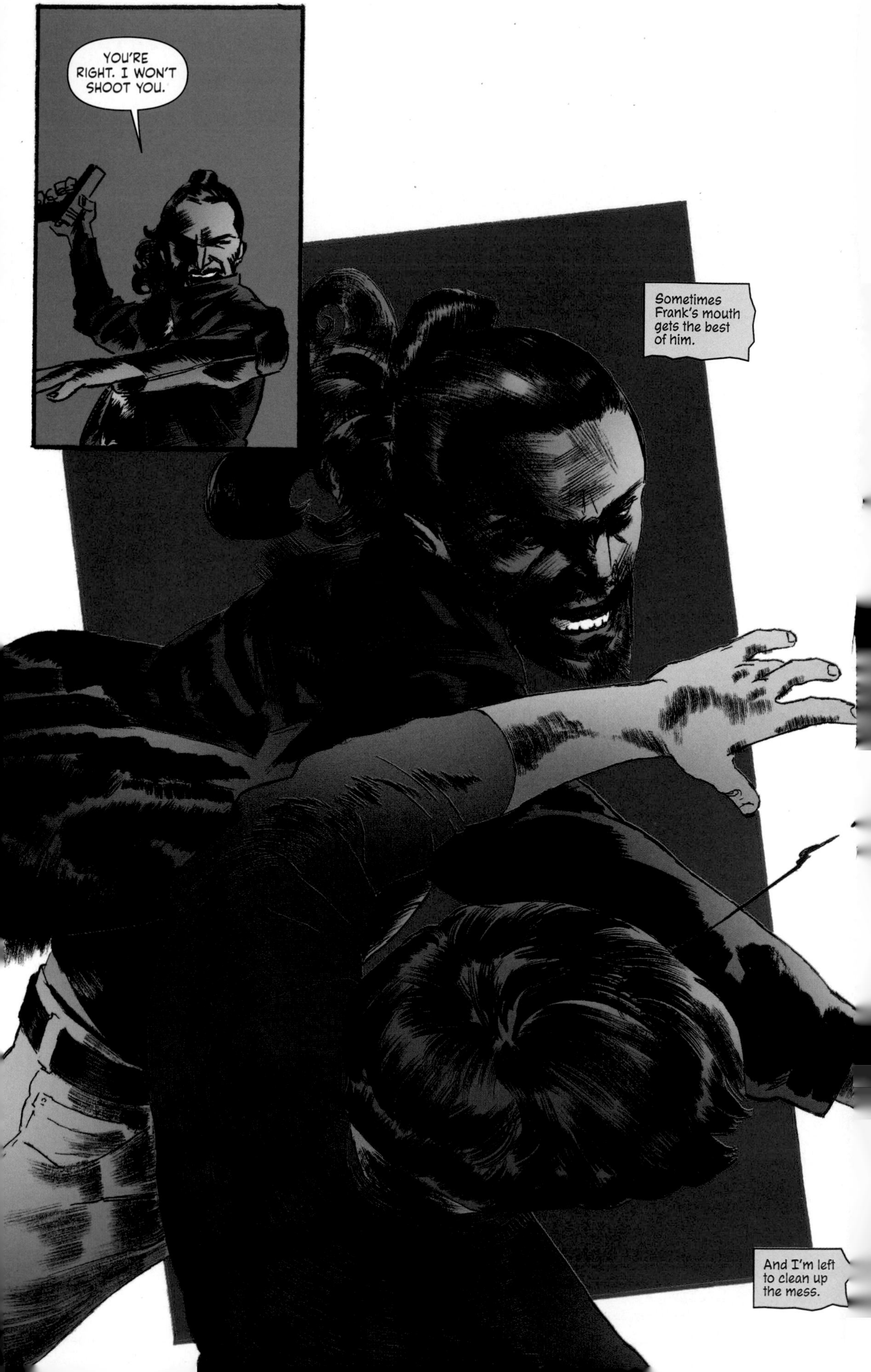
YOU'RE RIGHT. I WON'T SHOOT YOU.
Sometimes Frank's mouth gets the best of him.
And I'm left to clean up the mess.

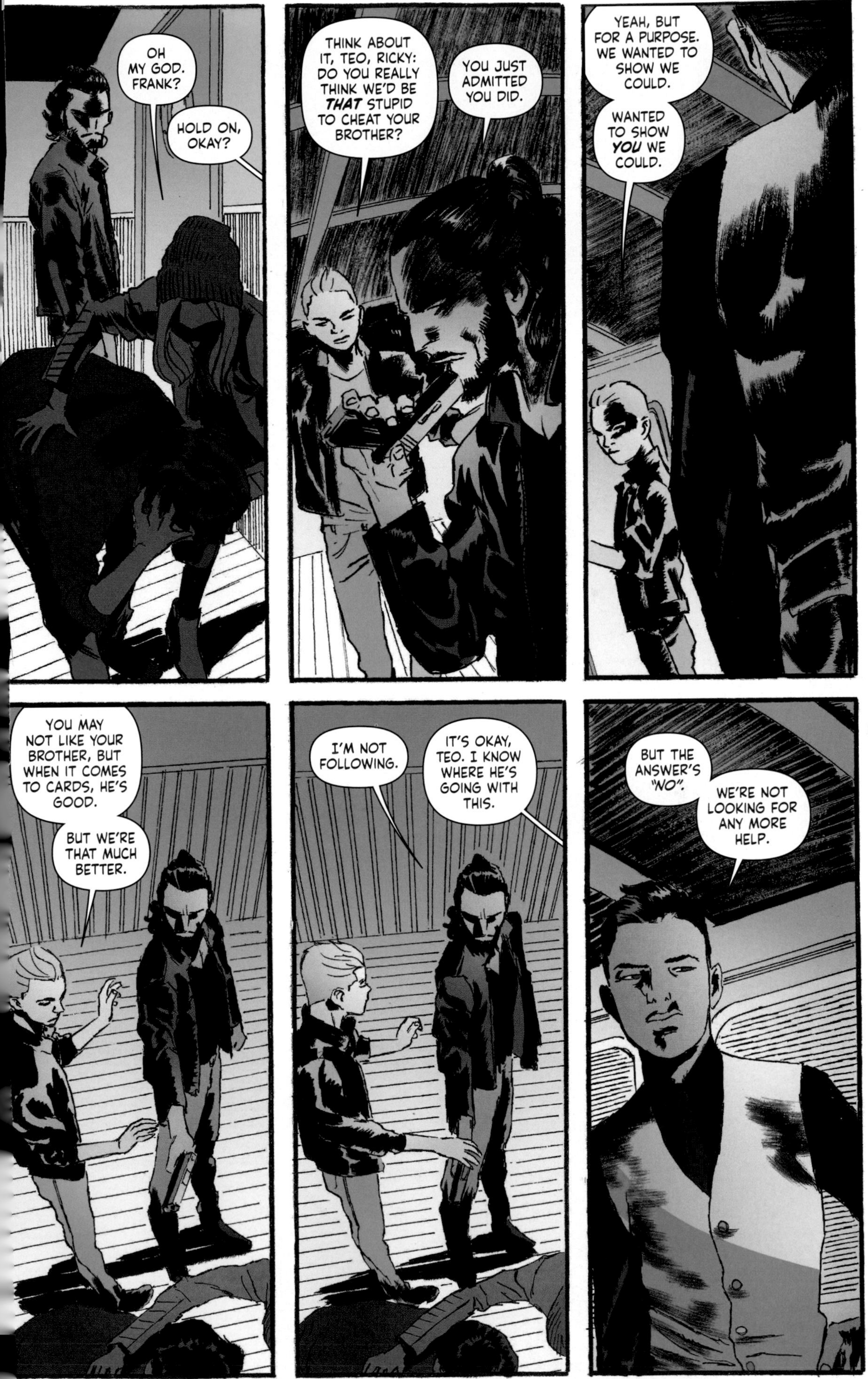
OH MY GOD. FRANK?
HOLD ON, OKAY?
THINK ABOUT IT, TEO, RICKY: DO YOU REALLY THINK WE'D BE *THAT* STUPID TO CHEAT YOUR BROTHER?
YOU JUST ADMITTED YOU DID.
YEAH, BUT FOR A PURPOSE. WE WANTED TO SHOW WE COULD.
WANTED TO SHOW *YOU* WE COULD.
YOU MAY NOT LIKE YOUR BROTHER, BUT WHEN IT COMES TO CARDS, HE'S GOOD.
BUT WE'RE THAT MUCH BETTER.
I'M NOT FOLLOWING.
IT'S OKAY, TEO. I KNOW WHERE HE'S GOING WITH THIS.
BUT THE ANSWER'S *"NO"*.
WE'RE NOT LOOKING FOR ANY MORE HELP.

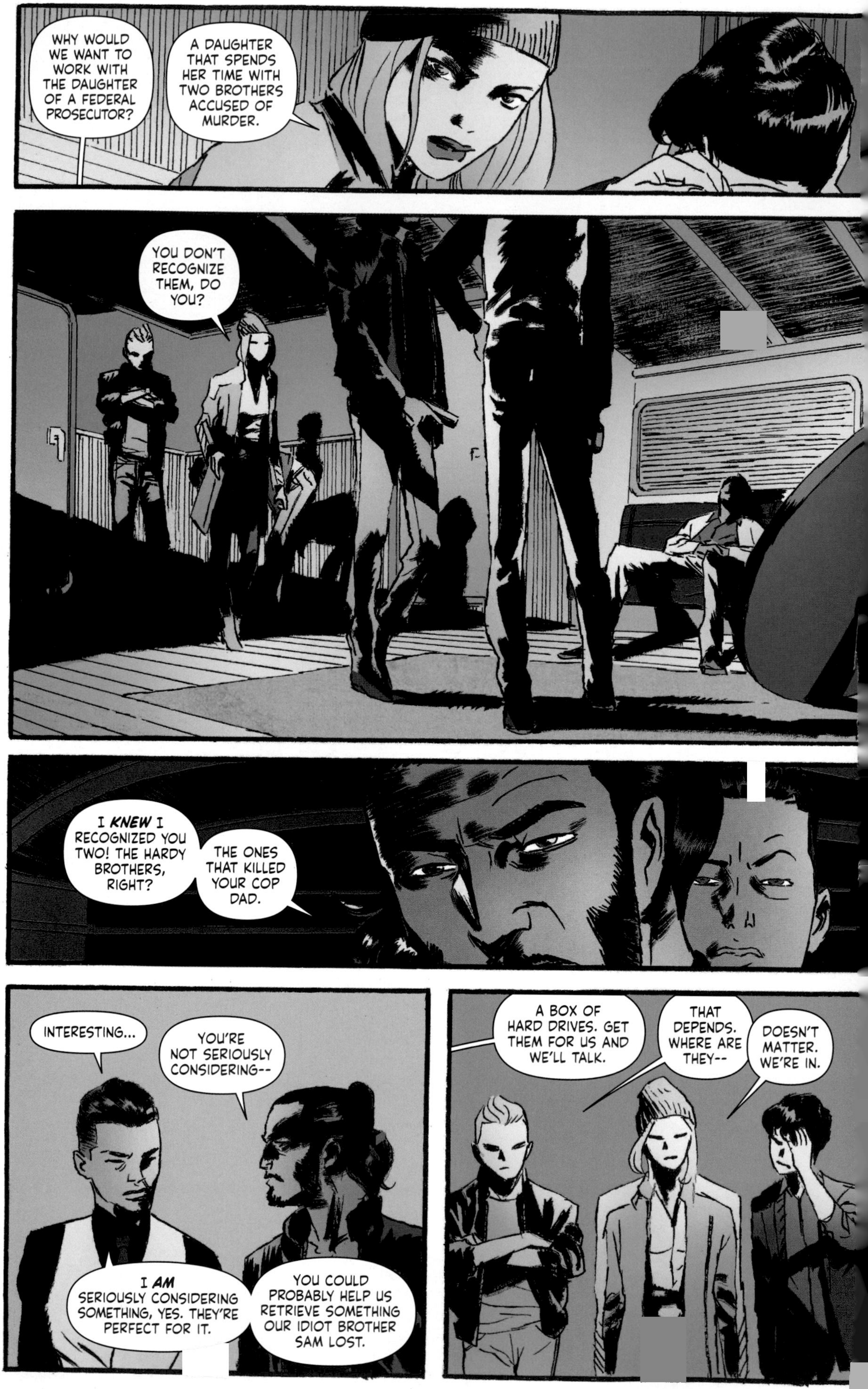
WHY WOULD WE WANT TO WORK WITH THE DAUGHTER OF A FEDERAL PROSECUTOR?
A DAUGHTER THAT SPENDS HER TIME WITH TWO BROTHERS ACCUSED OF MURDER.
YOU DON'T RECOGNIZE THEM, DO YOU?
I KNEW I RECOGNIZED YOU TWO! THE HARDY BROTHERS, RIGHT?
THE ONES THAT KILLED YOUR COP DAD.
INTERESTING...
YOU'RE NOT SERIOUSLY CONSIDERING--
I AM SERIOUSLY CONSIDERING SOMETHING, YES. THEY'RE PERFECT FOR IT.
YOU COULD PROBABLY HELP US RETRIEVE SOMETHING OUR IDIOT BROTHER SAM LOST.
A BOX OF HARD DRIVES. GET THEM FOR US AND WE'LL TALK.
THAT DEPENDS. WHERE ARE THEY--
DOESN'T MATTER. WE'RE IN.

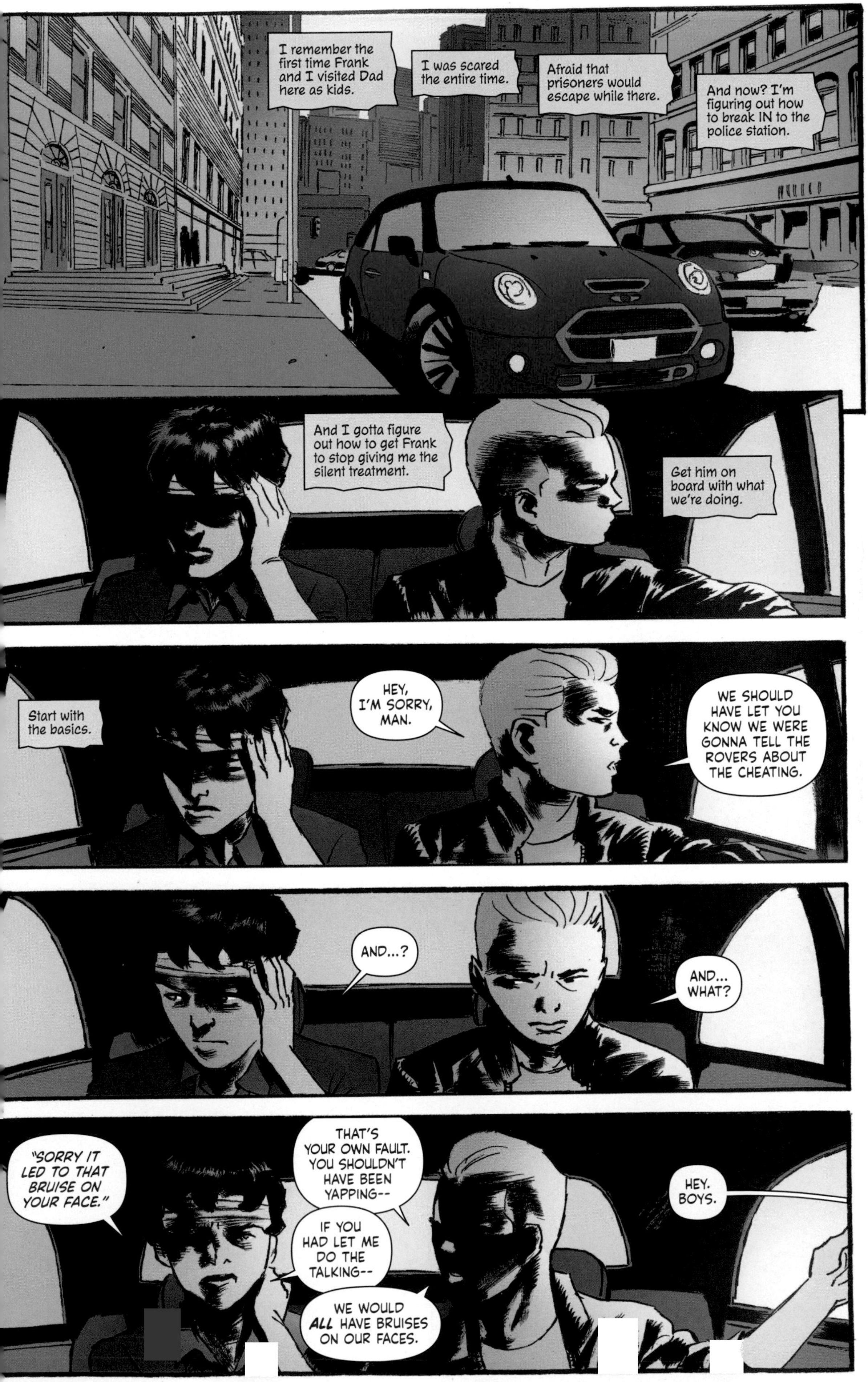
I remember the first time Frank and I visited Dad here as kids.
I was scared the entire time.
Afraid that prisoners would escape while there.
And now? I'm figuring out how to break IN to the police station.
And I gotta figure out how to get Frank to stop giving me the silent treatment.
Get him on board with what we're doing.
Start with the basics.
HEY, I'M SORRY, MAN.
WE SHOULD HAVE LET YOU KNOW WE WERE GONNA TELL THE ROVERS ABOUT THE CHEATING.
AND...?
AND... WHAT?
"SORRY IT LED TO THAT BRUISE ON YOUR FACE."
THAT'S YOUR OWN FAULT. YOU SHOULDN'T HAVE BEEN YAPPING--
IF YOU HAD LET ME DO THE TALKING--
WE WOULD ALL HAVE BRUISES ON OUR FACES.
HEY. BOYS.

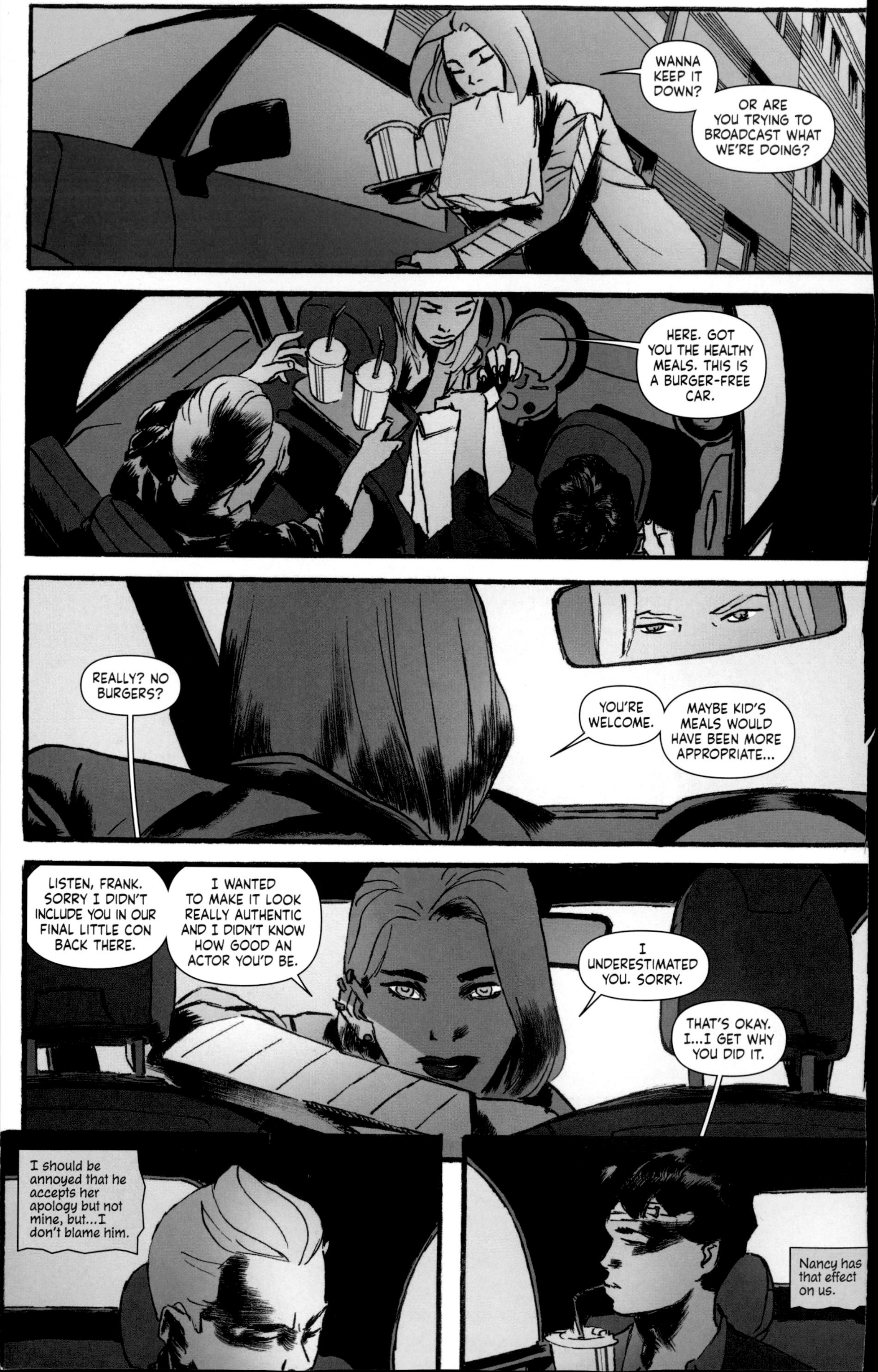
WANNA KEEP IT DOWN?
OR ARE YOU TRYING TO BROADCAST WHAT WE'RE DOING?
HERE. GOT YOU THE HEALTHY MEALS. THIS IS A BURGER-FREE CAR.
REALLY? NO BURGERS?
YOU'RE WELCOME.
MAYBE KID'S MEALS WOULD HAVE BEEN MORE APPROPRIATE...
LISTEN, FRANK. SORRY I DIDN'T INCLUDE YOU IN OUR FINAL LITTLE CON BACK THERE.
I WANTED TO MAKE IT LOOK REALLY AUTHENTIC AND I DIDN'T KNOW HOW GOOD AN ACTOR YOU'D BE.
I UNDERESTIMATED YOU. SORRY.
THAT'S OKAY. I...I GET WHY YOU DID IT.
I should be annoyed that he accepts her apology but not mine, but...I don't blame him.
Nancy has that effect on us.

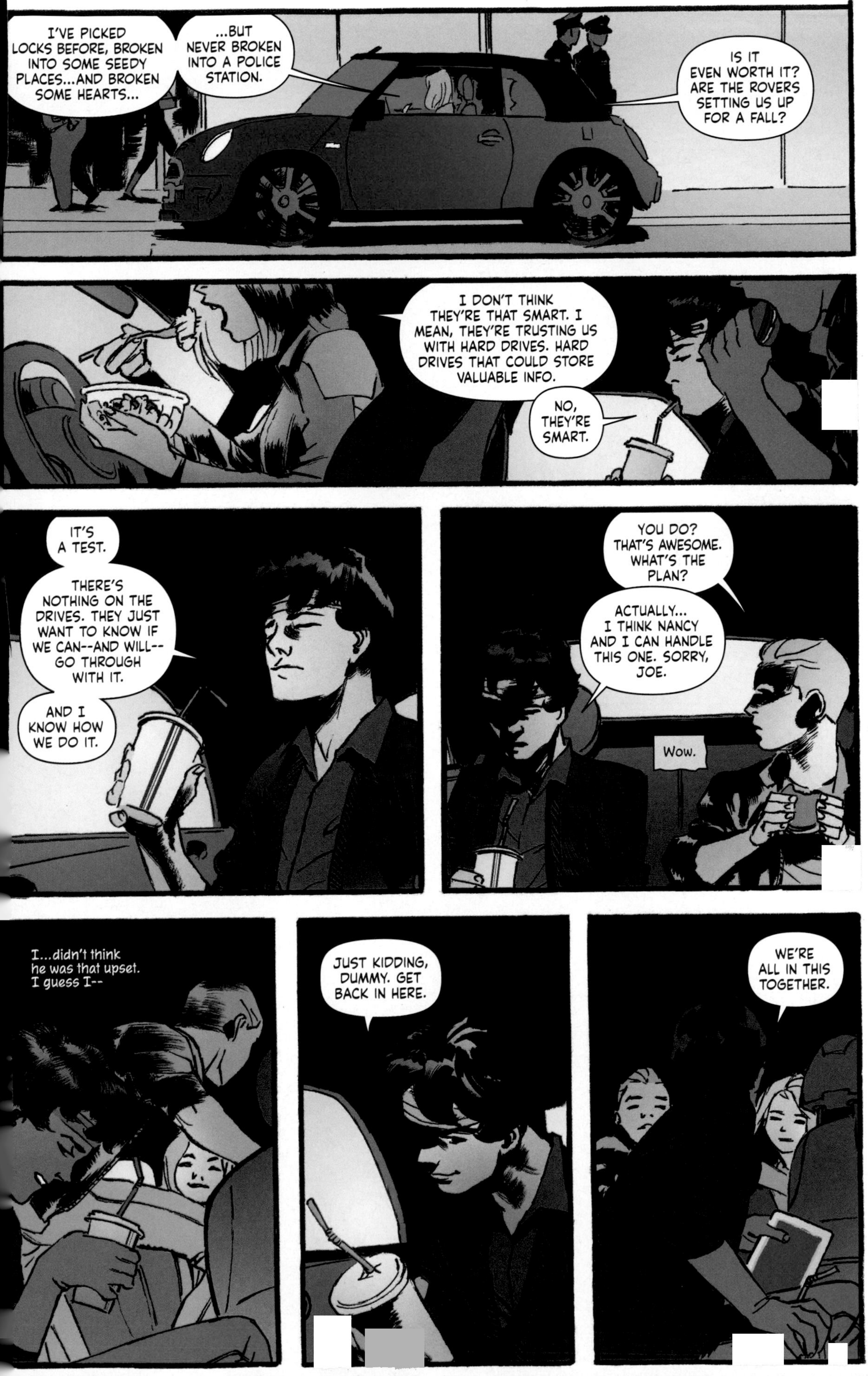
I'VE PICKED LOCKS BEFORE, BROKEN INTO SOME SEEDY PLACES...AND BROKEN SOME HEARTS...
...BUT NEVER BROKEN INTO A POLICE STATION.
IS IT EVEN WORTH IT? ARE THE ROVERS SETTING US UP FOR A FALL?
I DON'T THINK THEY'RE THAT SMART. I MEAN, THEY'RE TRUSTING US WITH HARD DRIVES. HARD DRIVES THAT COULD STORE VALUABLE INFO.
NO, THEY'RE SMART.
IT'S A TEST.
THERE'S NOTHING ON THE DRIVES. THEY JUST WANT TO KNOW IF WE CAN--AND WILL--GO THROUGH WITH IT.
AND I KNOW HOW WE DO IT.
YOU DO? THAT'S AWESOME. WHAT'S THE PLAN?
ACTUALLY... I THINK NANCY AND I CAN HANDLE THIS ONE. SORRY, JOE.
Wow.
I...didn't think he was that upset. I guess I--
JUST KIDDING, DUMMY. GET BACK IN HERE.
WE'RE ALL IN THIS TOGETHER.

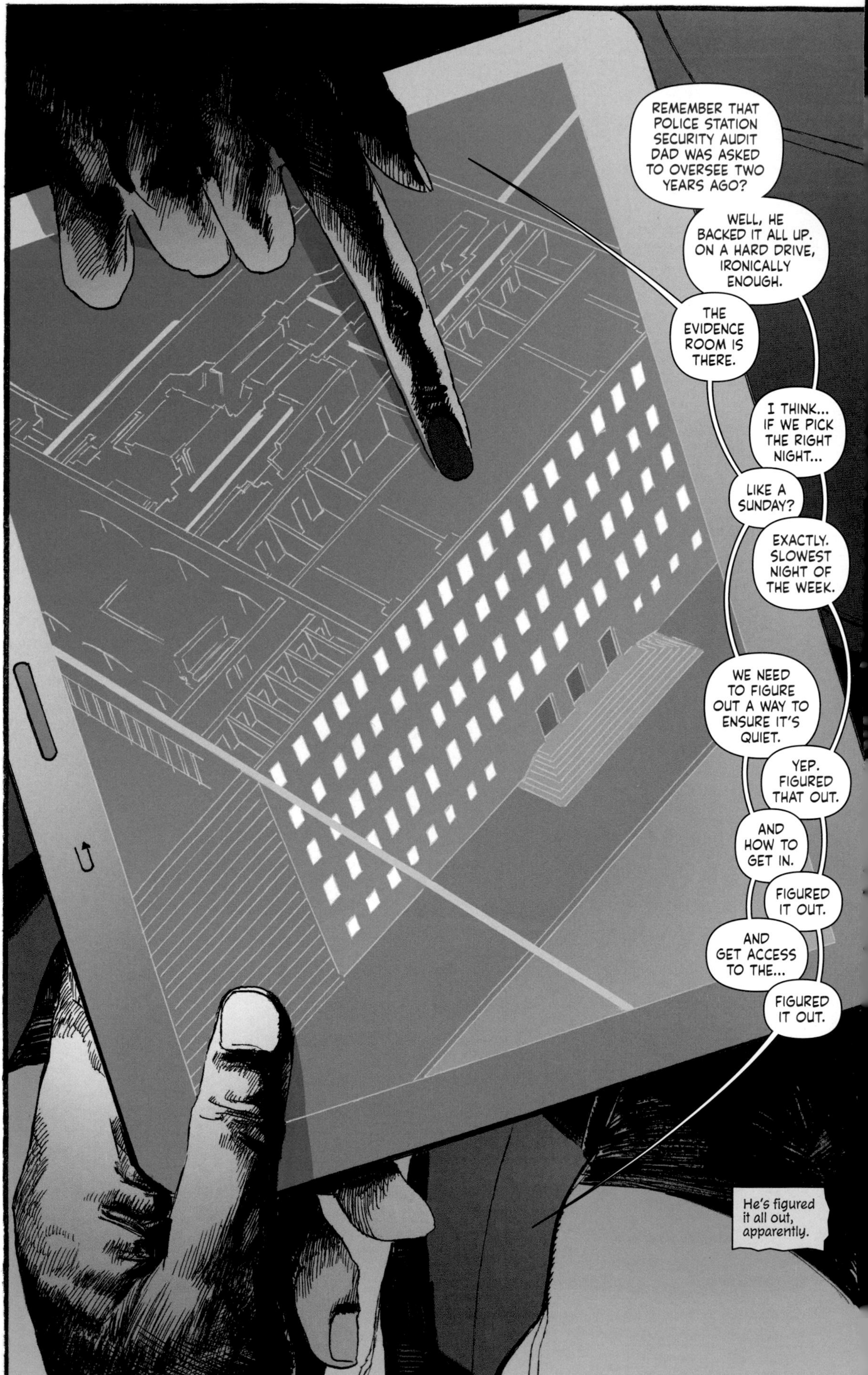
REMEMBER THAT POLICE STATION SECURITY AUDIT DAD WAS ASKED TO OVERSEE TWO YEARS AGO?
WELL, HE BACKED IT ALL UP. ON A HARD DRIVE, IRONICALLY ENOUGH.
THE EVIDENCE ROOM IS THERE.
I THINK... IF WE PICK THE RIGHT NIGHT...
LIKE A SUNDAY?
EXACTLY. SLOWEST NIGHT OF THE WEEK.
WE NEED TO FIGURE OUT A WAY TO ENSURE IT'S QUIET.
YEP. FIGURED THAT OUT.
AND HOW TO GET IN.
FIGURED IT OUT.
AND GET ACCESS TO THE...
FIGURED IT OUT.
He's figured it all out, apparently.

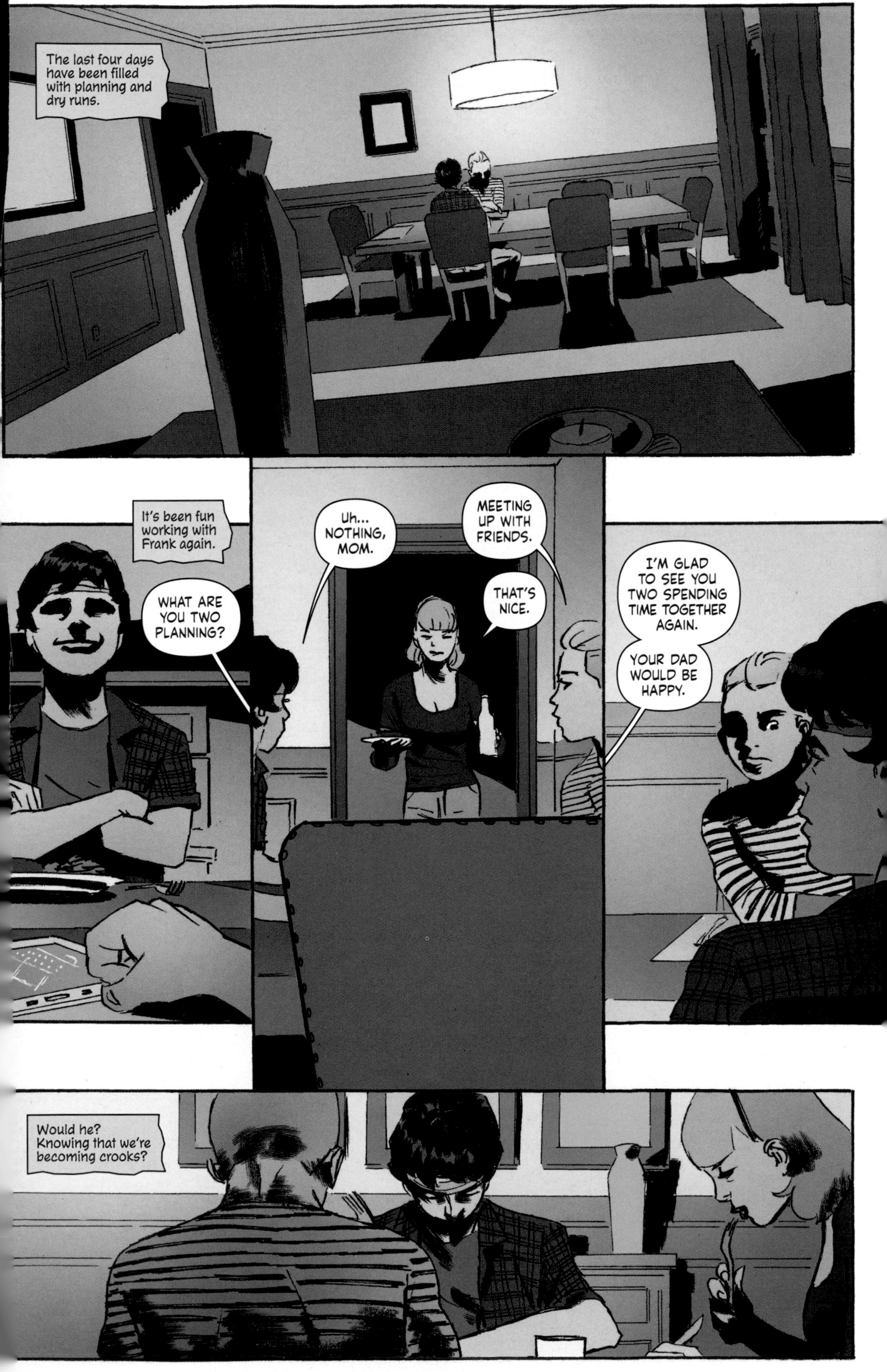
The last four days have been filled with planning and dry runs.
It's been fun working with Frank again.
WHAT ARE YOU TWO PLANNING?
Uh... NOTHING, MOM.
MEETING UP WITH FRIENDS.
THAT'S NICE.
I'M GLAD TO SEE YOU TWO SPENDING TIME TOGETHER AGAIN.
YOUR DAD WOULD BE HAPPY.
Would he? Knowing that we're becoming crooks?

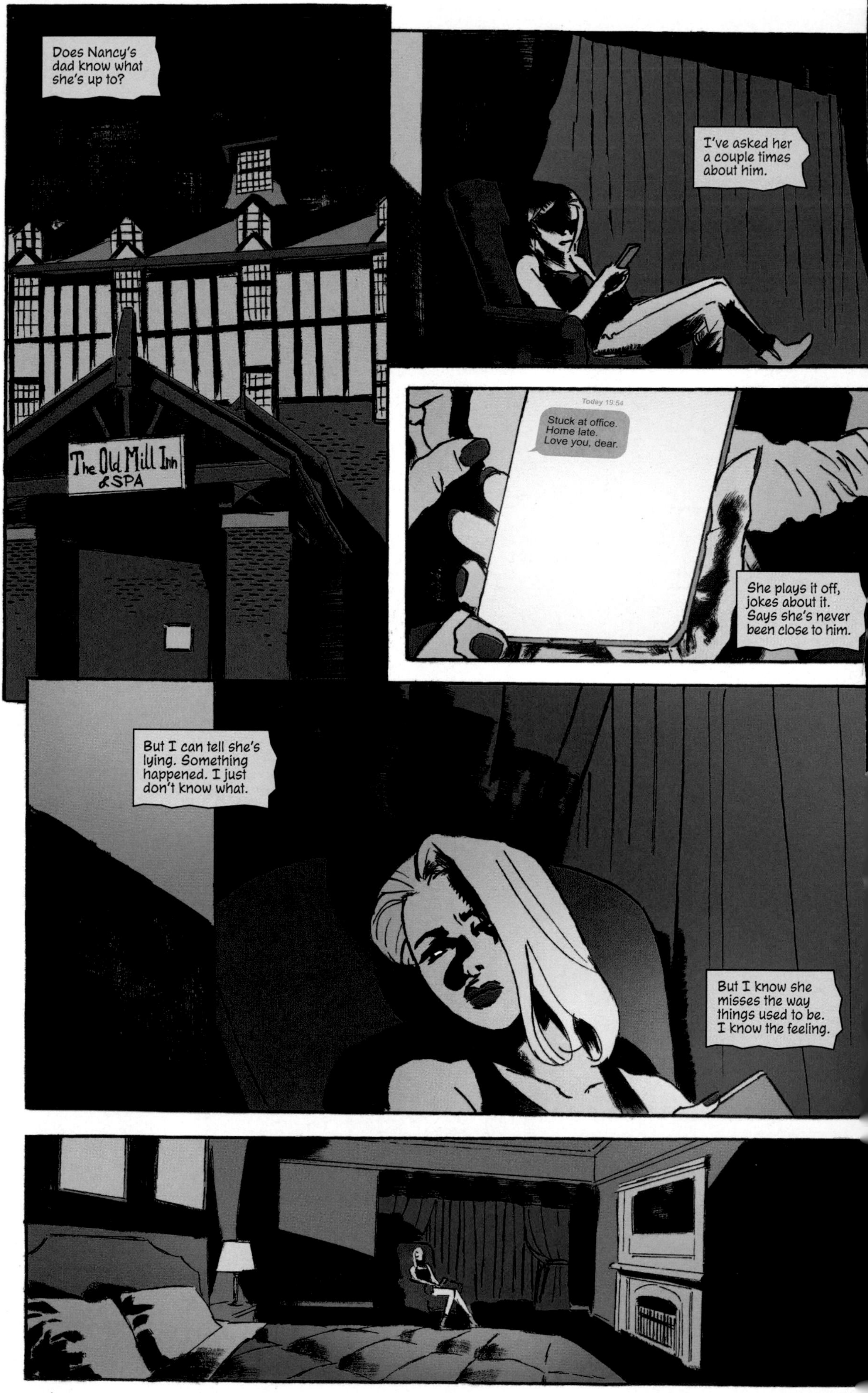
Does Nancy's dad know what she's up to?
The Old Mill Inn & SPA
I've asked her a couple times about him.
Today 19:54
Stuck at office. Home late. Love you, dear.
She plays it off, jokes about it. Says she's never been close to him.
But I can tell she's lying. Something happened. I just don't know what.
But I know she misses the way things used to be. I know the feeling.

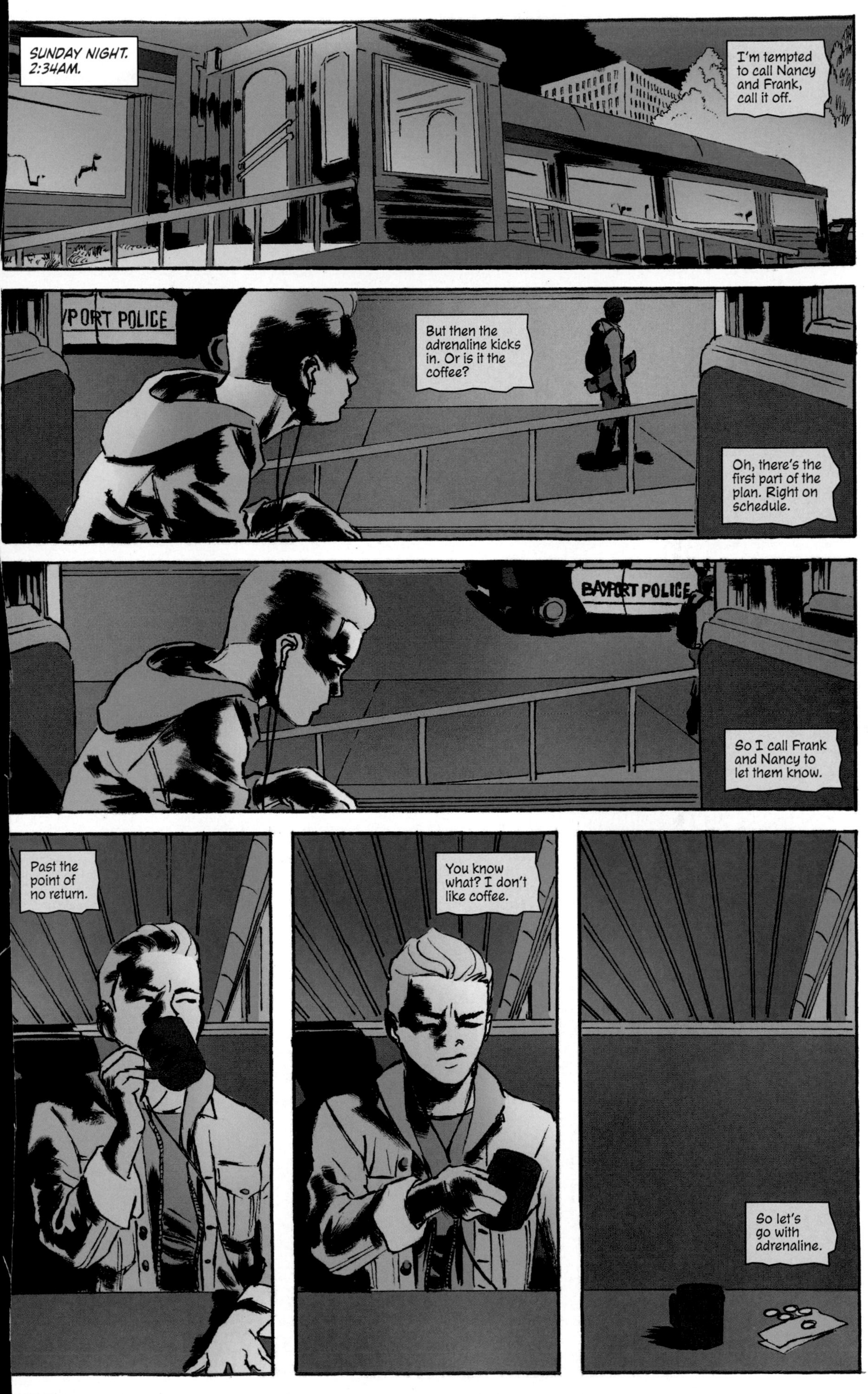
SUNDAY NIGHT. 2:34AM.
I'm tempted to call Nancy and Frank, call it off.
YPORT POLICE
But then the adrenaline kicks in. Or is it the coffee?
Oh, there's the first part of the plan. Right on schedule.
BAYPORT POLICE
So I call Frank and Nancy to let them know.
Past the point of no return.
You know what? I don't like coffee.
So let's go with adrenaline.

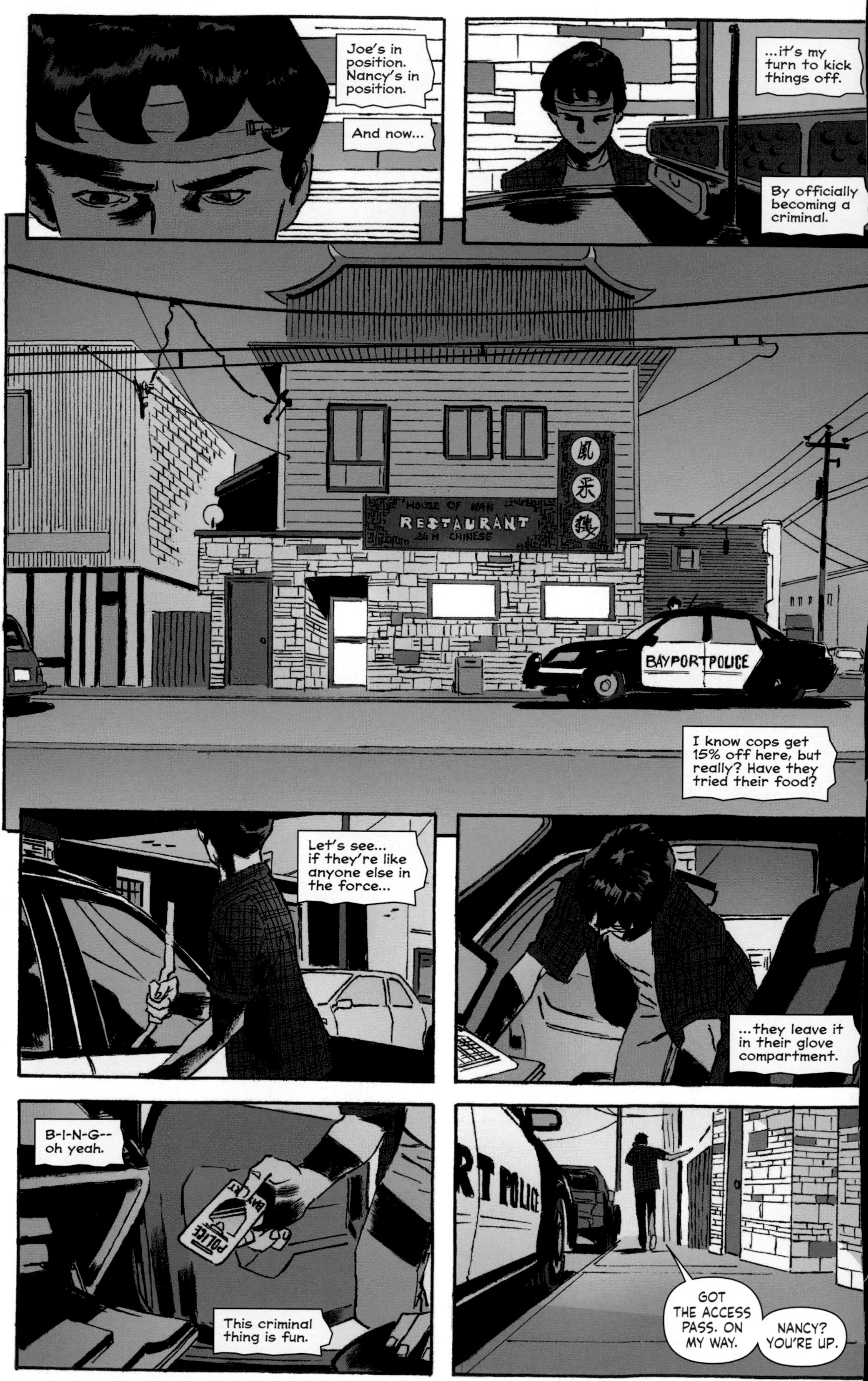
Joe's in position. Nancy's in position.
And now...
...it's my turn to kick things off.
By officially becoming a criminal.
HOUSE OF WAH
RESTAURANT
24 H CHINESE
BAYPORT POLICE
I know cops get 15% off here, but really? Have they tried their food?
Let's see... if they're like anyone else in the force...
...they leave it in their glove compartment.
B-I-N-G-- oh yeah.
POLICE
This criminal thing is fun.
GOT THE ACCESS PASS. ON MY WAY.
NANCY? YOU'RE UP.

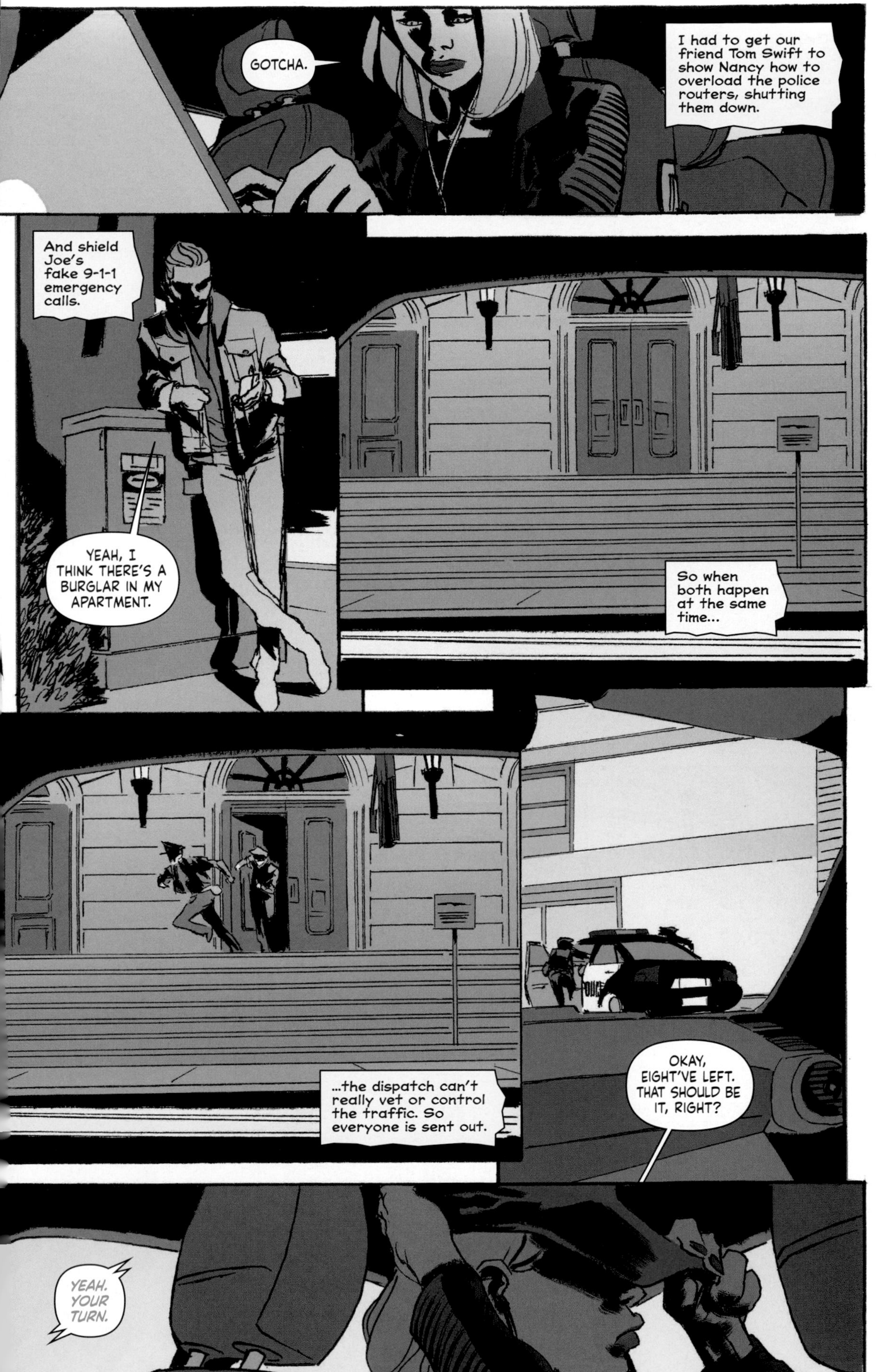

GOTCHA.
I had to get our friend Tom Swift to show Nancy how to overload the police routers, shutting them down.
And shield Joe's fake 9-1-1 emergency calls.
YEAH, I THINK THERE'S A BURGLAR IN MY APARTMENT.
So when both happen at the same time...
...the dispatch can't really vet or control the traffic. So everyone is sent out.
OKAY, EIGHT'VE LEFT. THAT SHOULD BE IT, RIGHT?
YEAH. YOUR TURN.

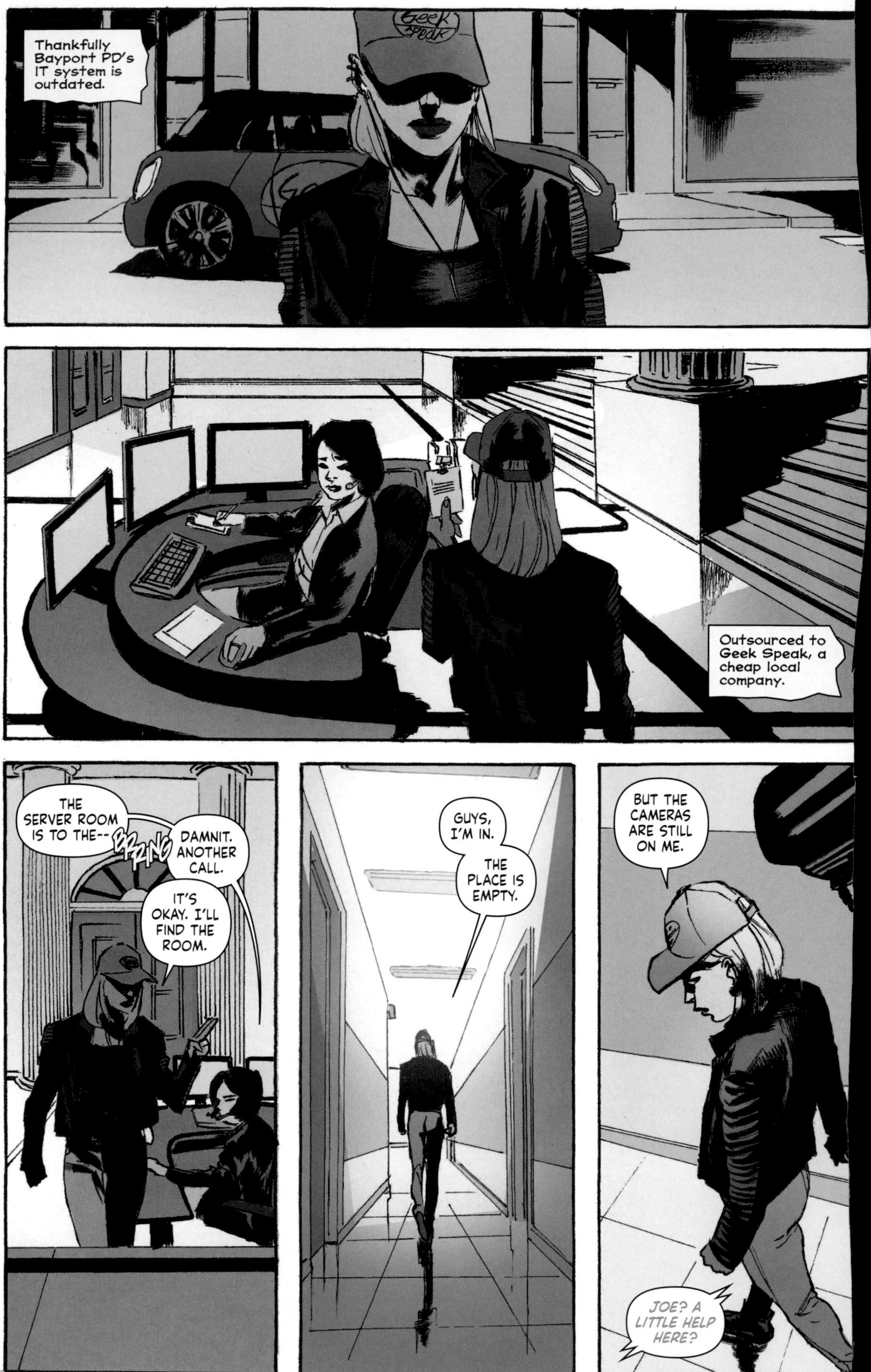

Thankfully Bayport PD's IT system is outdated.
Outsourced to Geek Speak, a cheap local company.
THE SERVER ROOM IS TO THE--
BRRING
DAMNIT. ANOTHER CALL.
IT'S OKAY. I'LL FIND THE ROOM.
GUYS, I'M IN.
THE PLACE IS EMPTY.
BUT THE CAMERAS ARE STILL ON ME.
JOE? A LITTLE HELP HERE?

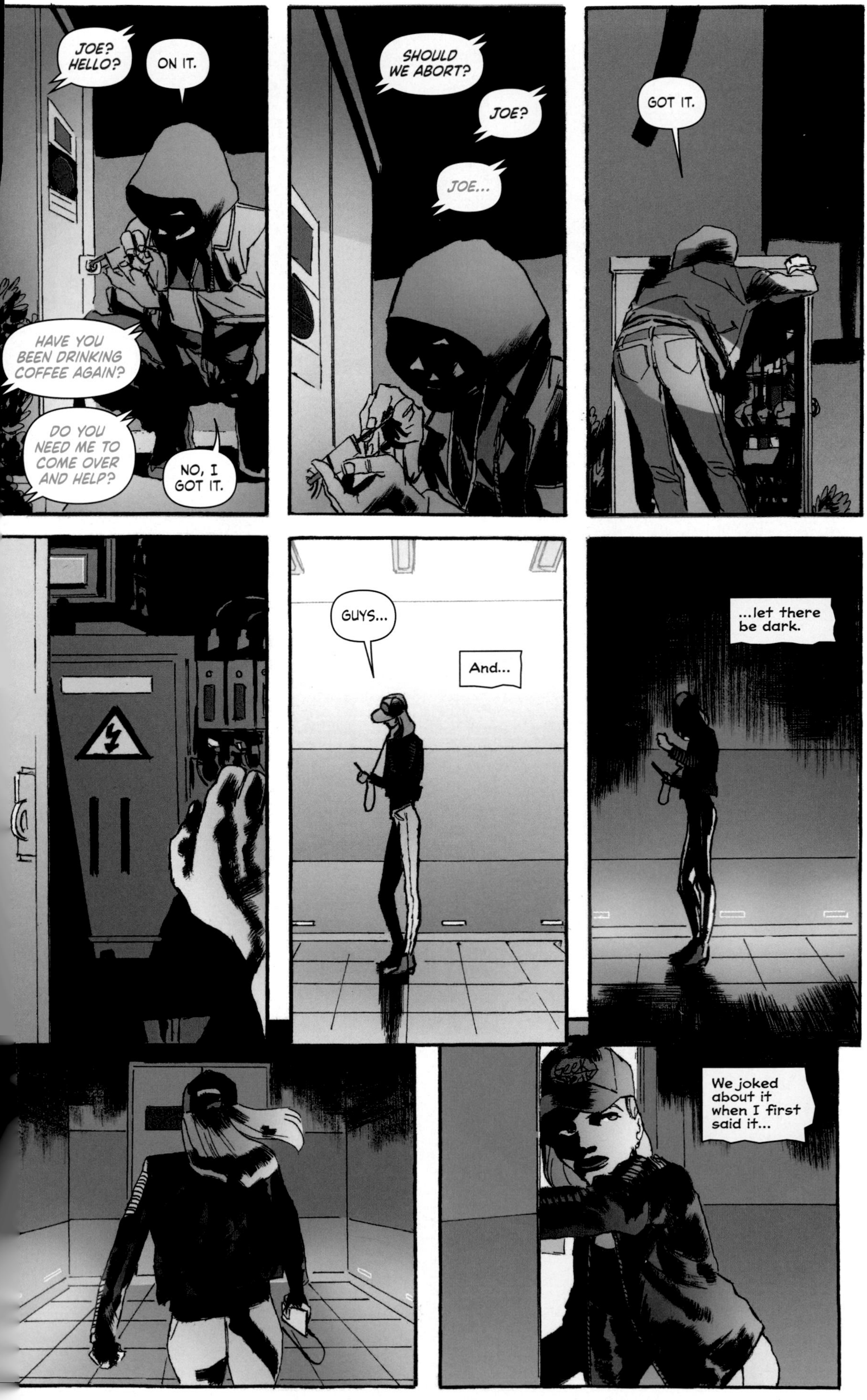
JOE? HELLO?
ON IT.
HAVE YOU BEEN DRINKING COFFEE AGAIN?
DO YOU NEED ME TO COME OVER AND HELP?
NO, I GOT IT.
SHOULD WE ABORT?
JOE?
JOE...
GOT IT.
GUYS...
And...
...let there be dark.
We joked about it when I first said it...

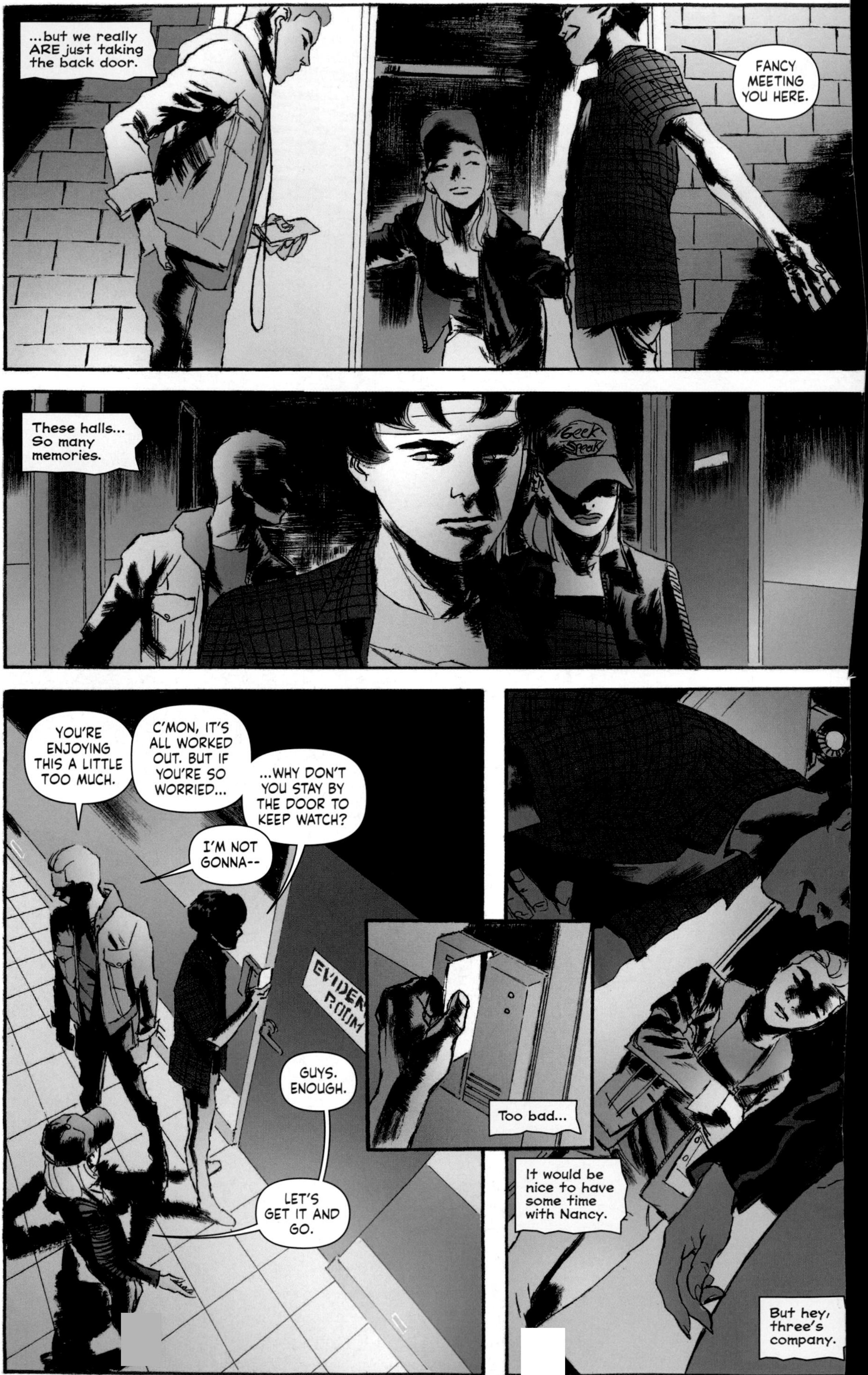
...but we really ARE just taking the back door.
FANCY MEETING YOU HERE.
These halls... So many memories.
YOU'RE ENJOYING THIS A LITTLE TOO MUCH.
C'MON, IT'S ALL WORKED OUT. BUT IF YOU'RE SO WORRIED...
...WHY DON'T YOU STAY BY THE DOOR TO KEEP WATCH?
I'M NOT GONNA--
EVIDENCE ROOM
GUYS. ENOUGH.
LET'S GET IT AND GO.
Too bad...
It would be nice to have some time with Nancy.
But hey, three's company.

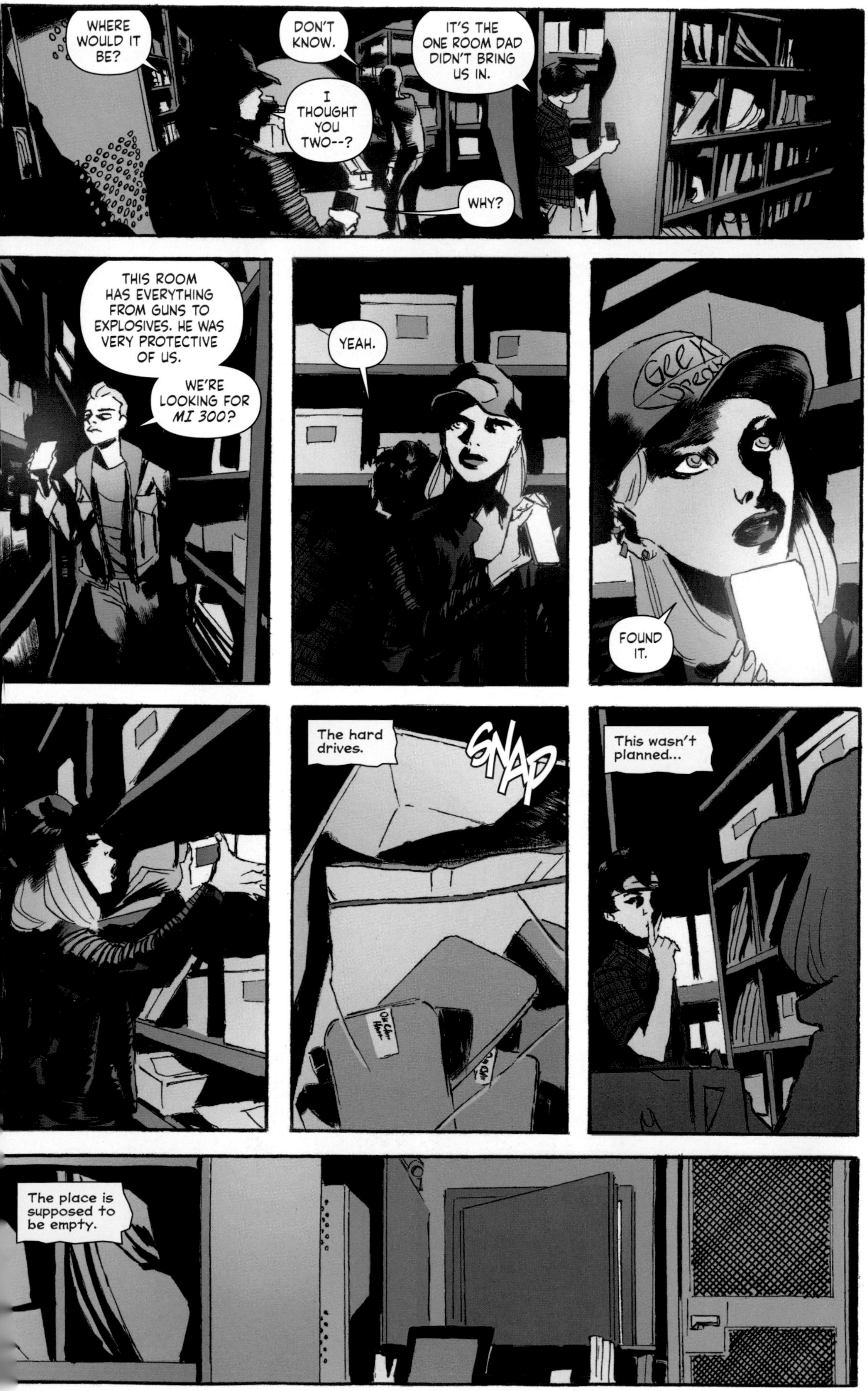

WHERE WOULD IT BE?
DON'T KNOW.
I THOUGHT YOU TWO--?
IT'S THE ONE ROOM DAD DIDN'T BRING US IN.
WHY?
THIS ROOM HAS EVERYTHING FROM GUNS TO EXPLOSIVES. HE WAS VERY PROTECTIVE OF US.
WE'RE LOOKING FOR *MI 300*?
YEAH.
FOUND IT.
The hard drives.
SNAP
This wasn't planned...
The place is supposed to be empty.

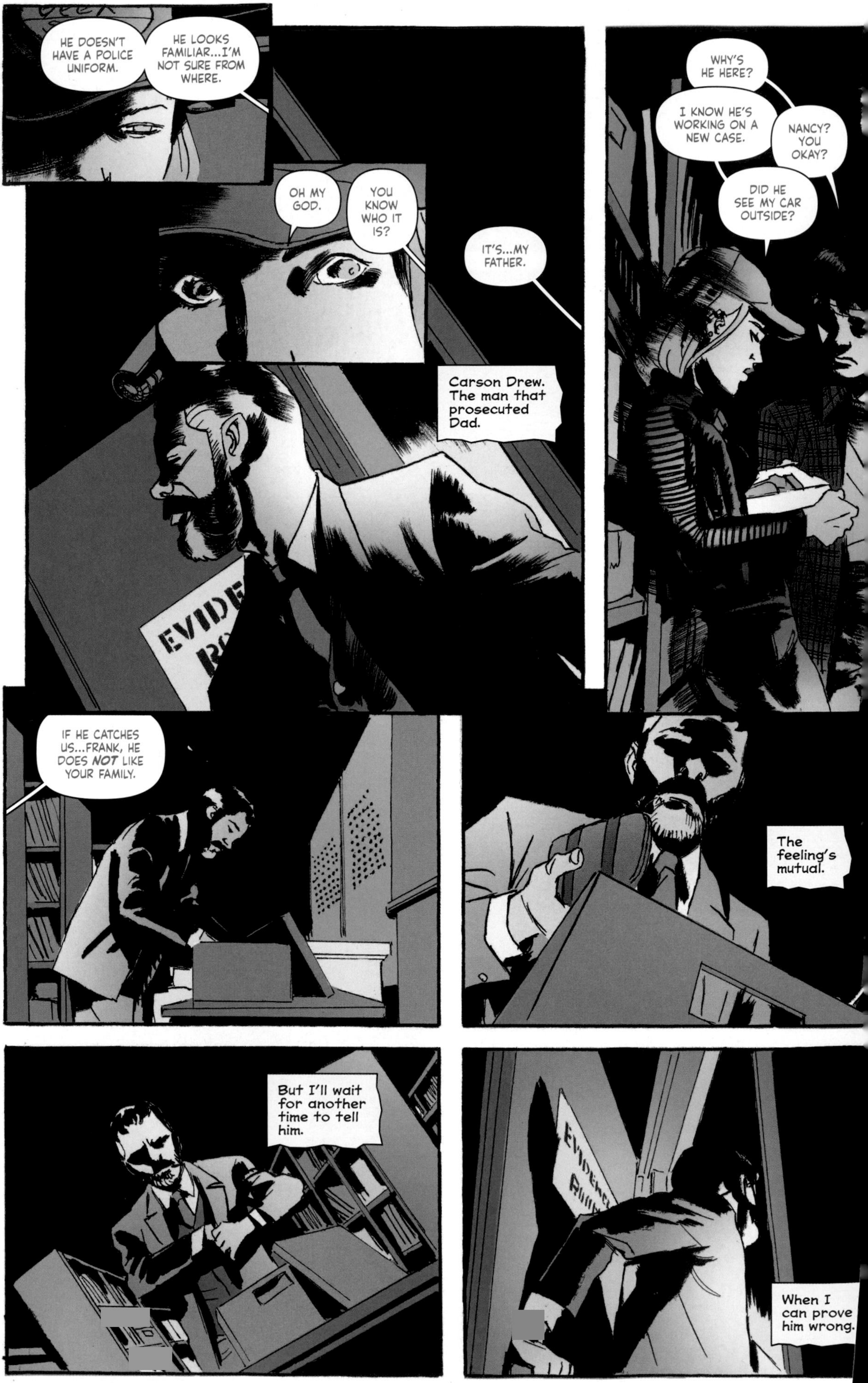

HE DOESN'T HAVE A POLICE UNIFORM.
HE LOOKS FAMILIAR...I'M NOT SURE FROM WHERE.
OH MY GOD.
YOU KNOW WHO IT IS?
IT'S...MY FATHER.
Carson Drew. The man that prosecuted Dad.
WHY'S HE HERE?
I KNOW HE'S WORKING ON A NEW CASE.
NANCY? YOU OKAY?
DID HE SEE MY CAR OUTSIDE?
IF HE CATCHES US...FRANK, HE DOES ***NOT*** LIKE YOUR FAMILY.
The feeling's mutual.
But I'll wait for another time to tell him.
When I can prove him wrong.

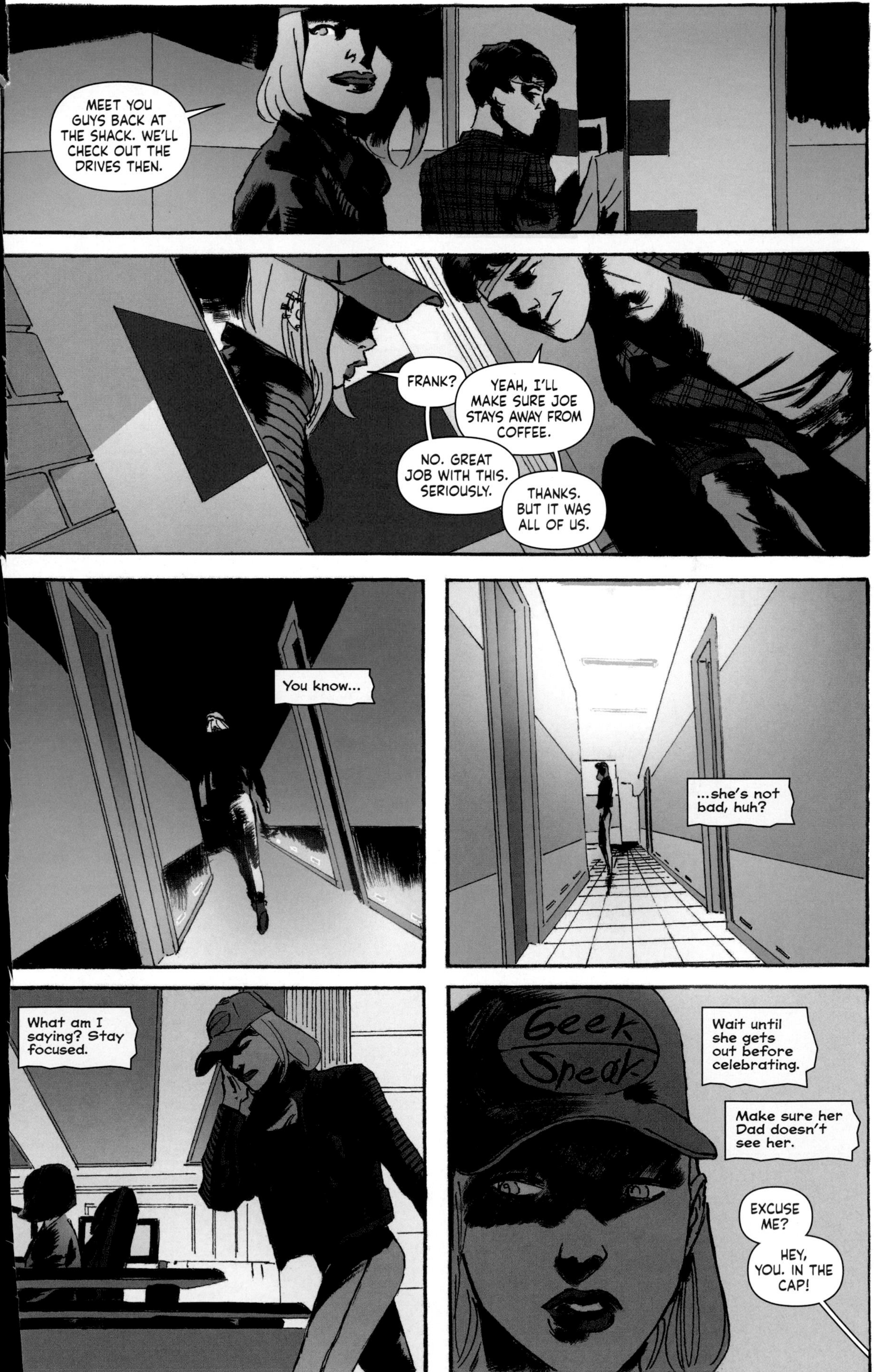
MEET YOU GUYS BACK AT THE SHACK. WE'LL CHECK OUT THE DRIVES THEN.
FRANK?
YEAH, I'LL MAKE SURE JOE STAYS AWAY FROM COFFEE.
NO. GREAT JOB WITH THIS. SERIOUSLY.
THANKS. BUT IT WAS ALL OF US.
You know...
...she's not bad, huh?
What am I saying? Stay focused.
Geek Speak
Wait until she gets out before celebrating.
Make sure her Dad doesn't see her.
EXCUSE ME?
HEY, YOU. IN THE CAP!

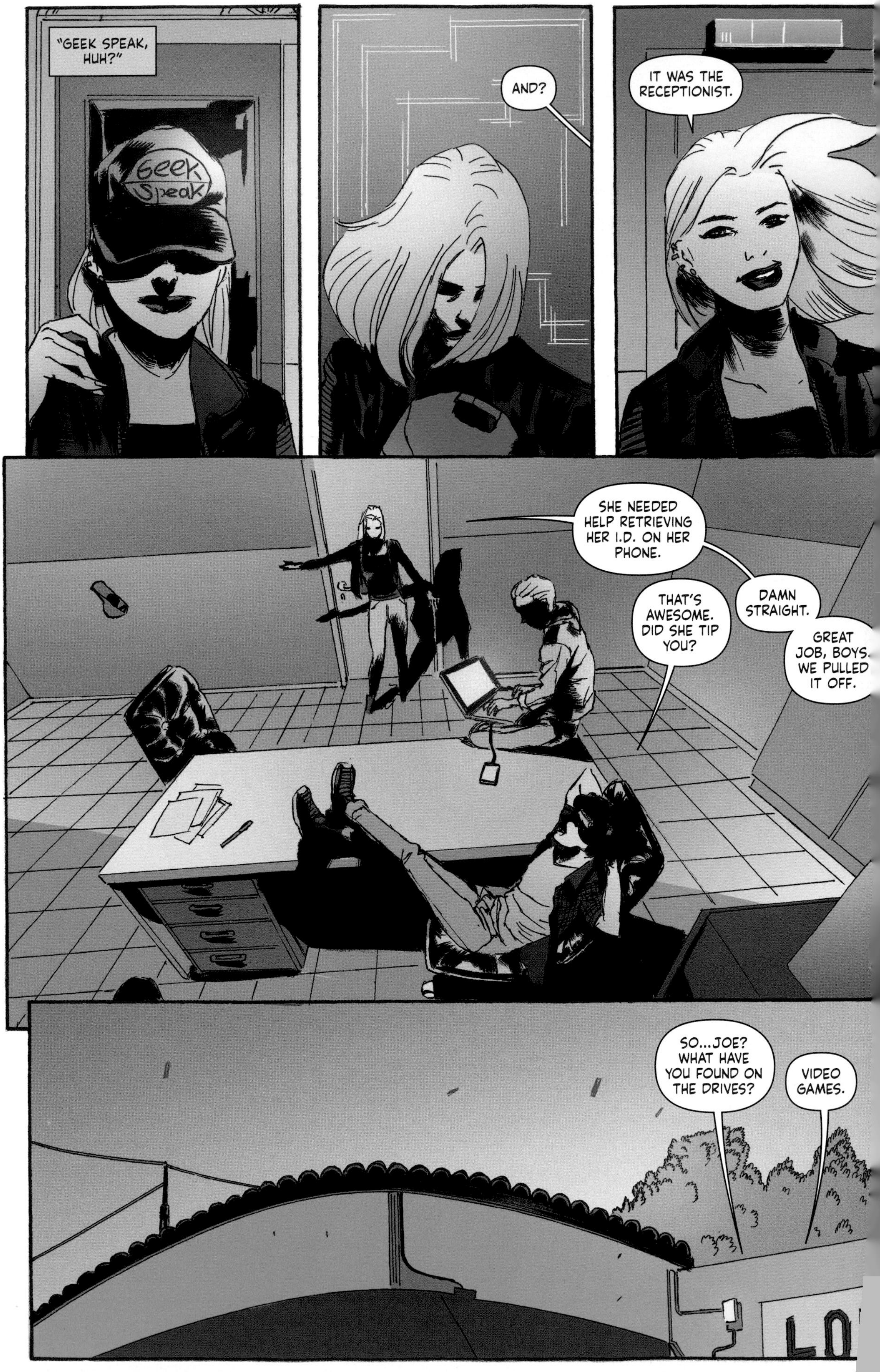
"GEEK SPEAK, HUH?"
Geek Speak
AND?
IT WAS THE RECEPTIONIST.
SHE NEEDED HELP RETRIEVING HER I.D. ON HER PHONE.
THAT'S AWESOME. DID SHE TIP YOU?
DAMN STRAIGHT.
GREAT JOB, BOYS. WE PULLED IT OFF.
SO...JOE? WHAT HAVE YOU FOUND ON THE DRIVES?
VIDEO GAMES.

HUH?

NOTHING BUT CLASSIC VIDEO GAMES. PONG, ASTEROIDS, CENTIPEDE...

HERE, LET ME SEE.

HEY, THESE GAMES ARE PRETTY COOL, BUT...HUH? ARE THERE ANY HIDDEN FILES?

CAN'T FIND ANY. I CAN CHECK WITH OUR FRIEND TOM. HE MIGHT BE ABLE TO FIND SOMETHING.

ARE YOU KIDDING ME? WE RISKED THIS ALL FOR...SOME GAMES?

THEY'RE SMART-ASSES. AND I SHOULD KNOW.

THIS HAS BEEN A GAME TO THEM. *WE'RE* A GAME TO THEM.

THEY NEVER TOOK US SERIOUSLY.

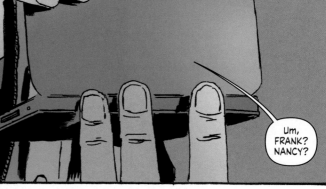

Um, FRANK? NANCY?

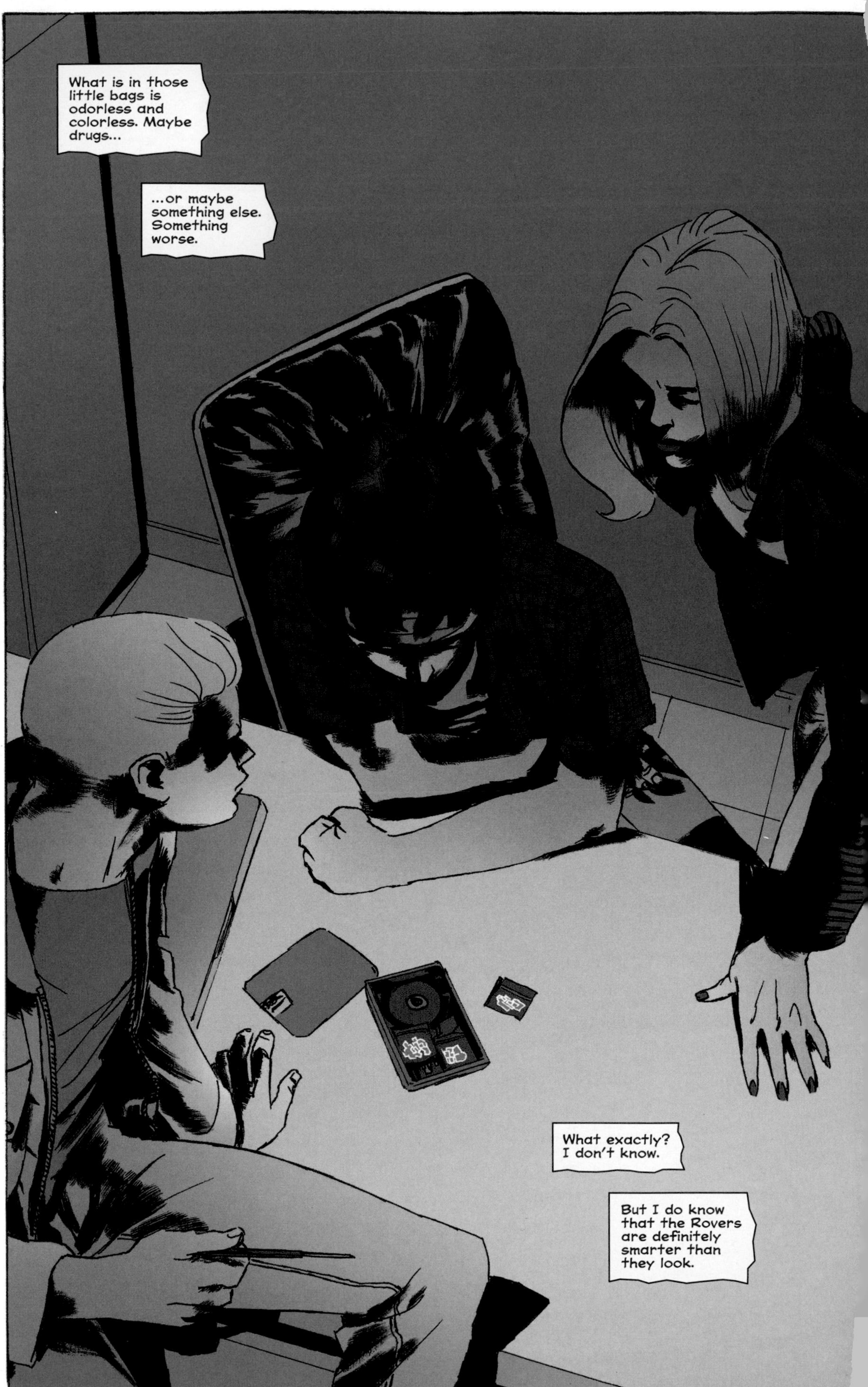
What is in those little bags is odorless and colorless. Maybe drugs...
...or maybe something else. Something worse.
What exactly? I don't know.
But I do know that the Rovers are definitely smarter than they look.

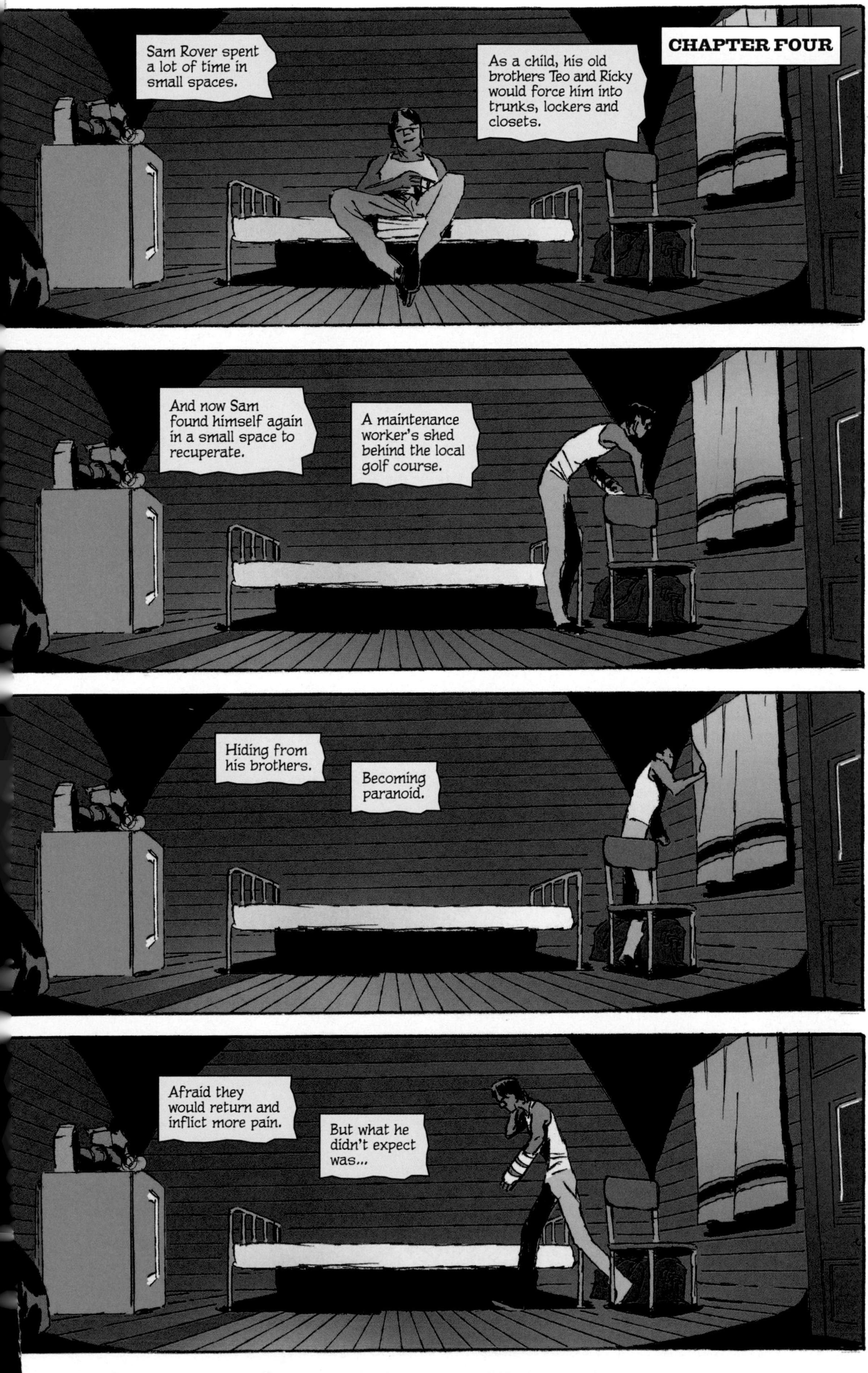
CHAPTER FOUR
Sam Rover spent a lot of time in small spaces.
As a child, his old brothers Teo and Ricky would force him into trunks, lockers and closets.
And now Sam found himself again in a small space to recuperate.
A maintenance worker's shed behind the local golf course.
Hiding from his brothers.
Becoming paranoid.
Afraid they would return and inflict more pain.
But what he didn't expect was...

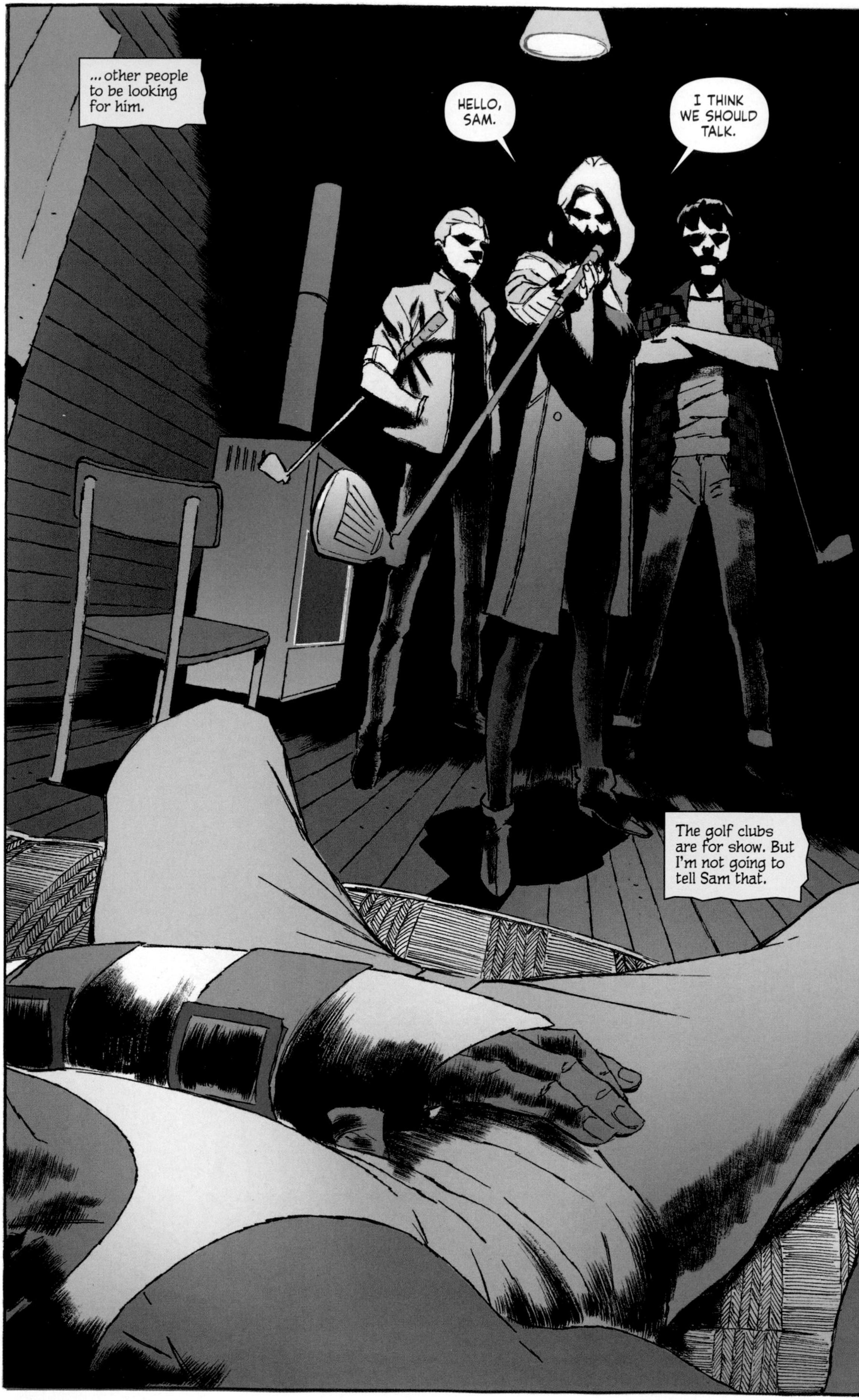
...other people to be looking for him.
HELLO, SAM.
I THINK WE SHOULD TALK.
The golf clubs are for show. But I'm not going to tell Sam that.

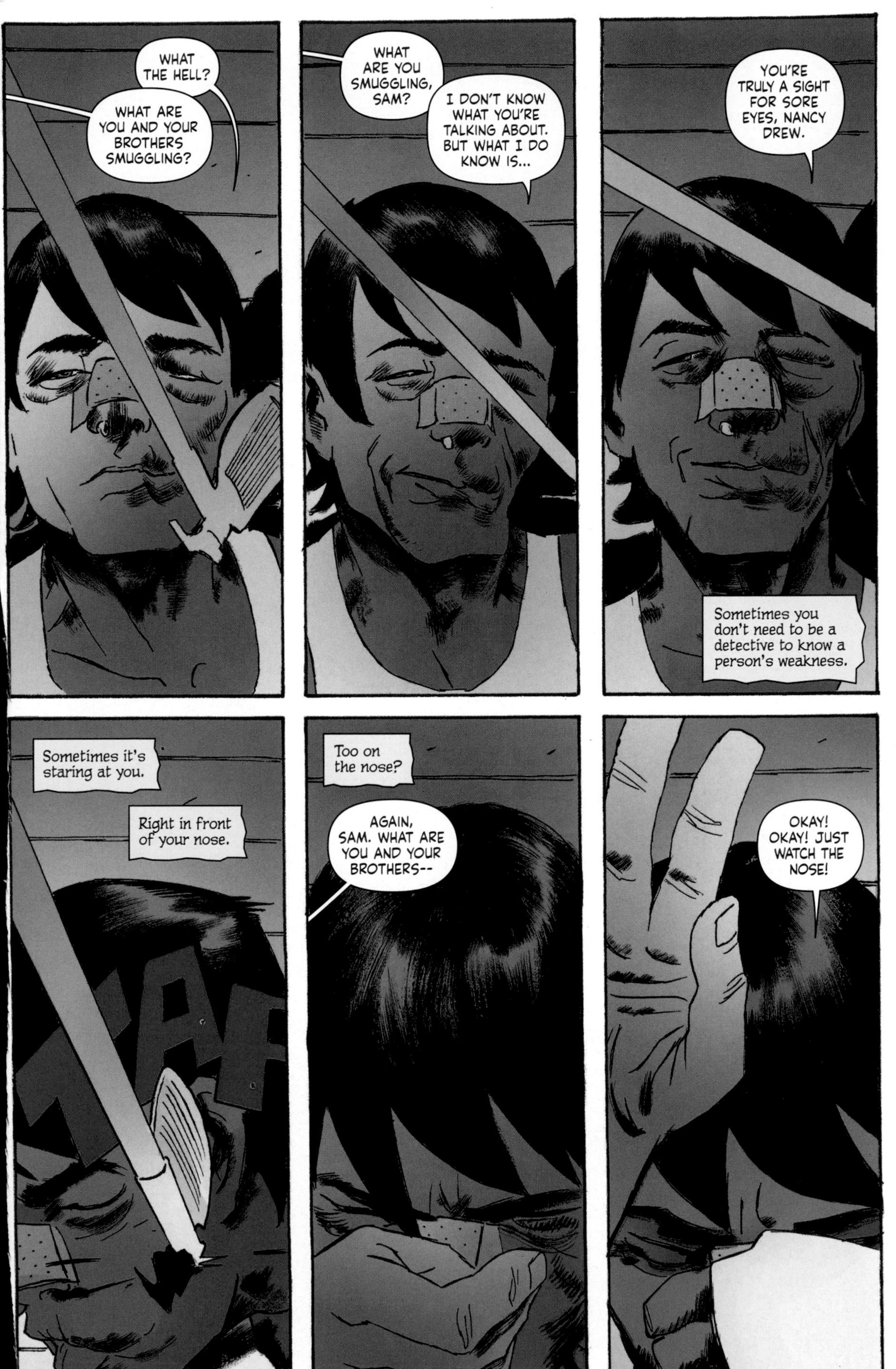
WHAT THE HELL?
WHAT ARE YOU AND YOUR BROTHERS SMUGGLING?
WHAT ARE YOU SMUGGLING, SAM?
I DON'T KNOW WHAT YOU'RE TALKING ABOUT. BUT WHAT I DO KNOW IS...
YOU'RE TRULY A SIGHT FOR SORE EYES, NANCY DREW.
Sometimes you don't need to be a detective to know a person's weakness.
Sometimes it's staring at you.
Right in front of your nose.
Too on the nose?
AGAIN, SAM. WHAT ARE YOU AND YOUR BROTHERS--
OKAY! OKAY! JUST WATCH THE NOSE!

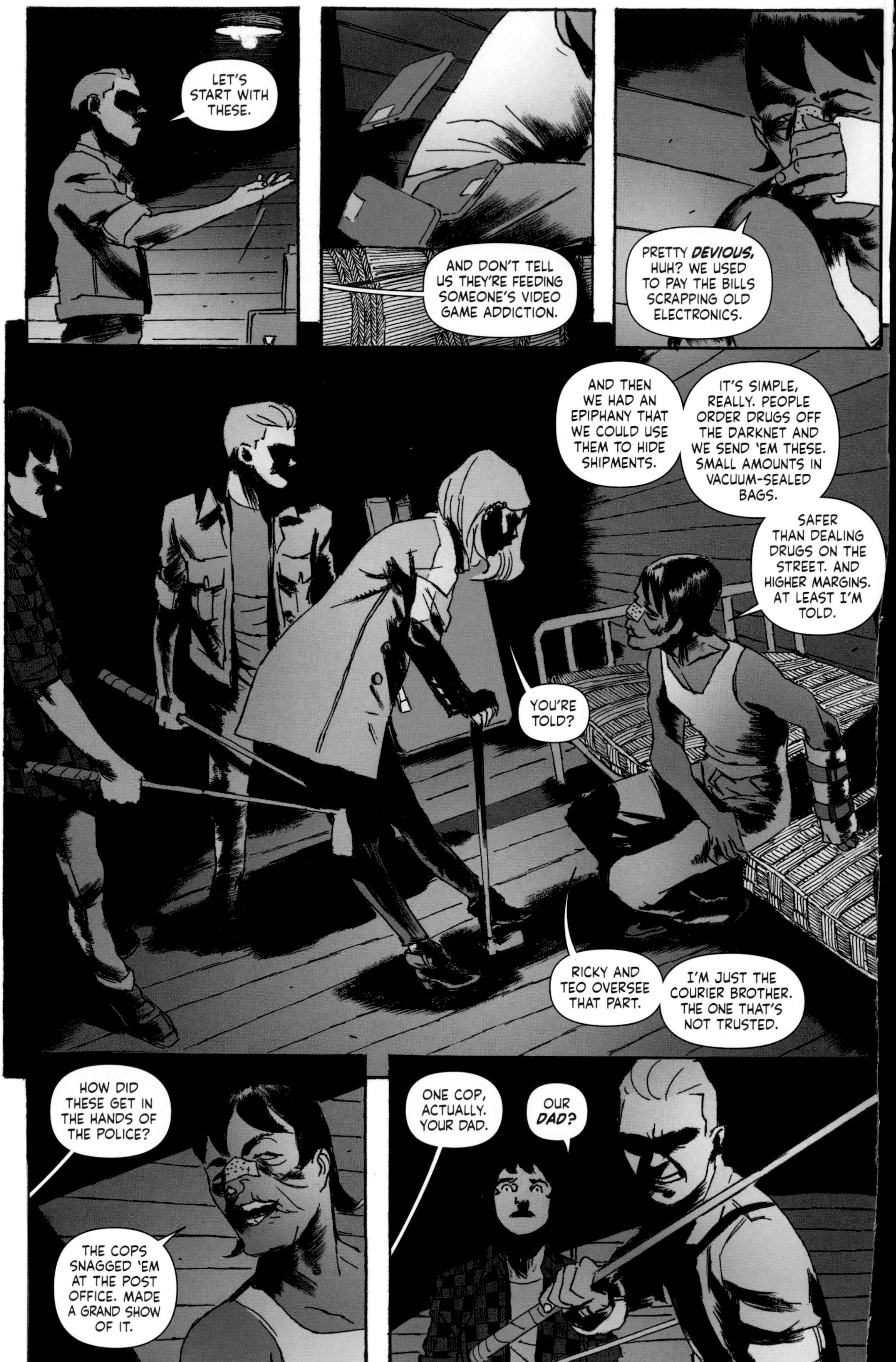
LET'S START WITH THESE.
AND DON'T TELL US THEY'RE FEEDING SOMEONE'S VIDEO GAME ADDICTION.
PRETTY DEVIOUS, HUH? WE USED TO PAY THE BILLS SCRAPPING OLD ELECTRONICS.
AND THEN WE HAD AN EPIPHANY THAT WE COULD USE THEM TO HIDE SHIPMENTS.
IT'S SIMPLE, REALLY. PEOPLE ORDER DRUGS OFF THE DARKNET AND WE SEND 'EM THESE. SMALL AMOUNTS IN VACUUM-SEALED BAGS.
SAFER THAN DEALING DRUGS ON THE STREET. AND HIGHER MARGINS. AT LEAST I'M TOLD.
YOU'RE TOLD?
RICKY AND TEO OVERSEE THAT PART.
I'M JUST THE COURIER BROTHER. THE ONE THAT'S NOT TRUSTED.
HOW DID THESE GET IN THE HANDS OF THE POLICE?
THE COPS SNAGGED 'EM AT THE POST OFFICE. MADE A GRAND SHOW OF IT.
ONE COP, ACTUALLY. YOUR DAD.
OUR DAD?

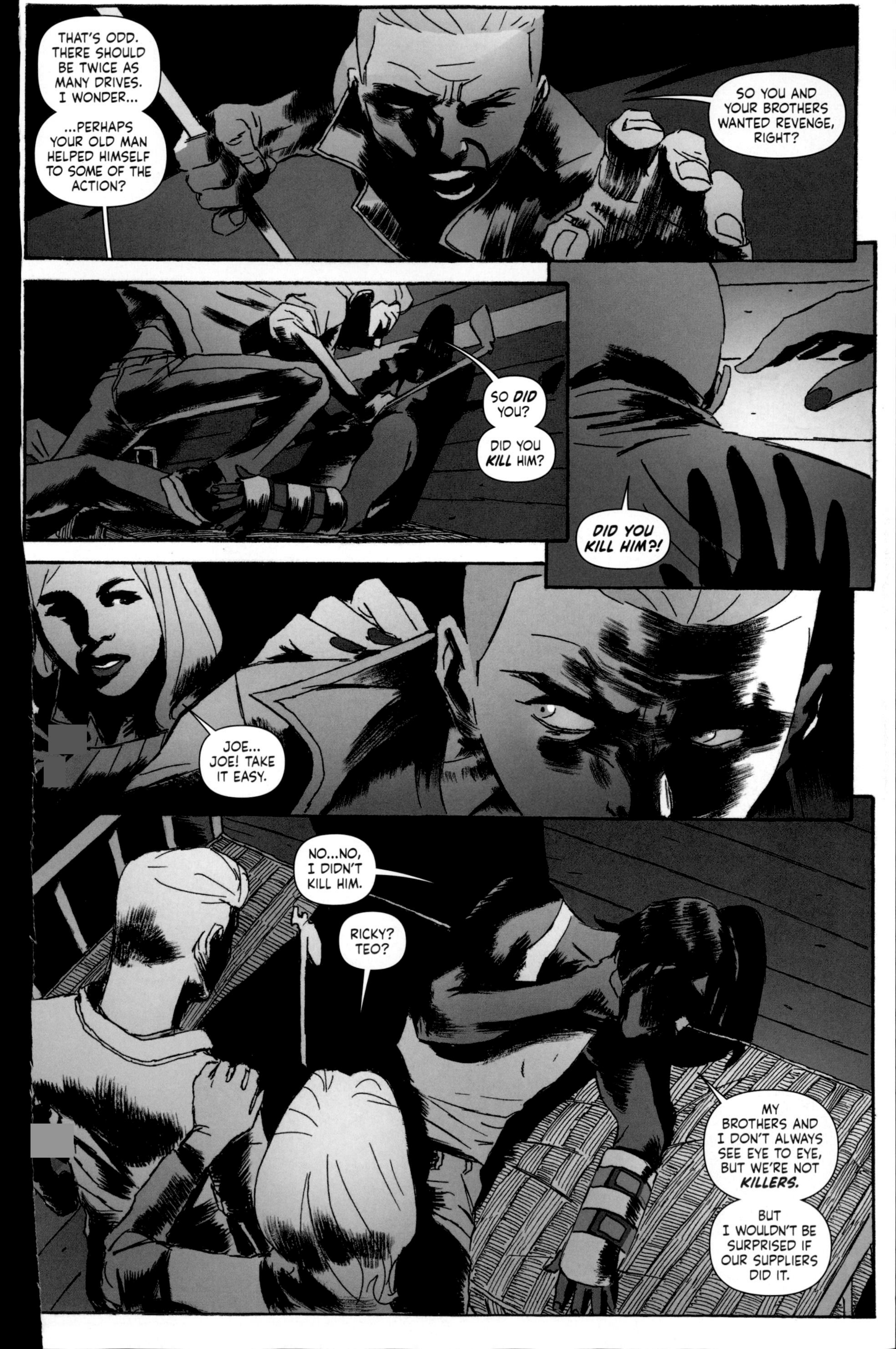
THAT'S ODD. THERE SHOULD BE TWICE AS MANY DRIVES. I WONDER...
...PERHAPS YOUR OLD MAN HELPED HIMSELF TO SOME OF THE ACTION?
SO YOU AND YOUR BROTHERS WANTED REVENGE, RIGHT?
SO *DID* YOU?
DID YOU *KILL* HIM?
DID YOU KILL HIM?!
JOE... JOE! TAKE IT EASY.
NO...NO, I DIDN'T KILL HIM.
RICKY? TEO?
MY BROTHERS AND I DON'T ALWAYS SEE EYE TO EYE, BUT WE'RE NOT *KILLERS.*
BUT I WOULDN'T BE SURPRISED IF OUR SUPPLIERS DID IT.

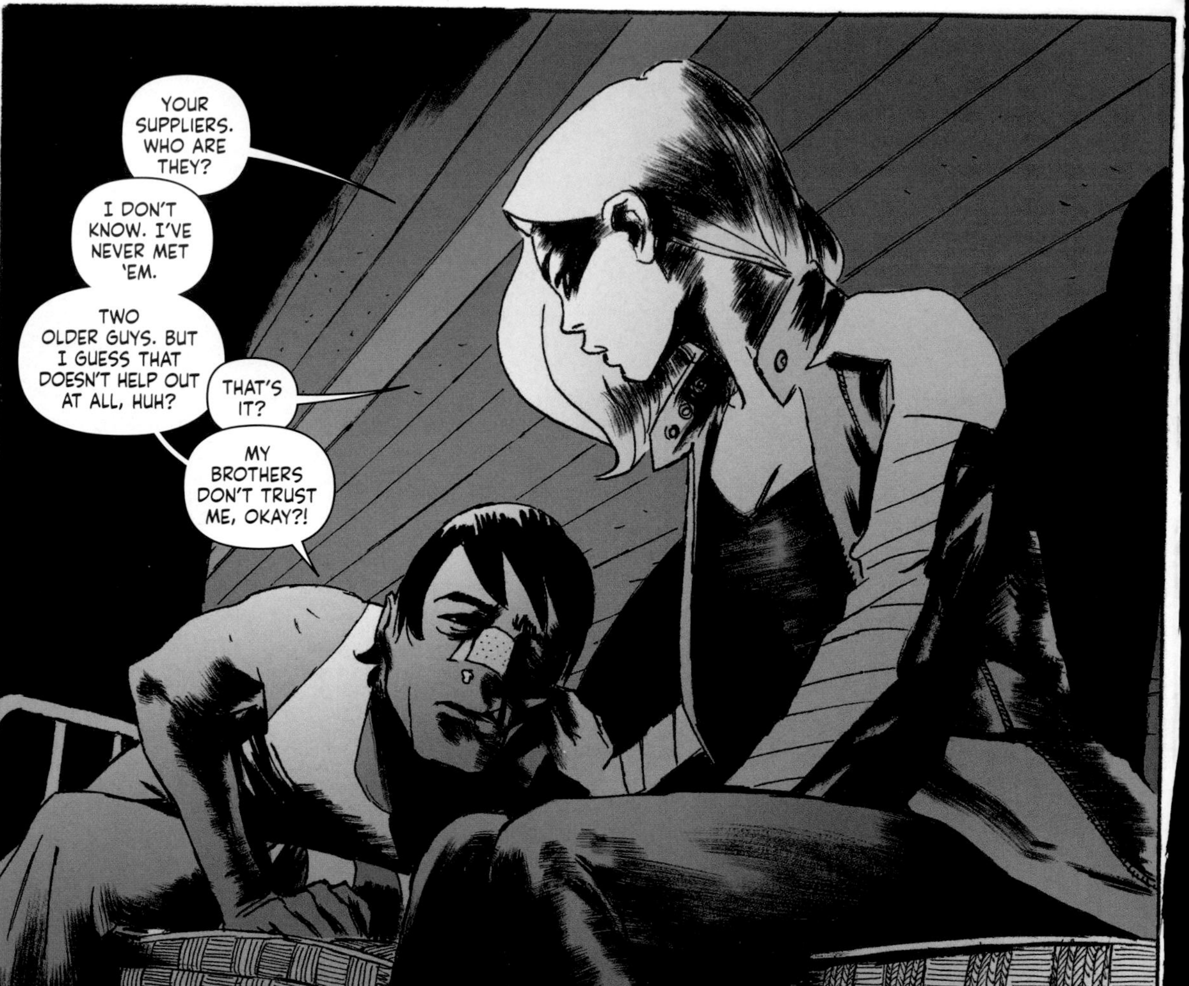
YOUR SUPPLIERS. WHO ARE THEY?
I DON'T KNOW. I'VE NEVER MET 'EM.
TWO OLDER GUYS. BUT I GUESS THAT DOESN'T HELP OUT AT ALL, HUH?
THAT'S IT?
MY BROTHERS DON'T TRUST ME, OKAY?!

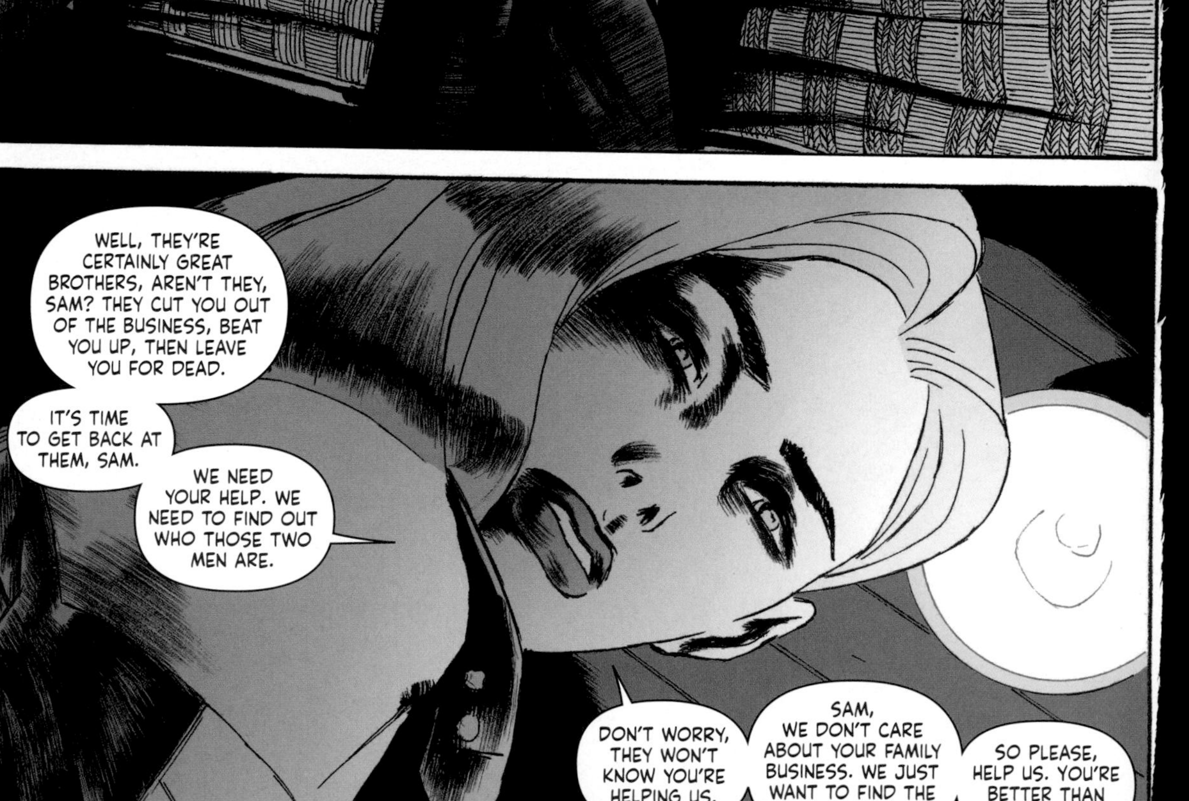
WELL, THEY'RE CERTAINLY GREAT BROTHERS, AREN'T THEY, SAM? THEY CUT YOU OUT OF THE BUSINESS, BEAT YOU UP, THEN LEAVE YOU FOR DEAD.
IT'S TIME TO GET BACK AT THEM, SAM.
WE NEED YOUR HELP. WE NEED TO FIND OUT WHO THOSE TWO MEN ARE.
DON'T WORRY, THEY WON'T KNOW YOU'RE HELPING US.
SAM, WE DON'T CARE ABOUT YOUR FAMILY BUSINESS. WE JUST WANT TO FIND THE MURDERER.
SO PLEASE, HELP US. YOU'RE BETTER THAN RICKY AND TEO.

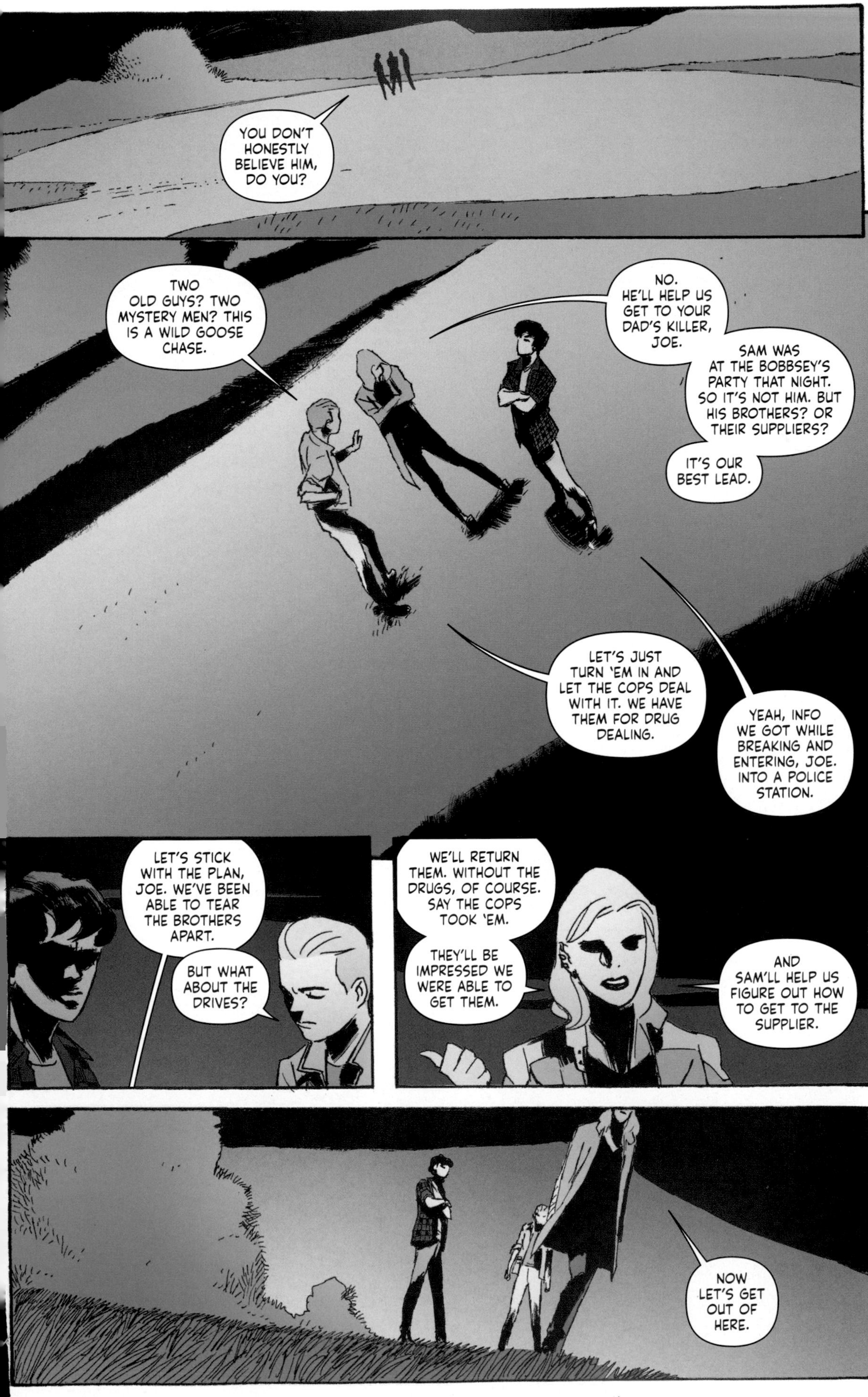
YOU DON'T HONESTLY BELIEVE HIM, DO YOU?
TWO OLD GUYS? TWO MYSTERY MEN? THIS IS A WILD GOOSE CHASE.
NO. HE'LL HELP US GET TO YOUR DAD'S KILLER, JOE.
SAM WAS AT THE BOBBSEY'S PARTY THAT NIGHT. SO IT'S NOT HIM. BUT HIS BROTHERS? OR THEIR SUPPLIERS?
IT'S OUR BEST LEAD.
LET'S JUST TURN 'EM IN AND LET THE COPS DEAL WITH IT. WE HAVE THEM FOR DRUG DEALING.
YEAH, INFO WE GOT WHILE BREAKING AND ENTERING, JOE. INTO A POLICE STATION.
LET'S STICK WITH THE PLAN, JOE. WE'VE BEEN ABLE TO TEAR THE BROTHERS APART.
BUT WHAT ABOUT THE DRIVES?
WE'LL RETURN THEM. WITHOUT THE DRUGS, OF COURSE. SAY THE COPS TOOK 'EM.
THEY'LL BE IMPRESSED WE WERE ABLE TO GET THEM.
AND SAM'LL HELP US FIGURE OUT HOW TO GET TO THE SUPPLIER.
NOW LET'S GET OUT OF HERE.

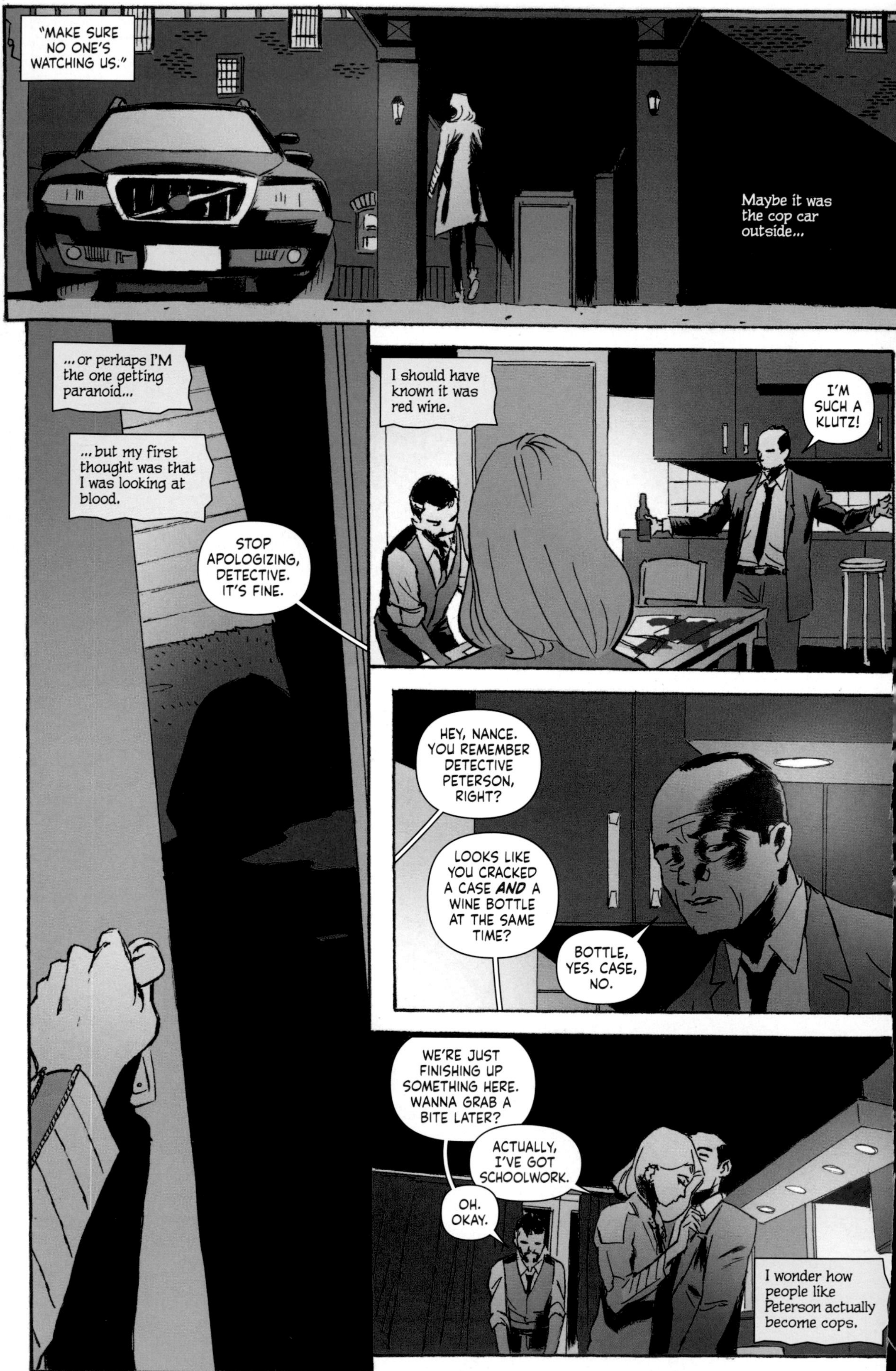
"MAKE SURE NO ONE'S WATCHING US."
Maybe it was the cop car outside...
...or perhaps I'M the one getting paranoid...
...but my first thought was that I was looking at blood.
STOP APOLOGIZING, DETECTIVE. IT'S FINE.
I should have known it was red wine.
I'M SUCH A KLUTZ!
HEY, NANCE. YOU REMEMBER DETECTIVE PETERSON, RIGHT?
LOOKS LIKE YOU CRACKED A CASE *AND* A WINE BOTTLE AT THE SAME TIME?
BOTTLE, YES. CASE, NO.
WE'RE JUST FINISHING UP SOMETHING HERE. WANNA GRAB A BITE LATER?
ACTUALLY, I'VE GOT SCHOOLWORK.
OH. OKAY.
I wonder how people like Peterson actually become cops.

But others...
are born cops.

CHIEF COLLIG? I DIDN'T KNOW YOU WERE HERE.

KNOCK
KNOCK
KNOCK

HAD A "CLEAN-UP IN AISLE FIVE" TO ATTEND TO.

GOTTA GIVE IT TO PETERSON: HE'S GOT GOOD AIM WITH THAT WINE.

YEAH. I GUESS HE DOESN'T CARE ABOUT PROMOTIONS, HUH?

HEY, LISTEN, I HAVEN'T SAID ANYTHING TO YOUR DAD, BUT...

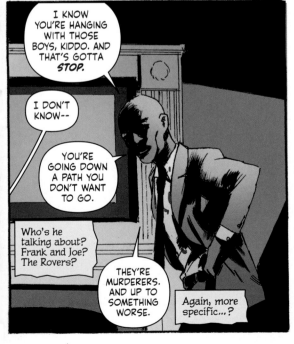

I KNOW YOU'RE HANGING WITH THOSE BOYS, KIDDO. AND THAT'S GOTTA STOP.

I DON'T KNOW--

YOU'RE GOING DOWN A PATH YOU DON'T WANT TO GO.

Who's he talking about? Frank and Joe? The Rovers?

THEY'RE MURDERERS. AND UP TO SOMETHING WORSE.

Again, more specific...?

JUST BE CAREFUL. 'CAUSE I KNOW EVERYTHING THAT GOES ON IN MY TOWN.

Do you really? 'Cause I'm about to find out what really happens in your town.

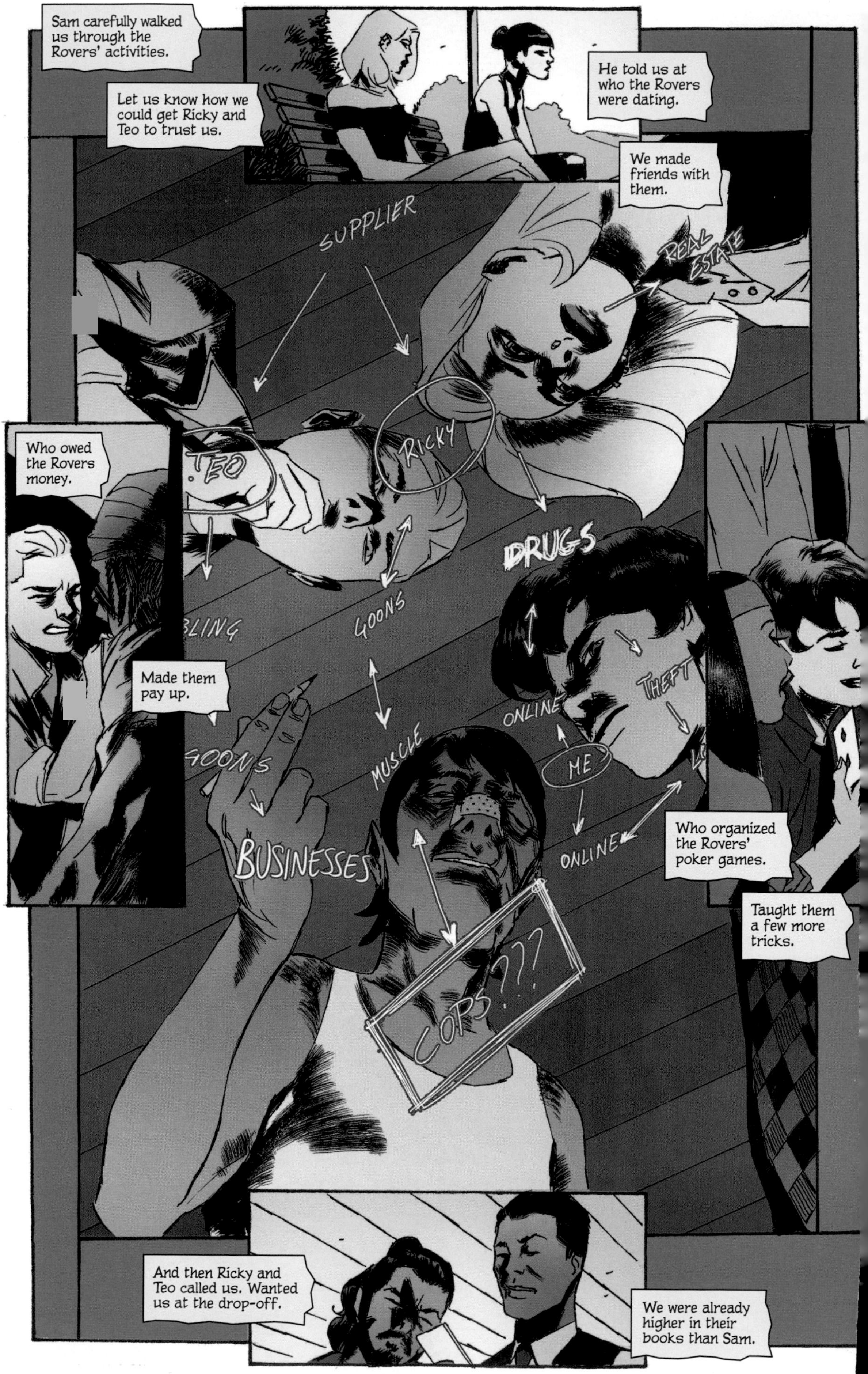

Sam carefully walked us through the Rovers' activities.
Let us know how we could get Ricky and Teo to trust us.
He told us at who the Rovers were dating.
We made friends with them.
SUPPLIER
REAL ESTATE
TEO
RICKY
DRUGS
Who owed the Rovers money.
GOONS
THEFT
Made them pay up.
ONLINE
GOONS
MUSCLE
ME
BUSINESSES
ONLINE
Who organized the Rovers' poker games.
Taught them a few more tricks.
COPS???
And then Ricky and Teo called us. Wanted us at the drop-off.
We were already higher in their books than Sam.

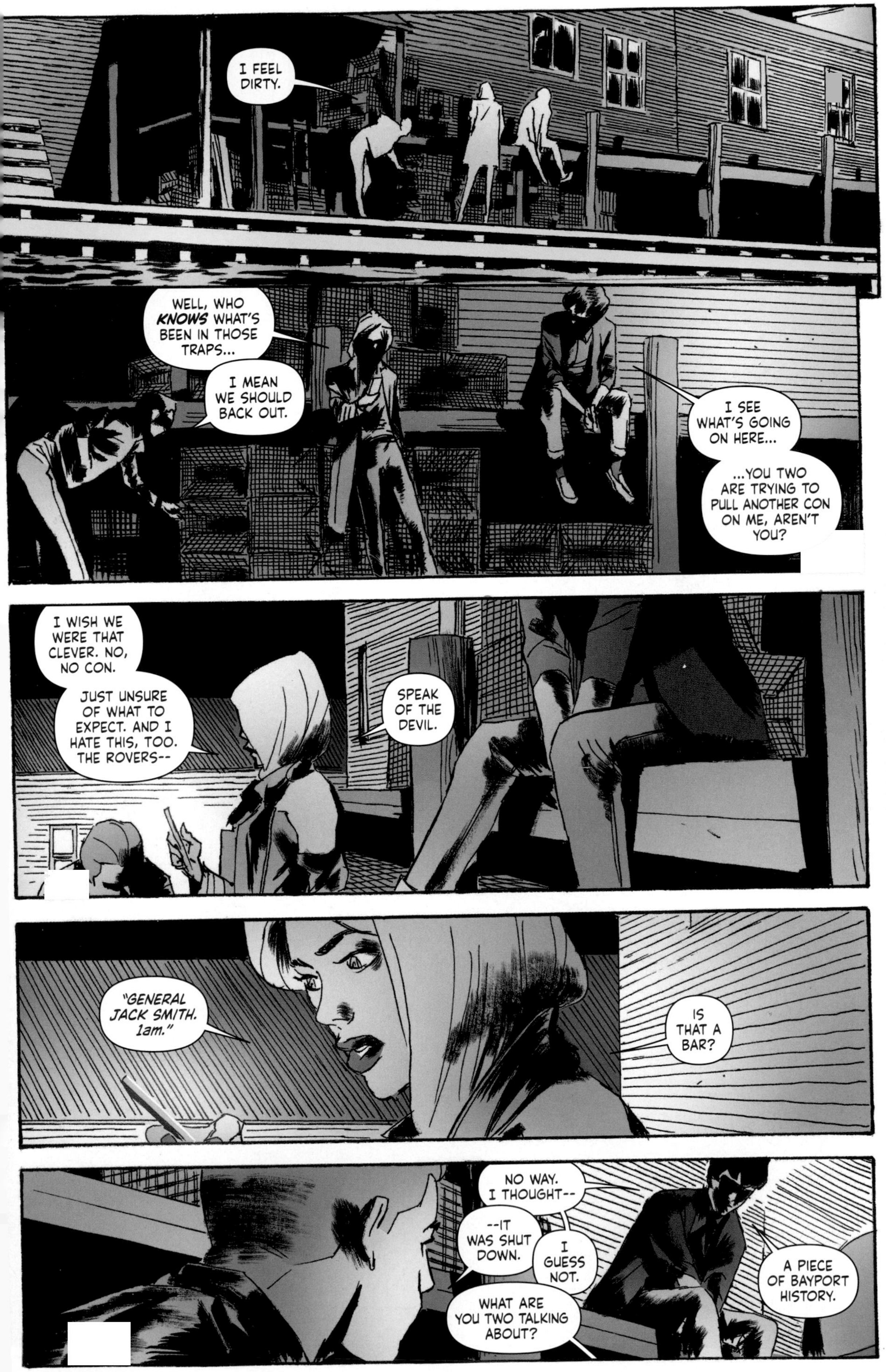
I FEEL DIRTY.
WELL, WHO *KNOWS* WHAT'S BEEN IN THOSE TRAPS...
I MEAN WE SHOULD BACK OUT.
I SEE WHAT'S GOING ON HERE...
...YOU TWO ARE TRYING TO PULL ANOTHER CON ON ME, AREN'T YOU?
I WISH WE WERE THAT CLEVER. NO, NO CON.
JUST UNSURE OF WHAT TO EXPECT. AND I HATE THIS, TOO. THE ROVERS--
SPEAK OF THE DEVIL.
"GENERAL JACK SMITH. 1am."
IS THAT A BAR?
NO WAY. I THOUGHT--
--IT WAS SHUT DOWN.
I GUESS NOT.
WHAT ARE YOU TWO TALKING ABOUT?
A PIECE OF BAYPORT HISTORY.

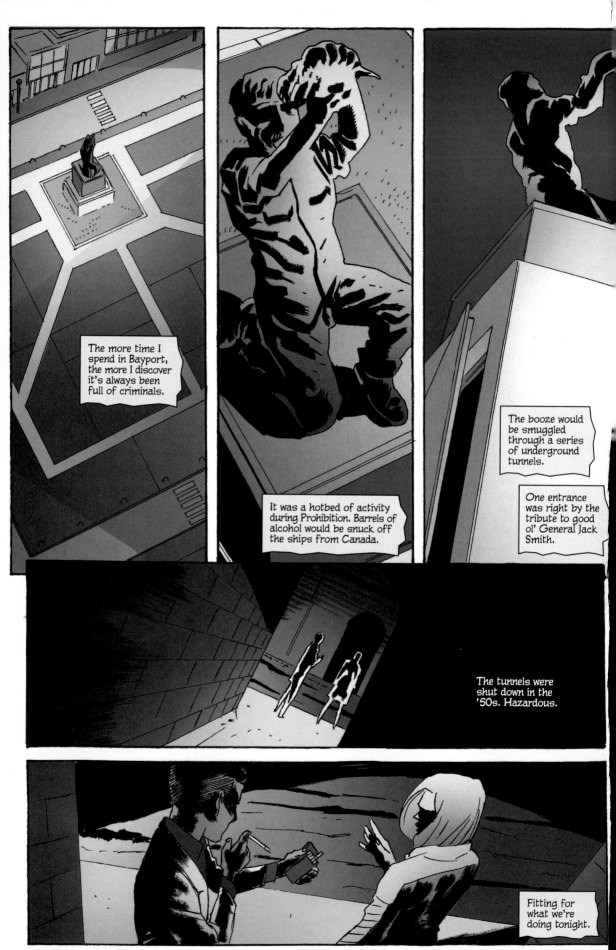

The more time I spend in Bayport, the more I discover it's always been full of criminals.

It was a hotbed of activity during Prohibition. Barrels of alcohol would be snuck off the ships from Canada.

The booze would be smuggled through a series of underground tunnels.

One entrance was right by the tribute to good ol' General Jack Smith.

The tunnels were shut down in the '50s. Hazardous.

Fitting for what we're doing tonight.

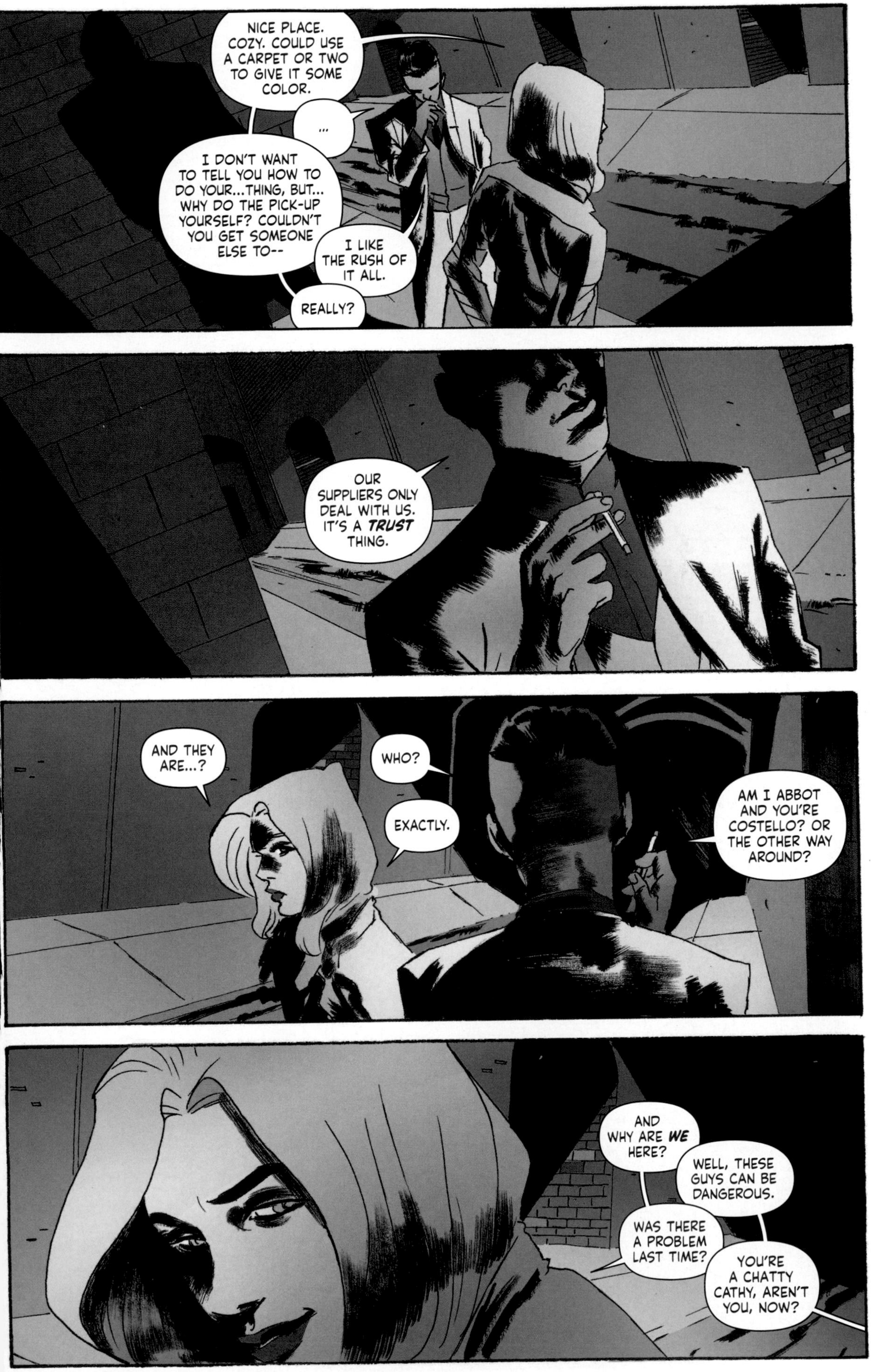
NICE PLACE. COZY. COULD USE A CARPET OR TWO TO GIVE IT SOME COLOR.
...
I DON'T WANT TO TELL YOU HOW TO DO YOUR...THING, BUT... WHY DO THE PICK-UP YOURSELF? COULDN'T YOU GET SOMEONE ELSE TO--
I LIKE THE RUSH OF IT ALL.
REALLY?
OUR SUPPLIERS ONLY DEAL WITH US. IT'S A TRUST THING.
AND THEY ARE...?
WHO?
EXACTLY.
AM I ABBOT AND YOU'RE COSTELLO? OR THE OTHER WAY AROUND?
AND WHY ARE WE HERE?
WELL, THESE GUYS CAN BE DANGEROUS.
WAS THERE A PROBLEM LAST TIME?
YOU'RE A CHATTY CATHY, AREN'T YOU, NOW?

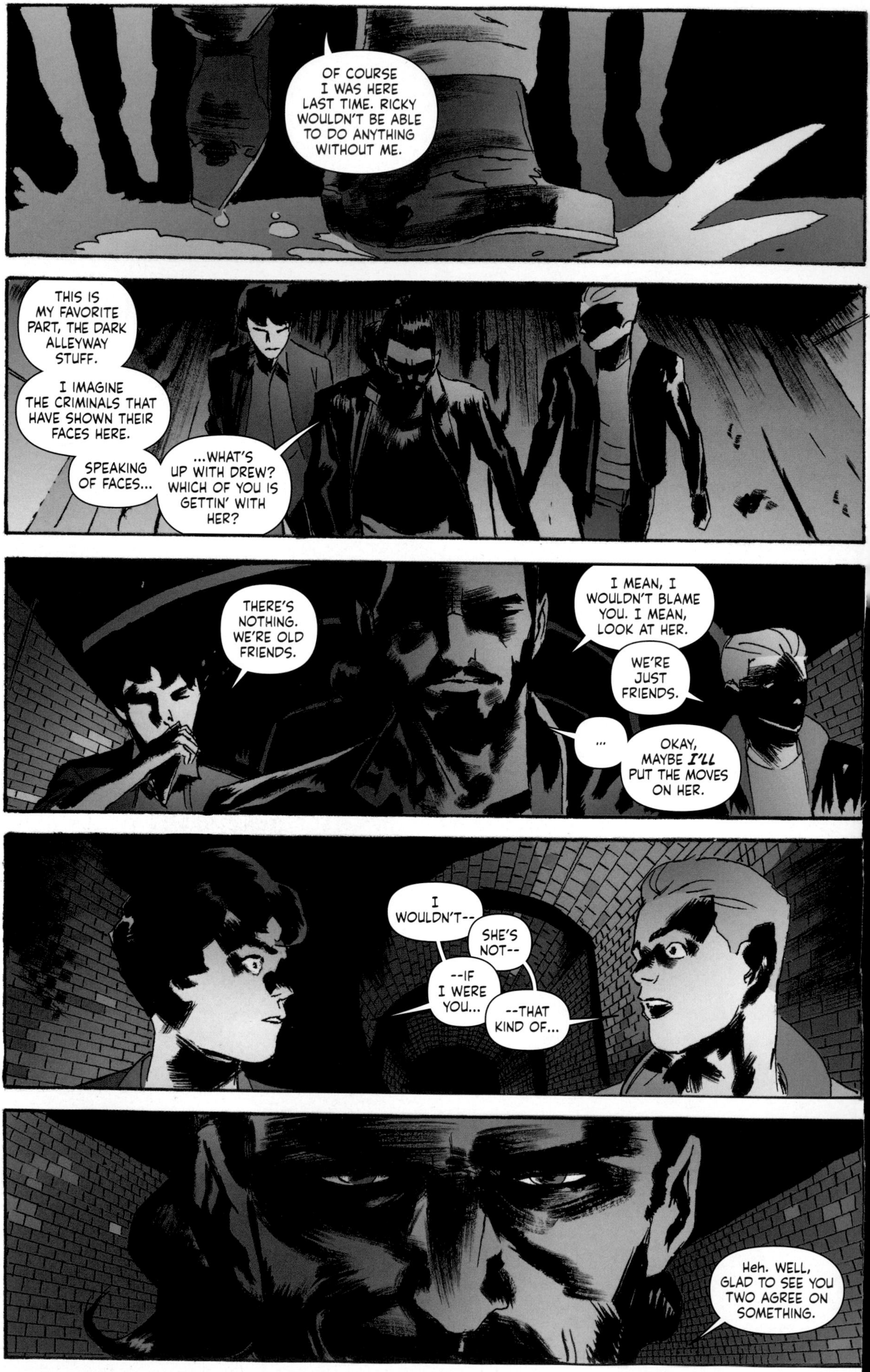
OF COURSE I WAS HERE LAST TIME. RICKY WOULDN'T BE ABLE TO DO ANYTHING WITHOUT ME.
THIS IS MY FAVORITE PART, THE DARK ALLEYWAY STUFF.
I IMAGINE THE CRIMINALS THAT HAVE SHOWN THEIR FACES HERE.
SPEAKING OF FACES...
...WHAT'S UP WITH DREW? WHICH OF YOU IS GETTIN' WITH HER?
THERE'S NOTHING. WE'RE OLD FRIENDS.
I MEAN, I WOULDN'T BLAME YOU. I MEAN, LOOK AT HER.
WE'RE JUST FRIENDS.
...
OKAY, MAYBE *I'LL* PUT THE MOVES ON HER.
I WOULDN'T--
SHE'S NOT--
--IF I WERE YOU...
--THAT KIND OF...
Heh. WELL, GLAD TO SEE YOU TWO AGREE ON SOMETHING.

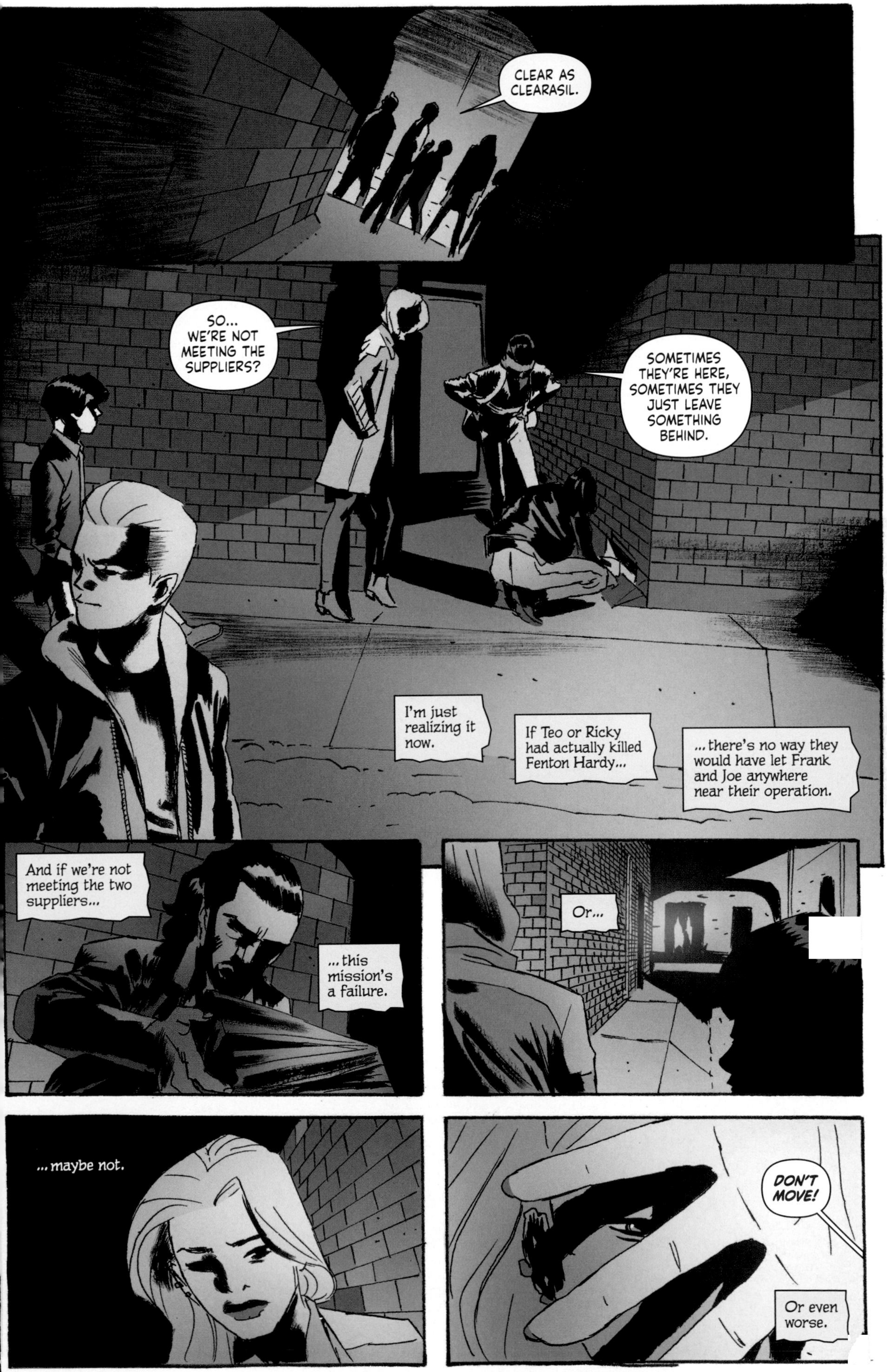
CLEAR AS CLEARASIL.
SO... WE'RE NOT MEETING THE SUPPLIERS?
SOMETIMES THEY'RE HERE, SOMETIMES THEY JUST LEAVE SOMETHING BEHIND.
I'm just realizing it now.
If Teo or Ricky had actually killed Fenton Hardy...
...there's no way they would have let Frank and Joe anywhere near their operation.
And if we're not meeting the two suppliers...
...this mission's a failure.
Or...
...maybe not.
DON'T MOVE!
Or even worse.

DROP THE BAG!
YOU'RE UNDER ARREST!
I recognize that voice.

Chief Collig.

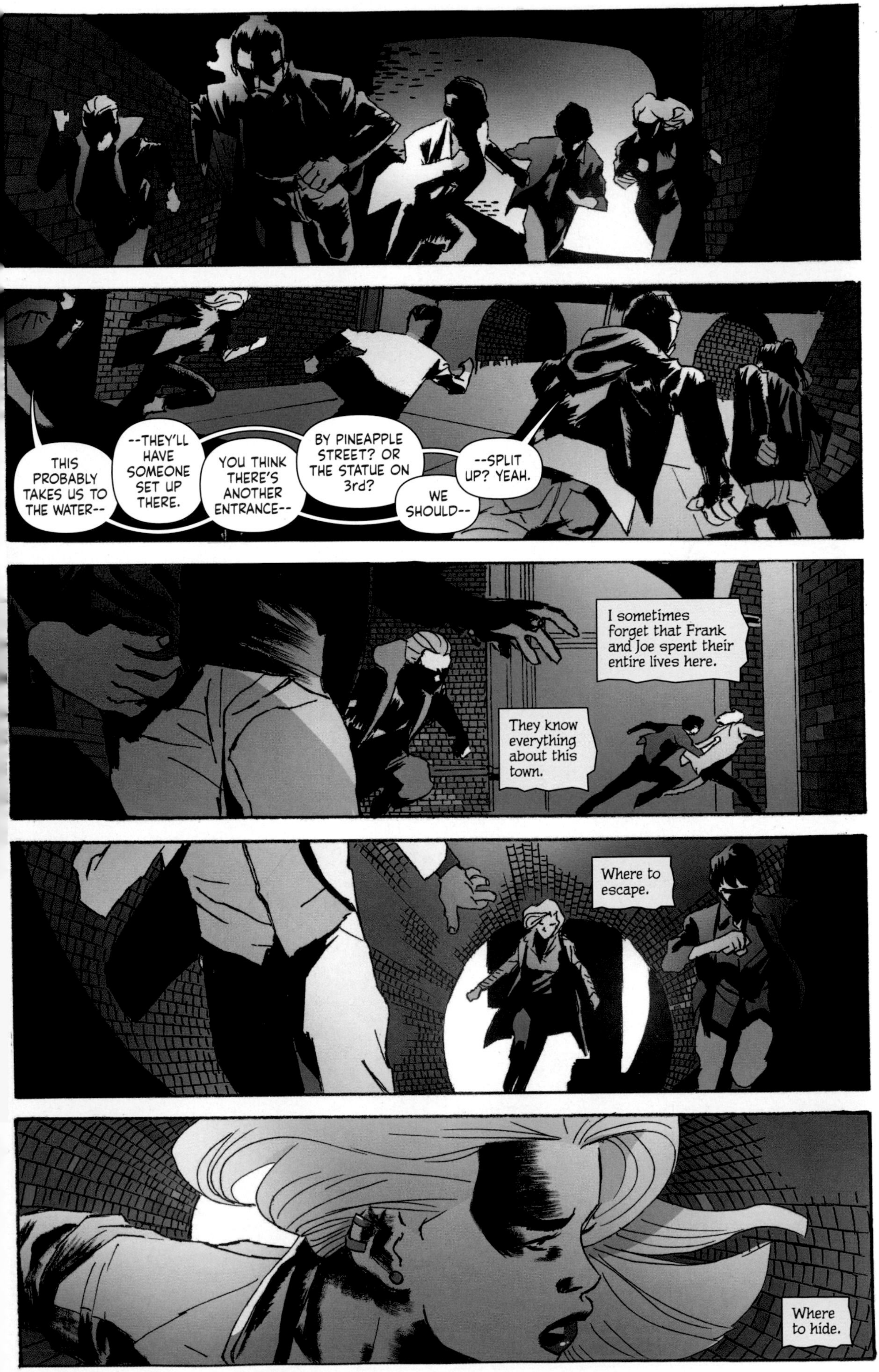
THIS PROBABLY TAKES US TO THE WATER--
--THEY'LL HAVE SOMEONE SET UP THERE.
YOU THINK THERE'S ANOTHER ENTRANCE--
BY PINEAPPLE STREET? OR THE STATUE ON 3rd?
WE SHOULD--
--SPLIT UP? YEAH.
I sometimes forget that Frank and Joe spent their entire lives here.
They know everything about this town.
Where to escape.
Where to hide.

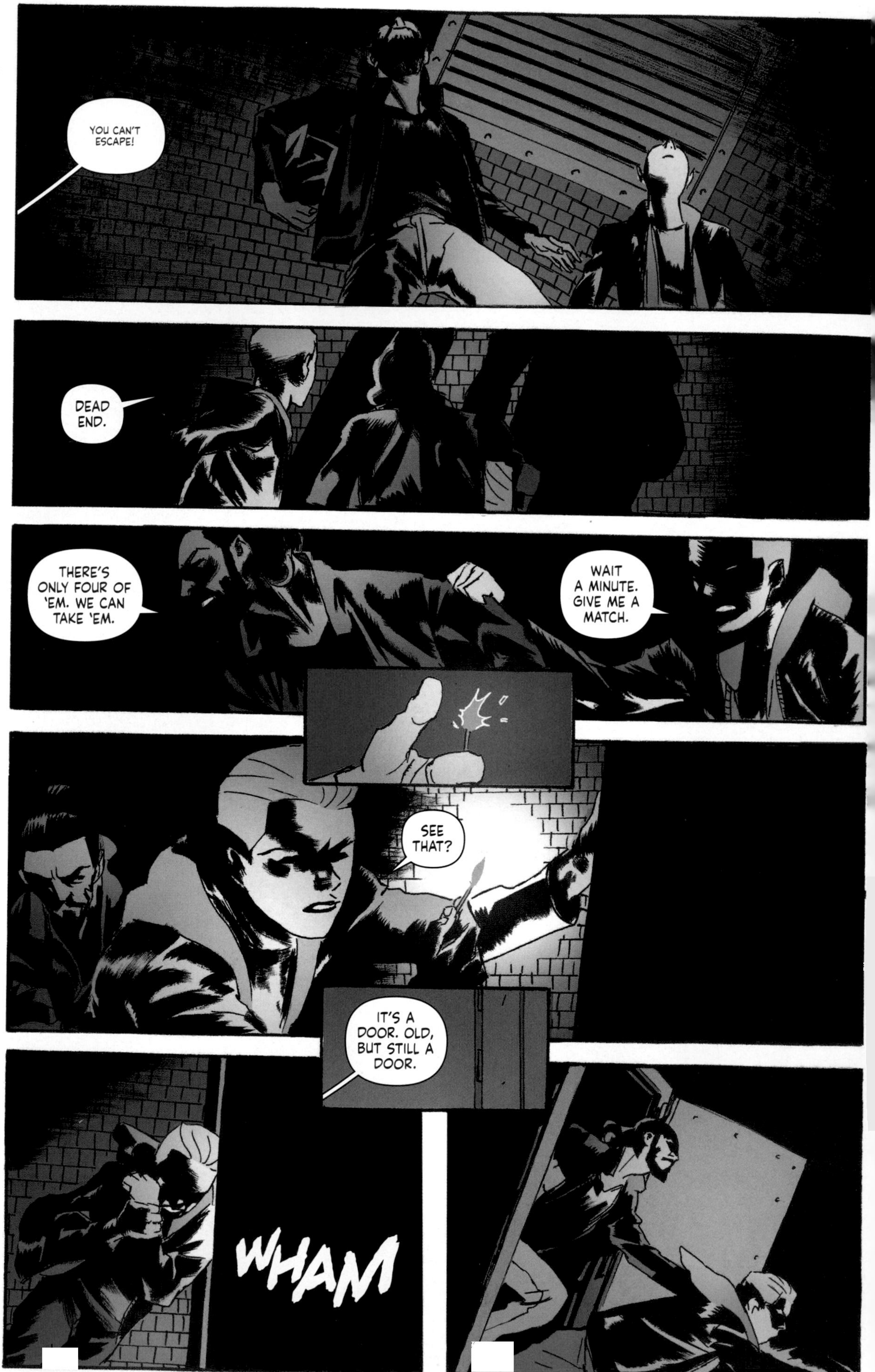
YOU CAN'T ESCAPE!
DEAD END.
THERE'S ONLY FOUR OF 'EM. WE CAN TAKE 'EM.
WAIT A MINUTE. GIVE ME A MATCH.
SEE THAT?
IT'S A DOOR. OLD, BUT STILL A DOOR.
WHAM

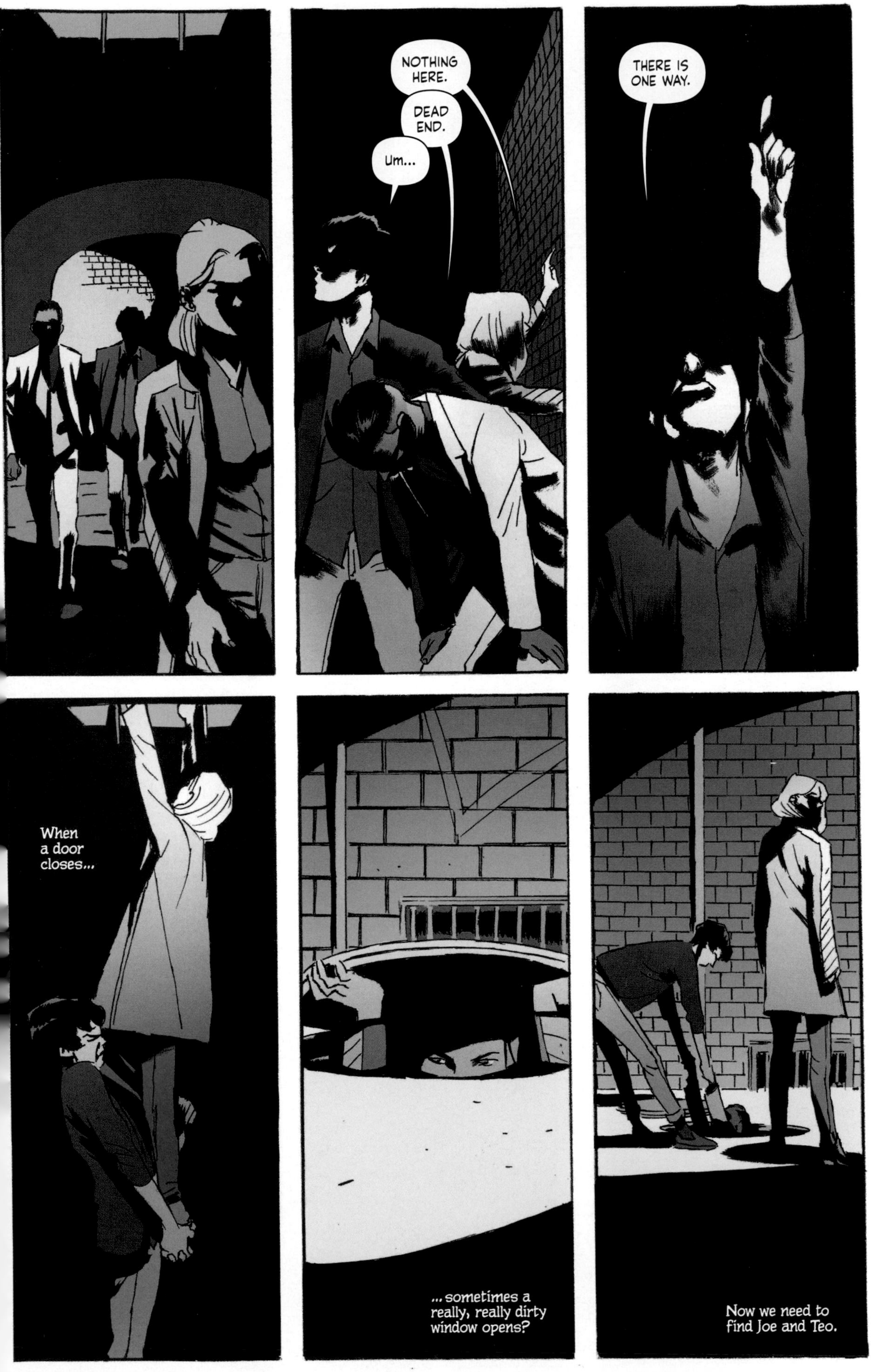
NOTHING HERE.
DEAD END.
Um...
THERE IS ONE WAY.
When a door closes...
... sometimes a really, really dirty window opens?
Now we need to find Joe and Teo.

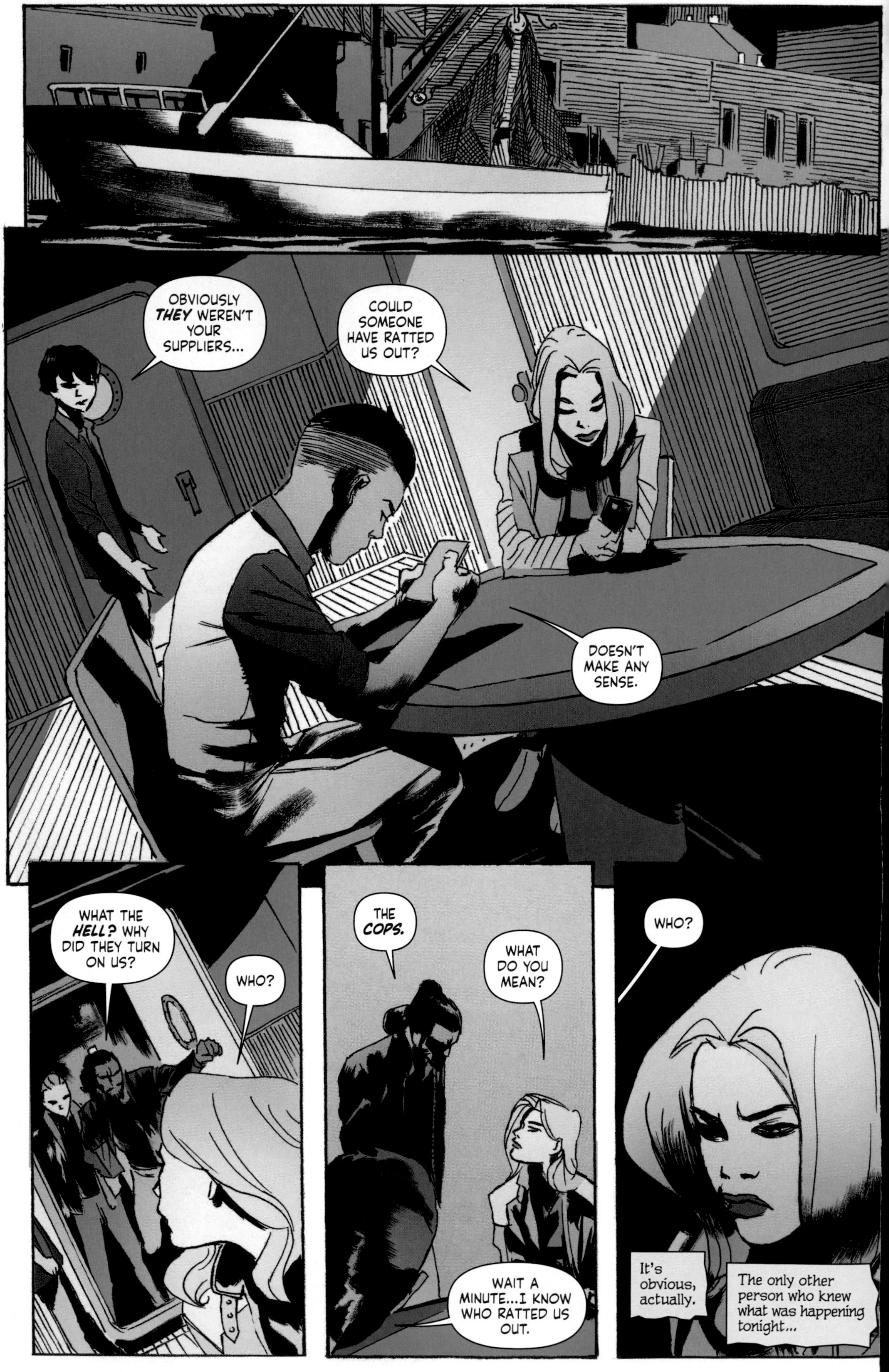
OBVIOUSLY THEY WEREN'T YOUR SUPPLIERS...
COULD SOMEONE HAVE RATTED US OUT?
DOESN'T MAKE ANY SENSE.
WHAT THE HELL? WHY DID THEY TURN ON US?
WHO?
THE COPS.
WHAT DO YOU MEAN?
WAIT A MINUTE...I KNOW WHO RATTED US OUT.
WHO?
It's obvious, actually.
The only other person who knew what was happening tonight...

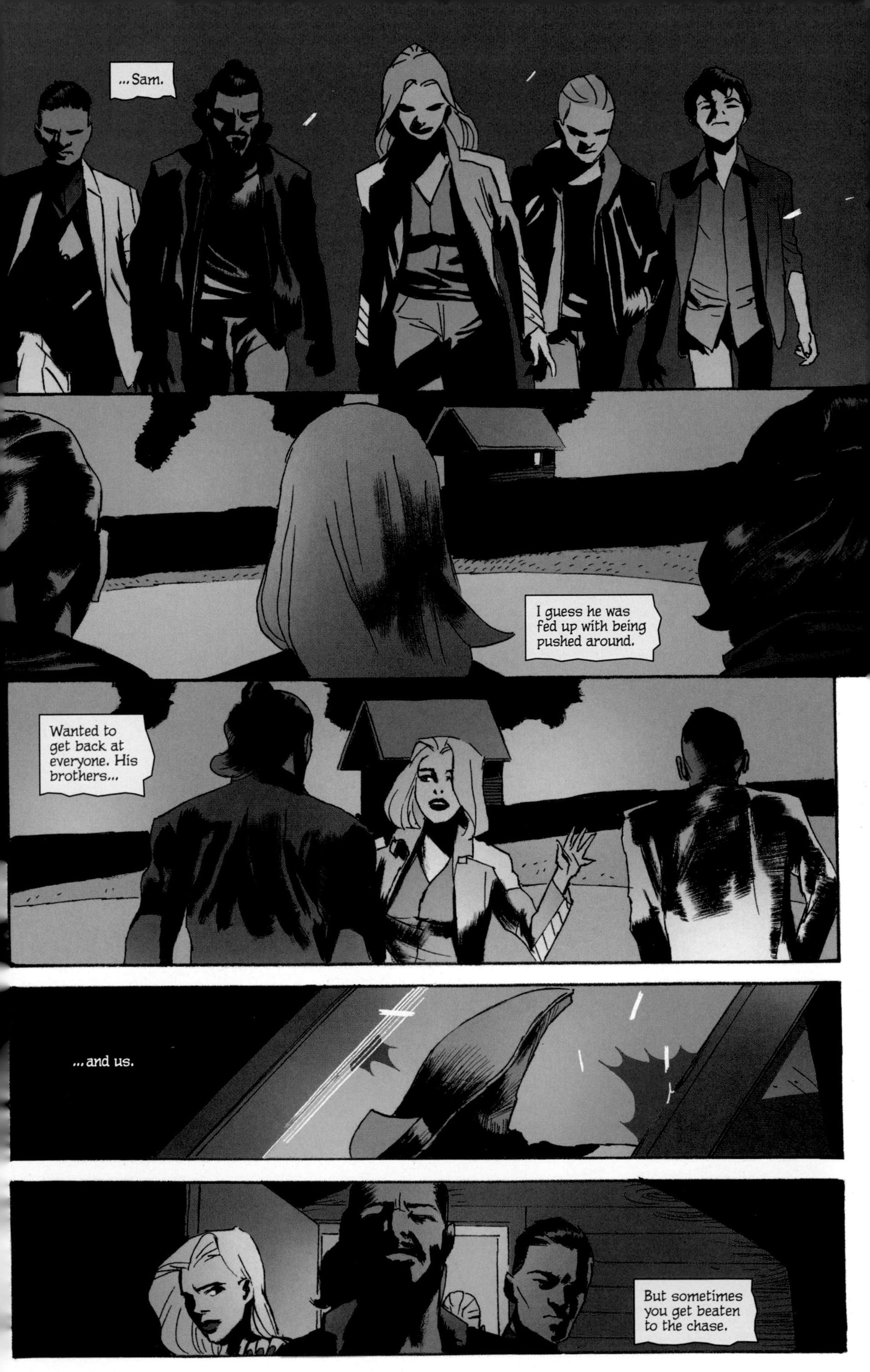
...Sam.
I guess he was fed up with being pushed around.
Wanted to get back at everyone. His brothers...
...and us.
But sometimes you get beaten to the chase.

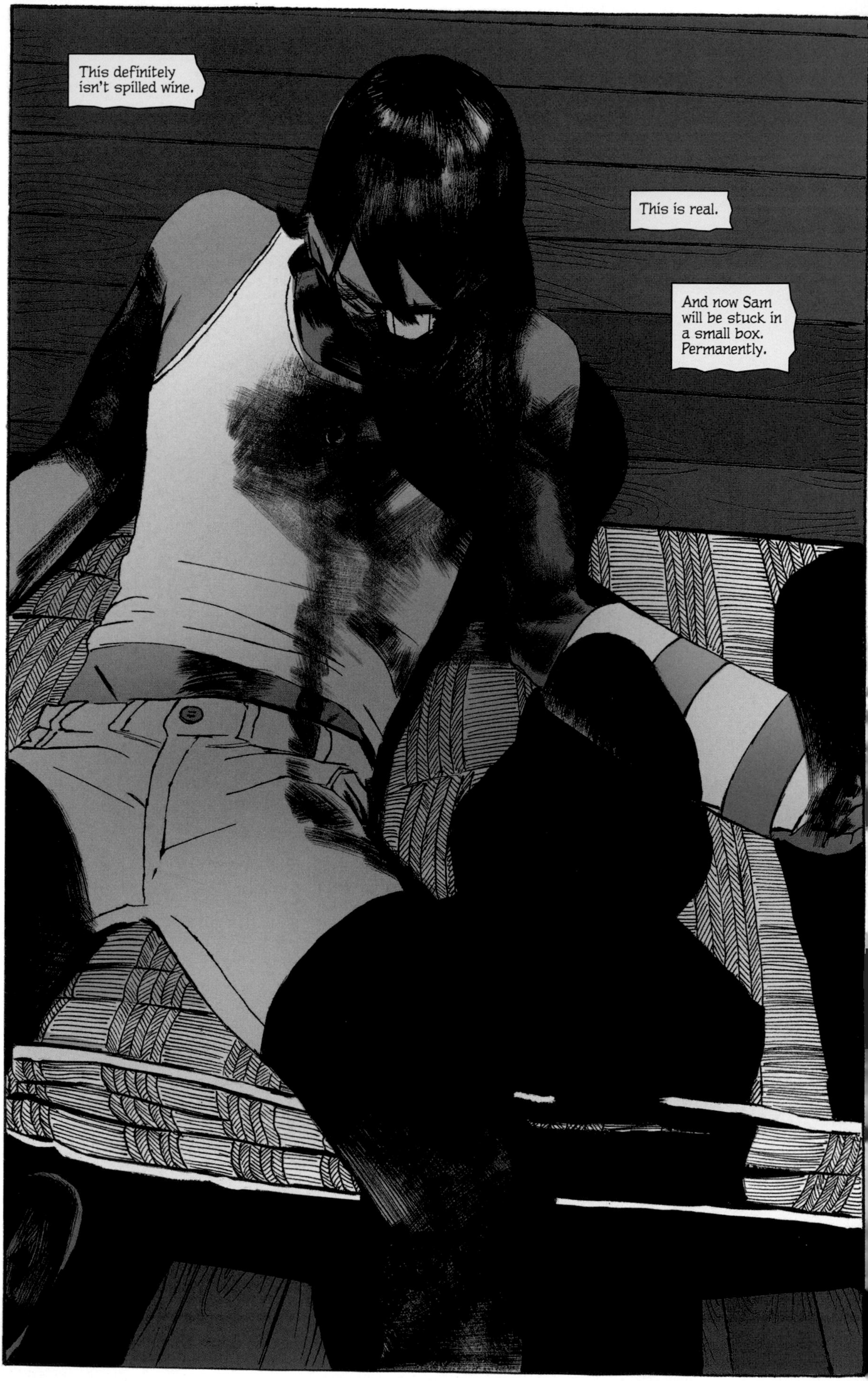
This definitely isn't spilled wine.
This is real.
And now Sam will be stuck in a small box. Permanently.

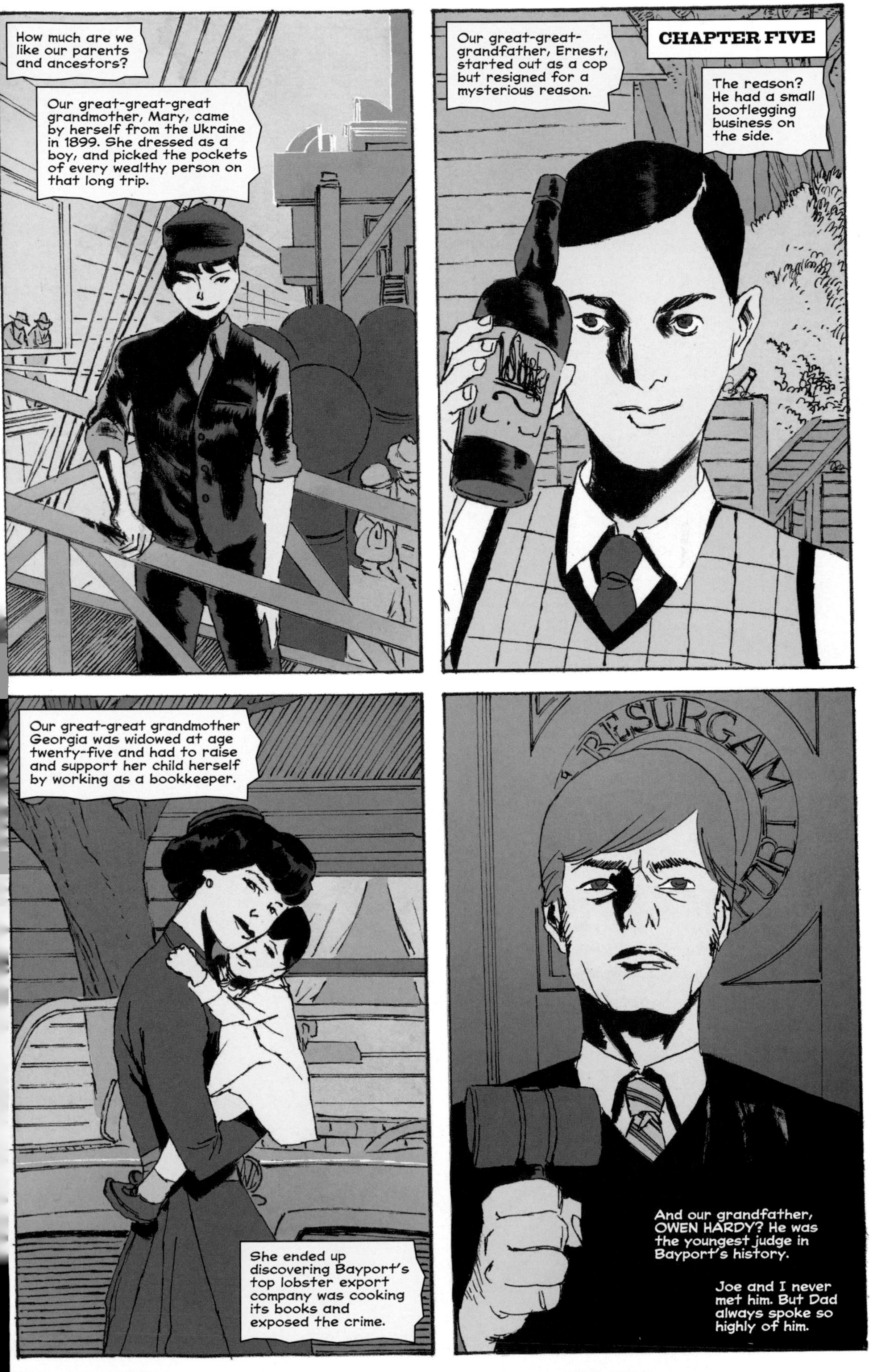
How much are we like our parents and ancestors?
Our great-great-great grandmother, Mary, came by herself from the Ukraine in 1899. She dressed as a boy, and picked the pockets of every wealthy person on that long trip.
CHAPTER FIVE
Our great-great-grandfather, Ernest, started out as a cop but resigned for a mysterious reason.
The reason? He had a small bootlegging business on the side.
Our great-great grandmother Georgia was widowed at age twenty-five and had to raise and support her child herself by working as a bookkeeper.
She ended up discovering Bayport's top lobster export company was cooking its books and exposed the crime.
RESURGAM
And our grandfather, OWEN HARDY? He was the youngest judge in Bayport's history.
Joe and I never met him. But Dad always spoke so highly of him.

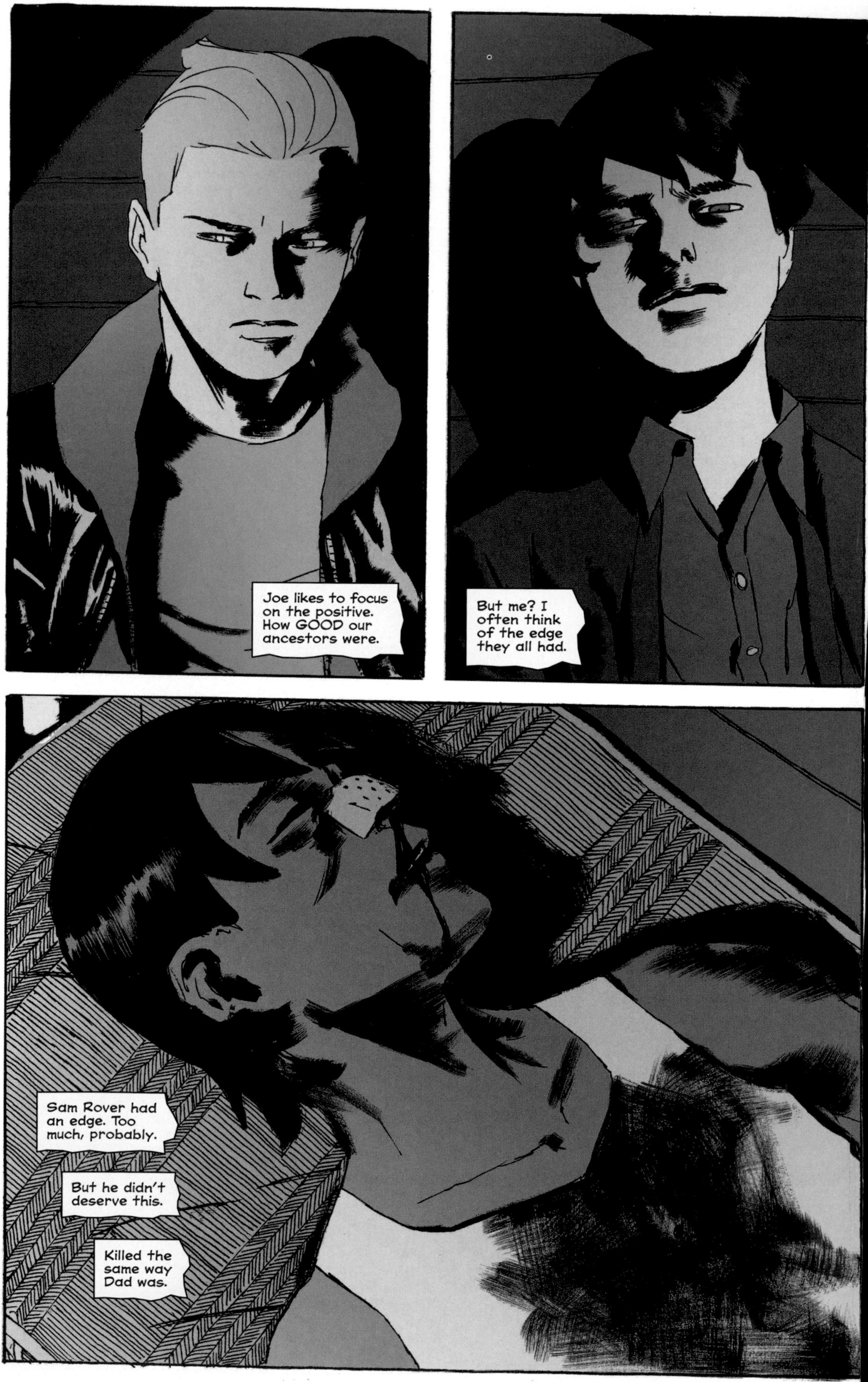
Joe likes to focus on the positive. How GOOD our ancestors were.
But me? I often think of the edge they all had.
Sam Rover had an edge. Too much, probably.
But he didn't deserve this.
Killed the same way Dad was.

YOU REALIZE, OF COURSE, THAT WHOEVER KILLED SAM ALSO KILLED OUR FATHER.

SO LET'S GET PUT ALL THE CARDS ON THE TABLE. WHAT DO YOU KNOW ABOUT FENTON HARDY'S DEATH?

WE DIDN'T KILL HIM, FRANK, IF THAT'S WHAT YOU'RE WONDERING.

THERE WAS NO REASON TO. HE WAS OUR GUY.

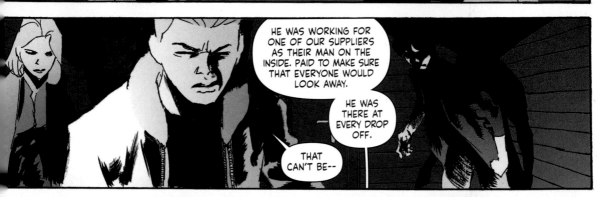

HE WAS WORKING FOR ONE OF OUR SUPPLIERS AS THEIR MAN ON THE INSIDE. PAID TO MAKE SURE THAT EVERYONE WOULD LOOK AWAY.

HE WAS THERE AT EVERY DROP OFF.

THAT CAN'T BE--

THE TRUTH *SUCKS*, RIGHT?

YOU'RE LYING!

WHY WOULD HE BE LYING, JOE? THINK ABOUT IT. WE'RE ALL ON THE SAME SIDE NOW.

I'M NOT WITH THESE... *THUGS*.

LIKE IT OR NOT, YOU ARE *NOW*.

DAD WAS PROBABLY UNDERCOVER, FRANK. THERE'S NO WAY--

MAYBE HE'S NOT WHO WE THOUGHT HE WAS.

DO YOU REALLY THINK SO?

IT'S TIME FOR US TO GROW UP, JOE.

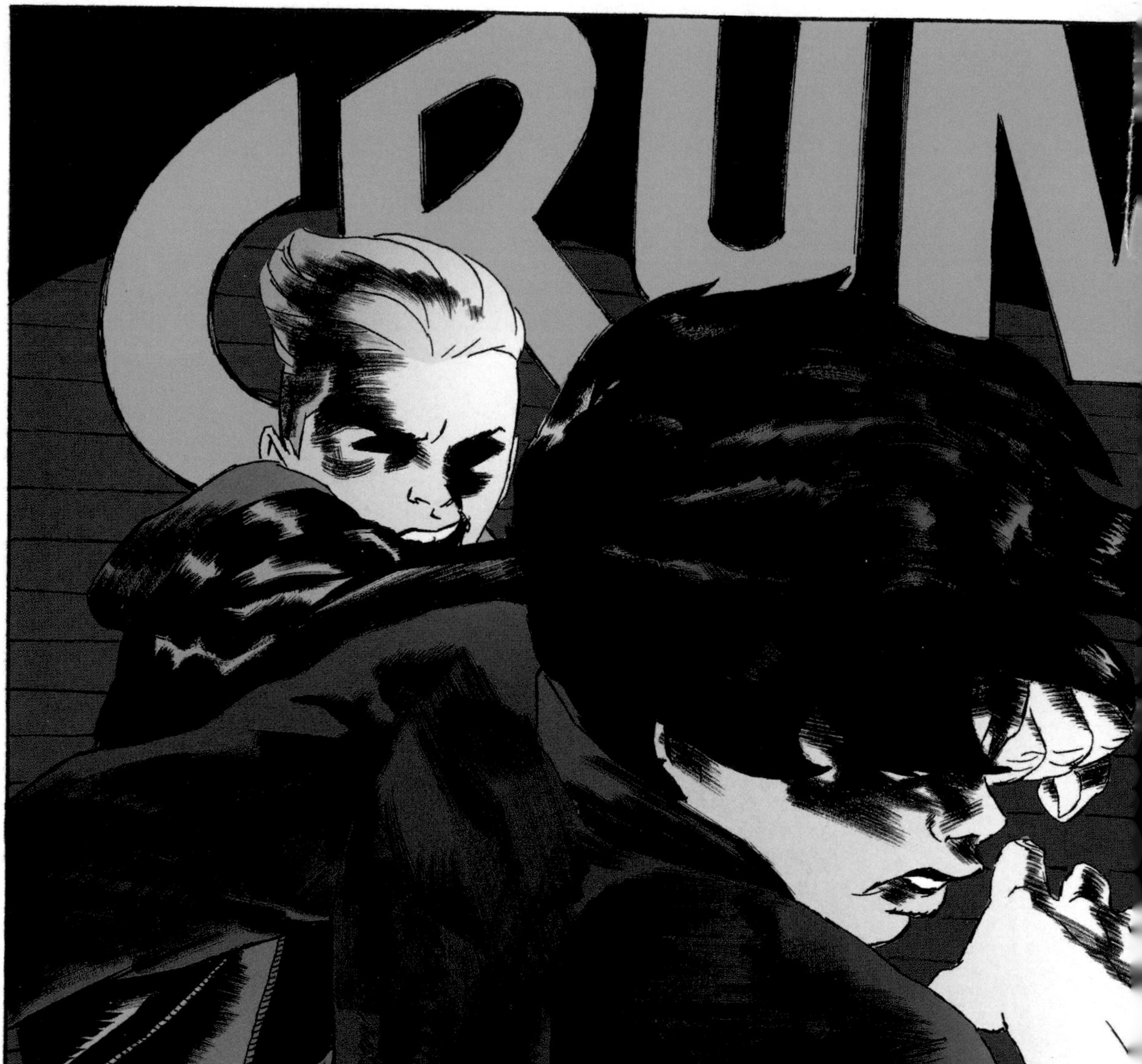
CRUN

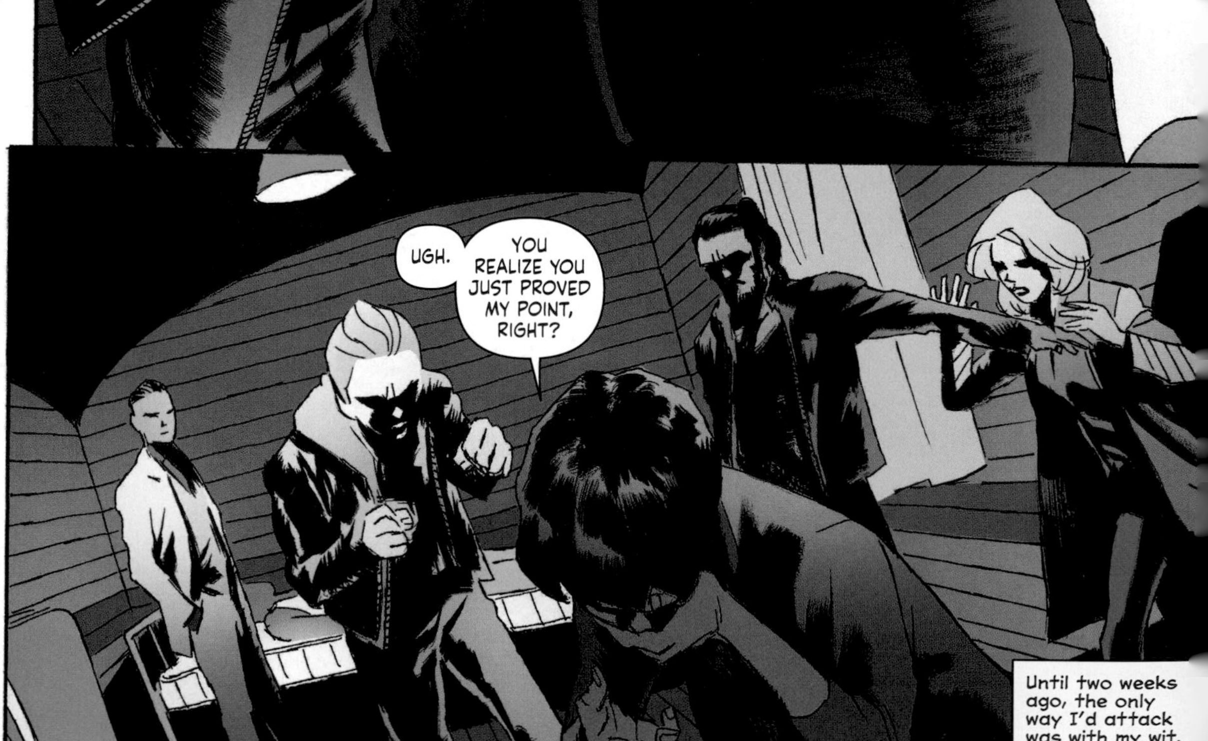
UGH.
YOU REALIZE YOU JUST PROVED MY POINT, RIGHT?
Until two weeks ago, the only way I'd attack was with my wit.

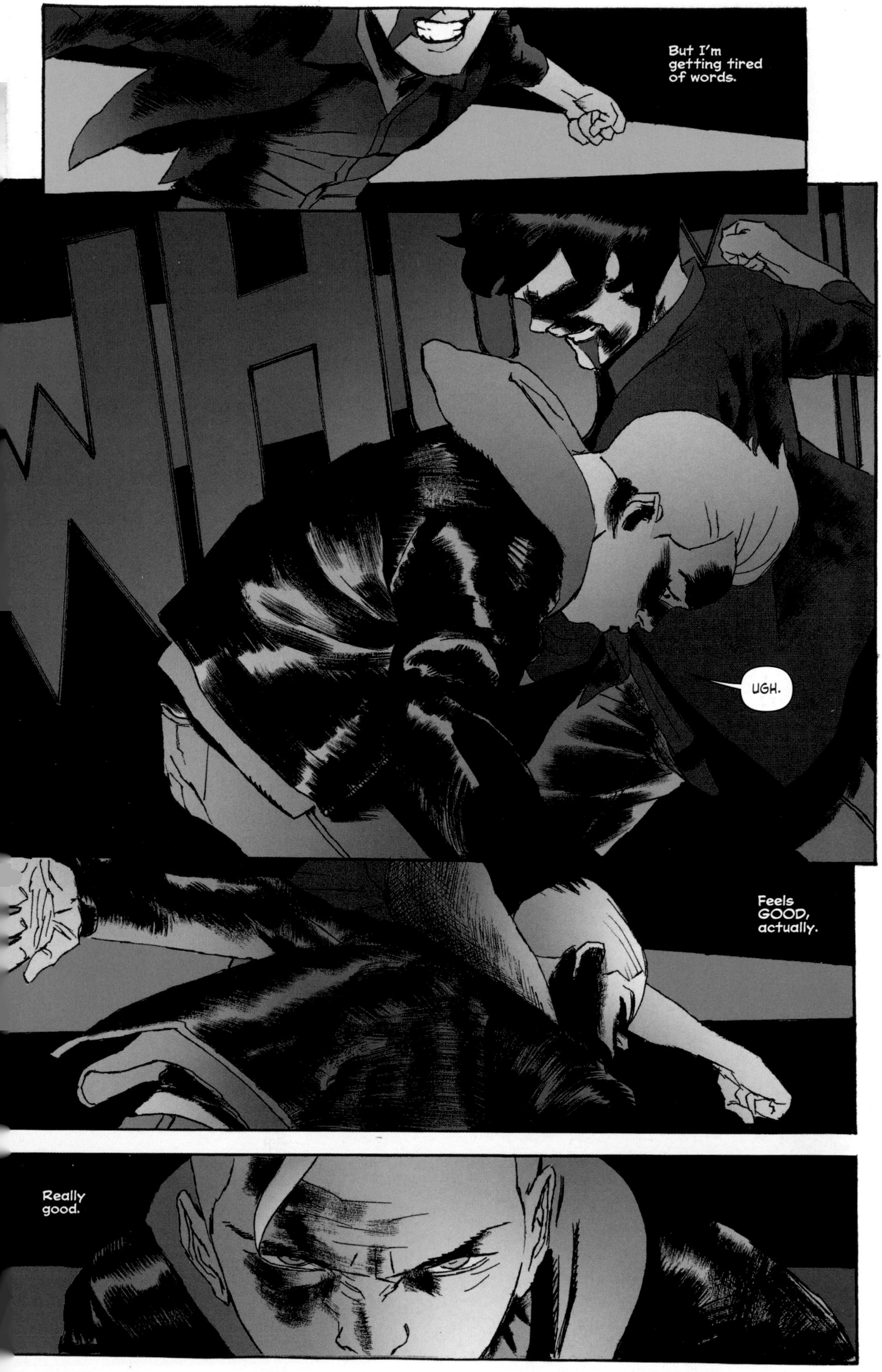
But I'm getting tired of words.
UGH.
Feels GOOD, actually.
Really good.

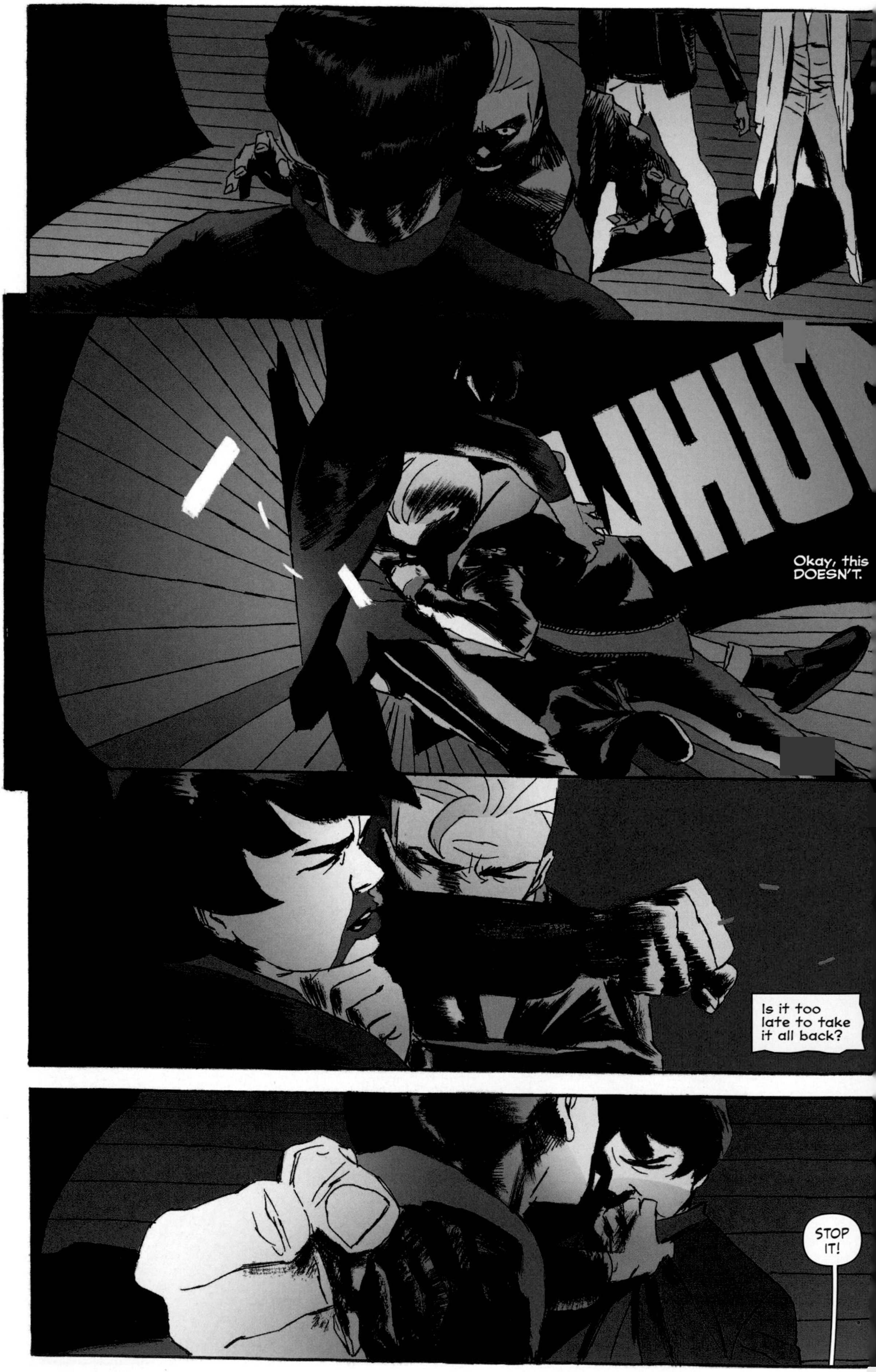
Okay, this DOESN'T.
Is it too late to take it all back?
STOP IT!

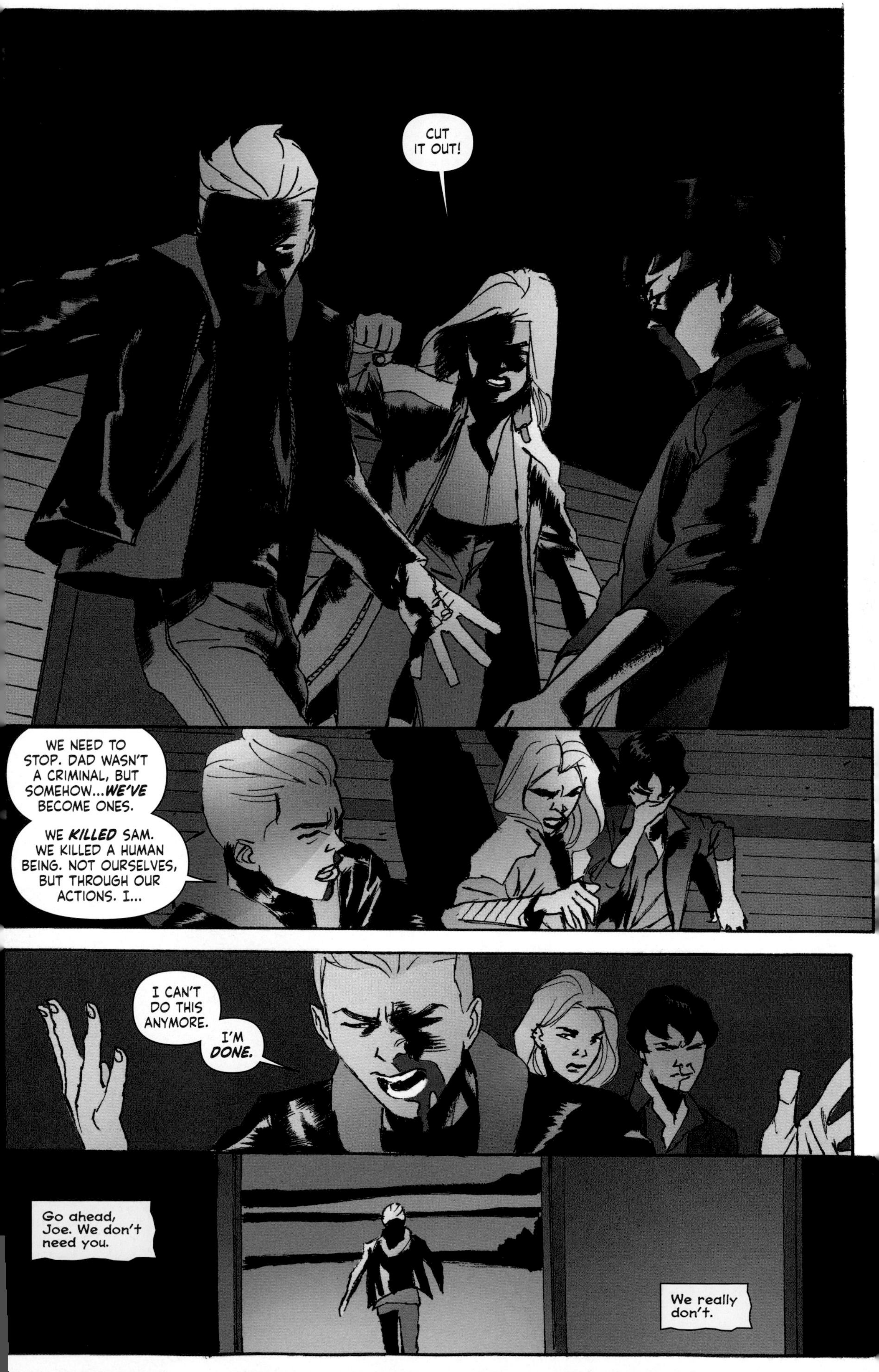
CUT IT OUT!
WE NEED TO STOP. DAD WASN'T A CRIMINAL, BUT SOMEHOW...WE'VE BECOME ONES.
WE KILLED SAM. WE KILLED A HUMAN BEING. NOT OURSELVES, BUT THROUGH OUR ACTIONS. I...
I CAN'T DO THIS ANYMORE.
I'M DONE.
Go ahead, Joe. We don't need you.
We really don't.

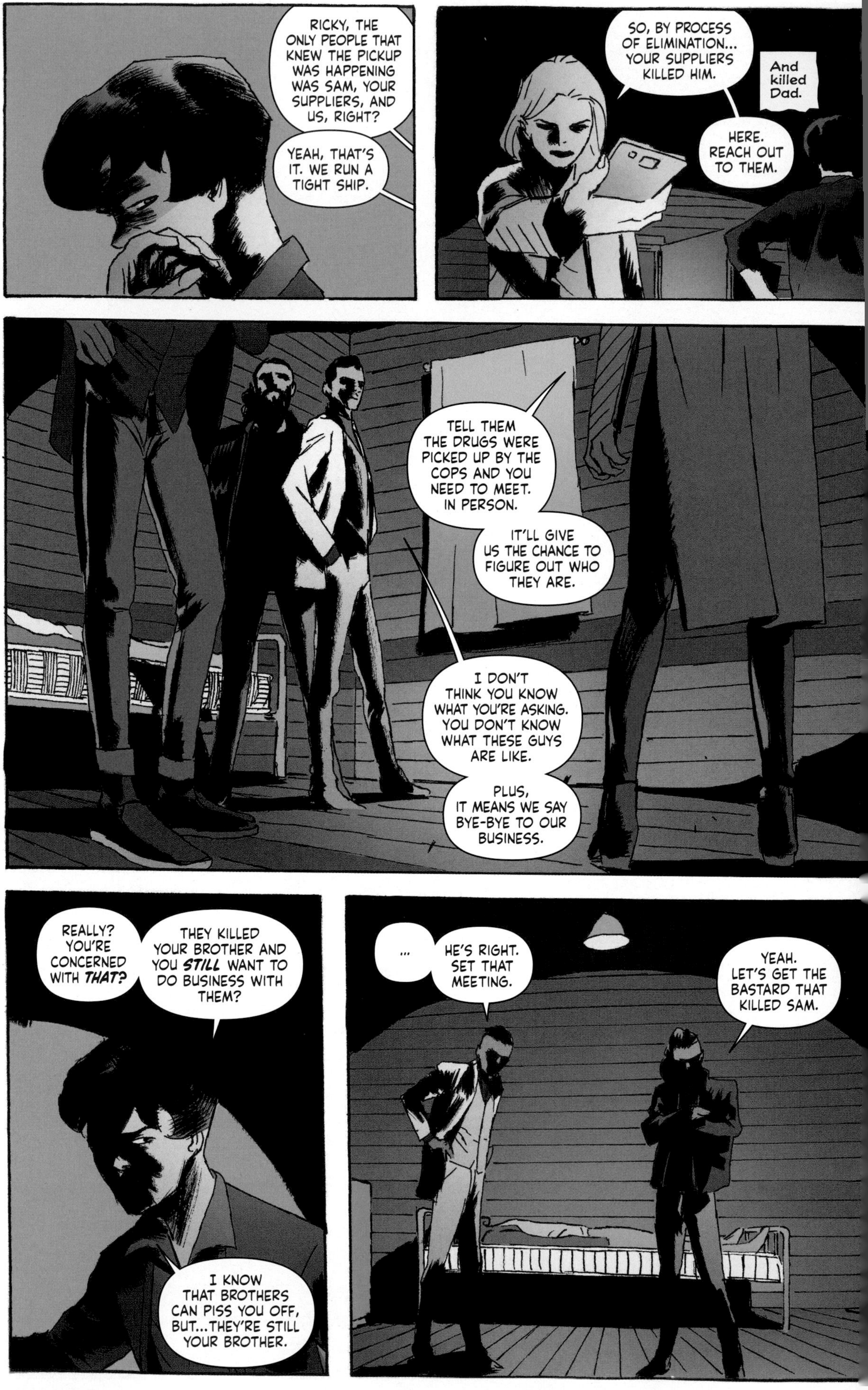
RICKY, THE ONLY PEOPLE THAT KNEW THE PICKUP WAS HAPPENING WAS SAM, YOUR SUPPLIERS, AND US, RIGHT?
YEAH, THAT'S IT. WE RUN A TIGHT SHIP.
SO, BY PROCESS OF ELIMINATION... YOUR SUPPLIERS KILLED HIM.
And killed Dad.
HERE. REACH OUT TO THEM.
TELL THEM THE DRUGS WERE PICKED UP BY THE COPS AND YOU NEED TO MEET. IN PERSON.
IT'LL GIVE US THE CHANCE TO FIGURE OUT WHO THEY ARE.
I DON'T THINK YOU KNOW WHAT YOU'RE ASKING. YOU DON'T KNOW WHAT THESE GUYS ARE LIKE.
PLUS, IT MEANS WE SAY BYE-BYE TO OUR BUSINESS.
REALLY? YOU'RE CONCERNED WITH ***THAT?***
THEY KILLED YOUR BROTHER AND YOU ***STILL*** WANT TO DO BUSINESS WITH THEM?
I KNOW THAT BROTHERS CAN PISS YOU OFF, BUT...THEY'RE STILL YOUR BROTHER.
...
HE'S RIGHT. SET THAT MEETING.
YEAH. LET'S GET THE BASTARD THAT KILLED SAM.

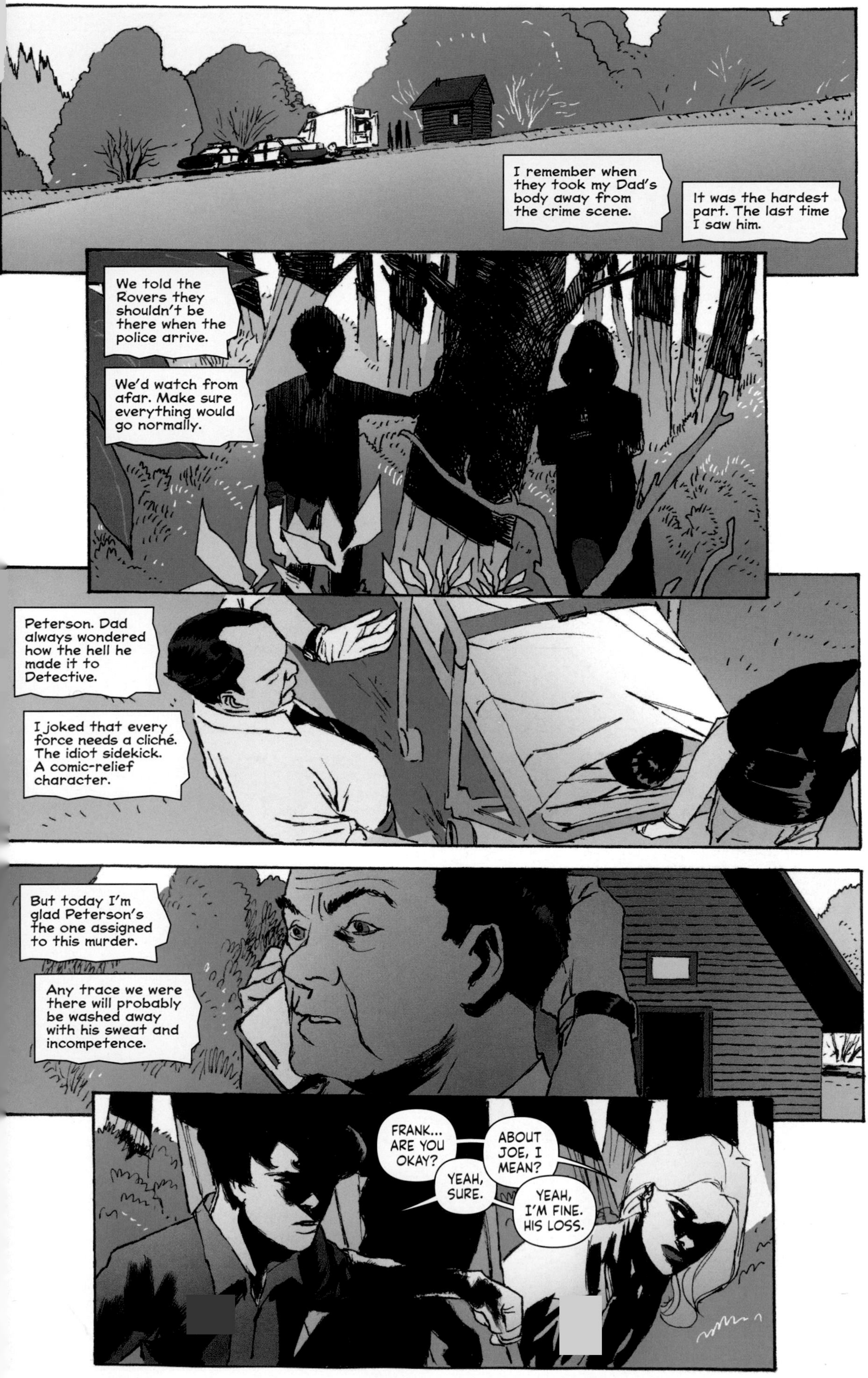
I remember when they took my Dad's body away from the crime scene.
It was the hardest part. The last time I saw him.
We told the Rovers they shouldn't be there when the police arrive.
We'd watch from afar. Make sure everything would go normally.
Peterson. Dad always wondered how the hell he made it to Detective.
I joked that every force needs a cliché. The idiot sidekick. A comic-relief character.
But today I'm glad Peterson's the one assigned to this murder.
Any trace we were there will probably be washed away with his sweat and incompetence.
FRANK... ARE YOU OKAY?
ABOUT JOE, I MEAN?
YEAH, SURE.
YEAH, I'M FINE. HIS LOSS.

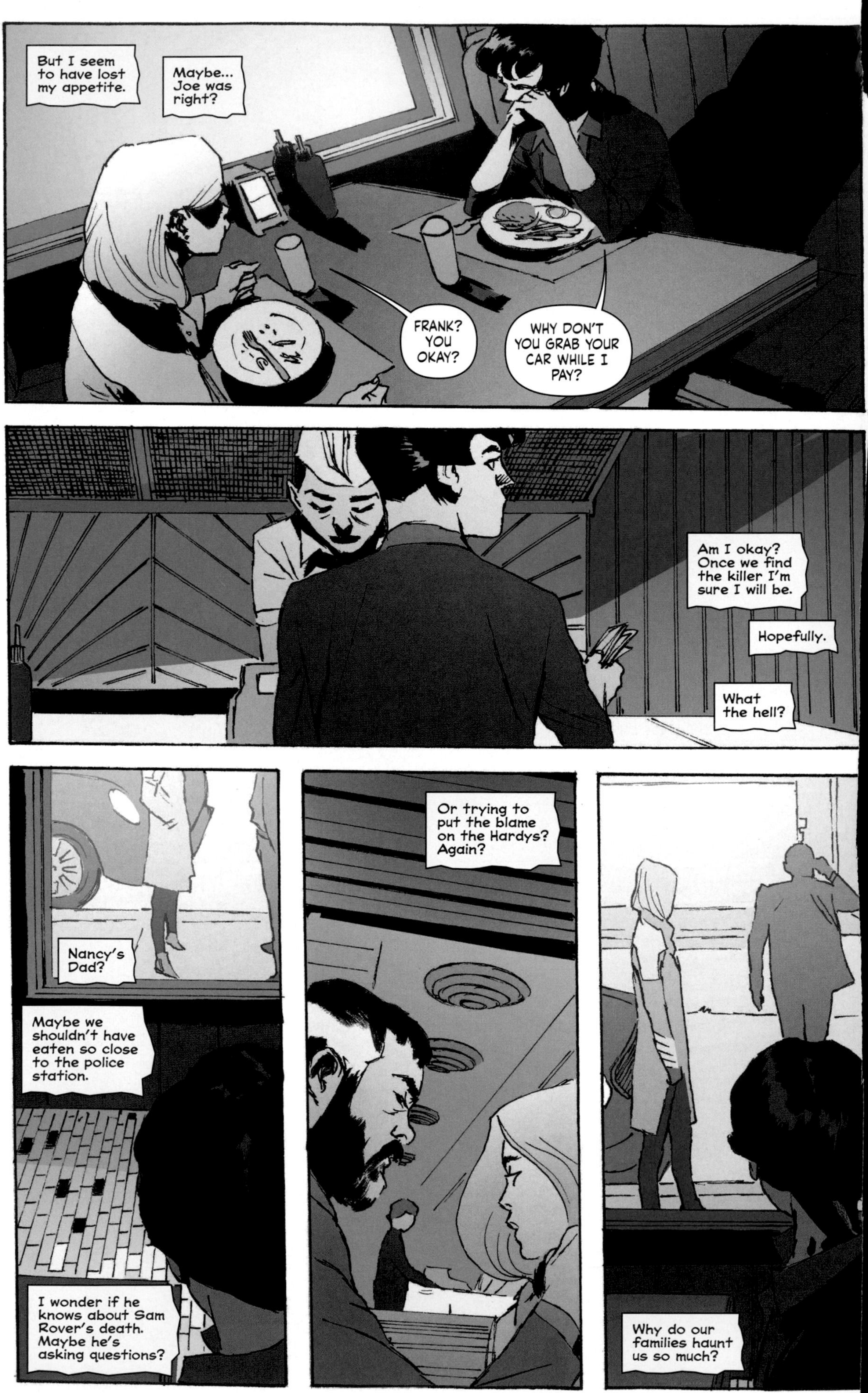
But I seem to have lost my appetite.
Maybe... Joe was right?
FRANK? YOU OKAY?
WHY DON'T YOU GRAB YOUR CAR WHILE I PAY?
Am I okay? Once we find the killer I'm sure I will be.
Hopefully.
What the hell?
Nancy's Dad?
Maybe we shouldn't have eaten so close to the police station.
I wonder if he knows about Sam Rover's death. Maybe he's asking questions?
Or trying to put the blame on the Hardys? Again?
Why do our families haunt us so much?

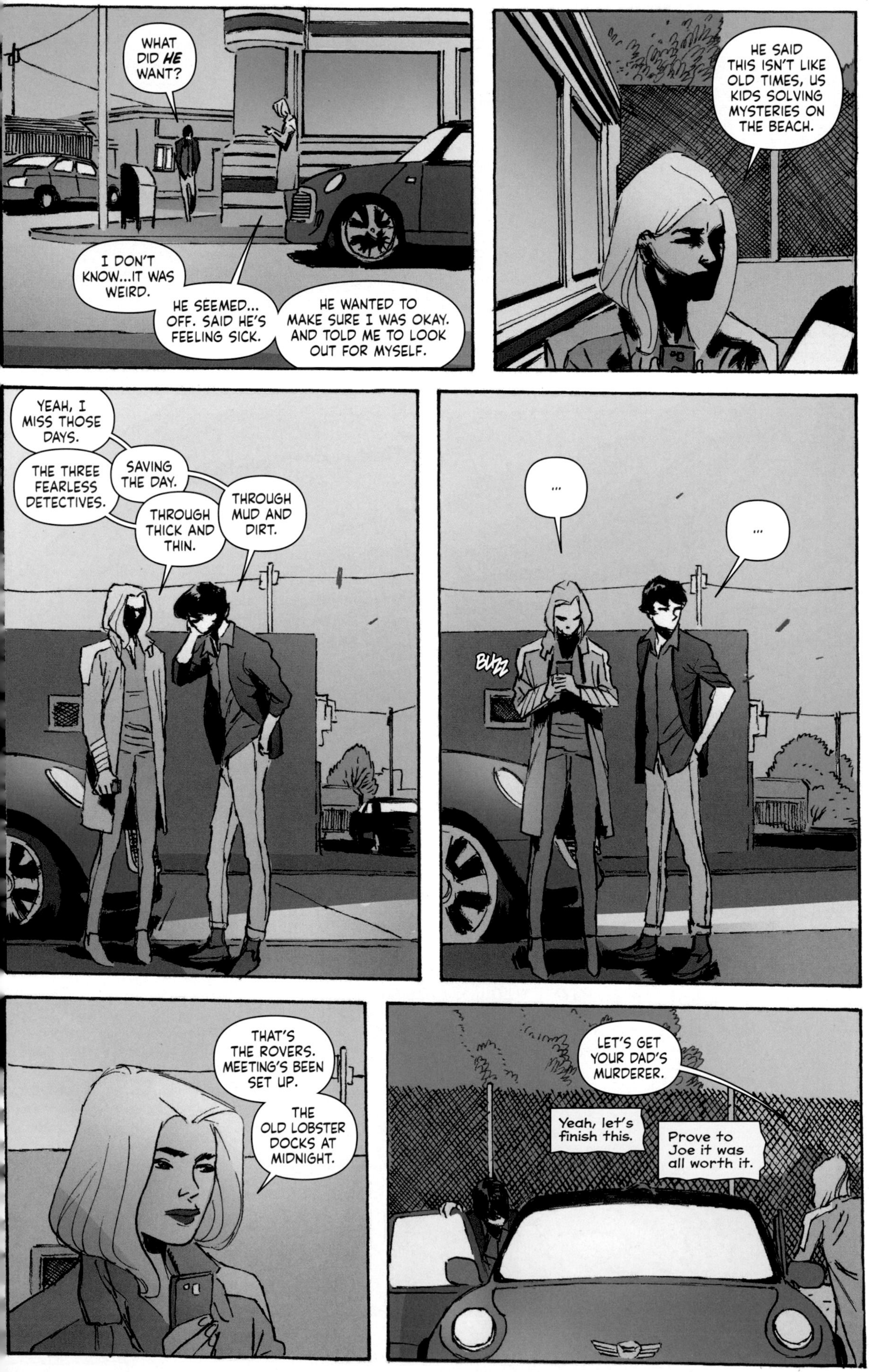
WHAT DID **HE** WANT?
I DON'T KNOW...IT WAS WEIRD.
HE SEEMED... OFF. SAID HE'S FEELING SICK.
HE WANTED TO MAKE SURE I WAS OKAY. AND TOLD ME TO LOOK OUT FOR MYSELF.
HE SAID THIS ISN'T LIKE OLD TIMES, US KIDS SOLVING MYSTERIES ON THE BEACH.
YEAH, I MISS THOSE DAYS.
THE THREE FEARLESS DETECTIVES.
SAVING THE DAY.
THROUGH THICK AND THIN.
THROUGH MUD AND DIRT.
...
...
BUZZ
THAT'S THE ROVERS. MEETING'S BEEN SET UP.
THE OLD LOBSTER DOCKS AT MIDNIGHT.
LET'S GET YOUR DAD'S MURDERER.
Yeah, let's finish this.
Prove to Joe it was all worth it.

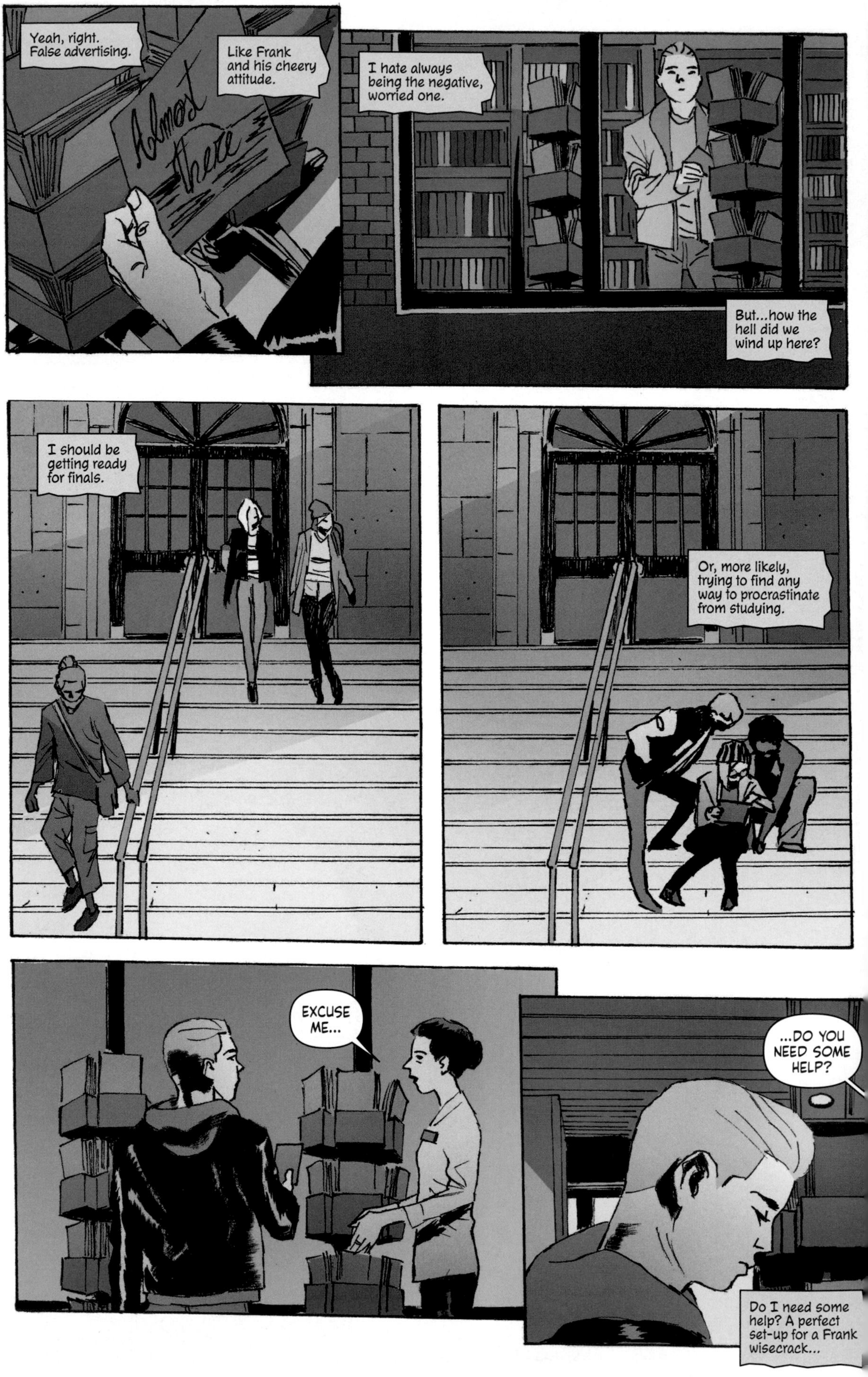
Yeah, right. False advertising.
Almost there
Like Frank and his cheery attitude.
I hate always being the negative, worried one.
But...how the hell did we wind up here?
I should be getting ready for finals.
Or, more likely, trying to find any way to procrastinate from studying.
EXCUSE ME...
...DO YOU NEED SOME HELP?
Do I need some help? A perfect set-up for a Frank wisecrack...

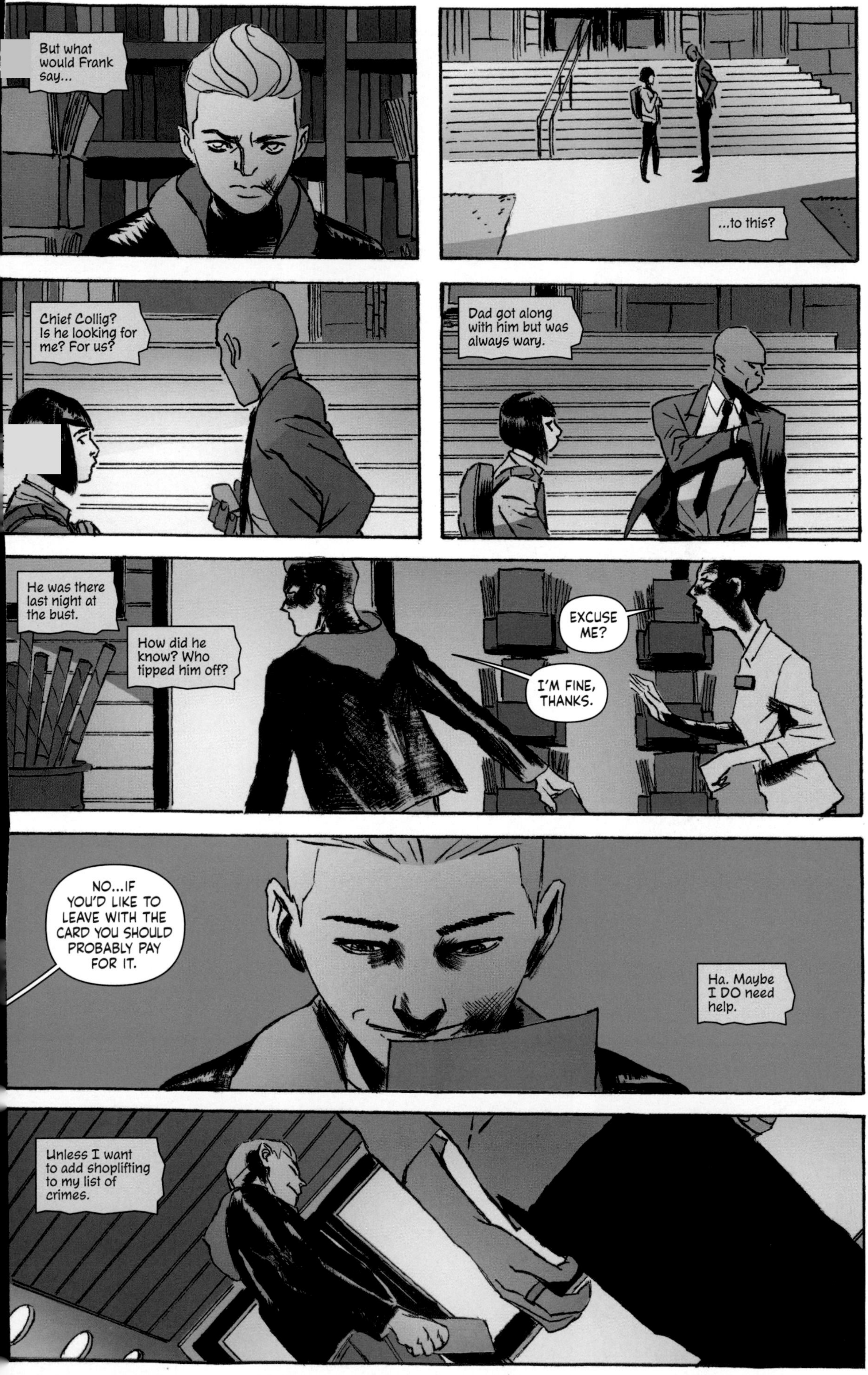
But what would Frank say...
...to this?
Chief Collig? Is he looking for me? For us?
Dad got along with him but was always wary.
He was there last night at the bust.
How did he know? Who tipped him off?
EXCUSE ME?
I'M FINE, THANKS.
NO...IF YOU'D LIKE TO LEAVE WITH THE CARD YOU SHOULD PROBABLY PAY FOR IT.
Ha. Maybe I DO need help.
Unless I want to add shoplifting to my list of crimes.

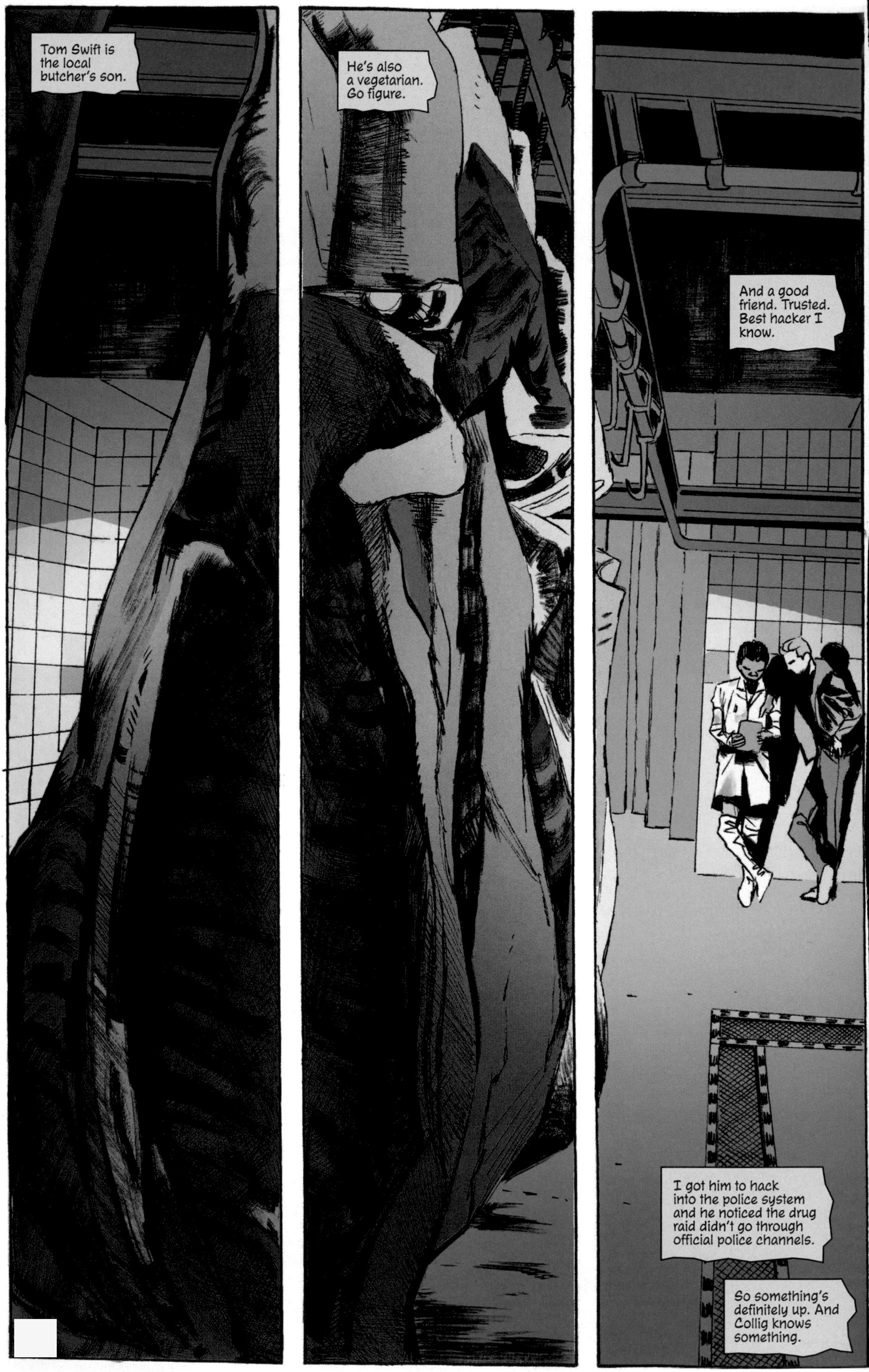
Tom Swift is the local butcher's son.
He's also a vegetarian. Go figure.
And a good friend. Trusted. Best hacker I know.
I got him to hack into the police system and he noticed the drug raid didn't go through official police channels.
So something's definitely up. And Collig knows something.

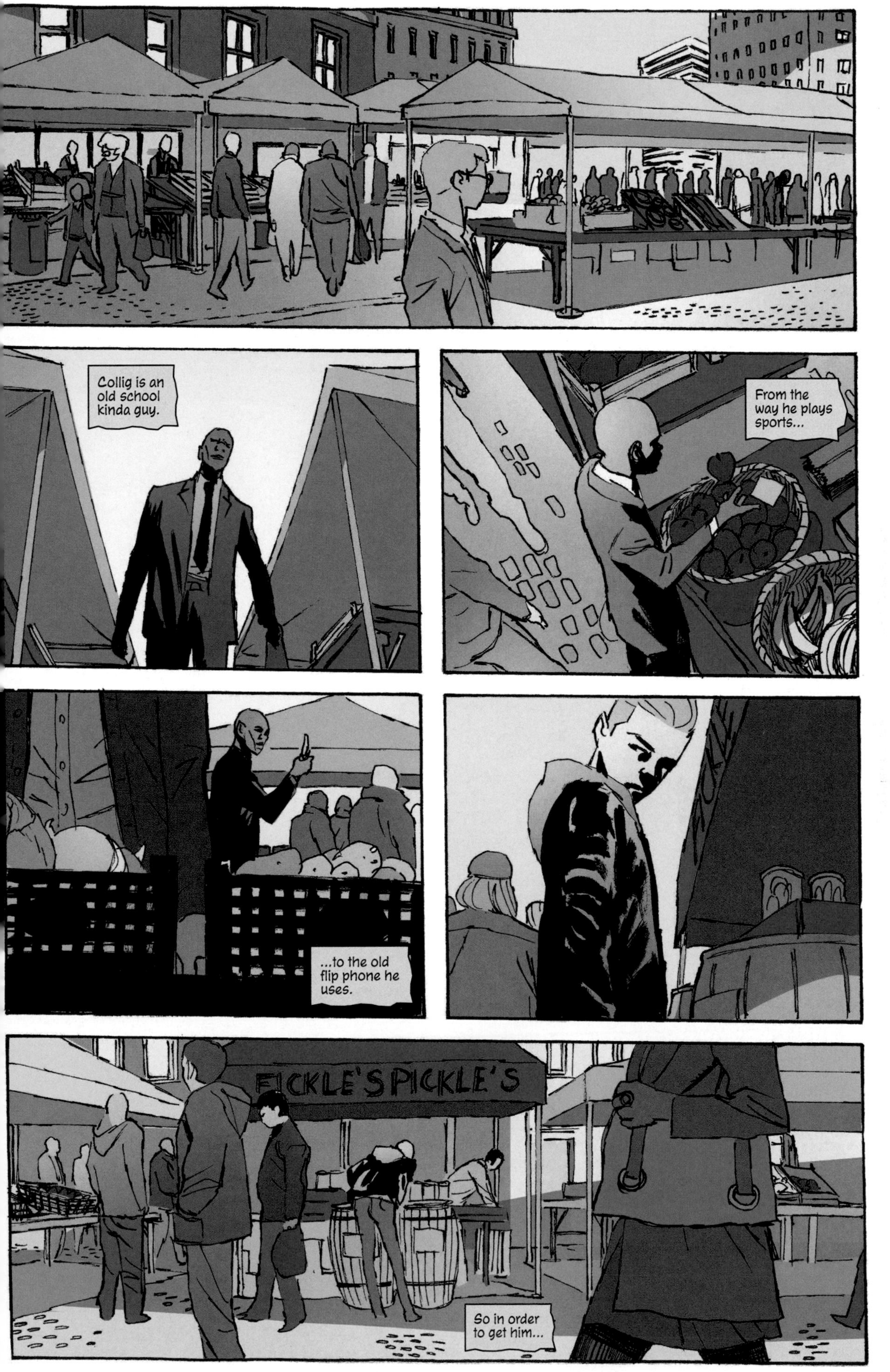
Collig is an old school kinda guy.
From the way he plays sports...
...to the old flip phone he uses.
FICKLE'S PICKLE'S
So in order to get him...

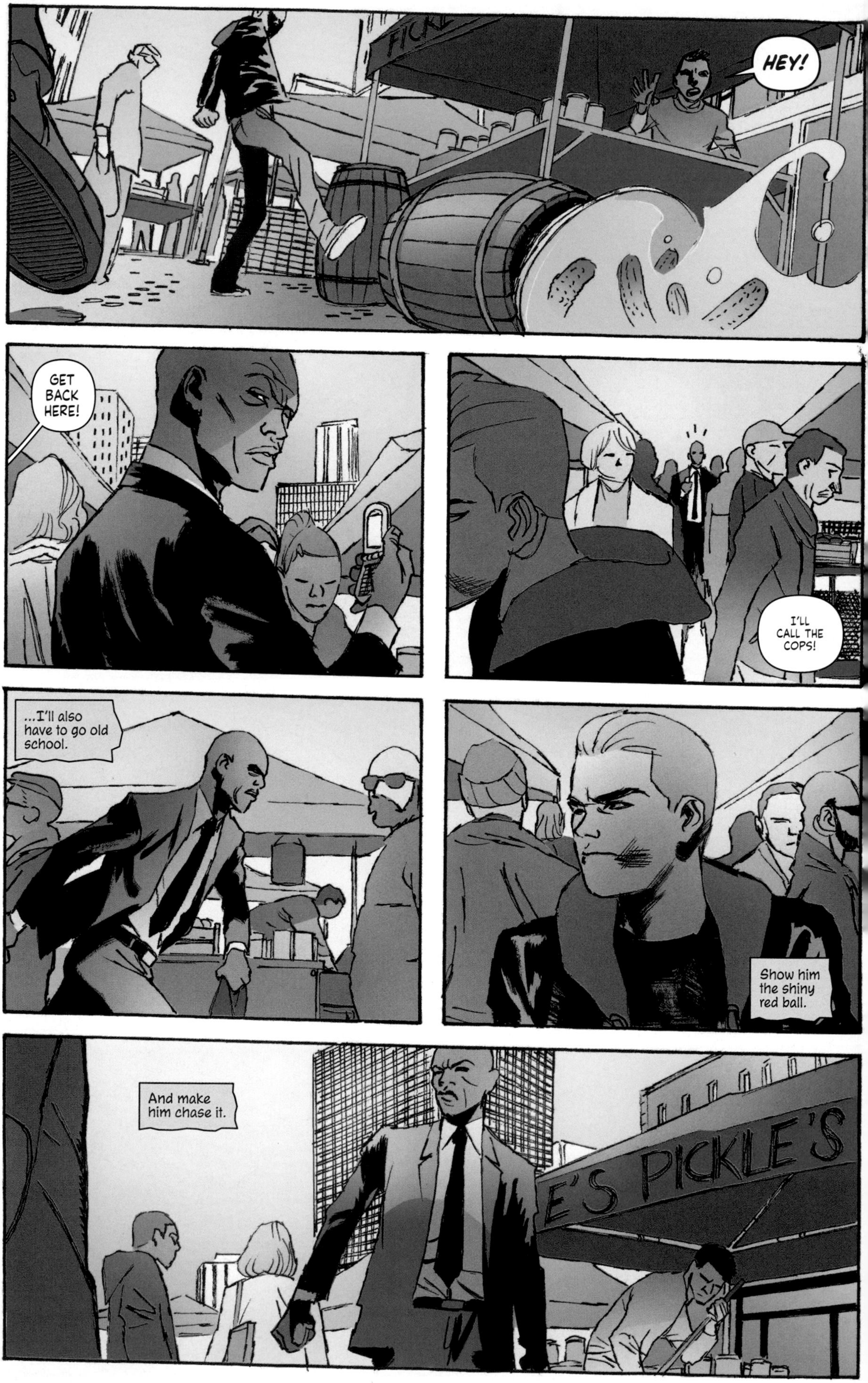
PICKLE
HEY!
GET BACK HERE!
I'LL CALL THE COPS!
...I'll also have to go old school.
Show him the shiny red ball.
And make him chase it.
E'S PICKLE'S

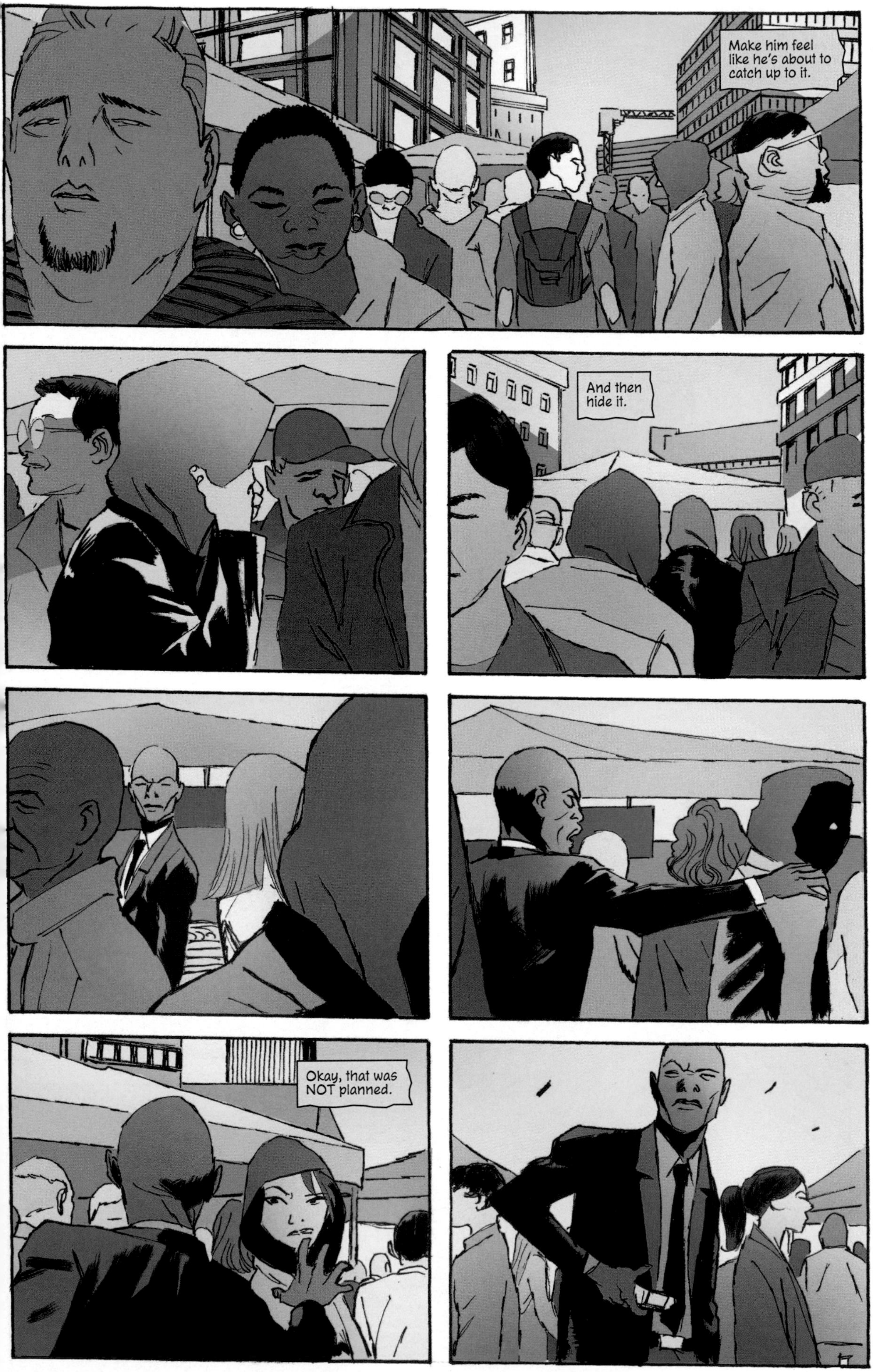
Make him feel like he's about to catch up to it.
And then hide it.
Okay, that was NOT planned.

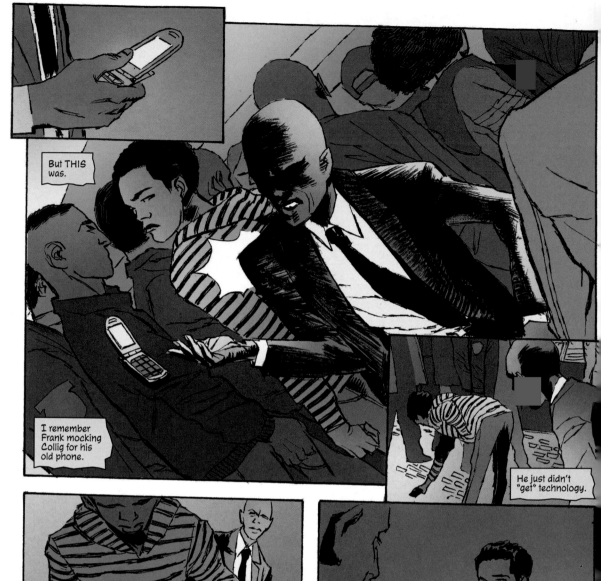

But THIS was.

I remember Frank mocking Collig for his old phone.

He just didn't "get" technology.

For some reason that stayed with me.

So if someone were to switch his phone with another one that looks the same...

...it would take him a while to notice.

Hacking, the old school way.

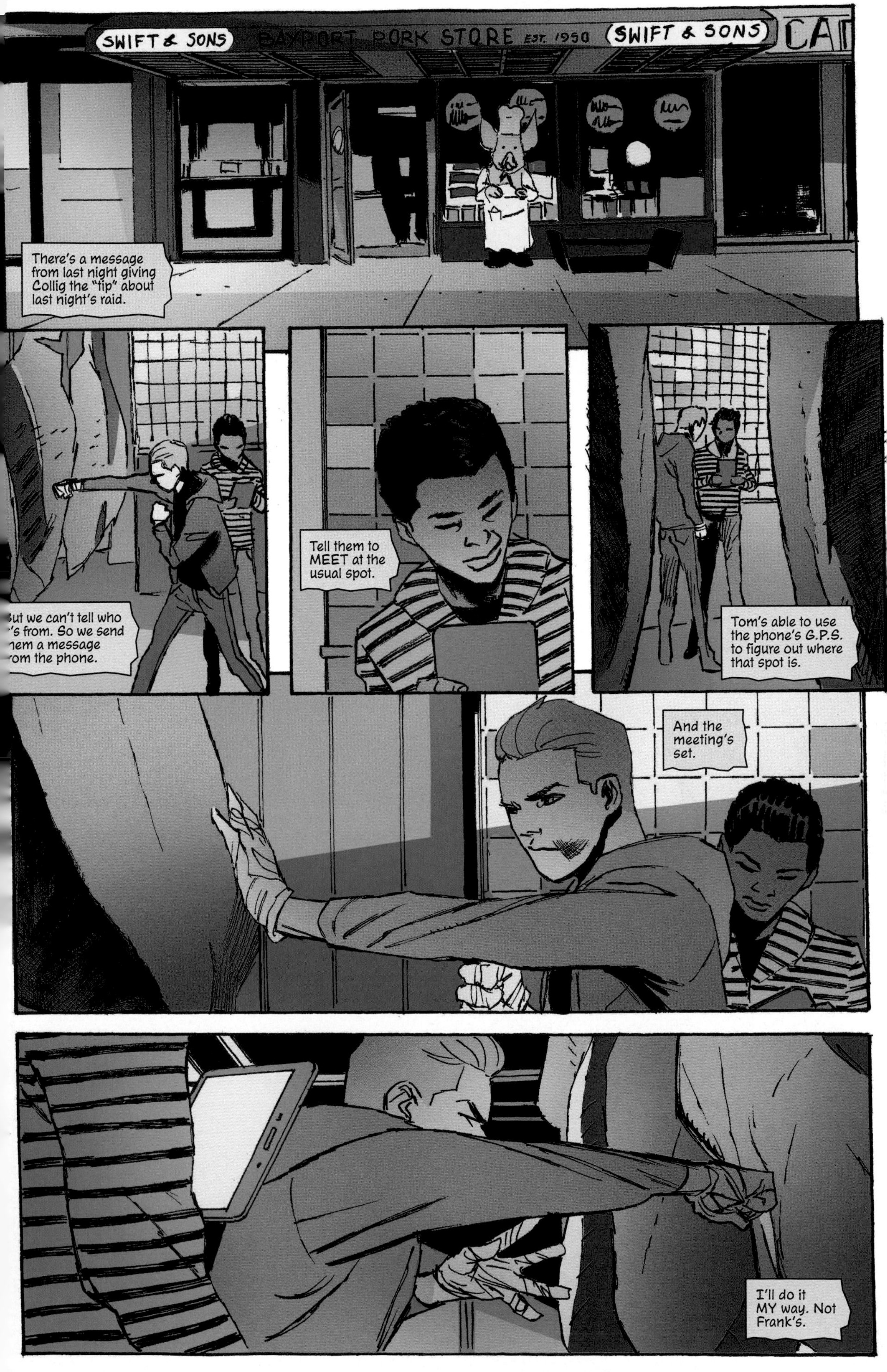
SWIFT & SONS
BAYPORT PORK STORE EST. 1950
SWIFT & SONS
CA
There's a message from last night giving Collig the "tip" about last night's raid.
ut we can't tell who 's from. So we send nem a message rom the phone.
Tell them to MEET at the usual spot.
Tom's able to use the phone's G.P.S. to figure out where that spot is.
And the meeting's set.
I'll do it MY way. Not Frank's.

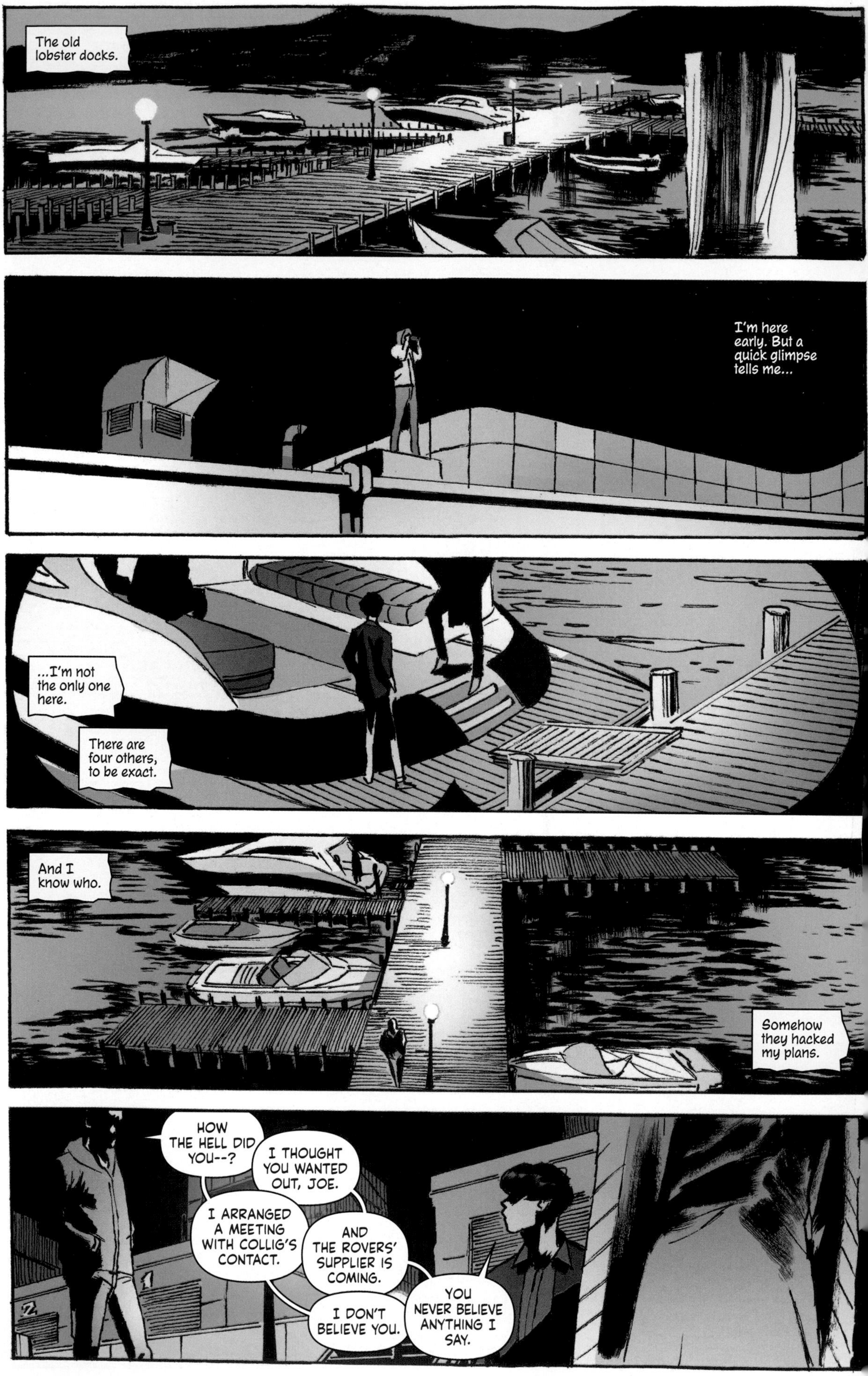
The old lobster docks.
I'm here early. But a quick glimpse tells me...
...I'm not the only one here.
There are four others, to be exact.
And I know who.
Somehow they hacked my plans.
HOW THE HELL DID YOU--?
I THOUGHT YOU WANTED OUT, JOE.
I ARRANGED A MEETING WITH COLLIG'S CONTACT.
AND THE ROVERS' SUPPLIER IS COMING.
I DON'T BELIEVE YOU.
YOU NEVER BELIEVE ANYTHING I SAY.

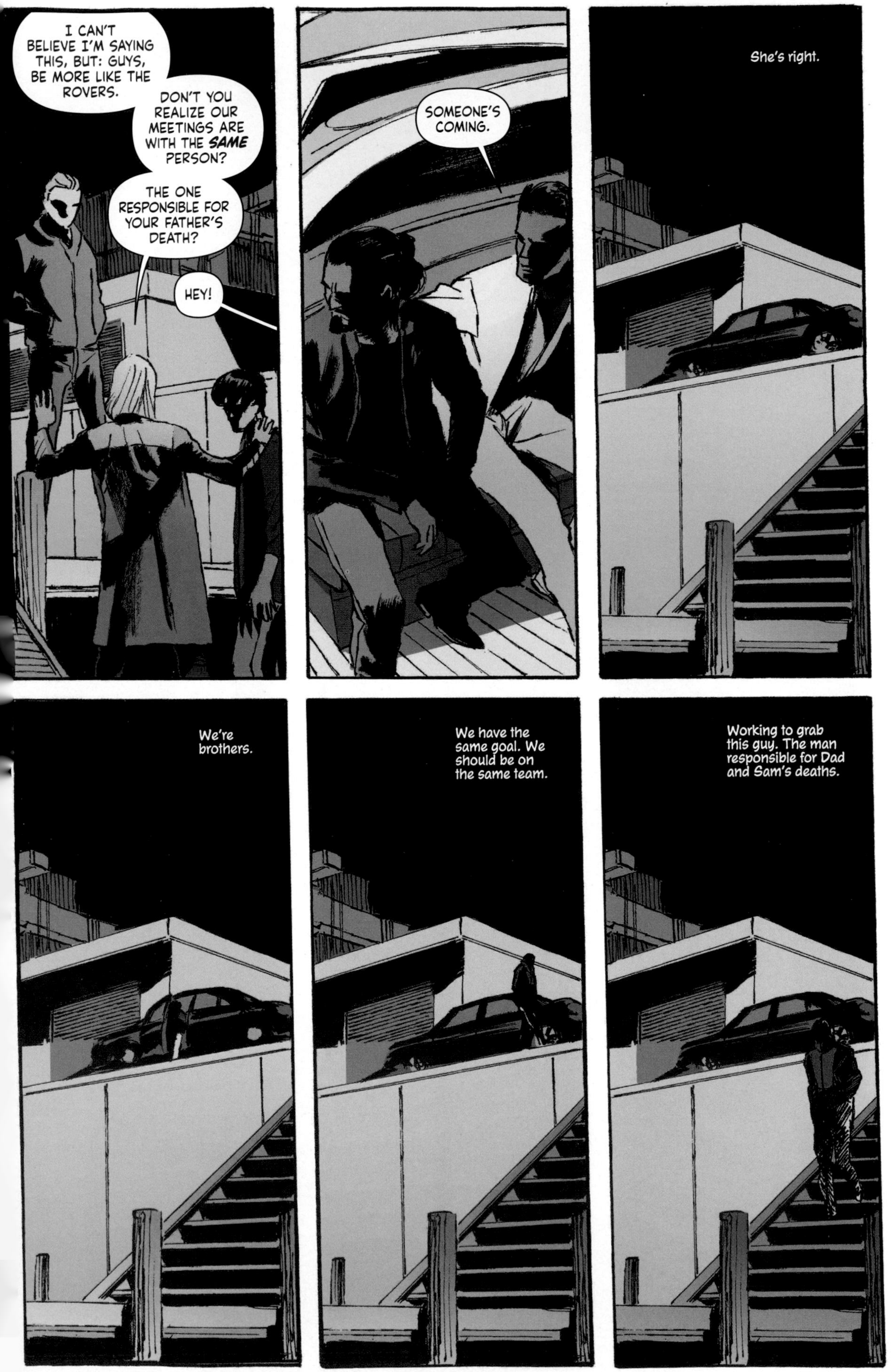
I CAN'T BELIEVE I'M SAYING THIS, BUT: GUYS, BE MORE LIKE THE ROVERS.
DON'T YOU REALIZE OUR MEETINGS ARE WITH THE *SAME* PERSON?
THE ONE RESPONSIBLE FOR YOUR FATHER'S DEATH?
HEY!
SOMEONE'S COMING.
She's right.
We're brothers.
We have the same goal. We should be on the same team.
Working to grab this guy. The man responsible for Dad and Sam's deaths.

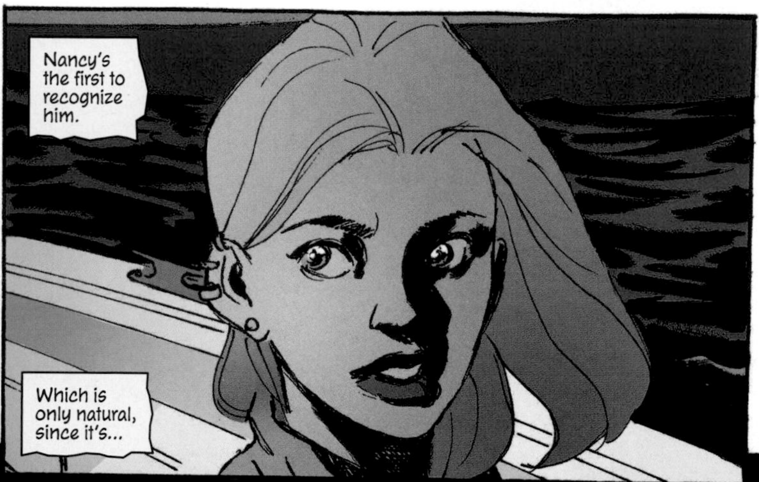
Nancy's the first to recognize him.
Which is only natural, since it's...

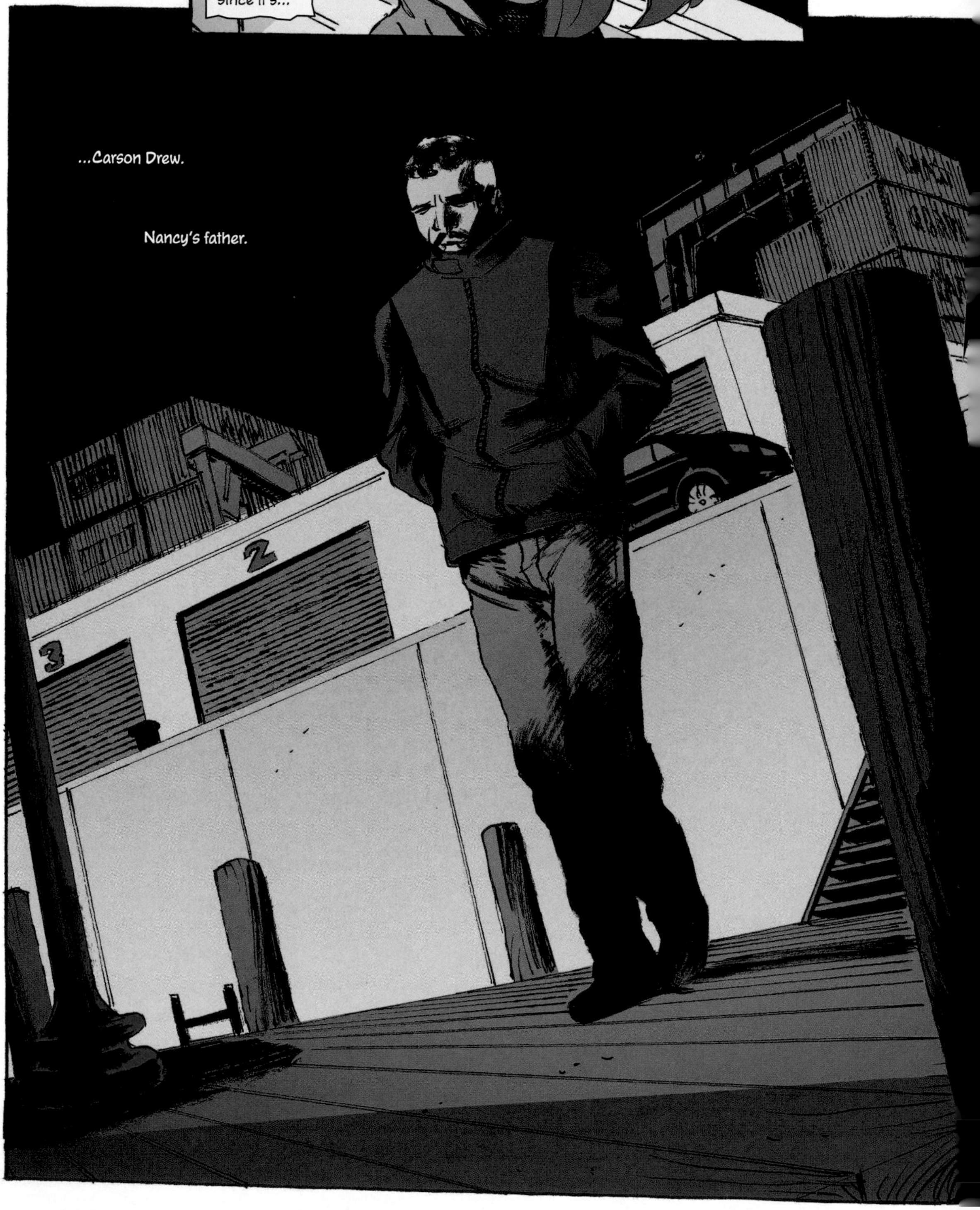
...Carson Drew.
Nancy's father.

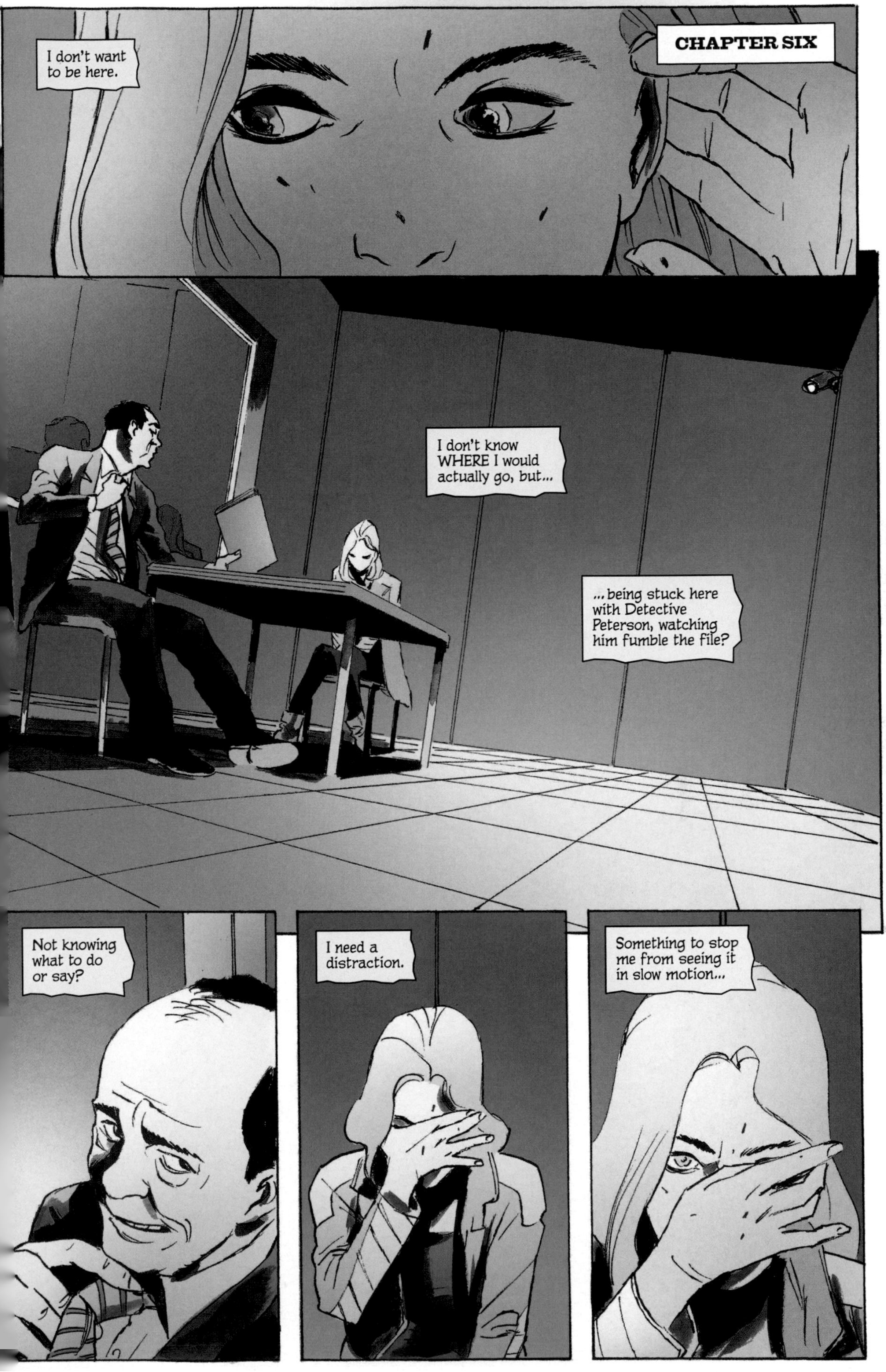
CHAPTER SIX
I don't want to be here.
I don't know WHERE I would actually go, but...
...being stuck here with Detective Peterson, watching him fumble the file?
Not knowing what to do or say?
I need a distraction.
Something to stop me from seeing it in slow motion...

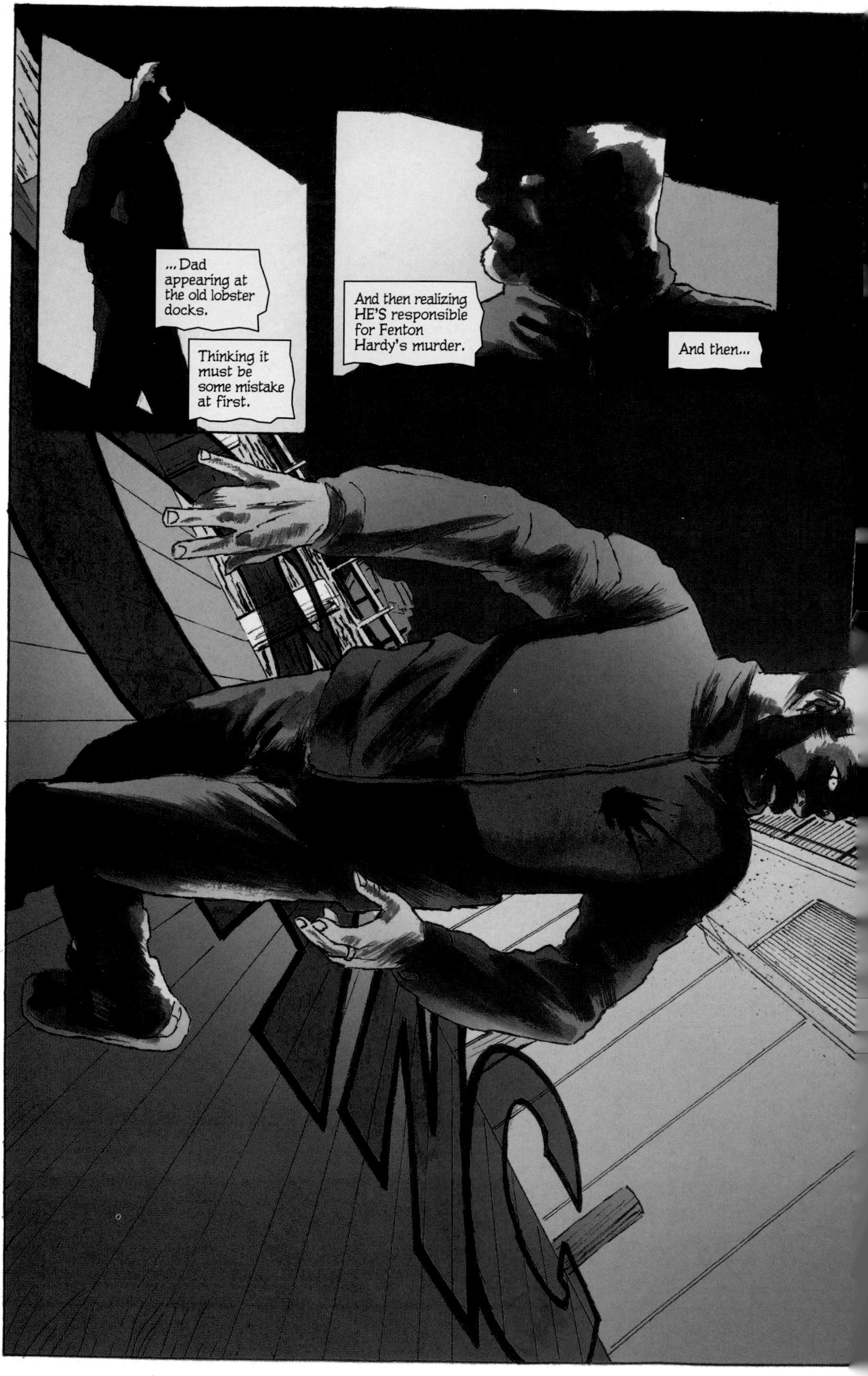
...Dad appearing at the old lobster docks.
Thinking it must be some mistake at first.
And then realizing HE'S responsible for Fenton Hardy's murder.
And then...

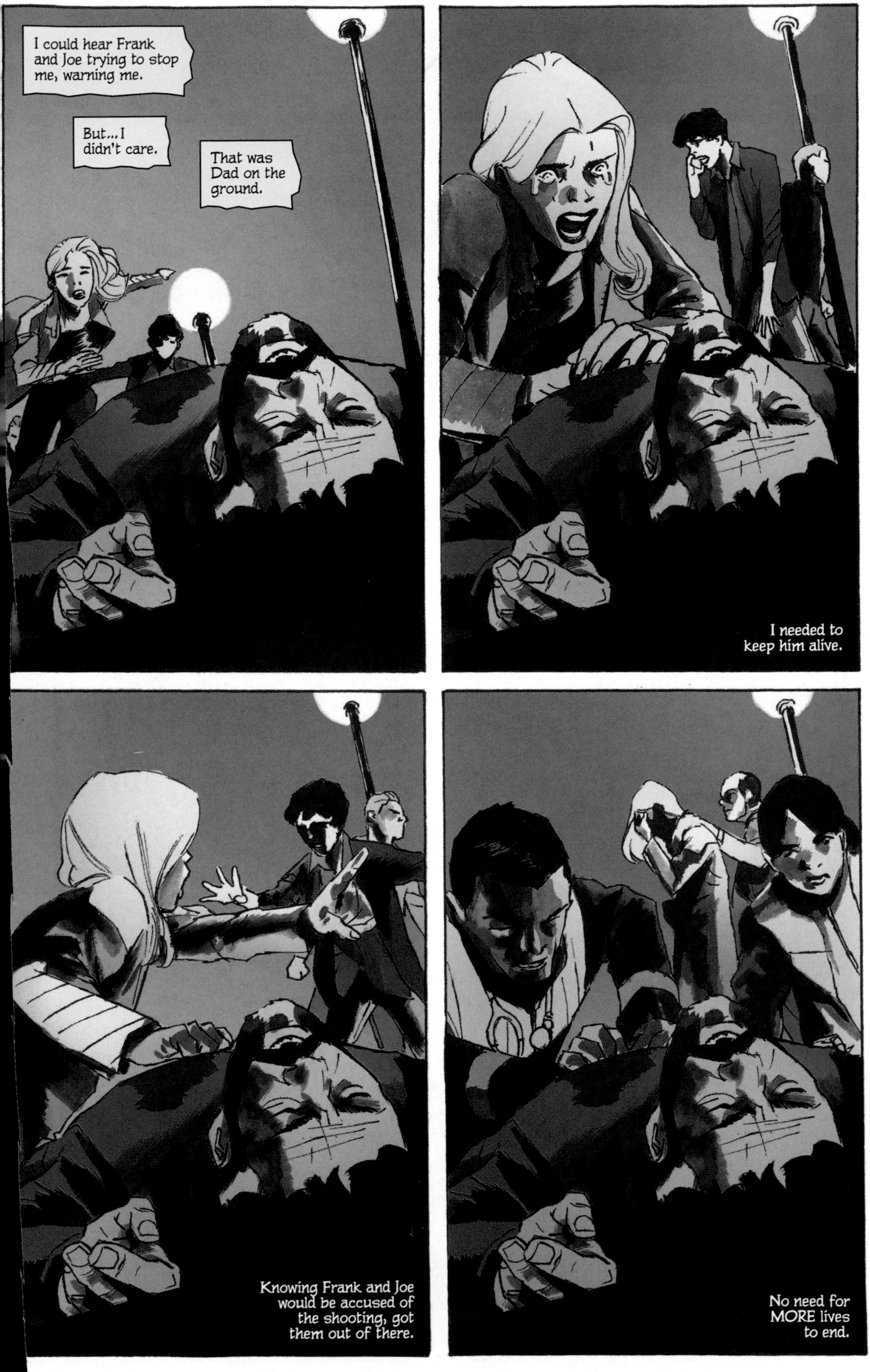

I could hear Frank and Joe trying to stop me, warning me.
But...I didn't care.
That was Dad on the ground.
I needed to keep him alive.
Knowing Frank and Joe would be accused of the shooting, got them out of there.
No need for MORE lives to end.

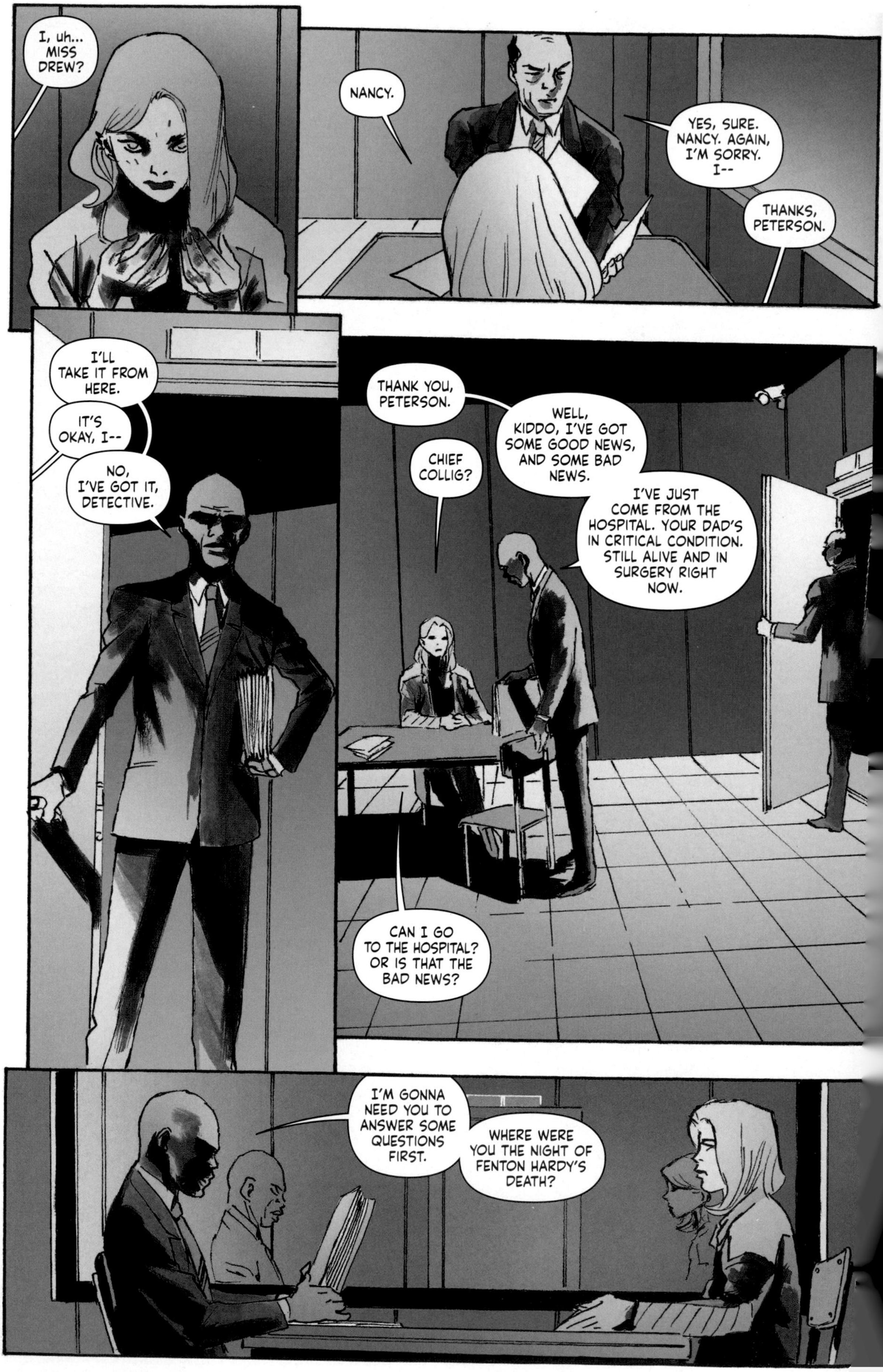
I, uh... MISS DREW?
NANCY.
YES, SURE. NANCY. AGAIN, I'M SORRY. I--
THANKS, PETERSON.
I'LL TAKE IT FROM HERE.
IT'S OKAY, I--
NO, I'VE GOT IT, DETECTIVE.
THANK YOU, PETERSON.
CHIEF COLLIG?
WELL, KIDDO, I'VE GOT SOME GOOD NEWS, AND SOME BAD NEWS.
I'VE JUST COME FROM THE HOSPITAL. YOUR DAD'S IN CRITICAL CONDITION. STILL ALIVE AND IN SURGERY RIGHT NOW.
CAN I GO TO THE HOSPITAL? OR IS THAT THE BAD NEWS?
I'M GONNA NEED YOU TO ANSWER SOME QUESTIONS FIRST.
WHERE WERE YOU THE NIGHT OF FENTON HARDY'S DEATH?

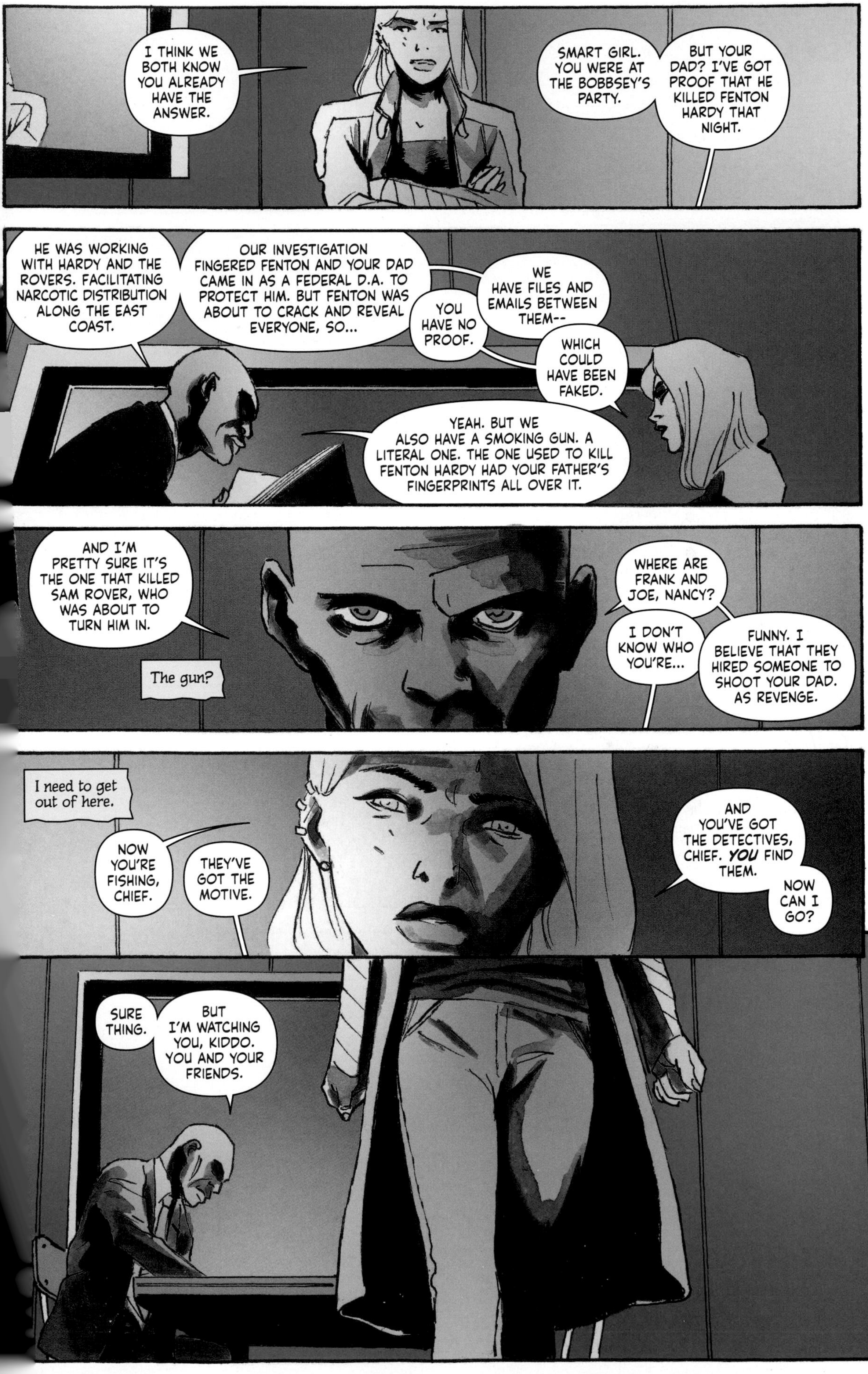
I THINK WE BOTH KNOW YOU ALREADY HAVE THE ANSWER.
SMART GIRL. YOU WERE AT THE BOBBSEY'S PARTY.
BUT YOUR DAD? I'VE GOT PROOF THAT HE KILLED FENTON HARDY THAT NIGHT.
HE WAS WORKING WITH HARDY AND THE ROVERS. FACILITATING NARCOTIC DISTRIBUTION ALONG THE EAST COAST.
OUR INVESTIGATION FINGERED FENTON AND YOUR DAD CAME IN AS A FEDERAL D.A. TO PROTECT HIM. BUT FENTON WAS ABOUT TO CRACK AND REVEAL EVERYONE, SO...
YOU HAVE NO PROOF.
WE HAVE FILES AND EMAILS BETWEEN THEM--
WHICH COULD HAVE BEEN FAKED.
YEAH. BUT WE ALSO HAVE A SMOKING GUN. A LITERAL ONE. THE ONE USED TO KILL FENTON HARDY HAD YOUR FATHER'S FINGERPRINTS ALL OVER IT.
AND I'M PRETTY SURE IT'S THE ONE THAT KILLED SAM ROVER, WHO WAS ABOUT TO TURN HIM IN.
The gun?
WHERE ARE FRANK AND JOE, NANCY?
I DON'T KNOW WHO YOU'RE...
FUNNY. I BELIEVE THAT THEY HIRED SOMEONE TO SHOOT YOUR DAD. AS REVENGE.
I need to get out of here.
NOW YOU'RE FISHING, CHIEF.
THEY'VE GOT THE MOTIVE.
AND YOU'VE GOT THE DETECTIVES, CHIEF. YOU FIND THEM.
NOW CAN I GO?
SURE THING.
BUT I'M WATCHING YOU, KIDDO. YOU AND YOUR FRIENDS.

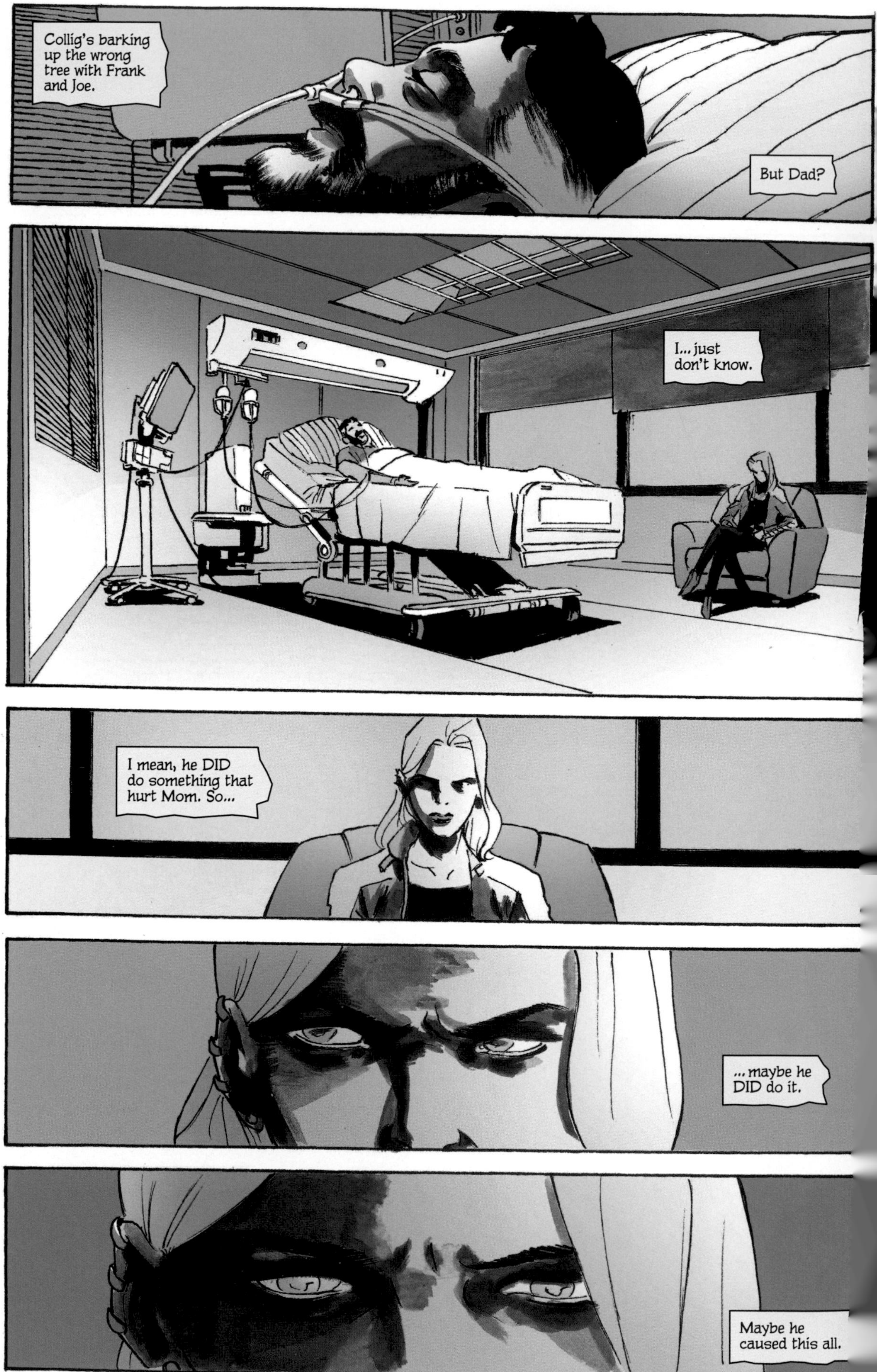
Collig's barking up the wrong tree with Frank and Joe.
But Dad?
I... just don't know.
I mean, he DID do something that hurt Mom. So...
...maybe he DID do it.
Maybe he caused this all.

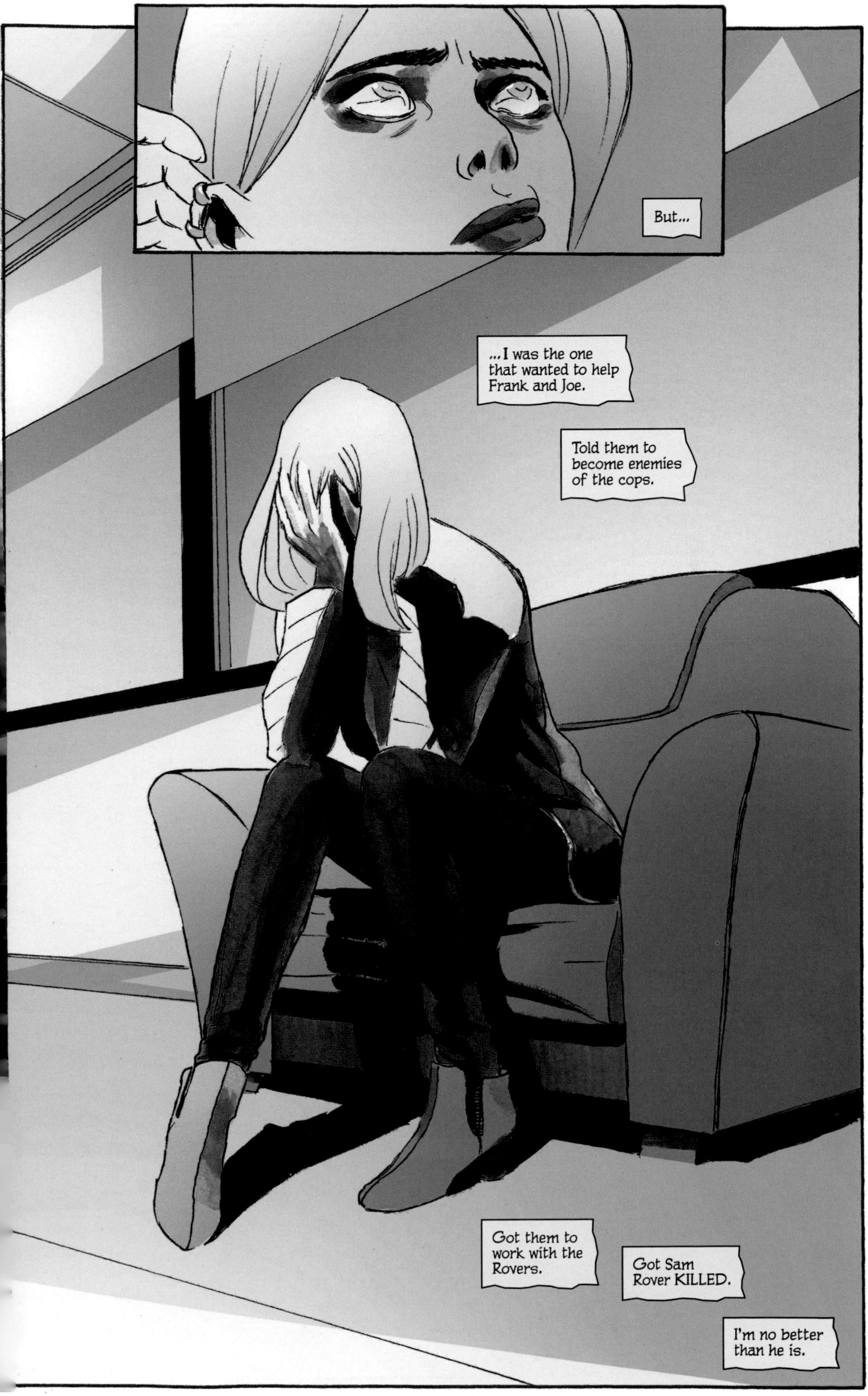
But...
...I was the one that wanted to help Frank and Joe.
Told them to become enemies of the cops.
Got them to work with the Rovers.
Got Sam Rover KILLED.
I'm no better than he is.

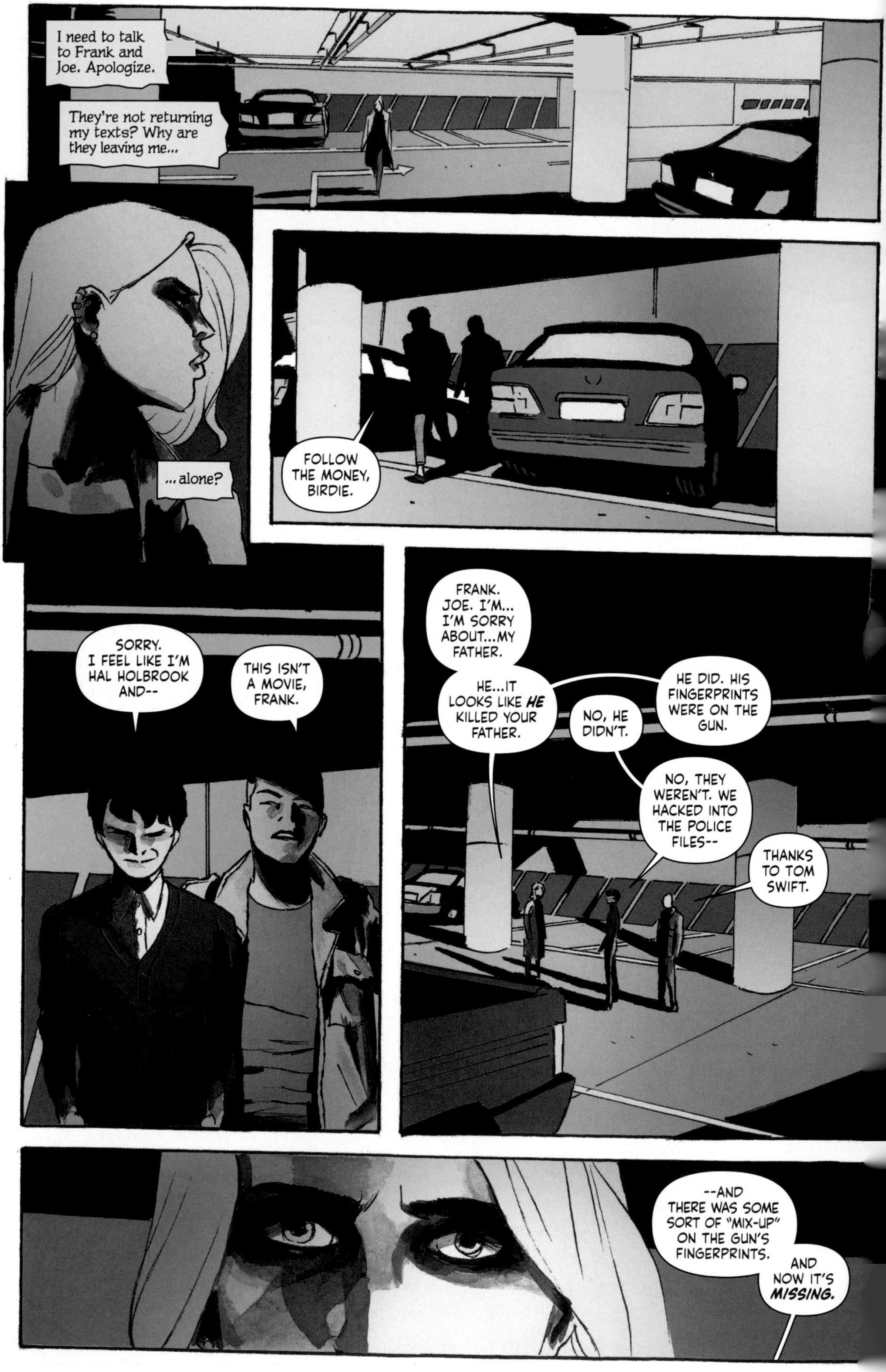
I need to talk to Frank and Joe. Apologize.
They're not returning my texts? Why are they leaving me...
...alone?
FOLLOW THE MONEY, BIRDIE.
SORRY. I FEEL LIKE I'M HAL HOLBROOK AND--
THIS ISN'T A MOVIE, FRANK.
FRANK. JOE. I'M... I'M SORRY ABOUT...MY FATHER.
HE...IT LOOKS LIKE HE KILLED YOUR FATHER.
HE DID. HIS FINGERPRINTS WERE ON THE GUN.
NO, HE DIDN'T.
NO, THEY WEREN'T. WE HACKED INTO THE POLICE FILES--
THANKS TO TOM SWIFT.
--AND THERE WAS SOME SORT OF "MIX-UP" ON THE GUN'S FINGERPRINTS.
AND NOW IT'S MISSING.

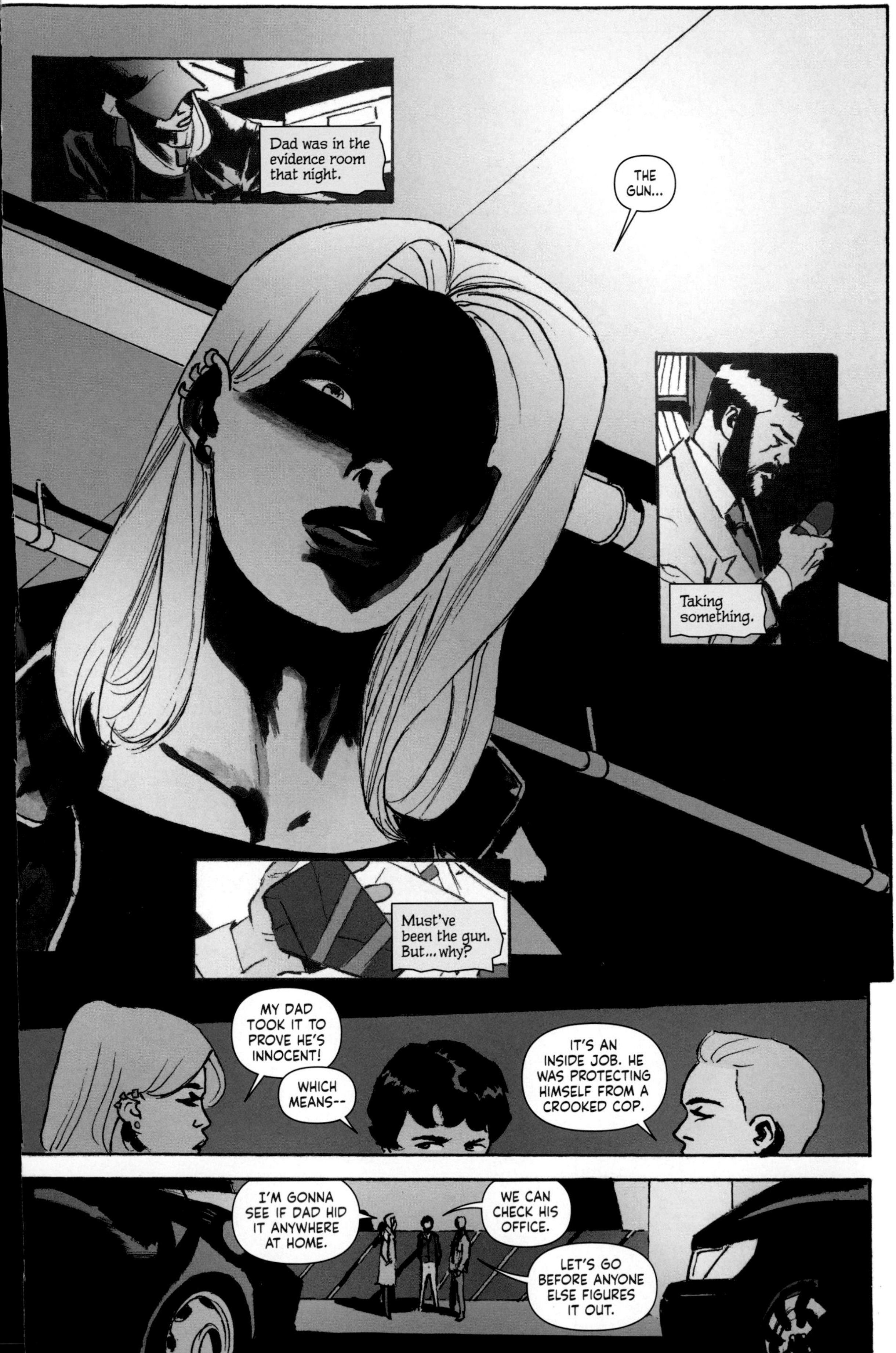
Dad was in the evidence room that night.
THE GUN...
Taking something.
Must've been the gun. But...why?
MY DAD TOOK IT TO PROVE HE'S INNOCENT!
WHICH MEANS--
IT'S AN INSIDE JOB. HE WAS PROTECTING HIMSELF FROM A CROOKED COP.
I'M GONNA SEE IF DAD HID IT ANYWHERE AT HOME.
WE CAN CHECK HIS OFFICE.
LET'S GO BEFORE ANYONE ELSE FIGURES IT OUT.

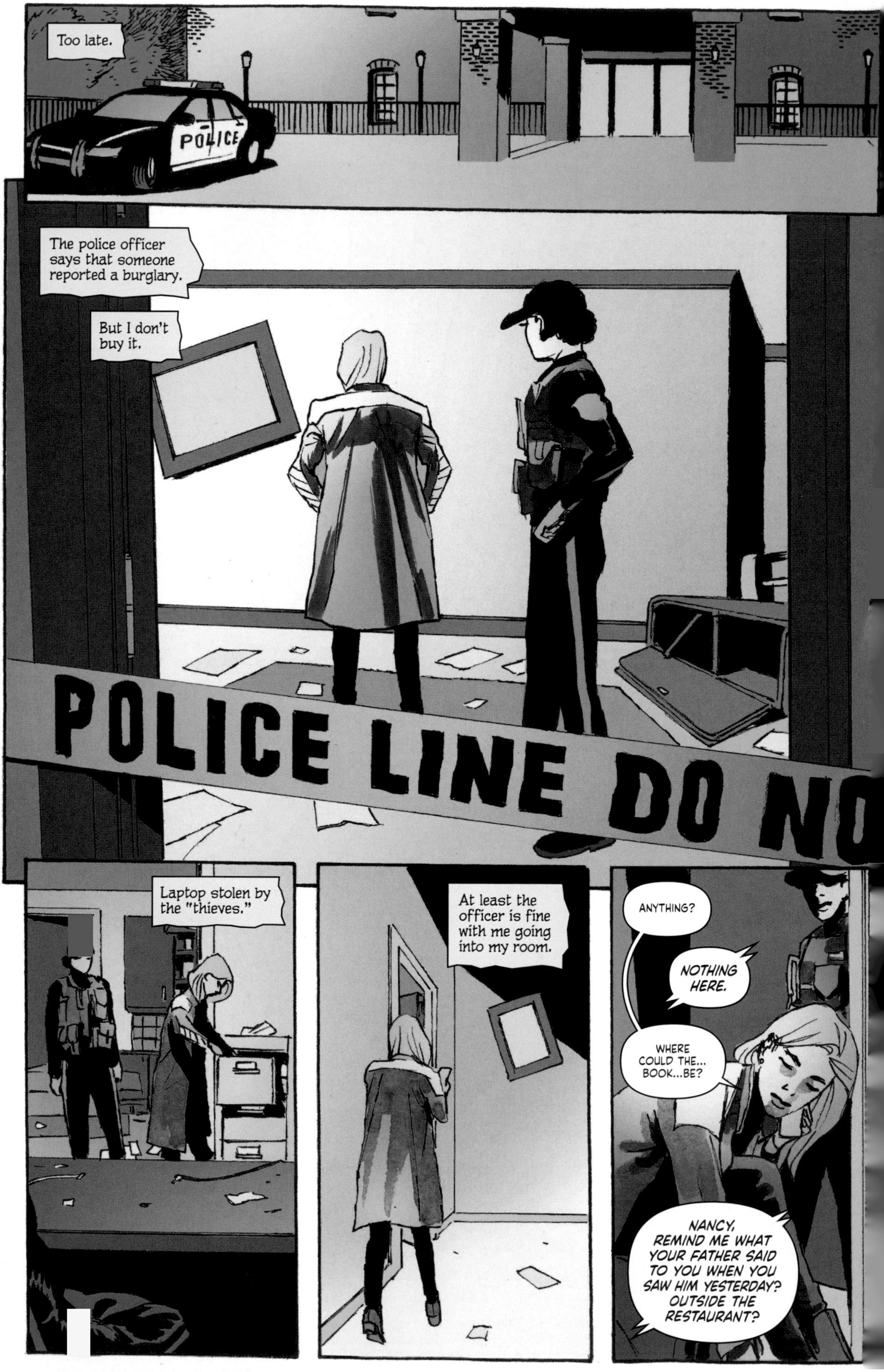

Too late.
POLICE
The police officer says that someone reported a burglary.
But I don't buy it.
POLICE LINE DO NO
Laptop stolen by the "thieves."
At least the officer is fine with me going into my room.
ANYTHING?
NOTHING HERE.
WHERE COULD THE... BOOK...BE?
NANCY, REMIND ME WHAT YOUR FATHER SAID TO YOU WHEN YOU SAW HIM YESTERDAY? OUTSIDE THE RESTAURANT?

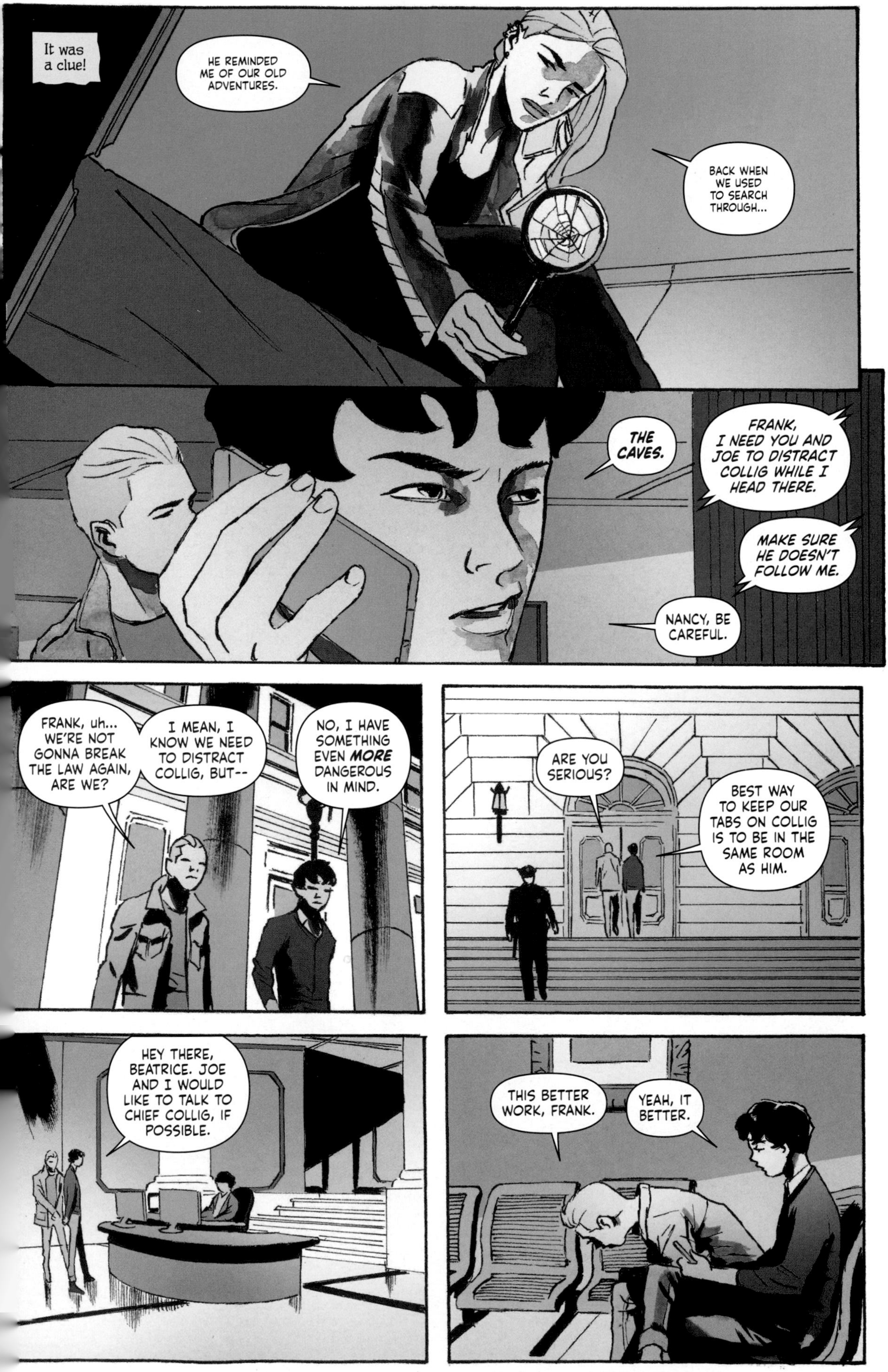
It was a clue!
HE REMINDED ME OF OUR OLD ADVENTURES.
BACK WHEN WE USED TO SEARCH THROUGH...
THE CAVES.
FRANK, I NEED YOU AND JOE TO DISTRACT COLLIG WHILE I HEAD THERE.
MAKE SURE HE DOESN'T FOLLOW ME.
NANCY, BE CAREFUL.
FRANK, uh... WE'RE NOT GONNA BREAK THE LAW AGAIN, ARE WE?
I MEAN, I KNOW WE NEED TO DISTRACT COLLIG, BUT--
NO, I HAVE SOMETHING EVEN MORE DANGEROUS IN MIND.
ARE YOU SERIOUS?
BEST WAY TO KEEP OUR TABS ON COLLIG IS TO BE IN THE SAME ROOM AS HIM.
HEY THERE, BEATRICE. JOE AND I WOULD LIKE TO TALK TO CHIEF COLLIG, IF POSSIBLE.
THIS BETTER WORK, FRANK.
YEAH, IT BETTER.

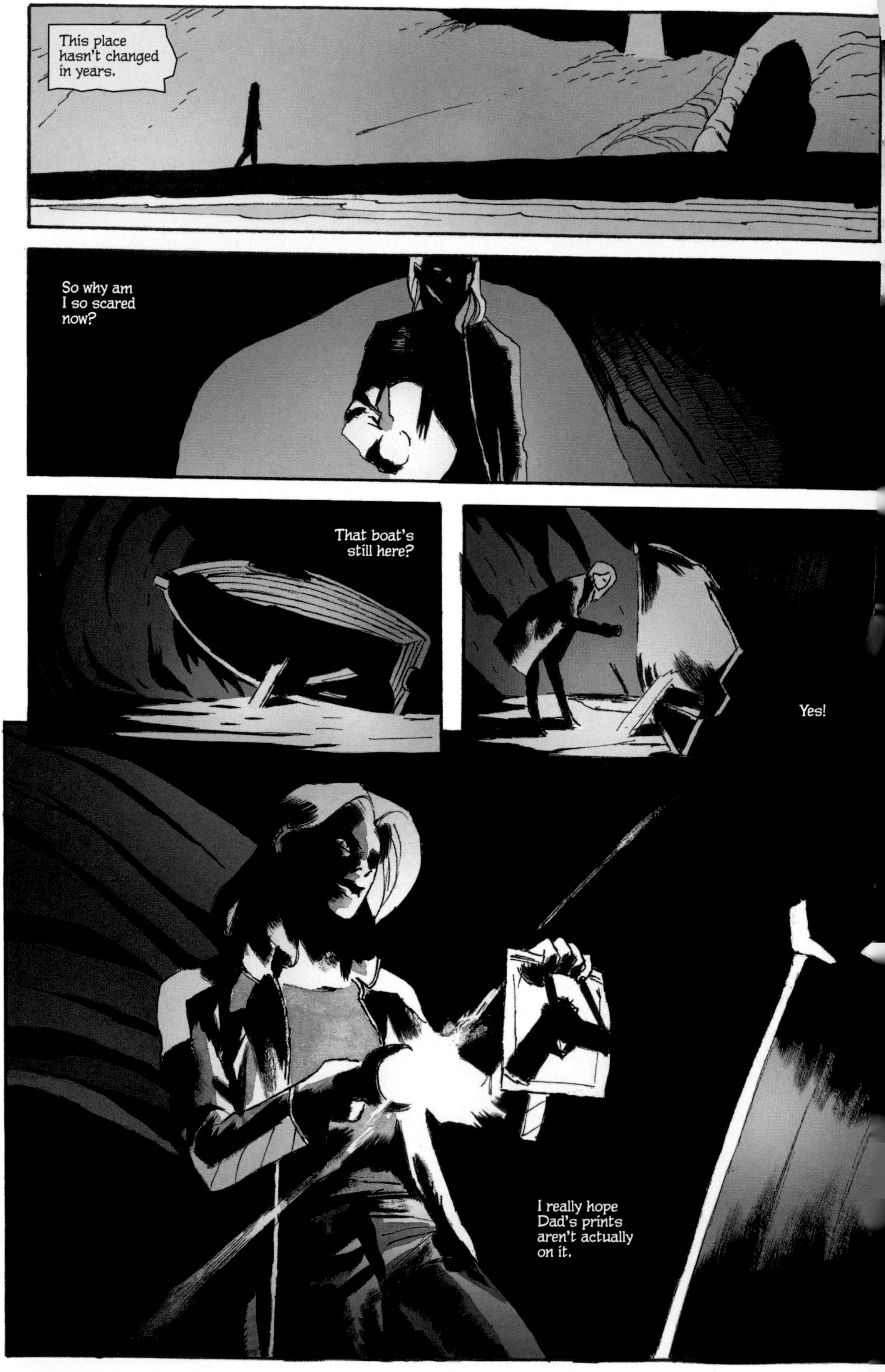
This place hasn't changed in years.
So why am I so scared now?
That boat's still here?
Yes!
I really hope Dad's prints aren't actually on it.

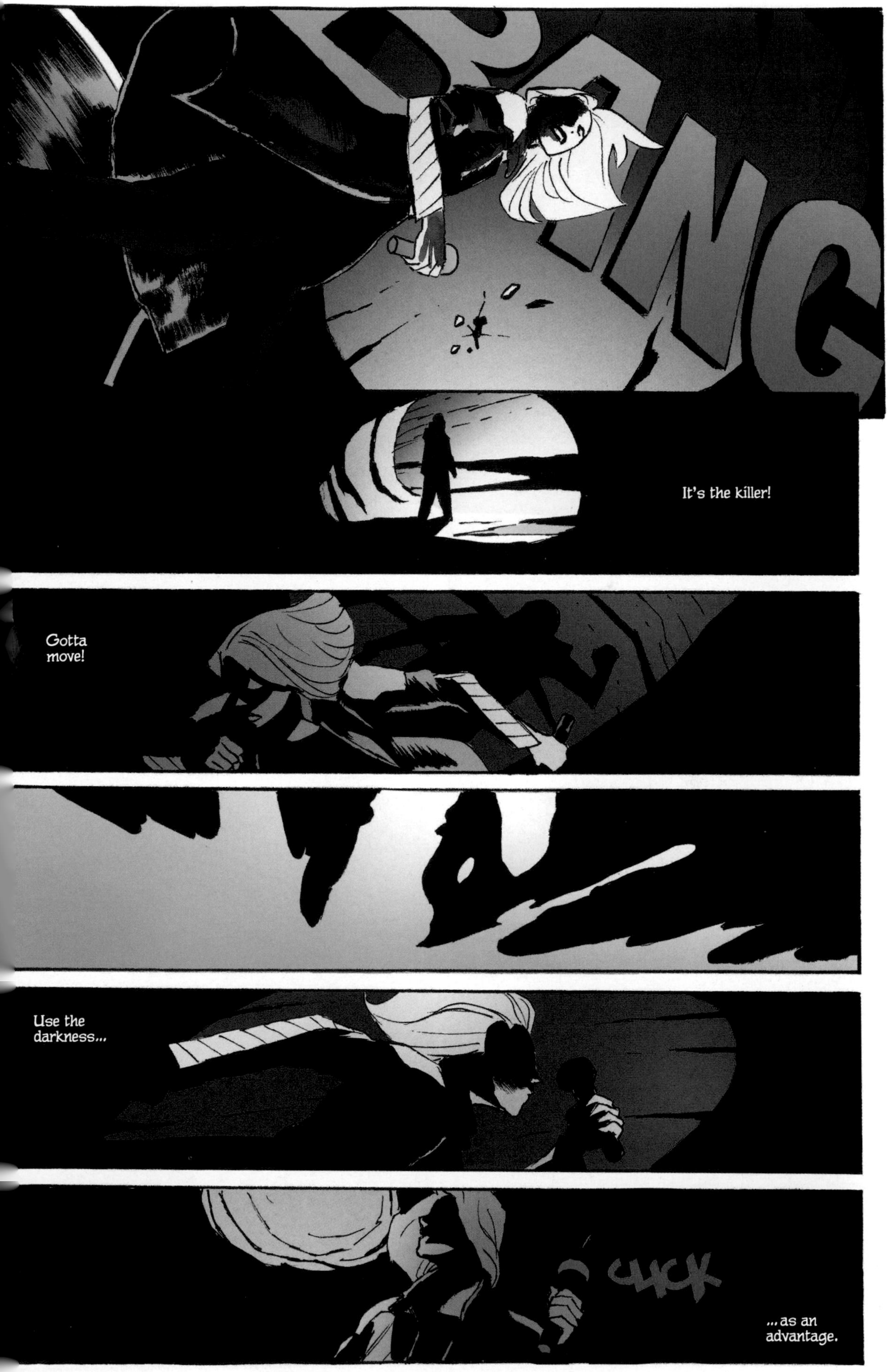
It's the killer!
Gotta move!
Use the darkness...
CLICK
...as an advantage.

There better be another exit here...

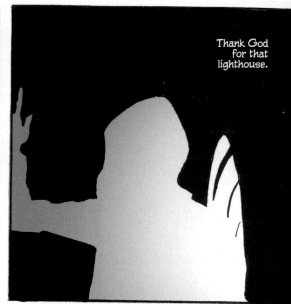

Thank God for that lighthouse.

Damn.

Gotta go.

Gotta get out of here.

No! I was so close...

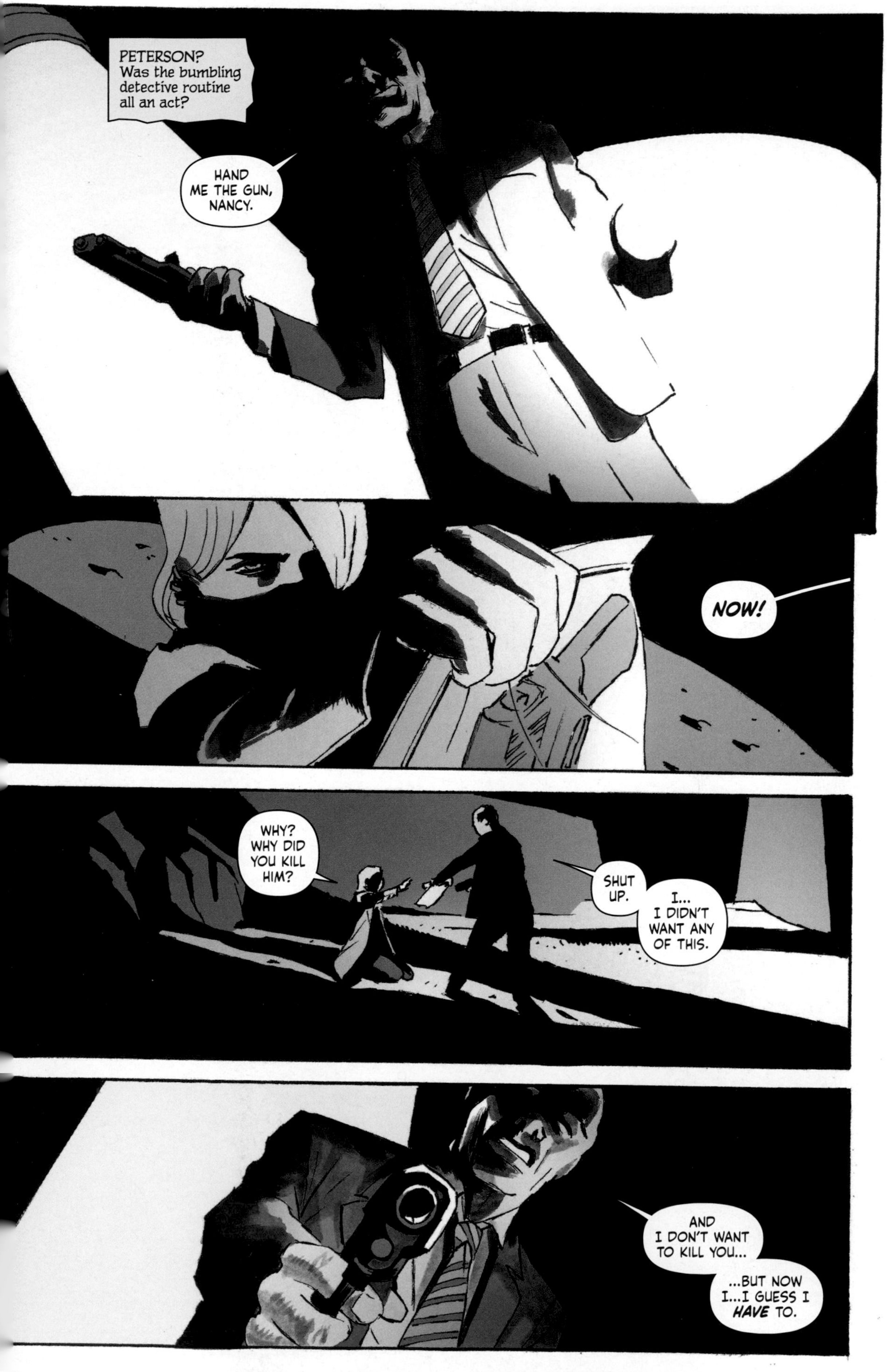
PETERSON? Was the bumbling detective routine all an act?
HAND ME THE GUN, NANCY.
NOW!
WHY? WHY DID YOU KILL HIM?
SHUT UP.
I... I DIDN'T WANT ANY OF THIS.
AND I DON'T WANT TO KILL YOU...
...BUT NOW I...I GUESS I *HAVE* TO.

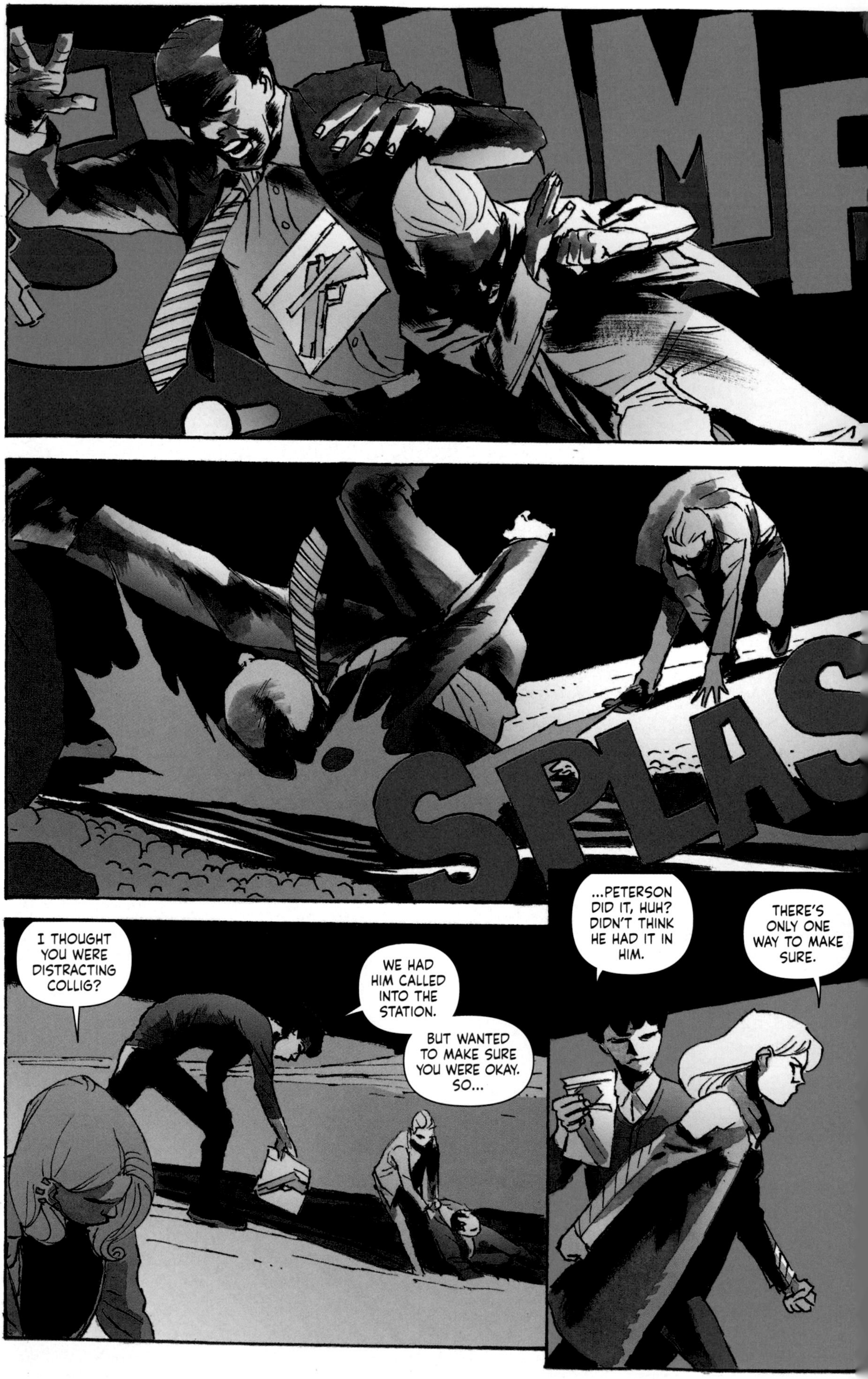
SPLAS
I THOUGHT YOU WERE DISTRACTING COLLIG?
WE HAD HIM CALLED INTO THE STATION.
BUT WANTED TO MAKE SURE YOU WERE OKAY. SO...
...PETERSON DID IT, HUH? DIDN'T THINK HE HAD IT IN HIM.
THERE'S ONLY ONE WAY TO MAKE SURE.

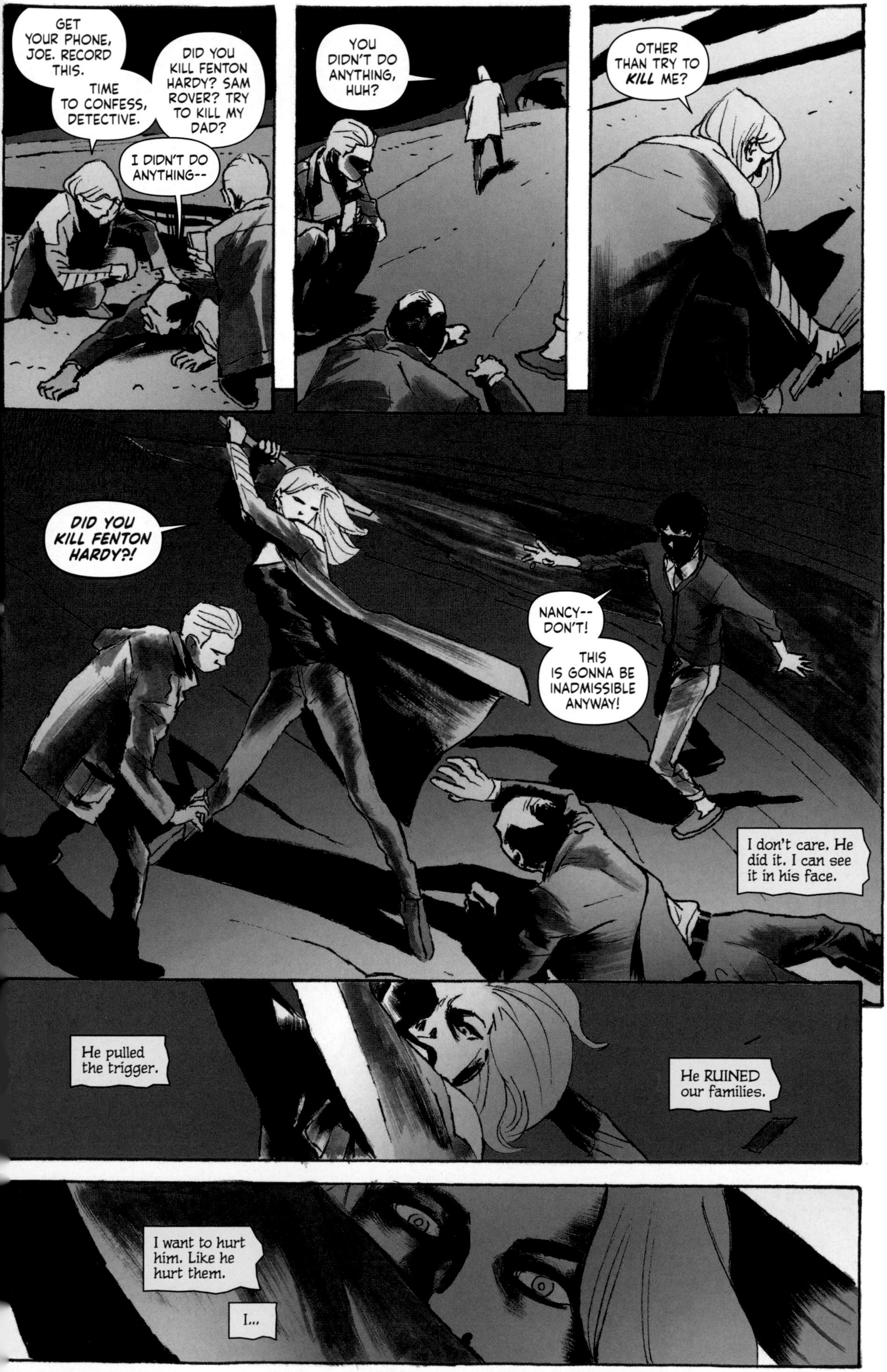
GET YOUR PHONE, JOE. RECORD THIS.
TIME TO CONFESS, DETECTIVE.
DID YOU KILL FENTON HARDY? SAM ROVER? TRY TO KILL MY DAD?
I DIDN'T DO ANYTHING--
YOU DIDN'T DO ANYTHING, HUH?
OTHER THAN TRY TO KILL ME?
DID YOU KILL FENTON HARDY?!
NANCY-- DON'T!
THIS IS GONNA BE INADMISSIBLE ANYWAY!
I don't care. He did it. I can see it in his face.
He pulled the trigger.
He RUINED our families.
I want to hurt him. Like he hurt them.
I...

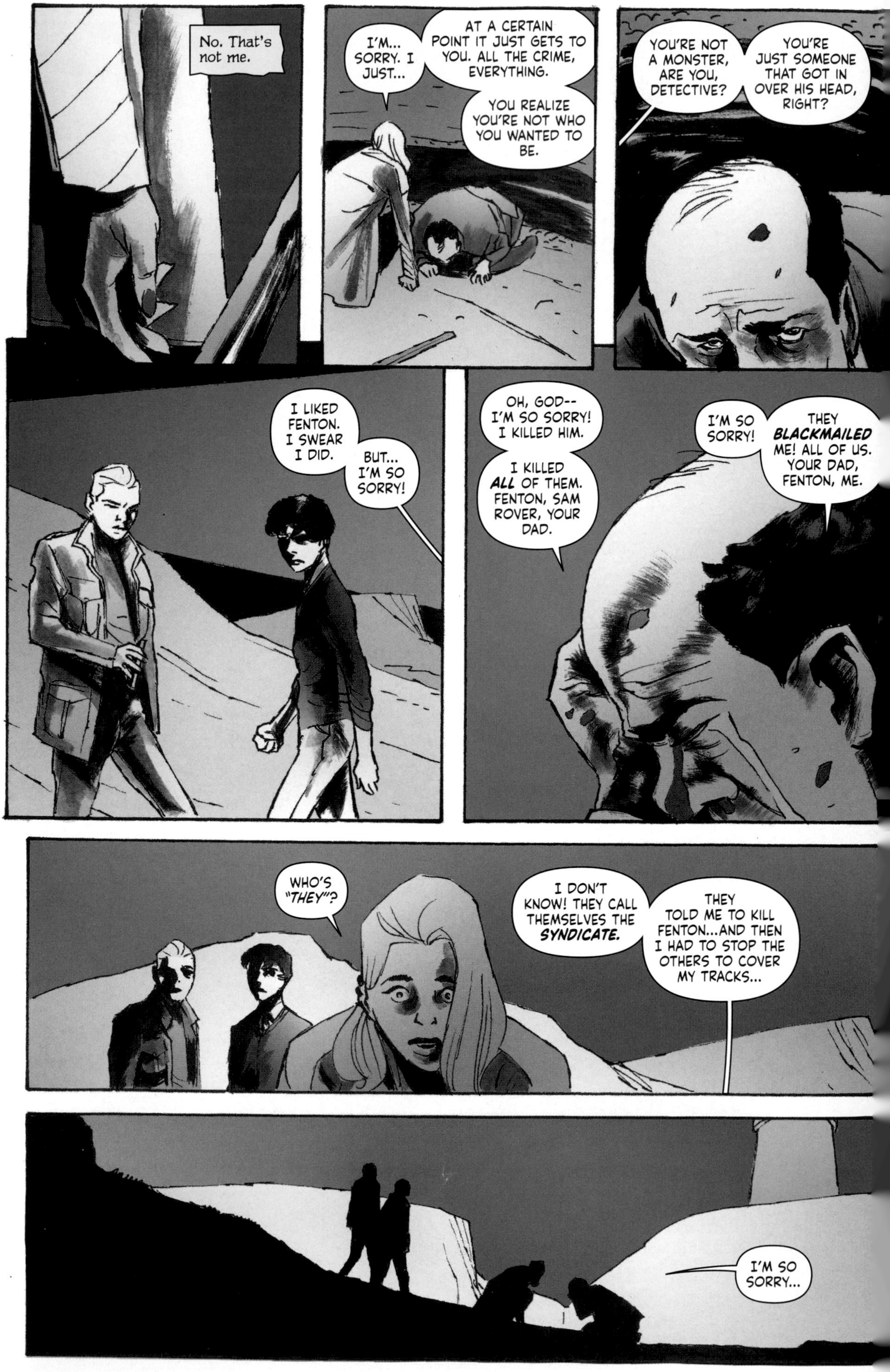
No. That's not me.
I'M... SORRY. I JUST...
AT A CERTAIN POINT IT JUST GETS TO YOU. ALL THE CRIME, EVERYTHING.
YOU REALIZE YOU'RE NOT WHO YOU WANTED TO BE.
YOU'RE NOT A MONSTER, ARE YOU, DETECTIVE?
YOU'RE JUST SOMEONE THAT GOT IN OVER HIS HEAD, RIGHT?
I LIKED FENTON. I SWEAR I DID.
BUT... I'M SO SORRY!
OH, GOD-- I'M SO SORRY! I KILLED HIM.
I KILLED ALL OF THEM. FENTON, SAM ROVER, YOUR DAD.
I'M SO SORRY!
THEY BLACKMAILED ME! ALL OF US. YOUR DAD, FENTON, ME.
WHO'S "THEY"?
I DON'T KNOW! THEY CALL THEMSELVES THE SYNDICATE.
THEY TOLD ME TO KILL FENTON...AND THEN I HAD TO STOP THE OTHERS TO COVER MY TRACKS...
I'M SO SORRY...

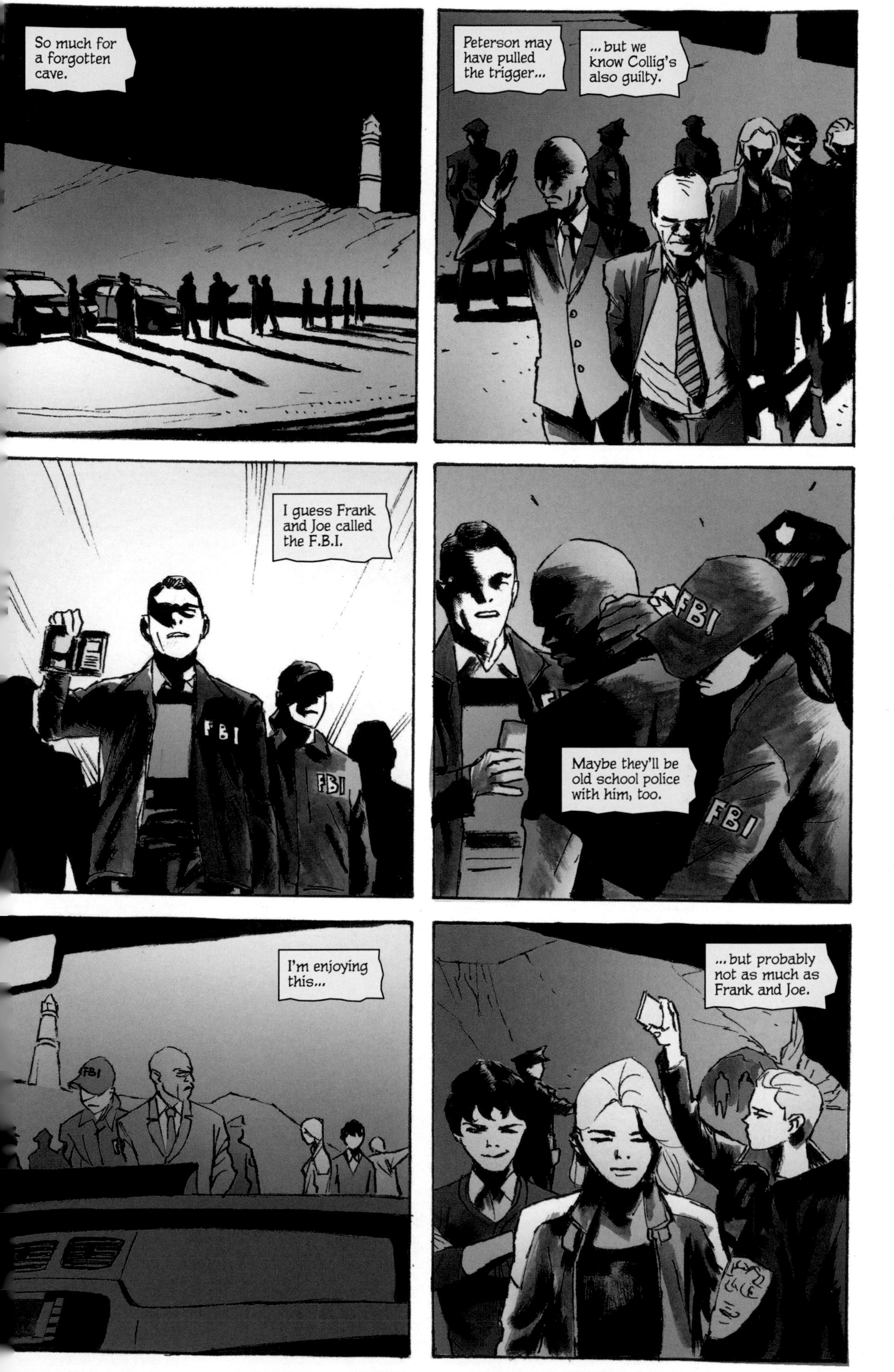
So much for a forgotten cave.
Peterson may have pulled the trigger...
...but we know Collig's also guilty.
I guess Frank and Joe called the F.B.I.
Maybe they'll be old school police with him, too.
I'm enjoying this...
...but probably not as much as Frank and Joe.

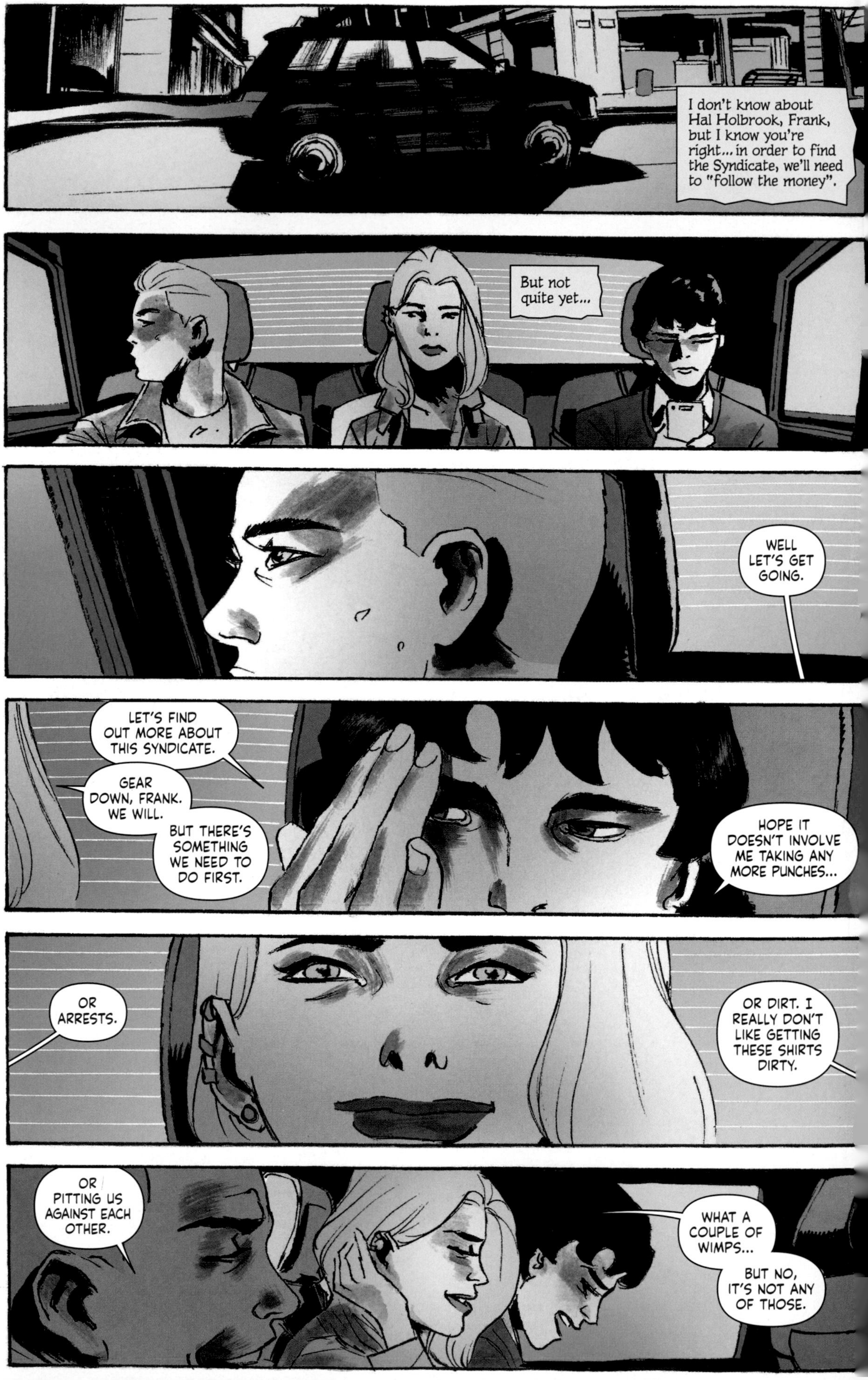
I don't know about Hal Holbrook, Frank, but I know you're right... in order to find the Syndicate, we'll need to "follow the money".
But not quite yet...
WELL LET'S GET GOING.
LET'S FIND OUT MORE ABOUT THIS SYNDICATE.
GEAR DOWN, FRANK. WE WILL.
BUT THERE'S SOMETHING WE NEED TO DO FIRST.
HOPE IT DOESN'T INVOLVE ME TAKING ANY MORE PUNCHES...
OR ARRESTS.
OR DIRT. I REALLY DON'T LIKE GETTING THESE SHIRTS DIRTY.
OR PITTING US AGAINST EACH OTHER.
WHAT A COUPLE OF WIMPS...
BUT NO, IT'S NOT ANY OF THOSE.

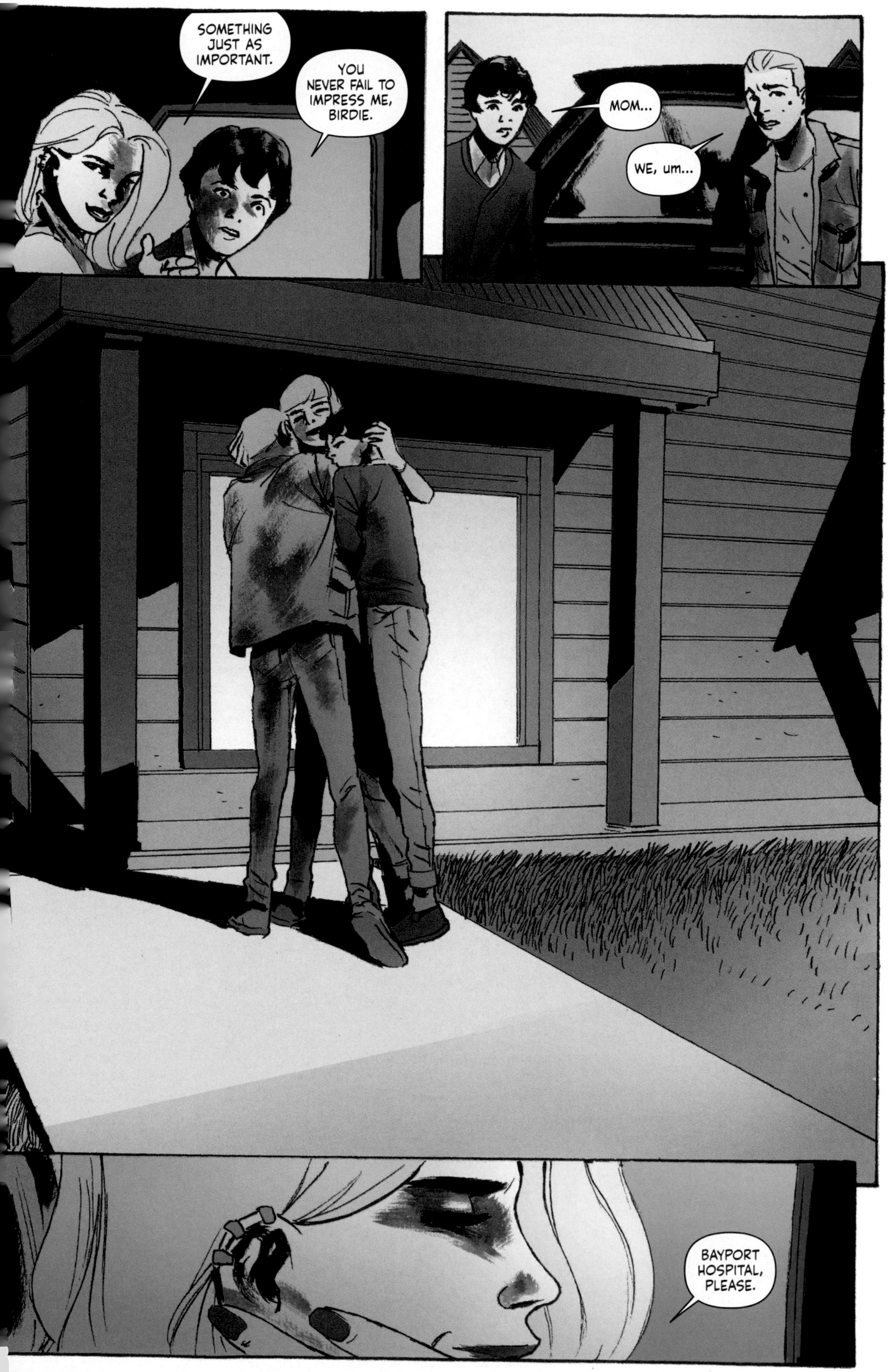
SOMETHING JUST AS IMPORTANT.
YOU NEVER FAIL TO IMPRESS ME, BIRDIE.
MOM...
WE, um...
BAYPORT HOSPITAL, PLEASE.

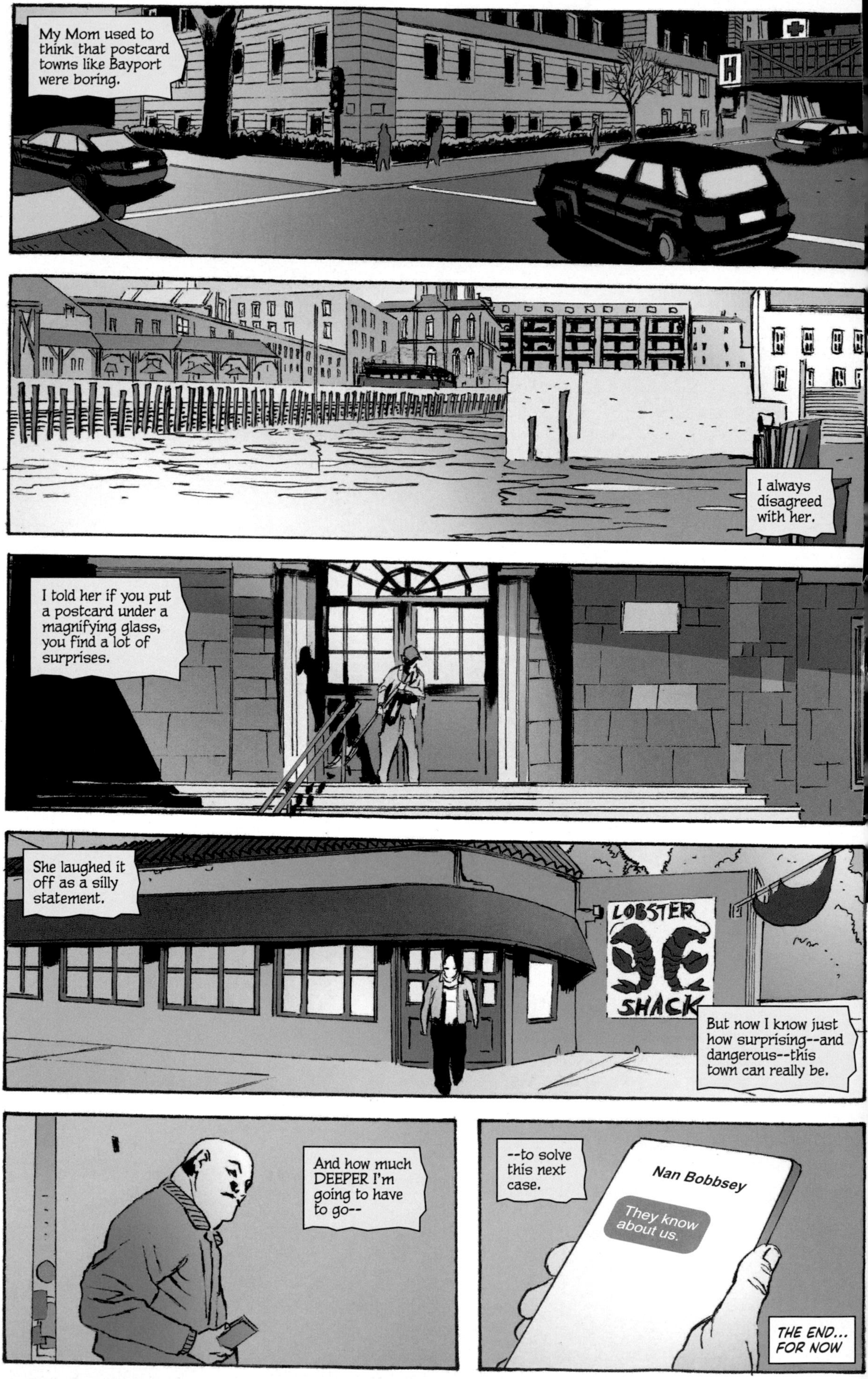

My Mom used to think that postcard towns like Bayport were boring.
H
I always disagreed with her.
I told her if you put a postcard under a magnifying glass, you find a lot of surprises.
She laughed it off as a silly statement.
LOBSTER SHACK
But now I know just how surprising--and dangerous--this town can really be.
And how much DEEPER I'm going to have to go--
--to solve this next case.
Nan Bobbsey
They know about us.
THE END... FOR NOW

BIOS

and drew *Semplice (Tunué), Ogni Piccolo Pezzo* and *Diciottovoltevirgolatre* (Bao Publishing). When he's not working on comics, he illustrates trees and flowers for *Vivi e Vegeta*, a series by Bao Publishing. He's also a proud member of Skeleton Monster.

Simon Bowland

Born and bred in Cheshire, England, Simon has been lettering comics full-time since 2004 and has now produced work for all of the mainstream publishers in both the UK and the USA. Projects past and present include *The Boys*, *Incredible Hulk*, *The Wild Storm*, *Nameless*, *Judge Dredd*, *James Bond*, and now *Nancy Drew and The Hardy Boys*. Simon still lives in Cheshire, alongside his partner and their cat. He dedicates his work on this book to the memory of his beloved mother.

Anthony Del Col

Writer and creator Anthony Del Col is the co-creator and co-writer of the award-winning IDW Publishing series *Kill Shakespeare*, which has been adapted into a stage show, board game and audio. He co-wrote the *Assassin's Creed* (Titan Comics) comic series, and created the Audible UK audio found footage thriller *Inheard*. In addition, Del Col has been involved in music, film and television projects, most notably as the producer of two feature films and a stint as a manager for international pop star Nelly Furtado. Though a proud Canadian, Del Col lives in Brooklyn with his amazing wife Lisa.

Fay Dalton

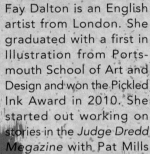

Fay Dalton is an English artist from London. She graduated with a first in Illustration from Portsmouth School of Art and Design and won the Pickled Ink Award in 2010. She started out working on stories in the *Judge Dredd Megazine* with Pat Mills and is now a sought-after cover artist for publishers including Titan (*Triggerman, Peepland*) and Dynamite (*Nancy Drew and The Hardy Boys, Casino Royale*). Previous work includes film posters and storyboard work for Empire designs and a number of high-profile ad campaigns. Fay is currently illustrating a series of deluxe editions of Ian Fleming's original James Bond stories for the Folio Society.

Werther Dell'edera

Born in the south of Italy, Werther Dell'edara has worked for the biggest publishers both in Italy and the US. His works range from *Loveless* and *Hellblazer: Dark Entries* for DC Comics, to the *Punisher Annual* and the graphic novel *Spider-Man: Family Business* (both of which he penciled). Werther has also worked on *The Mission* for Image and *G.I. Joe: Cobra* for IDW, and now the miniseries *Nancy Drew and The Hardy Boys: The Big Lie* for Dynamite.

Stefano Simeone

Born in 1985, illustrator and comic book artist Stefano Simeone has collaborated with The Walt Disney Company, Dynamite, Red Bull, Image Comics, il Mucchio, XL di Repubblica, Sergio Bonelli Editore, Aurea Editoriale, IDW, Archaia, Boom!Studios and Piemme. He wrote

Anthony Del Col & Werther Dell'Edera

AKA "When in Rome, do as Nancy, Frank and Joe Do..."

Anthony: Buon giorno, Werther!

Werther: Buon giorno, Antonio. Come va? Certo fa ridere che tu, Americano, ti chiami Antonio e io, Italiano, mi chiamo Werther... che poi è un nome Tedesco!

Se te lo stai chiedendo, il mio nome si pronuncia come inverter senza ininiziale o verter in spagnolo, che significa girare.

Anthony: Um... yeah... Okay, you called my bluff. Though I have an Italian name, and my grandfather's from Northern Italy, I don't actually know any Italian. I know, you're disappointed in me.

Werther: Oh My God! Please tell me that you are able to cook spaghetti at least!

Werther hard at work in the studio

Anthony: Yeah, Chef Boyardee is Italian, right...? Right? *[Editor's note: Anthony can actually cook pasta – we think.]* Speaking of wet noodles, I'll abstain from asking anything about Italian politics here but instead... how did you get your start in comics? As someone not familiar with the comic book industry overseas, are there a lot of art schools that feature comic book courses and programs?

Werther: Yes, there are a lot of comic art schools in Italy. I've hung out at one of those schools. It was cool, because they gave me the fundamentals for this job. After that I've worked a lot, alone or with other people, trying desperately to join this business. A lot!

Anthony: How did you get your start in the North American comic book industry? What was your first big break?

Werther: I have to thank a lot of guys for this. Too many, maybe. So I will just talk about two of them: Will Dennis and Brian Azzarello. They gave me the chance to start in the North American comic book industry and it was a huge one, because my first work was on *Loveless*, a western series by Brian Azzarello for DC/Vertigo, edited by Will Dennis.

Anthony: What is your favorite Italian comic book series or character? Of course, I'm not familiar with any of them so if you make up something completely here I probably wouldn't be able to tell... but do it anyway.

Werther: Well, there are a lot of them. One for all? Tex! It's an Italian western comic book, pretty famous all over the world too. But If I may, I would prefer to speak about Authors instead of comic books. People like Hugo Pratt, Attilio Micheluzzi, Dino Battaglia, Sergio Toppi! They haven't worked on regular characters (except for Pratt and his Corto Maltese), but they have done a lot of beautiful comics, real pieces of art and of great inspirations too!

Anthony: I took an Italian film course in my third year of university and watched some of the greats (*Cinema Paradiso*, *La Dolce Vita*) and some of the worst (you may hate me when I say this but I'm not an Antonioni fan). What's your favourite Italian film of all-time?

Werther: This is a difficult one, because I'm not a real fan of Italian films. Anyway I would pick some of Mario Monicelli's film, like *Il Marchese del Grillo* or *La grande guerra*. And I really like *La Dolce Vita* too or *Il Mestiere delle Armi* by Ermanno Olmi. That is outstanding.

Anthony: I'm always curious about the process of an artist. What hours do ou work? Where do you work (a studio at home, a studio with other artists)?

Werther: When I turned 40 I stopped working at night-time. I find myself too tired to work after 9 p.m. (unless I really have to). So I work in a studio with other (great) artists from 9 a.m. till 6.30 p.m. every day.

Anthony: As a writer I find my influences all over the place – books, comics, TV, film, etc. Where do you find yourself turning to most for inspiration?

Werther: It's the same for me. Sometime it's something that I read in a book or that I see somewhere. Obviously due to my kind of job it's easier that it's something visual that influences me in the strongest way. And it can come from everywhere. From a painting, from another comic book, from a movie, from a picture. In these days, for example, it's easy that I find inspiration from painters, most of all during the inking process. It probably sounds weird, but I assure you that it helps me a lot.

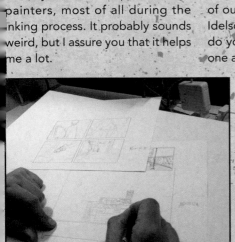

Pencilled panels for issue three

Anthony: So had you read any Nancy Drew or Hardy Boys books before working on this project? Don't worry, you can be honest here. This is a safe zone.

Werther: Ok, now it's your turn to be disappointed in me. I haven't

read them ever. I'm sorry for this and I ask you and all the other Nancy Drew and Hardy Boys' fan for forgiveness!

Anthony: Wow. That may be too much. I'll see if we can get the editors to cut this part out… So, here's the toughest question of the day… which of our three main characters do you enjoy drawing most? Nancy? Frank? Joe? None of them?

Werther: I love each of them because each character has a unique trait that makes him very fun to draw. Nancy is the one that maybe I have to explore more as character. She is beautiful and she is smart, of course, but most of all she should be real and every person has their moments in sadness, sweetness, anger. I like to make my characters alive as more as possible.

Anthony: Okay, I lied. Another even tougher question: which editor of ours do you prefer most? Matt Idelson or Matt Humphreys? Or… do you think that perhaps they're one and the same…?

Werther: You are really mean! How can I choose one, they are both great and kind! So I can tell you this: I love Matt!

Anthony: Wow. Playing the political game, huh? Impressive. Thanks so much, Werther (pronounced like "inverter" – see, I was able to Google Translate your first answer!).

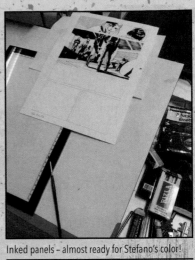

Inked panels – almost ready for Stefano's color!

Anthony Del Col & Colorist Stefano Simeone
AKA "All Roads Lead to Bayport... via Rome?"

Anthony: Buon giorno, Stefano! I'm not sure if you read my interview with (artist) Werther last month, but he really embarrassed me by proving how little Italian I actually know (this despite the fact that I have an Italian background).

Stefano: Ciao Anthony! Partiremo dalle basi allora: "buongiorno", non "buon giorno"! (so, let's start from the base: "buongiorno", not "buon giorno")

Anthony: Um... since you and Werther both live in Rome, did you collude here or something? Is this "make fun of the Ukrainian-Italian-Canadian guy day"?

Stefano: Ok ok, this insult just doesn't work fine. Anyway, we and Werther are working in the same studio, Skeleton Monster. It's a very small place so, you know, we need to organize the UICG (Ukrainian Italian Canadian Guy) day twice in a month. You should coming, it's a big convention in a very beautiful park. Oh, and we have beers and popcorns. THAT was an insult.

Anthony: Why do I find that hard to believe...? Anyways, I'm sure people aren't reading this to find out ways to insult me. Well, unless my family's reading this... in that case, they're DEFINITELY trying to figure that out...

But seriously, I'm so glad that you and I are chatting like this. MORE importantly, I'm so glad to have you as colorist on this series! You've been doing an amazing job thus far and I've gotten so many compliments on your work. So... let's start with some really tough questions. First off... favorite color?

Stefano: I'm quite hesitant, but now I think it is magenta.

Anthony: Second favorite color?

Stefano: Ultramarine Blue.

Anthony: I have so much respect for colorists— it's really a hard job, isn't it, with all the flatting that takes place. Can you walk me (well, the reader, I guess) on the coloring process? Perhaps use a specific panel from this issue for an example?

Stefano hard at work.

Stefano: Let's take on exam panel 3 from Nancy Drew issue #02, page 10. An introduction: every artist, I think, have a "correct color way", sometimes you must complete the artwork, some other you need colors to focus on an element. This is not the case of Werther. He's a great storyteller (I'll have two beers at the next UICG day for this) so what I usually do, in order to make sense of coloring, is to add of glorify informations we have in the B/W art. In this panel, Nancy is alone, dancing, she's "in" the party, but just physically. So I colored her like as a foreign element of the composition. She have different lights, she doesn't mix to other people. The only thing that brings her back to the party is the drink in her hand, so I made it pink like the room. This is the kind of process I'm trying to figure out in every panel, I know it's quite philosophical, but this give me back a sense of my job.

Anthony: Like I said, really hard. How did you start as a colorist? Was it something you studied in school?

Stefano: I write and draw comics, but I must be honest: coloring is the only part of making art in which I'm a natural. I didn't study in a specific school for this, so I guess I've been quite lucky.

Anthony: Is there a colorist you like the best (other than yourself, that is). You know, someone who you look to for inspiration? As a comics writer it's people like Brian K Vaughan, Ed Brubaker, etc.

Stefano: In comics, I always look at Dave Stewart colors. I think at him as the parent engine of my arguments about coloring. I also look at 50's magazine illustrators, most of all Coby Whitmore.

Anthony: I myself didn't fall in love with comics until my 20s. Is there a specific moment that you remember thinking/knowing that you loved comics?

Stefano: I read comics since I was a child. I started about thinking at them as a job quite late, nine years ago, when I realized that comics could give you the power of telling what you need to without (or with a lot less) be compromised.

Issue 4 colors underway!

least? Don't worry, you can be honest here…

Stefano: The page I enjoyed most are the double pages 14 and 15 of Nancy Drew issue #02. It's been quite complicated to find an equilibrium, we've a static situation but I'll need to put strong colors into that, in order to give tension to the reader, without using reds. You know, reds are a shortcut.

Anthony: Last month Werther revealed that he hadn't really read any Nancy Drew or Hardy Boys books growing up. I know, you're as shocked as I am. Don't worry, I won't ask you the same question… but instead will ask you three silly questions… First off, when you think of Joe Hardy, what color do you think of?

Stefano: Phtalo green.

Anthony: Frank Hardy?

Stefano: Burnt Sienna.

Anthony: Nancy Drew?

Stefano: Pale slate grey.

Anthony: And Anthony Del Col?

Stefano: Smettila!

Anthony: That doesn't sound like a color…

Stefano: …

Stefano and Werther discuss a panel.

Anthony: What panel (or page) in our series have you enjoyed working on the most? And the

Anthony Del Col & Cover Artist Fay Dalton

Anthony: First off, every time I visit the UK (for vacations or to attend comic shows) I always try to pick up a new Cockney-ism (like "I'm cream crackered" which means "I'm knackered" or "I'm tired"). What's your favorite UK expression?

success. I was first brought to attention to your work on Titan Comics' Triggerman series and I immediately brought it to (series editors) Matt Idelson and Matt Humphreys. We were all blown away by them and knew that you were the right fit for this series.

Fay Dalton at work with various versions of the first cover

Fay: Hmm... I guess I don't have a favorite phrase, they're just part of my vocab. I tend to fanny around a lot (procrastinate) and I like a nice glass of plonk (cheap wine) when I'm buckling down on a deadline! I sound nuts, I'd like to hear the ones you've picked up! I'm not sure how far too go with British expressions, or how well known they are in the US!

Anthony: Well, the one I use the most (I think it's British?) is "Bob's your uncle". But I can't say it around my wife, because her father and brother have that as their first name, so she always corrects me...

But blimey! Enough about me... I'd like to focus on you. And your incredible work on *Nancy Drew & The Hardy Boys: The Big Lie*. Your covers for each of the books have been so evocative thus far and a huge part of our

What made you interested in the project when you were first approached (other than getting paid, of course)?

Fay: When I was first told about new Noir direction on the iconic Nancy Drew and the Hardy Boys I was excited to visualize the characters in modern times with a twist. The opportunity to be involved in transforming a vintage classic and being able to combine my vintage style with a noir vibe and contemporary writing was a perfect fit!

Anthony: It is a perfect fit. Can you walk us through the process of creating a cover? Perhaps we should focus on the first cover (which is complimented SO many times). How did you come up with the initial idea, and what are the steps involved from start to finish?

Fay: I wanted to keep Nancy the mysterious, femme fatale of this episode but emphasize her power and position to the boys, so it made sense making her the biggest impact of the cover without revealing her character. I roughly knew I wanted to run with the concept as it is in final and the idea of the lights as her eyes came to me as I was sketching it out, adding to the intrigue of her character.

There were a few changes to make to the final draft like the positioning of her arms and making sure she wasn't too femme fatale for the story, but it was a really fun cover to work on. The hardest part was finding the balance between the noir vibe and modern times. I was tempted to make it all smoky and much more noir but it was important to keep the boys and detectives current.

From doing quick sketches I was pretty certain of the concept so I ran to color before getting much feedback! I roughly painted it out traditionally after getting the comp and proportions right, scanned it in and digitally painted details, finessed the whole piece in Photoshop. Some parts I painted separately to scan in for extra textures, keeping that vintage look.

Anthony: Wow. You put me and my failed stick figures to shame. What was the first cover you did for comics?

Fay: The first comic cover I did was for the *Judge Dredd Megazine* for *American Reaper*, and my debut for the spin off series *Reaper Files*.

Anthony: When did you know you wanted to be an artist?

Fay: Since I was a child! It was always my passion and I think it just came naturally to me to pursue. It's been my path from as earlier as I can remember.

Anthony: What's your process? What time(s) of the day do you work? And do you work out of a studio or your flat?

Fay: I work in my studio and I'm quite the night owl, I'm always working to music and enjoying myself, getting stuck in to the brief!

Anthony: So... we're going into a lightning round of questions here.

First off — when you draw Nancy, what's the first thing you focus on?

Fay: I'm always aware of giving her that no-nonsense intelligent femme fatale vibe but keeping her youthful and current. I like to keep her quite serious and reserved, keeping that intrigue and a sense of depth.

Anthony: Interesting. And Frank?

Fay: His charisma, slightly nerdy look, his distinctive hair and collection of checked shirts. I like him to look confident but a little sulky.

Anthony: Wow. And Joe?

Fay: I think of Joe as the modern rebel without a cause, he's the handsome lad but can rely on his brother's tongue to get them out of trouble. I think of his sleek sandy hair, classic features and leather jacket.

Anthony: And me?

Fay: Teehee I think you ask too many questions.

Anthony: Do I?

Fay: See? Told you so.

I think you certainly knew what you wanted to create and I'm glad you had me rework a couple of the concepts so we nailed the series!

Anthony: Thanks, Fay! And again, you've done some incredible work on the series. So glad to have you as part of the team.

If you'd like to check out more of Fay's work, head to faydaltonillustration.com.

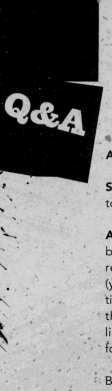

Anthony Del Col
& Letterer Simon Bowland

Anthony: Top of the morning, Simon!

Simon: Morning? I'm getting ready to go to bed.

Anthony: Oh, right. I forgot that you're based in the UK. You know what? I just realized that the entire creative team (you, Werther, Stefano, Fay) are international. And I'm Canadian, so that means… this reboot of All-American characters like Nancy, Joe and Frank are done by foreigners! Psst… Don't tell anyone!

But seriously, you've done an amazing job on the series thus far. I remember talking to our editors (Matt Idelson and Matt Humphreys) and I told them I wanted someone that wouldn't do just the normal "lettering" job but instead bring a new style to it. And you brought it. What attracted you to this work in the first place (other than a pay cheque, of course)?

Simon: Matt and Matt pay me in chocolate biscuits, but what attracted me to the project was memories of reading the Nancy Drew novels when I was younger. Plus my partner, Pippa, was a huge Nancy Drew fan when she was young and it made me really keen on being a part of the team.

Anthony: I'm quite fascinated by the lettering process. For those reading this that know very little (or nothing at all), can you explain the steps involved in putting together the lettering?

Simon: Sure! I'll receive a copy of the script and scans of the artwork via the wonders of the modern technology. It's my job to add all of the dialogue/balloons/tails to the pages, along with any sound effects (SFX), as per the script. But at the same time, it's my job to make sure that the reader's eye will seamlessly flow from balloon to balloon, panel to panel, without a second thought. Even if the artwork doesn't make that an easy task, I still have to make it work – all the

time trying to ensure that as little of the artwork as possible is covered up.

Anthony: And here's the most important question of this entire interview (okay, thus far)… for years I have ridiculed anyone that uses "Comic Sans" font in Powerpoint presentations or in any regular document. What are your thoughts on it?

Simon: Comic Sans is much maligned, and rightly so in most circumstances — it shouldn't ever been seen in a company logo, for example, and definitely shouldn't go anywhere near the pages of a comic book. But it has its uses; for example, many people

with learning difficulties find reading to be easier when material is typeset in Comic Sans. I'm not just a pretty face, y'know!

Anthony: Well, I'm still not… Hey, is there something wrong with this font?
[Editor's note: yes, there is, Anthony…]

How did you get started doing lettering work?

Simon: I'd always had a fascination with the lettering in comics, right back to the early 80s when I first started reading them. It was immediately clear to me that when my favourite letterers – Richard Starkings and Tom Orzechowski — skipped an issue of their regular series, the books just didn't look as good during their absence. From then on, I took a keen interest in lettering as an art form. Fast forward a good few years, I'm working in a design studio and bored out of my brains, and I decide to quit. With a mortgage to pay, and still being a huge fan of lettering in comics, I wanted to see if I could combine the

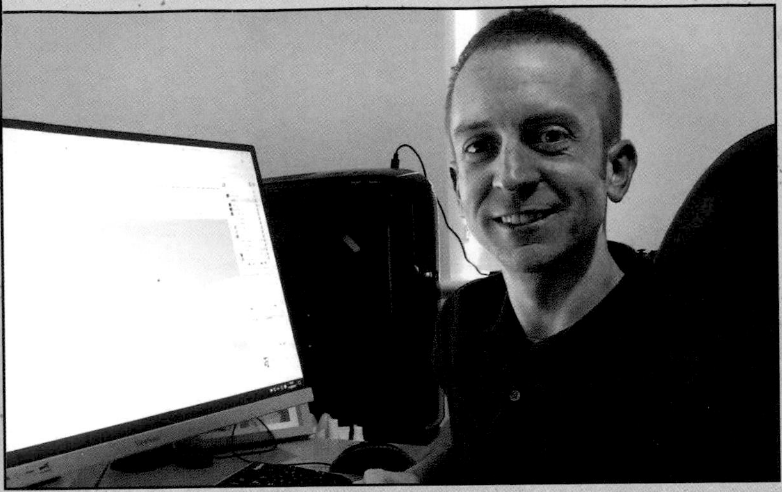

Letterer Simon Bowland at work in his home studio

knowledge from my design career with my passion for comics and, in particular, lettering. Once I'd got myself to what I thought was a reasonable level of ability as a letterer, I started knocking on the doors of publishers with a copy of my portfolio. Nobody opened the door, so I kept knocking. And one day, Dynamite opened that door and I've been working with them, as well as pretty much all the other major comic publishers, ever since.

Anthony: Um... why am I still speaking in Comics Sans...?

One of the challenges for this series is that we have three different narrators (Frank and Joe always split the odd-numbered issues, Nancy the even-numbered ones). How do you differentiate between the three with their captions?

Simon: The Matt twins asked me to go "old school" with the captions – something akin to the Joe Rosen-lettered ones from classic 80s *Daredevil* comics, so I tried to blend that concept with more modern lettering techniques. I'm fairly pleased with how they turned out, and once we had a basic design it was just a case of adjusting them so each narrator's caption had its own individual style.

Anthony: Now I just read on your Twitter account that you despise writers who fail to provide the exact SFX words (like "BANG!") and leave it blank for the letterer to devise. You can be honest... have I ever done that in this series??

Simon: Honestly? No, you're in the clear! And "despise" isn't what I said, but I do think it's very much the writer's job to write their own SFX. Speaking of SFX, I have to give a big shout-out to our wonderful series artist, Werther, for some of his incredible hand-drawn SFX in the Nancy Drew comic.

Anthony: You're absolutely right - I love how Werther's able to incorporate some of the SFX into the panels - a couple times in this issue, for instance. One other technical question.... For you, what is the ideal number of balloons on a page? I've heard it shouldn't be any more than eight (something I only break 2-3 times an issue). Is that a rubbish number, or accurate?

Simon: Hmm, it all depends on the number of panels on any given page, as well as the number of words in each balloon. But it's worth remembering that comics are, at their heart, a visual medium and as such the art should be allowed room to breathe. Personally, I don't like reading comics where the pages are smothered with excessive dialogue. Most of the time it's unnecessary, because the artwork is telling the story on its own.

Anthony: And finally... What is the best SFX that can be done to represent the end of this interview?

Simon:

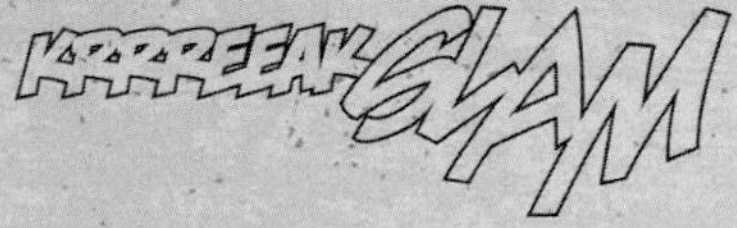
KRRREEAK SLAM

Anthony: KRRREEAK SLAM! See? It just doesn't look as good in Comic Sans...

You can follow Simon Bowland at @simonbowland.

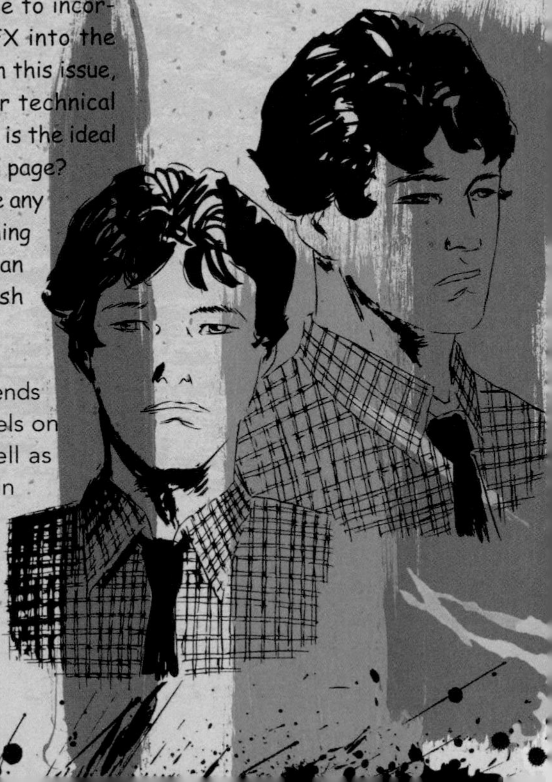

ISSUE #1
Cover Art: Fay Dalton

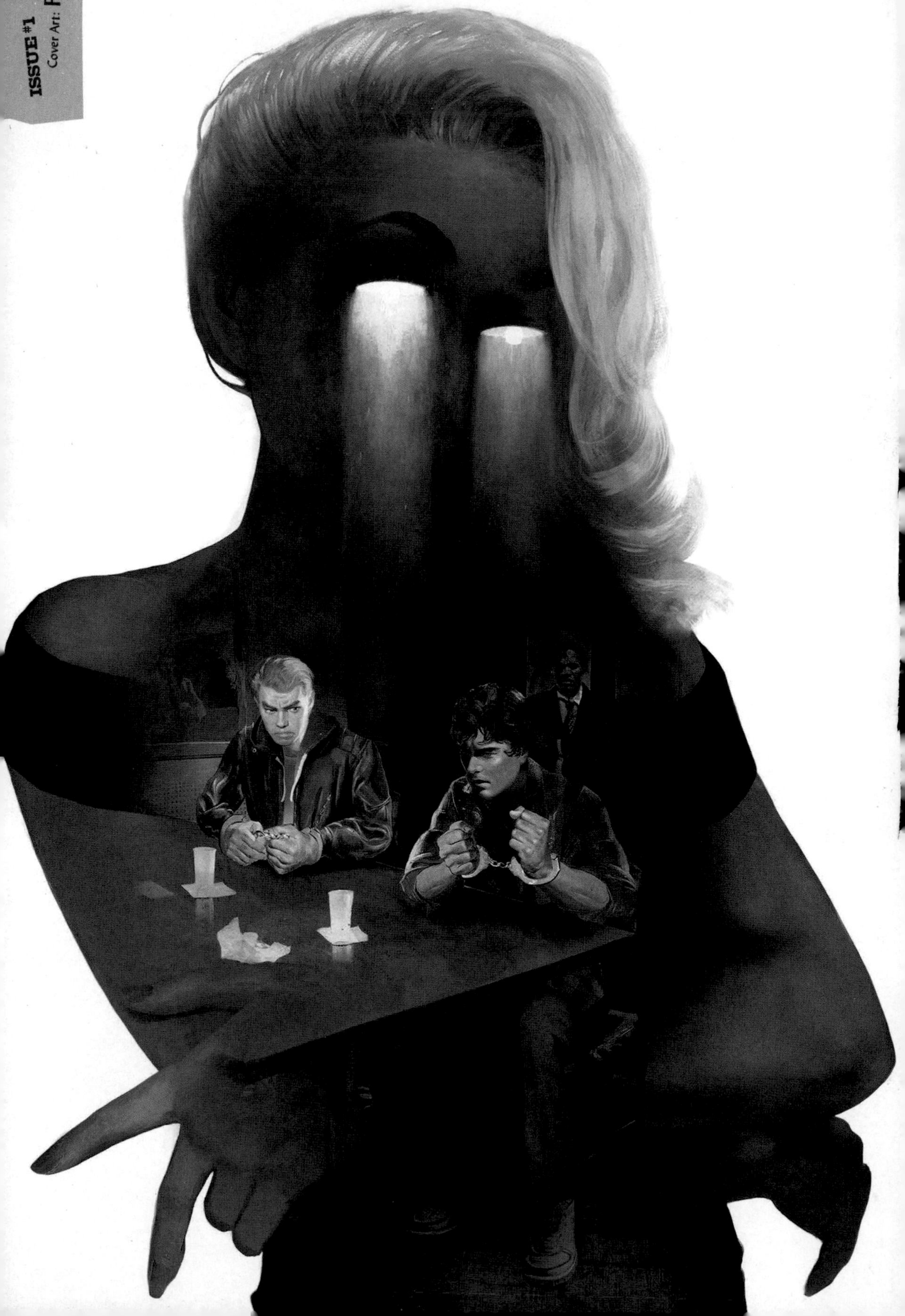

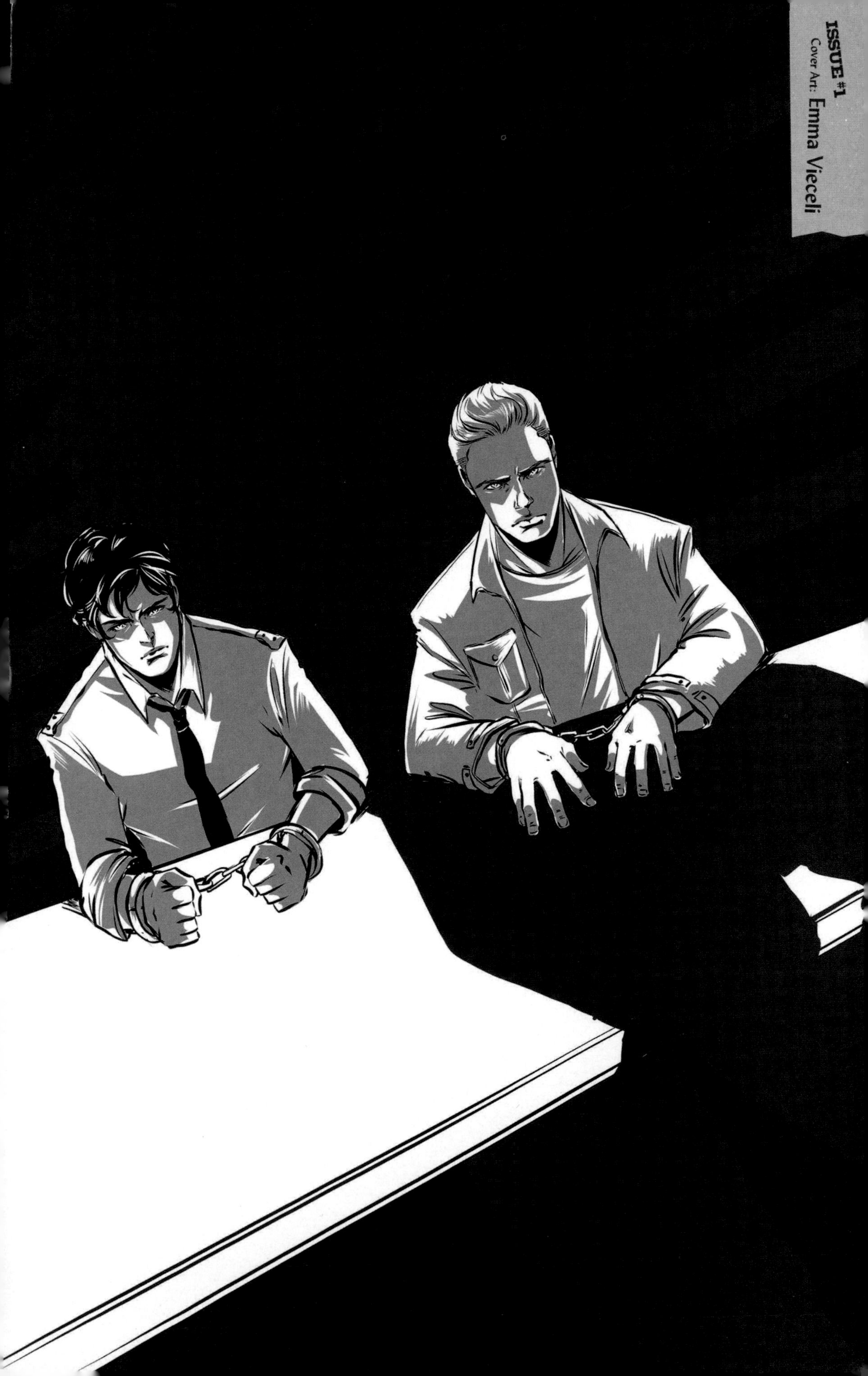

ISSUE #1
Cover Art: Emma Vieceli

ISSUE #1
Cover Art: Robert Hack

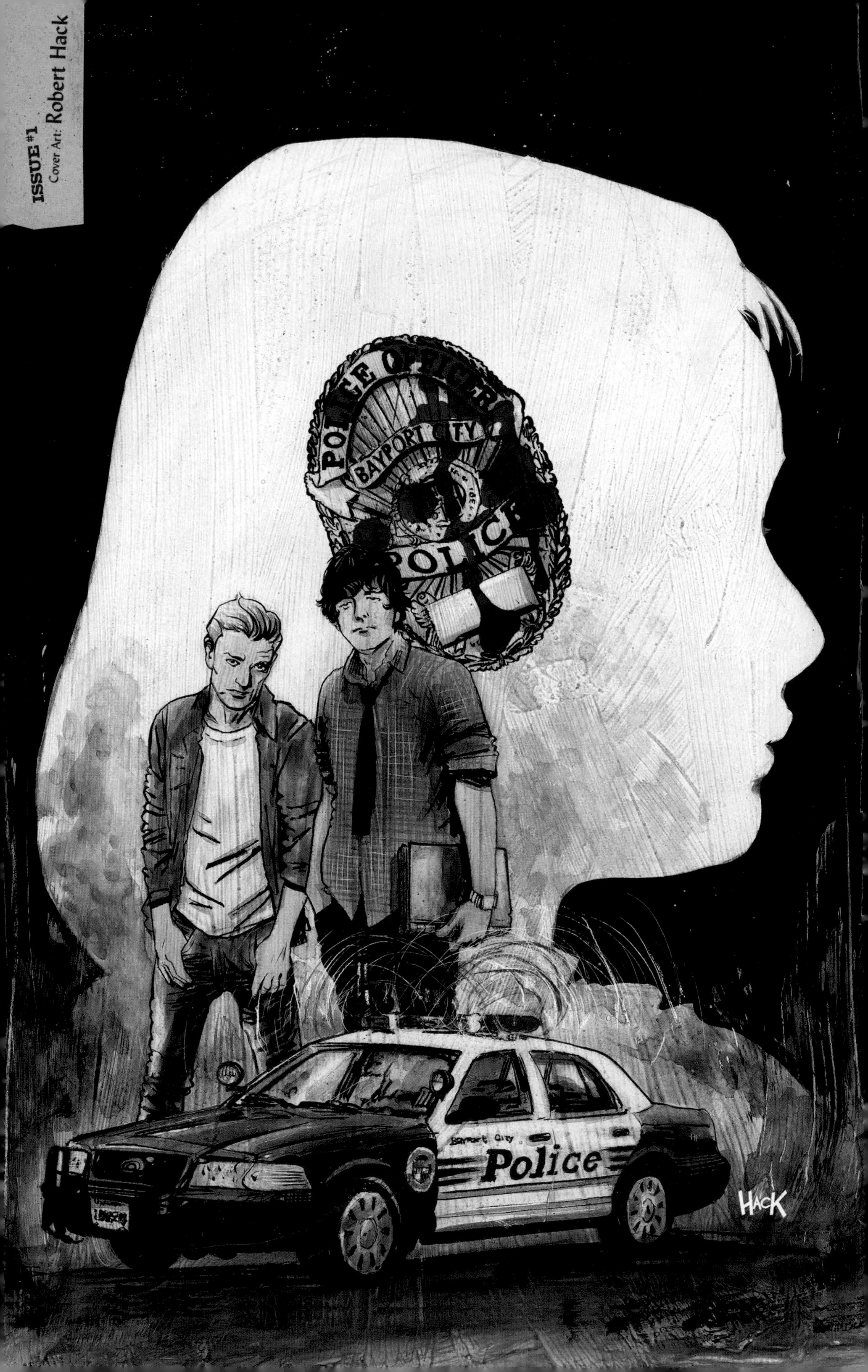
POLICE OFFICER
BAYPORT CITY
POLICE
Bayport City
Police
HACK

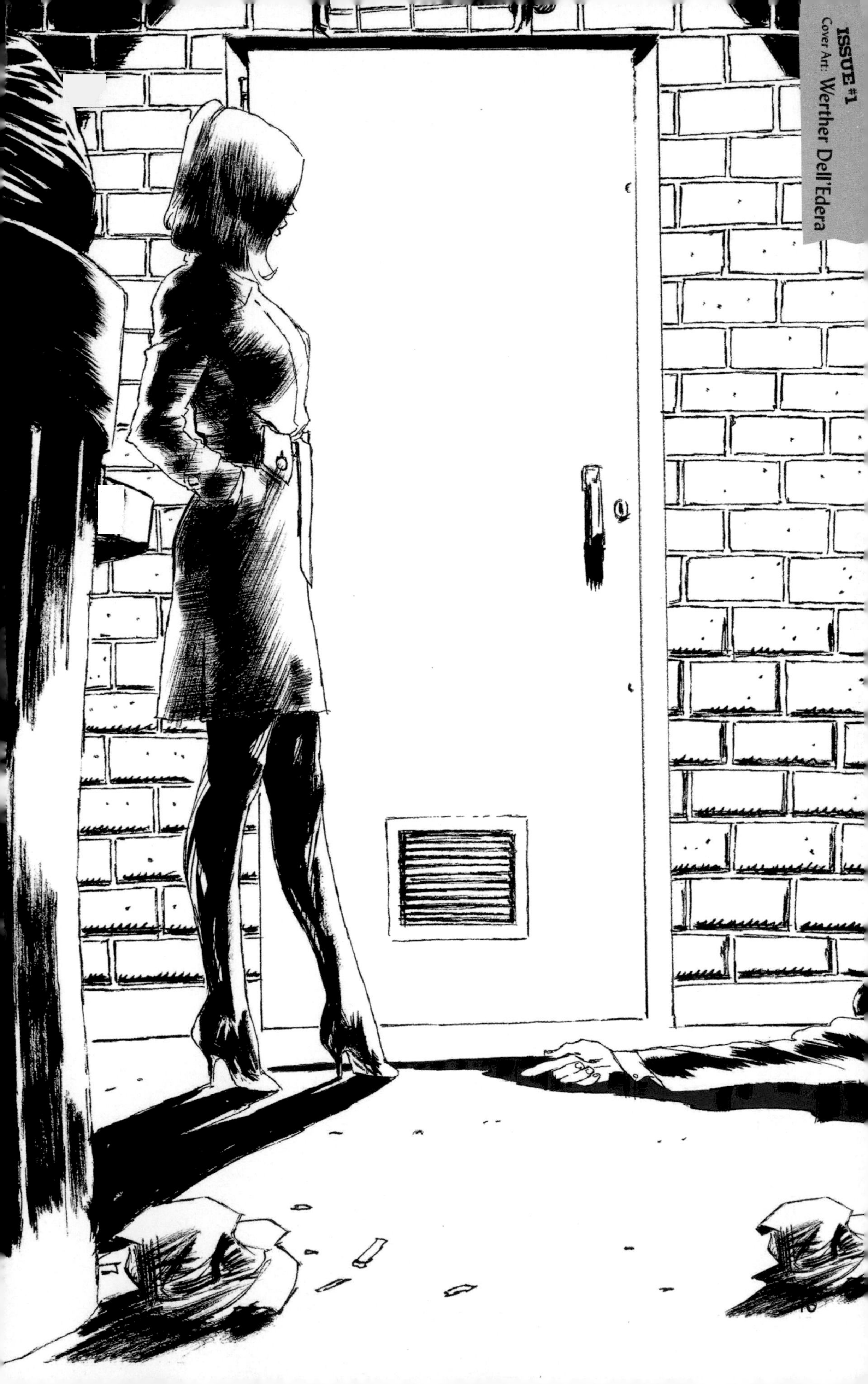

ISSUE #1
Cover Art: Werther Dell'Edera

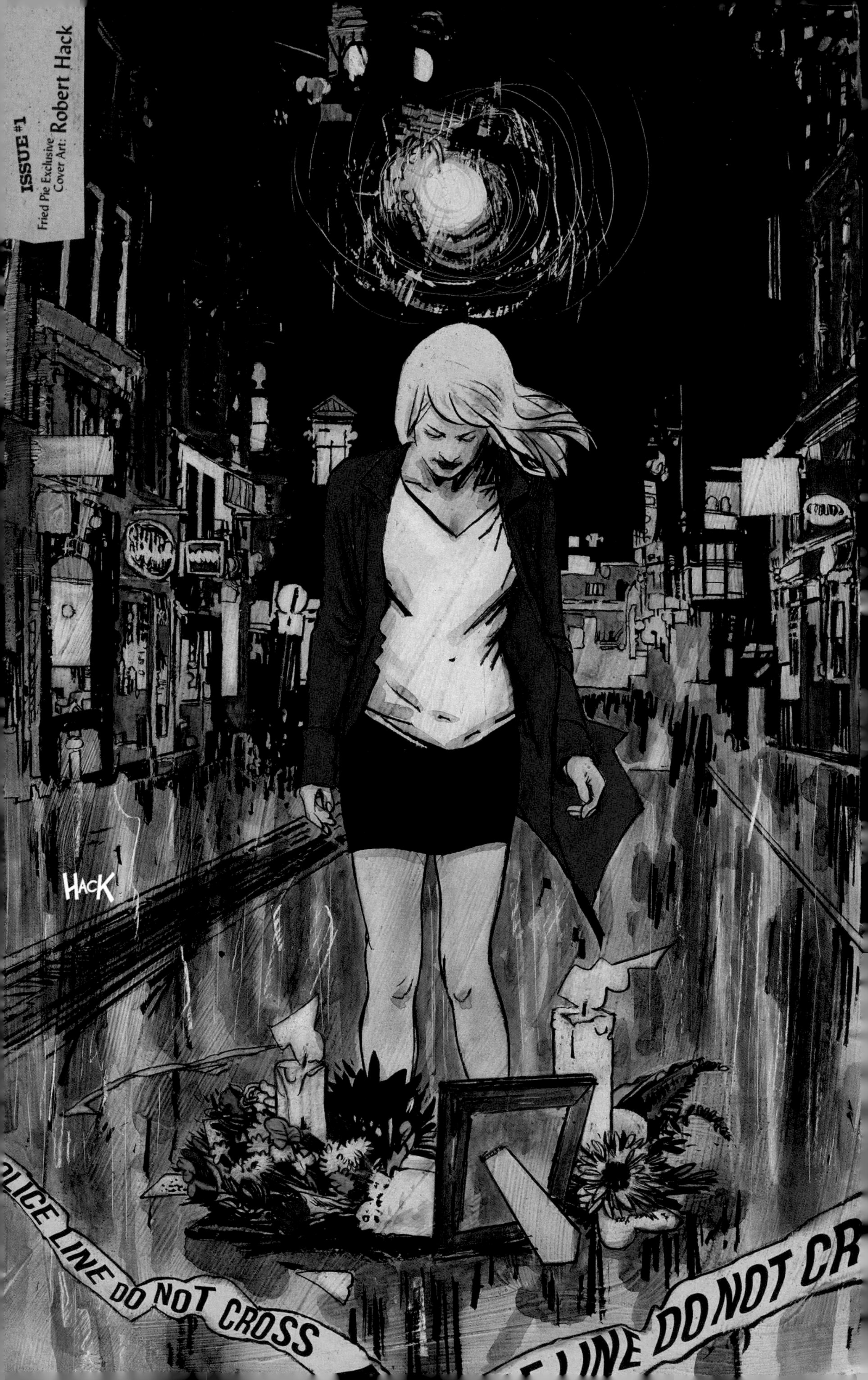
ISSUE #1
Fried Pie Exclusive
Cover Art: Robert Hack
HACK
OLICE LINE DO NOT CROSS
E LINE DO NOT CR

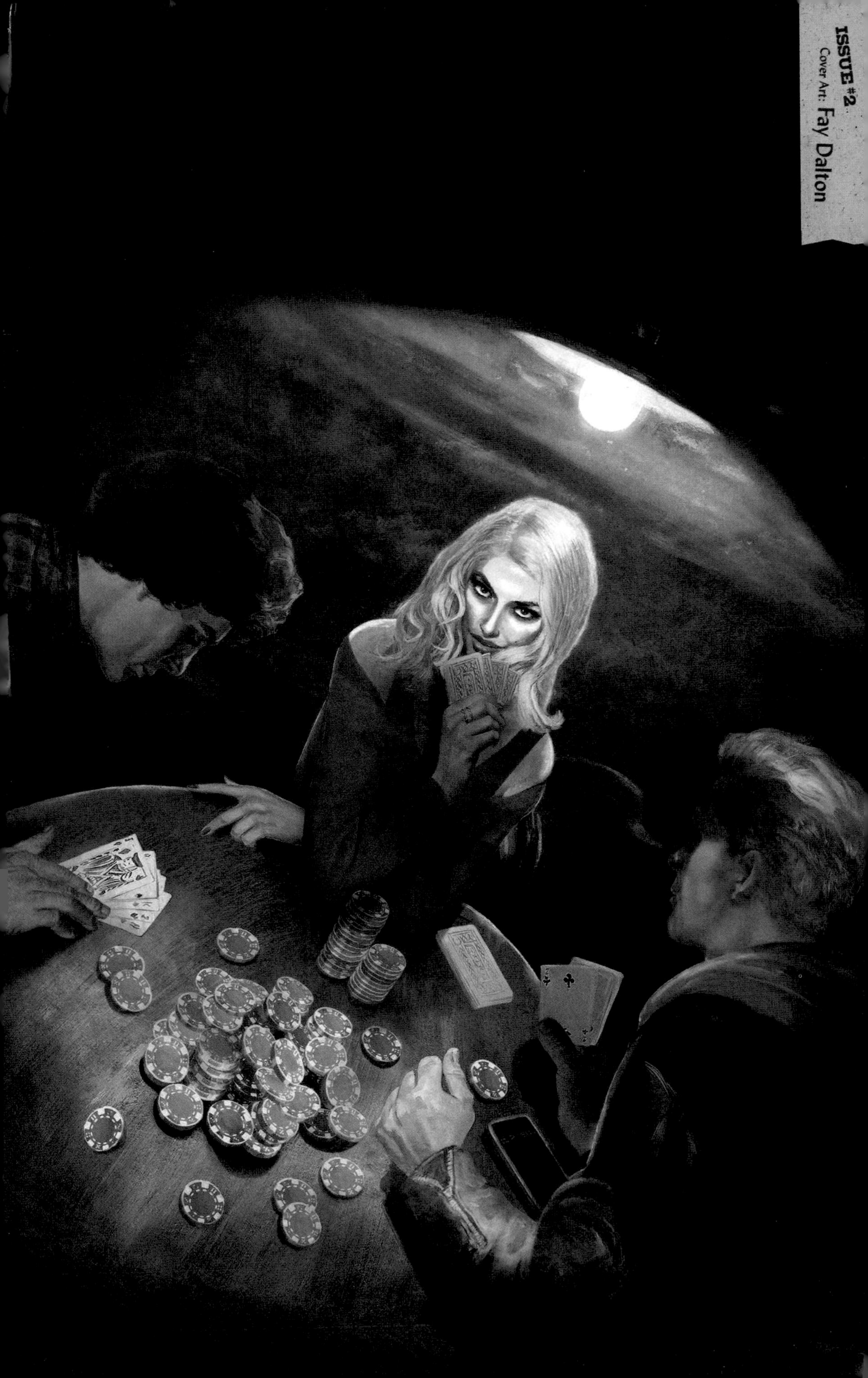

ISSUE #2
Cover Art: Fay Dalton

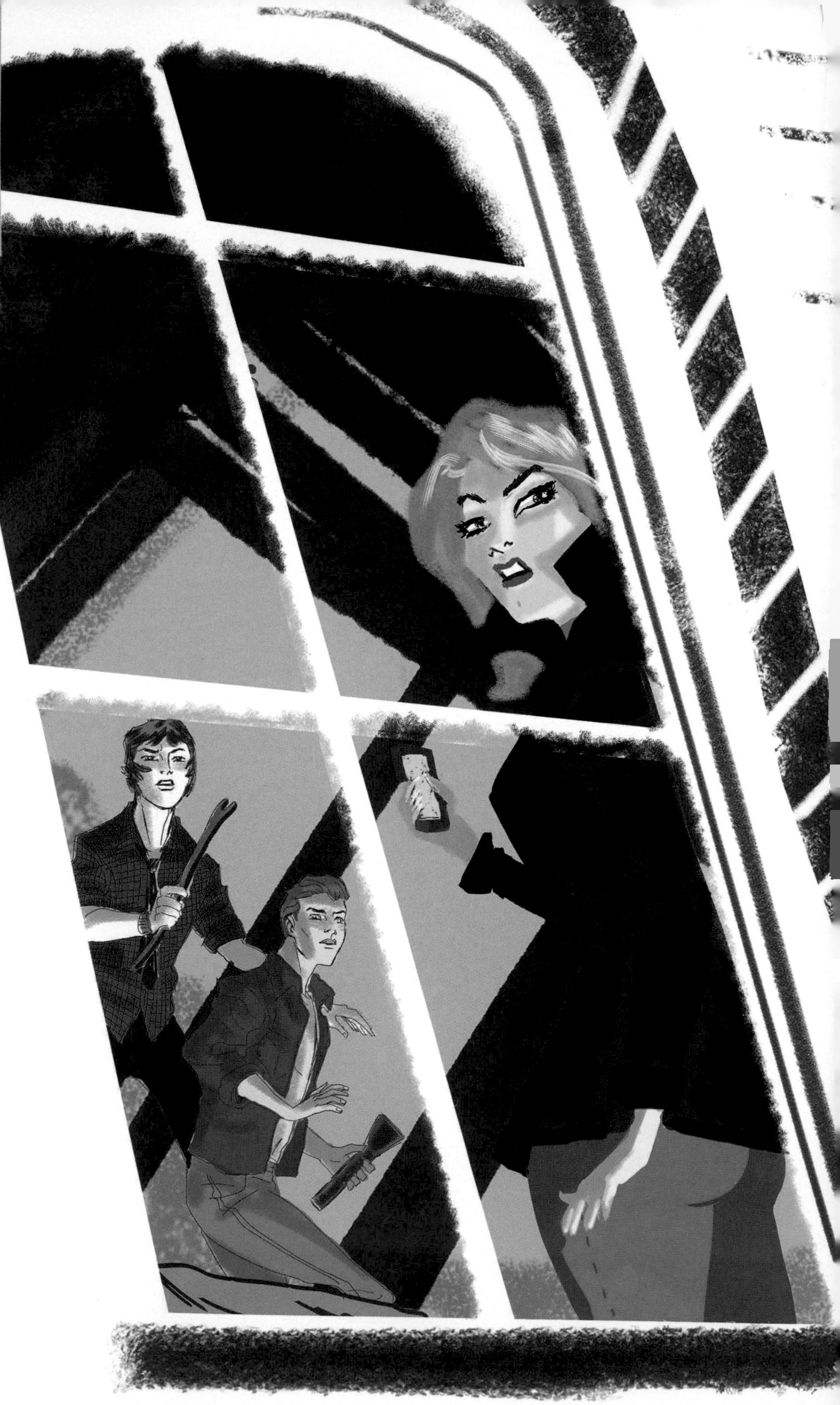

ISSUE #2
Cover Art: Dave Bullock

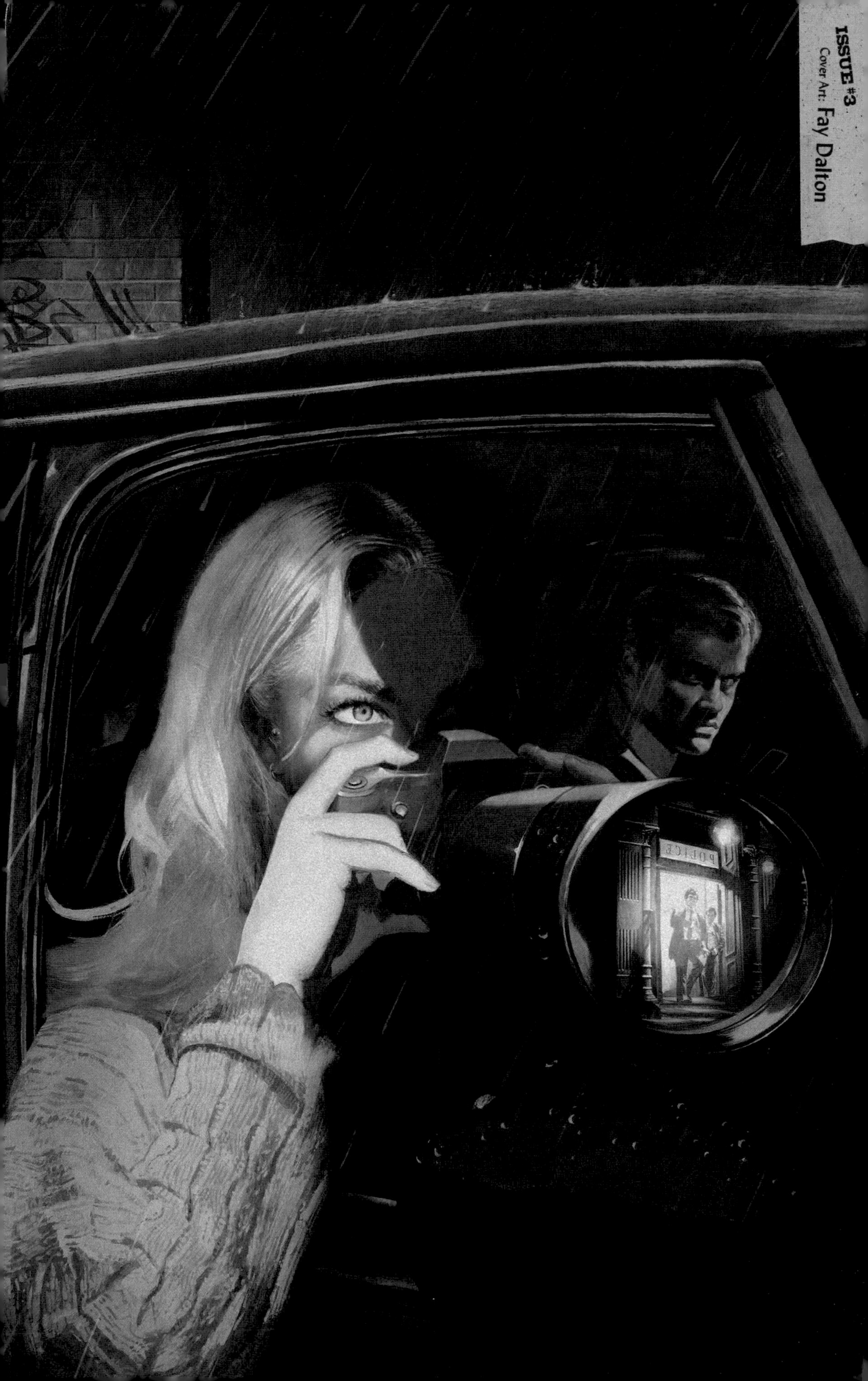
ISSUE #3
Cover Art: Fay Dalton

ISSUE #3
Cover Art: Elsa Charretier

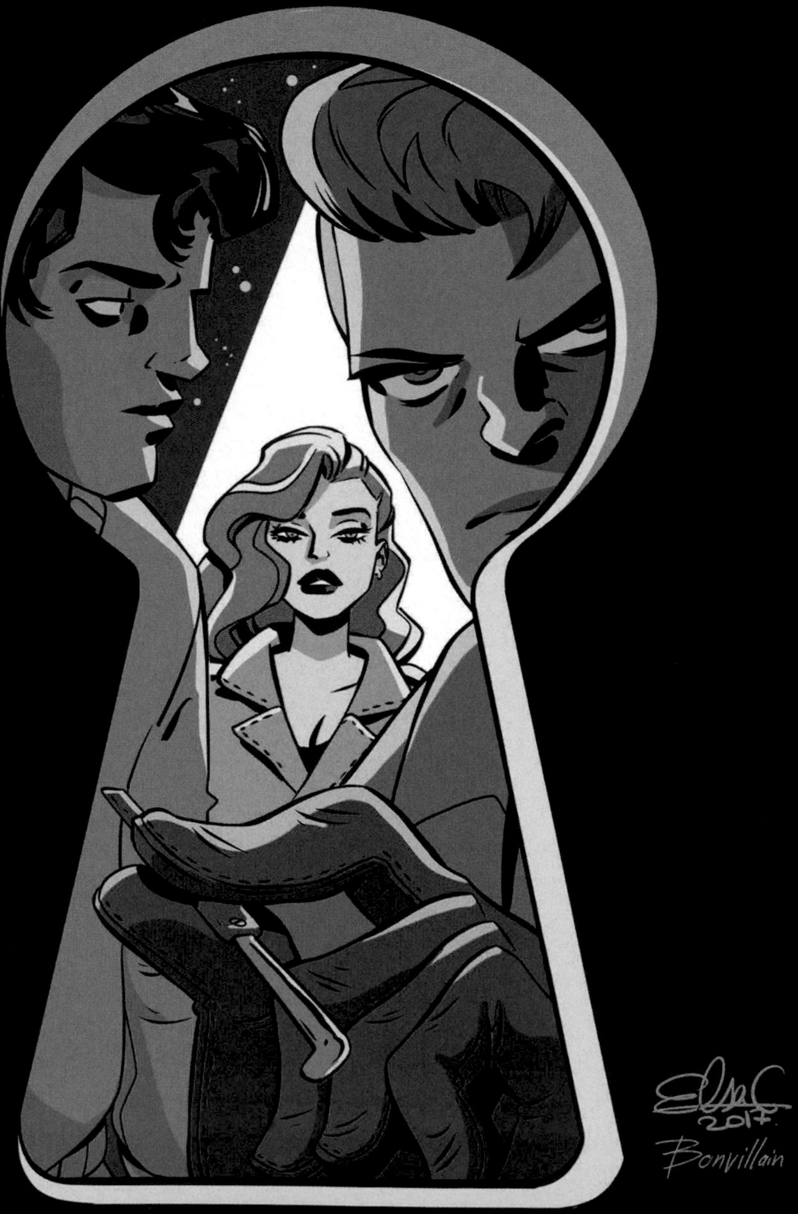
Bonvillain

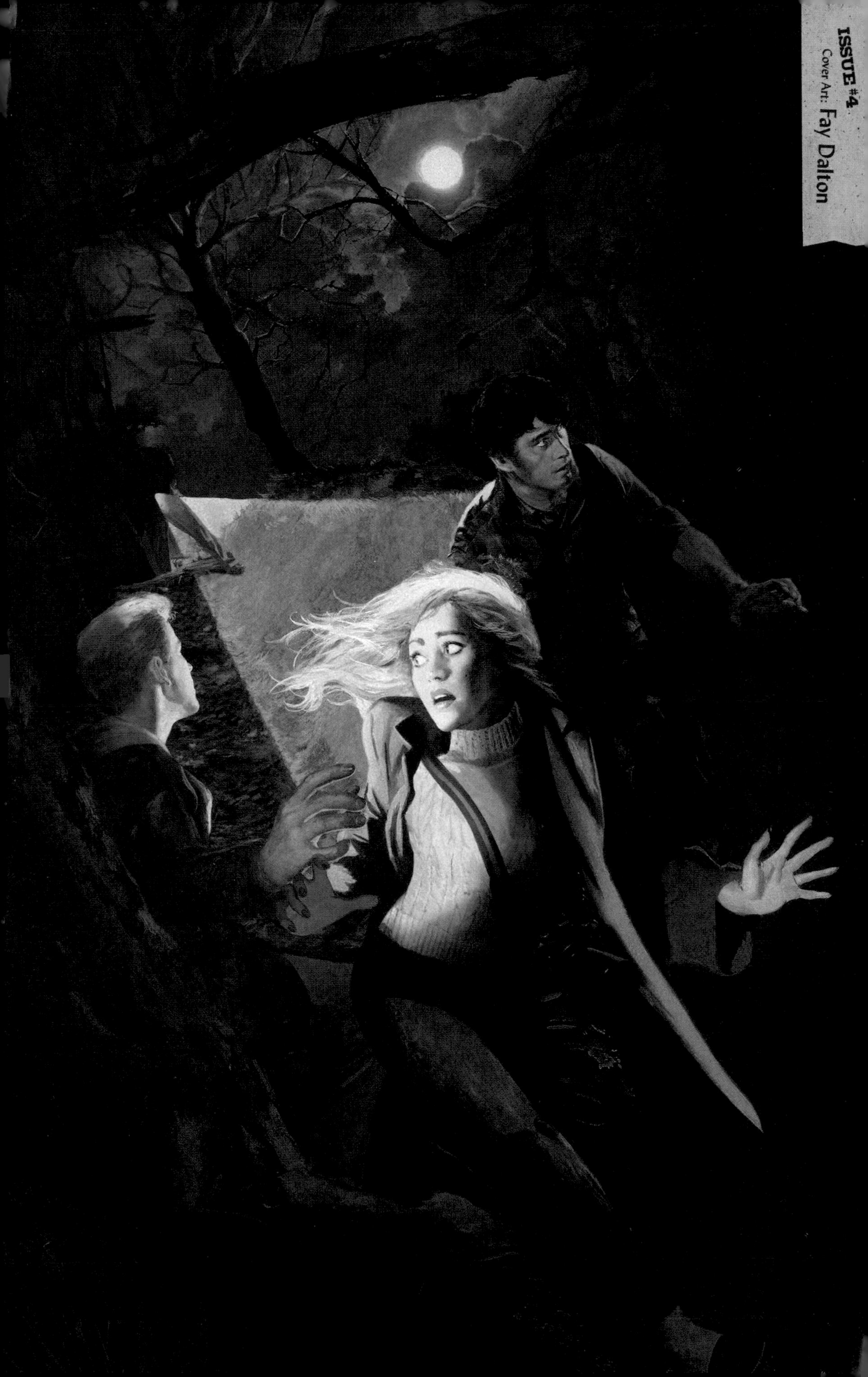

ISSUE #4
Cover Art: Fay Dalton

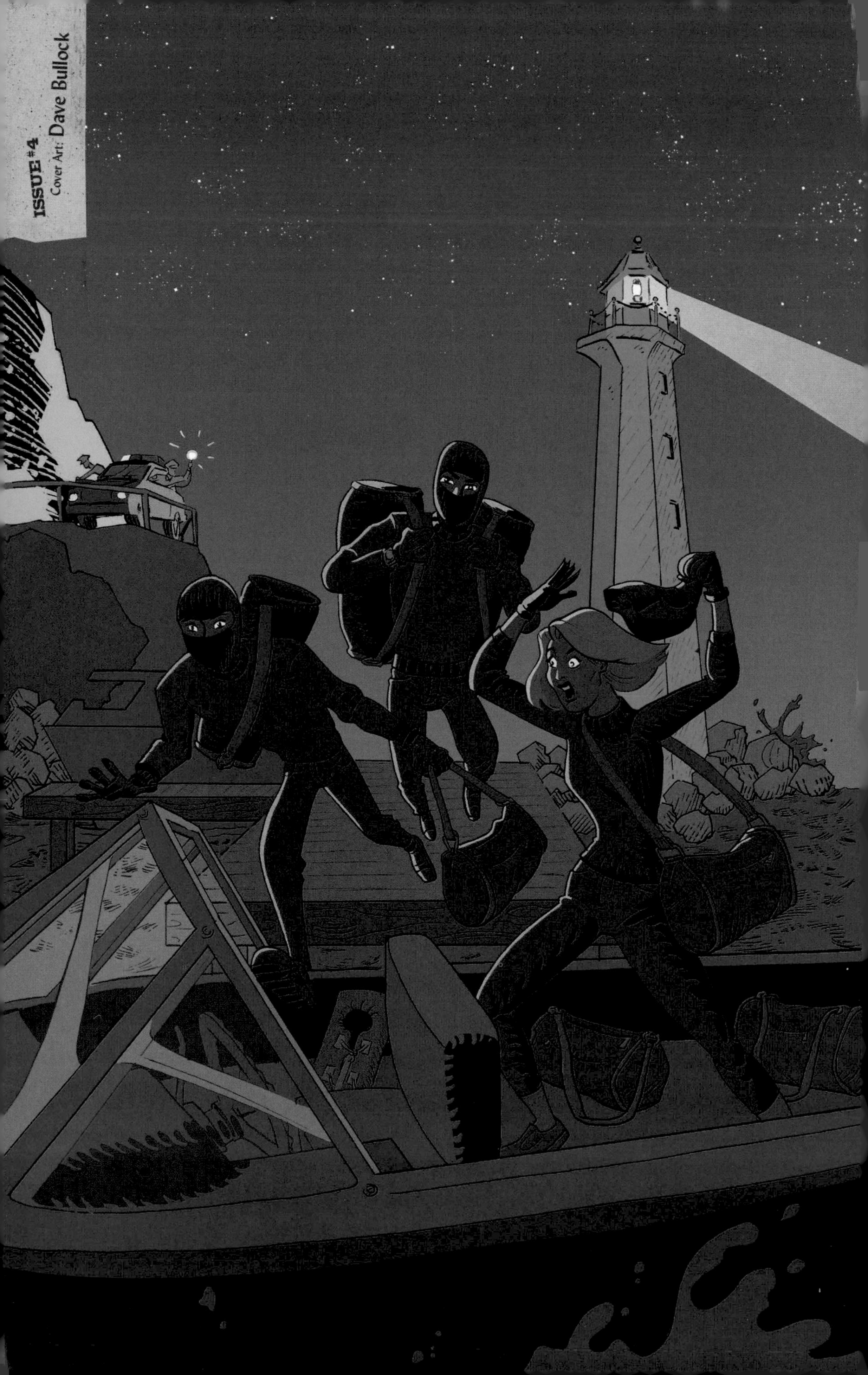

ISSUE #4
Cover Art: Dave Bullock

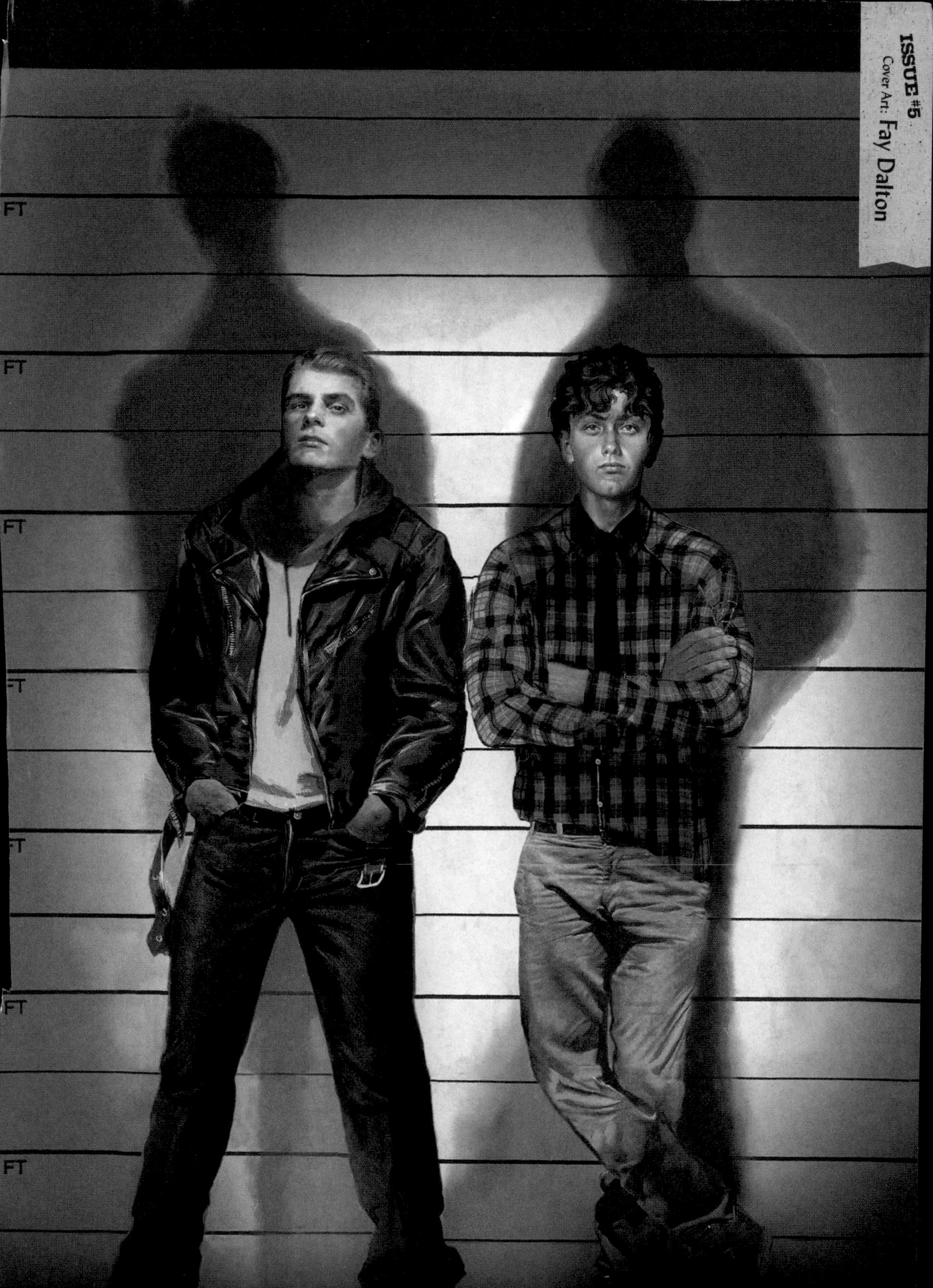
FT
FT
FT
FT
FT
FT
FT

ISSUE #5
Cover Art: Fay Dalton

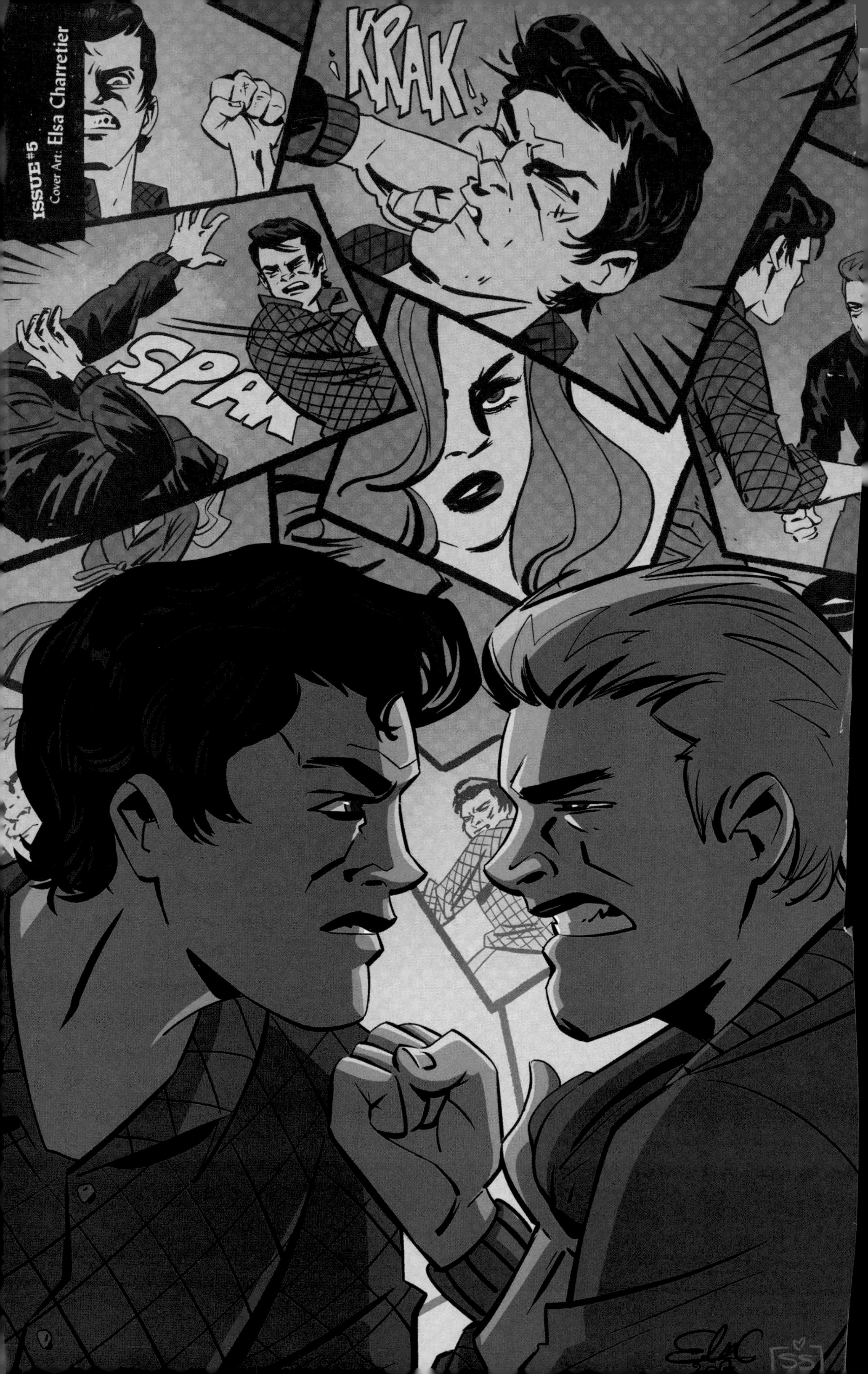
ISSUE #5
Cover Art: Elsa Charretier
KRAK